Also by Jonathan D. Spence

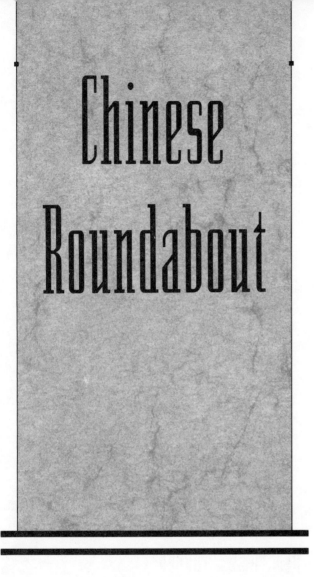

Chinese Roundabout

W W NORTON & COMPANY

NEW YORK   LONDON

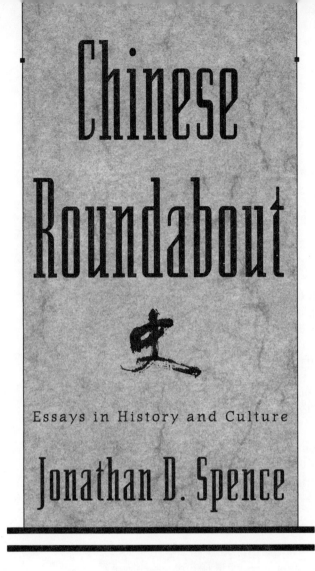

Chinese Roundabout

Essays in History and Culture

Jonathan D. Spence

The text of this book is composed in Stempel Garamond
with the display set in Senator Tall
Manufacturing by The Maple-Vail Book Manufacturing
Group
Book design by Guenet Abraham

Library of Congress Cataloging-in-Publication Data

Spence, Jonathan D.
Chinese roundabout : essays in history and culture /
Jonathan D. Spence.
p.   cm.
Includes bibliographical references and index.
1. China—History.   2. China—Civilization.   I. Title.
DS736.S625   1992
951—dc20   91-34393

ISBN: 3-393-03355-4
W. W. Norton & Company, Inc.
500 Fifth Avenue, New York, N.Y. 10110
W. W. Norton & Company Ltd.
10 Coptic Street, London WC1A 1PU
1 2 3 4 5 6 7 8 9 0

For
KEITH, NICHOLAS, AND SANDRA

                                        We seek
Nothing beyond reality. Within it,

Everything, the spirit's alchemicana
Included, the spirit that goes roundabout
And through included, not merely the visible,

The solid, but the movable, the moment,
The coming on of feasts and the habits of saints,
The pattern of the heavens and high, night air.

from "An Ordinary Evening in New Haven," by

Wallace Stevens

Contents

Poetry and Physics: The Spirits of Opposition

TEACHERS

Illustrations: following page 56, and pages 191, 201

NOTES

ACKNOWLEDGMENTS

INDEX

Introduction

"It happened one night by moonshine," Gaspar da Cruz recalled of a moment in south China during the winter of 1556–57, "that I and certain Portugals were sitting on a bench at the riverside by the door of our lodging, when a few young men came along the river in a boat passing the time, playing on divers instruments; and we, being glad to hear the music, sent for them to come near where we were, and that we would invite them. They as gallant youths came near with the boat and began to tune their instruments, in such sort that we were glad to see them fit themselves that they might make no discord." Da Cruz and his Portuguese friends enjoyed the music so much that they asked the Chinese players to come back the next day, this time bringing some singers. The Chinese promised to do so, but did not appear. Yet, as if sensing the sincerity of da Cruz's interest, "at daybreak one morning they came with the same instruments to give us a dawn-song, so as not to disappoint us altogether."[1]

We know, from other remarks of da Cruz, that he had not been altogether without music while he was awaiting the musicians' return. For he had followed the local Cantonese custom of buying two nightingales, one male and one female, feeding them cooked rice grains coated with yolk of egg and placing them in adjacent partially covered cages so that they could "feel but not see each other." With this treatment, as da Cruz delightedly noted, "the male melted himself in music" and the female responded accordingly, the two birds filling December with song "as if it had been in April."[2]

We can make of such a moment, snatched out of the past, what we will. Gaspar da Cruz was a Dominican friar, who had gone to Canton to convert the Chinese to Christianity. Failing in this endeavor, he returned to Portugal in leisurely stages, arriving in Lisbon just in time to succor the sick and dying in the terrible plague of 1569. This selflessness cost him his life, but not before he had seen to the press his "Treatise in which the things of China are related at great length, with their particularities." Published in late February 1570, two weeks after da Cruz's death, this "Treatise" in twenty-nine chapters was the first full-length book devoted entirely to China published in the West.

To someone like me, coming at China from the outside, da Cruz's work remains a model and an inspiration. Despite his ambitious religious goals, his clerical habit, his friendships with Portuguese adventurers, and his minimal knowledge of the Chinese language, da Cruz never lost his generosity of spirit or wavered in his attempt to balance precision with comprehensiveness in all his writings. To him, the music in the moonshine and his nightingales' songs were an integral part of the story of a vast country that could also be cruel and baffling. Da Cruz sought the elusive elements that would give a complete picture of China, even while he acknowledged the impossibility of the task. As he told his readers in the prologue to his "Treatise," he held to the hope that "by the things which are related herein, those which are as yet unknown could be conjectured."[3] China contradicted the experience of any other societies of which da Cruz had read or heard, where "distant things often sound greater than they really are." China, however, was "clean contrary, because China is much more than it sounds."[4]

If, in my studies of China, I must often plead guilty with Gaspar da Cruz of a certain overestimation of the object of affection, so I must also admit—as a reading of the essays collected here will surely show—to a certain overenthusiastic or even harebrained eclecticism. In this weakness I again find a precursor who offers a kind of solace, this time in the person of Theophilus Siegfried Bayer. Born in 1694 in the East Prussian town of Königsberg, the son of a painter, Bayer had a conventional enough school and university education in Latin, Greek, and Hebrew until, when he was nineteen, the thunder struck. Bayer later described the moment in an autobiographical essay:

> In the year 1713, while I was staying in the country, something happened to me—all of a sudden I was overwhelmed by a desire to learn Chinese. In the period that followed I worked and thought—or rather dreamed—about how to penetrate that mysterious discipline. If only I could produce some small thing in that field I would count myself grandson of the gods and king of kings. Like a pregnant rabbit, I collected everything in my burrow, whatever I could find to make up some kind of dictionary and some introduction to the rules of the Chinese language and to Chinese literature.[5]

The result, after seventeen years of grinding labor in Königsberg, Berlin, and St. Petersburg, was the publication in 1730 of Bayer's two-volume *Museum sinicum*, the first book about the Chinese language to be published in Europe.

The *Museum sinicum* is a wild and strange tribute to the capaciousness of Bayer's burrow and the length of his pregnancy. It was not a success, and indeed Bayer died shortly after reading a savage dismissal of the book by France's most eminent scholar of oriental studies. But, just as da Cruz had done in his book 160 years before, so had Bayer, despite his own ignorance, tried to be both fair and comprehensive. The obstacles in his way were daunting, perhaps insurmountable. In the first place, Bayer knew almost no Chinese and had only a scattering of inaccurate fragments and poorly reproduced Chinese characters to work from. As an academician in the newly founded St. Petersburg, he had some prestige and a small stipend yet almost no books, and it often took years of correspondence to tease out the answers to quite simple linguistic problems.

Bayer, furthermore, was heir to the European orientalist tradition that sought either a "key" or some totally comprehensive guide to the ideas behind the Chinese language that would yield all their mysteries at one fell swoop: thus his work was as full of false starts as of dead ends. But as Bayer wrote in a letter to a friend, with his customary (and somewhat playful) erudition, he "bravely shouldered the enormous burden. Why not? The Greeks got into Troy by trying, everything is done by trying, as the old woman of Alexandria says in Theocritus's *Bucolics.*"[6]

In the lengthy introduction to his *Museum sinicum*, Bayer reflected on the change in Western perceptions of China that had occurred between the mid-fourteenth and the mid-sixteenth centuries. In the period following Marco Polo's sojourn in China, with the collapse of the Mongol empire and the disruption of all the known trade routes, the "country seemed more and more to fade away, to disappear as a star declining in the skies"; but once China was "unveiled to us again it appeared as a new world, inhabited by a people that cultivated politeness, refined manners and elegance according to the teaching and the principles of their ancestors, thus vying for this kind of glory with the European nations."[7]

Yet in their studies of China, the many courageous scholarly and missionary pioneers spent little time or energy trying to analyze the Chinese language itself. It was this failure—fascinating and enigmatic to Bayer—that he set out to remedy. In his pageant of precursors, Bayer handled, with apparent equanimity, a number of theorists of colossal eccentricity; it was as if, in lining the walls of his burrow with their words, he felt it incumbent upon himself to give them his full compassion. Bayer's list gives us some sense of the range of linguistic approaches that he was attempting to synthesize: the Englishman John Webb, for instance, devoted much of his scholarly life to proving that Chinese was the world's first language and hence the "mother" of all others; the Dutchman Isaac Vossius praised the arts and sciences of China above all others and "indicated that he would rather have been born in China than in our part of the world"; the Frenchman Philippe Masson "proved" that Chinese was an old Hebrew dialect, knowledge of which could solve many a knotty Old Testament linguistic problem—thus the nature of the "Manna" that God fed to the children of Israel in the desert was easily understood when one realized the word was simply a variant of "Man-tou," the common steamed dumplings of China. For the Swedish scholar Olaus Rudbeck (who made his points, says Bayer, "with nearly terrifying force and verbosity"), Chinese was the closest parallel to the language of the Goths. Yet none of these men, according to Bayer, should be simply dismissed, even if their theories were "vague and superficial" or "steeped in mist," for behind their passionate theorizing lay much "sharpness of wit and assiduity."[8]

Bayer's balance between fairness and a sense of absurdity was given its greatest test when he considered the case of Andreas Müller. This prodigy from Pomerania claimed to have designed a simple *clavis sinica* ("key to Chinese") that would teach anyone to read the language in a few days, or a month at most; but having resolutely refused to share the details of this key with the European community, and having failed to find a purchaser who would come up with his asking price of two thousand thaler, Müller burned all his scholarly papers, including the famous key, shortly before his death. In assessing Müller's scholarship, Bayer admitted that Müller was "greedy," "created" sources to corroborate his arguments, wrote Chinese characters "badly," demonstrated an "utter helplessness" in some of his misinterpretations, and constructed an entire theory of the tones of Chinese characters by using the musical scale, "as if he were to imagine a whole nation singing at a party—quarts, octaves and double octaves!" And yet, despite all this and more, Bayer would never dismiss Müller's work, any more than that of the other scholars he analyzed: for what Müller showed throughout his scholarly life, however misjudged it might have been, was "a passionate desire for understanding and an admirable productivity."[9]

Of his own work, Bayer simply wrote, "I have called my book 'Museum Sinicum,' because that was the name that first occurred to me and because I could not find any better." As to its worth, "it is not for me to set forth in detail what it is that I have accomplished in these two volumes, nor how or to what extent I have failed—it is up to the reader to judge it for himself."[10] Even after he had read, in 1738, how "contemptuously and harshly" the French scholar Etienne Fourmont had dismissed his life's work, Bayer still wrote in a letter to a friend that his own respect for Fourmont's scholarship had not been "diminished" on that account: "I admire true excellence and merit in an adversary and even in an enemy."[11]

Now that we are in a scholarly world bulging with dictionaries, glossaries, and bibliographies and have comparatively easy access to China and Chinese scholars, Bayer and da Cruz might seem no more than curiosities. Bayer himself had apparently not heard of da Cruz, and few read Bayer after his flaying by Fourmont. Both scholars were swiftly superseded by others, of greater range and perspicacity—or with better access to publishing houses and the publicity mills. Yet I like thinking about these two men and reading their musings, because all of us will be superseded also, one way or another, before too long. The long years of research and writing will be shown to have been fugitive or inadequate. New texts will appear or old ones be reevaluated; new topics will absorb the scholars and their readers; new approaches to the past will thrust aside the old ones. Scholarship itself is full of a kind of barely contained craziness, as Bayer kept reminding us. We do what we can at the time we can do it, and take our lumps or receive the rewards—or maybe both at once. If we choose to do nothing with all our research, not to write it down, weigh it, and make our thoughts public, then we are protected in a way, but it is a weak kind of protection, one that dodges the quest for true knowledge. In our reticence, we can still be watchdogs to the field, maybe even gaze serenely across the whole panorama, but we can never truly be engaged at the deepest part of the fray.

An image occurs to me, from a walk in the rain with my father long ago. My father's terrier, Toms, is convulsed with excitement, keening into a rabbit burrow, his front paws drumming in a frenzy of exultation, the earth flying out in a cloud between his splayed hind legs. I stand nearby, astonished at the sight. The earth piles up, the dog barks on, the rain falls; and no rabbits ever appear. Forewarned by Toms's vociferous advances, they have presumably withdrawn to a quieter haven down adjacent tunnels.

Perhaps that is my own messy modernist version of Bayer's burrow. And doubtless, like da Cruz, I make more of all this than I should. But the earth did pile up, and along with the books that I wrote over the last twenty-five years, I wrote a good many essays on China as well; here are the ones that I think best represent my own attempts to think about China with precision and—as much as I could at each given time—to be fair and thorough.* The essays seem to fall rather naturally into five blocks: those about Chinese and Westerners who tried to cross over into each other's cultures; those related to Confucian theory and Chinese

---

* My thanks to many editors over many years who worked on these various essays, and especially to Robert Silvers at the *New York Review of Books*, for he edited the most, and always with sharpness and care. My deep thanks, also, to Steven Forman at Norton. This collection was his idea, and he saw it through from start to finish with his usual blend of patience, skill, and tenacity.

These essays are reprinted here as they were originally written or published, with some small exceptions: punctuation and phrasing have occasionally been altered for consistency or clarity, long quotations have been identified, a few names are now accompanied by an identifying phrase, and some passages originally cut for reasons of space have been reinserted. Both the old (Wade-Giles) and new (pinyin) systems of romanization appear, following usage in the original versions. I have not "updated" my conclusions in any way, nor sought to revise the bibliographies.

state power; those about varied aspects of Chinese social history; those concerned with revolutionary China; and those reflecting on my own teachers and mentors.

I call this collection my *Chinese Roundabout,* partly out of homage to Wallace Stevens, who has been part of my life for a long time now, but also because I love the word "roundabout." It is a word about a meandering that is yet somehow purposive. It is a word (at least in England, where it is the equivalent for the American "traffic circle") that attempts to sort out, with some kind of logic, the conveyances converging on a given point from many directions. And above all, in its sense of "carousel" it conjures up the children, those scholars of the future, knees gripping the painted wood, hands holding on for dear life, heads thrown back with laughter in the vertiginous wind.

New Haven, Connecticut
July 12 and 13, 1991

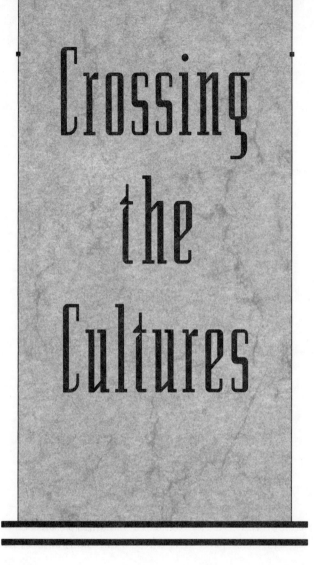

Crossing the Cultures

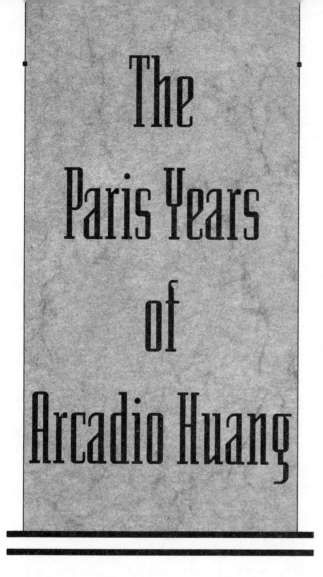

The Paris Years of Arcadio Huang

Life was hard for Arcadio Huang in the autumn and early winter of 1713.[1] The weather in Paris was vile, bitterly cold with swirling fog. France's apparently endless war over the Spanish succession had demoralized everyone, driven up the cost of food, and led to frequent drops in the value of money. Though Arcadio had married a young Parisian

---

An abbreviated version of this essay first appeared in *Granta*, in 1990.

woman, Marie-Claude Regnier, in April 1713, their life was a constant struggle. Their rented room in the Rue Guénégaud, on the south bank across the Seine from Notre Dame cathedral, was always cold since they had not enough money for a regular supply of wood or coal. Their furniture was sparse, they had few clothes, and they could not afford a decent matrimonial bed. They could not even afford salt to give some savor to their simple meals. And, alarmingly, Huang would awaken on some mornings spitting blood. After these episodes he felt a terrible lassitude and often had to rest in his bed for hours.

How Huang had ever come to be in Paris was a saga in itself. Huang was born in 1679 in the coastal Chinese province of Fujian. His father was a Catholic convert, baptized as Paul; anxious to live the celibate life of a Christian religious, Paul had tried not to marry, but had been forced to by his parents, since he was their only son and they could not allow the family line to die out. But after Paul's wife bore a succession of four daughters, the family was in despair. When she became pregnant for the fifth time, Paul and his wife pledged privately that if this child were a boy, that boy would be dedicated to the religious life. The child was a male, later baptized as Arcadio. Paul Huang died when his son was only seven, but Arcadio's mother stuck to her vow, though she was not sure how to implement it. The solution was provided by the arrival in their hometown of Philibert le Blanc, a French missionary of forty-two working with the papacy's Société des Missions Etrangères. Arcadio's mother took her son to see le Blanc, and explained the vow that she and her late husband had made; touched, le Blanc agreed to educate the boy and prepare him for the church. To prevent any misunderstandings as to le Blanc's motives, and to conform with Qing dynasty law, Arcadio was formally adopted by le Blanc, and the two studied and worked together for three years.

Le Blanc had the foresight to ensure that Huang continued his Chinese studies under good local tutors, as well as introducing him to Catholic theology and to Latin. For unexplained reasons, le Blanc passed the boy on to Artus de Lionne, the titular bishop of Rosalie, who continued to train Arcadio in the same range of subjects. Probably around 1695, in his midteens, Arcadio set off on a series of travels around south and central China, staying with various relatives from the Huang lineage and exploring the different customs of each area. It never occurred to him, he wrote later, that the knowledge acquired in these travels would later serve to allow him "an honest subsistence in a foreign land."

Before Huang, only a handful of Chinese had reached the West. Such a journey was not only a terrifying leap into the unknown; it also defied Chinese law, which held that those traveling overseas were rejecting the values of their own land. Huang's reasons for going seem to have been the accumulation of a number of coincidences: his mother had just died, his eldest sister was ready and willing to take over the management of the family, he was still restless and in a traveling mood, and he ran into de Lionne (whom he had not seen for several years) in a Fujian provincial town. When de Lionne told him he had been summoned back to Europe and suggested they travel together, Huang at once accepted. They sailed out of Amoy (Xiamen) on February 17, 1702, aboard a British ship, and reached London eight months later. The War of the Spanish Succession, pitting Louis XIV's France against Britain, made the cross-Channel journey almost impossible, but after some travails the two booked passage with an envoy of the duke of Bavaria, who traveled with diplomatic immunity. In late 1702 they were in Paris, and shortly after that in Rome.

Had Huang been a little less adventurous, or a little more devout, he would doubtless have stayed in Rome for further education and eventually been ordained a priest and sent back to China to work as a missionary. But in Rome he seems to have developed doubts about a life in holy orders, doubts exacerbated when he was sent back to Paris to live with the priests at the Société des Missions Etrangères. Through a lucky series of chance encounters, Huang met the king's librarian, the abbé Bignon. Bignon, who knew no Chinese language, was just beginning the daunting task of attempting to sort and catalog the miscellaneous treasure trove of books in Chinese and Manchu that had gradually been accumulating in the King's Library. Bignon needed a Chinese assistant; Huang needed a job. It was a perfect match, and by 1711 Huang had rented a room of his own and acquired the sonorous title of Chinese interpreter to the King's Library, along with a small stipend.

In Paris, Huang applied himself to the study of French. He was given shelter and library resources by the fathers of the Société des Missions Etrangères, who were regretful over his decision to abandon the priesthood but not vindictive. As his French became moderately fluent, he used his mission contacts to get translation jobs and began courting Marie-Claude Regnier. By the spring of 1713, Huang was supplementing his small stipend by translating letters to and from China for members of the mission society and by translating difficult works for French scholars, such as texts on astronomy and passages from the Chinese classics. It was a frail enough financial basis for a marriage, and several senior churchmen warned there would be trouble. But Marie-Claude's parents seem to have liked Huang and to have felt it right to give the young couple a chance. They came regularly to the Rue Guénégaud, sometimes bringing little gifts of wine and food, or making small cash loans to tide the couple over when payments to the tradesmen fell too far in arrears.

In late November 1713, the financial skies suddenly cleared for Huang and his wife. For months, the king's librarian Bignon had been petitioning for some sort of cash payment for the Chinese bibliographer and had traveled in person to Versailles to obtain it. A firm promise for five hundred livres was finally given by the king's chancellor in mid-November after Bignon had used his richest rhetoric: "Our little Chinese, for whom you have already shown some favor, has no means for staying alive other than the king's bounty. . . . He hasn't a sou; in the name of God, give him a few pistols on account." There were still a few bureaucratic hurdles, but on November 27 the whole sum of five hundred livres was handed over personally to Huang. He and Marie-Claude at once went on a tour of all their local creditors. "Everything is paid off," Huang wrote delightedly in the informal journal he had begun to keep in a small soft-bound notebook. He had anticipated the windfall by buying his wife two eggs for her Sunday breakfast on the twenty-sixth. Now he followed up by buying salt, and at eight in the morning on Tuesday the twenty-eighth a fresh load of firewood was delivered to their room. As if the world of international politics shared in their joy, peace was at last ratified to conclude France's long war over Spain, and Arcadio and Marie-Claude went to church to join with other Parisians in a Te Deum of thanks.

With solvency, little luxuries came into the Huangs' lives: loaves of bread, cheeses, two kinds of pâté, a cake, mushrooms to garnish a stew. A tailor began the fittings on a three-piece suit for Huang, to consist of britches, embroidered waistcoat, and a black topcoat. Scissors, silk, and thread were obtained for Marie-Claude so that she could do some dressmaking. A new bed was scrutinized, but rejected at the last minute by Marie-Claude. Huang was still sometimes sick and feverish, but now he could purchase medicines and visit local doctors. The weather followed the trend of politics with the gentlest of December days ("tems fort doux," as Huang wrote).

Warm weather and good food turned Huang's thoughts to the future. He wanted a child. Some sense of his excitement and expectation can be gleaned from brief notes in his journal, usually written out in Chinese-romanized form, presumably to hide these intimate details from prying eyes, and perhaps even from Marie-Claude herself, if she peeped at his book to see what he was writing. The first such note, inscribed on December 11, 1713, mentioned that she had had a menstrual flow a week before, during a full moon. Did Huang see that as a good omen for fertility? If so, the notation for December 28 reflected a disappointment. Marie-Claude had had her period again; indeed, it had begun on the way back from a post-Christmas mass, at the church of the Augustinians. Another period followed on January 25, and again in late February. More cryptic notations scattered across the pages probably refer to their love-making, with Sundays either before or after mass a favored time.

Other notations give us a taste of the couple's life together: Marie-Claude's visits to the shops, the markets, and the butcher; her making a special rice pudding for Huang, or his favorite fritters; there is tobacco to smoke, wine or tea to drink, and Huang's foray out on the town with friends to the "carbaret." The couple love to play cards, especially piquet, with their in-laws, and husband and wife are constantly buying lottery tickets—that new institution feeding the people's hopes for immense profits that were so much a part of the speculative fever of the time. There are plenty of tensions, too. Both are often sickly or querulous. Marie-Claude erupts occasionally into an anger Huang cannot decipher, retiring silently to her bed and sleeping late, refusing her dinner—which Huang quite often cooked—or bursting out in a tantrum while walking along the street. Money remains scarce, and there are signs of the minor catastrophes that could overwhelm those on the edge of poverty: a loaf of bread missing from the batch purchased, the loss of twenty-seven sous (later recovered), the spilling of oil (whether from a lamp or from cooking is not clear) on one of Marie-Claude's good dresses. The couple are faithful in their attendance at mass, but Huang nearly always records them as going at different times and to different churches. If he goes to the church of the Augustinians, she goes to St. Sulpice. If he goes to St. Sulpice, she goes to St. Germain. Is there a rhythm here we cannot understand? Was Marie-Claude perhaps ashamed or embarrassed to be seen in the streets among the Sunday crowds with her exotic husband?

Whatever the reason, by February 1714 Huang had done everything possible to make himself look like an elegant French man-about-town. A meticulous clerk on the staff of the King's Library kept a record of the clothes, furnishings, bedding, kitchen ware, and writing utensils that were given to Huang as he set himself up after his marriage in the Rue Guénégaud. There, neatly listed, are his shirts, a suit, stockings, shoes, hat, umbrella, and a sword and belt. Apart from the sword, there are no surprises here. But a supplementary list, carefully labeled "Memorandum of monies spent by Mr. Arcade Oange from his own earnings," shows how Huang upgraded the state's basic handouts. Here we find six muslin cravats and six sets of frills for the sleeves of his suit, with two silver buttons to fasten them; two wigs, one extremely expensive, one more modestly priced; a tasseled cane; and, most expensive of all, a flowing knee-length cape, buttoned down the front, of the type known as a "Roquelaure," only recently made fashionable by the duke of the same name.

In what is surely an ebullient response to his newly found splendor, shaven head under powdered wig, flowing cloth at neck and wrist, cape languidly thrown across his shoulders and tasseled cane in hand, Huang suddenly introduces a new element into his journal. Before February 8, 1714, he had always referred to himself in the third person as plain Mr. Houange (or Hoange), or as "H." Now, in entries scattered across February and early March, we find him referring to himself as "Mgr. le Duc du St. Houange," "son Eminence Monseigneur le Cardinal de Fonchan Houange," "Monseigneur le Maréchal Hoange," and "Mgr. le Patriarche Hoange." Marie-Claude, presumably better dressed than before, if not as sumptuously as he, gets similar promotions in status. One day she is "Son Altesse serenissime Hoange" and another "Mme la Duchesse son épouse." His mother-in-law Regnier becomes "Son Altesse Royale."

In one of these lightheartedly grandiose passages, entered on February 17, 1714, Huang wrote in semiparody of the popular novels of the day, "So you can see, my dear reader, that Monseigneur l'ambassadeur Hoange still has a great deal to do, and has been giving audiences to all kinds of people." The work on which Huang was concentrating was the compilation of a French-Chinese dictionary, which the librarian Bignon had decided was a top priority if the royal collection was ever to be of use to French scholars generally. Bignon believed that to put the study of China on a firm base it was necessary to compile the underpinnings of language instruction. The task was extraordinarily hard, given the absence of any systematic prior study of the Chinese language in Europe, and the absence of parallels between the syntxes of the two cultures. Accordingly, to help Huang in his task, Bignon assigned him a rising young scholar named Nicolas Fréret, who had recently been appointed a student member of the Académie des Inscriptions et Belles Lettres. Nine years younger than Huang, Fréret was also (like Huang) an only son with four sisters, and the two men soon became close friends. Fréret wrote after their first meeting that he found Huang to be "a charming, modest young man, who seemed . . . to have a natural intelligence." The only problem was that Huang

> had no idea at all of European sciences and methods. Even his way of speaking French was almost unintelligible, since he found nothing in his native language at all similar to the European languages of which he had acquired a smattering; thus the French grammars that he had been advised to take as his models were incomprehensible to him, since he could find no way to attach distinct ideas to the abstract grammatical terms with which these books were filled.

There followed, in 1713 and 1714, a truly remarkable collaboration. Fréret worked steadily and patiently, during lengthy question and answer sessions, to get Huang to understand the grammatical structures that lay at the heart of the French language and that could be applied in turn to making a fruitful analysis of the Chinese language. Huang's French improved under this regimen, and he became able to formulate the major analytical questions himself and to provide tentative answers that Fréret would check over for him. Huang in his turn began to introduce Fréret to the structure and significance of the Chinese written characters, weaning Fréret away from the currently fashionable idea that they were similar to Egyptian hieroglyphic scripts. Huang showed Fréret how the seventy thousand or more different Chinese characters that one would find in the larger dictionaries were almost all, in fact, composed of 214 components or groups of strokes, which the Chinese called "radicals." By listing these radicals according to a set sequence, one could comparatively easily find a way into the otherwise baffling universe of the Chinese written word.

Buoyed by their mutual excitement, the two men completed a tentative vocabulary list of two thousand Chinese words translated into French. These words were chosen for their practicability in forming simple sentences or in describing common objects and needs. Fréret wrote in admiration of Huang's adaptability and tenacity: "I was touched by the gentleness, the modesty, but above all the more than stoic calmness of this young Chinese who found himself in a situation that would have seemed desperate to us Europeans. Four or five thousand leagues away from home, without wealth, special skills, or any help apart from a pension conditional on work at which he was sure he could not succeed

alone, at which it was very hard to help him, and in which success would
never be very great, he nevertheless kept an equanimity and a good humor
which astonished me, and which made me believe in what various accounts
have said about the Chinese character." In a Western literature all too
often replete with racist innuendos, this is one of the grandest and most
affectionate exceptions.

A Chinese living in Paris was, of course, intriguing in and of himself
to the French. Probably only two Chinese had visited Paris before Huang,
one in the 1680s and one in 1700, and neither of them had stayed for
long. So Huang was both asked out fairly often and received visitors at
his lodgings; these visitors were often friends of Fréret, or of the scholar
and astronomer François-Joseph Delisle, who lived nearby. Doubtless
some were merely curious, but others wanted to pump Huang seriously
for information about his homeland. Among these latter, none achieved
greater fame later than the young Montesquieu, fresh from completing
his studies of law, who visited Huang in the summer or autumn of 1713,
when Montesquieu was twenty-four.

Montesquieu was turning countless ideas over in his head, as always,
but for two of them Huang had particular resonance. One idea was for
a book that would look at French society through Asian eyes, to poke
fun at French people's beliefs in their own superiority and to make a
moral critique of European values. Though Montesquieu chose to construct this book in the form of Lettres Persanes (1721), we know that
Huang was one of the models for the naive Persian questioners whose
views turn European pretensions upside down. Montesquieu was particularly intrigued to learn that Huang had so trusted the Christian values
of the French that he had left his handsome hat in a church while he
went outside for a stroll. When Huang returned, he found the hat had
been stolen. Huang also, according to Montesquieu, had believed Europeans to be so moral that they had dispensed with capital punishment,
and he was amazed when some criminals were executed in Paris.

Of greater importance to Montesquieu were the social and legal structures of China, which were to emerge as a basic component of the analysis of comparative politics comprising his masterpiece, De l'Esprit des
lois (1748). The Montesquieu-Huang connection was documented by the
English scholar Robert Shackleton in the late 1940s when, rummaging
through cupboards in Montesquieu's former library at the Château de la
Brède, he came across a bound volume of Montesquieu's reading notes
entitled "Geographica." To a twenty-page section of these notes, Montesquieu had appended the title "Quelques remarques sur la Chine, que

j'ai tirées des conversations que j'ai eues avec M. Hoange." That Montesquieu writes "conversations" in the plural suggests that he visited Huang several times; since he himself left Paris on receiving news of his father's death in November 1713, the visits must have taken place before that date.

Just as there was a mutuality of interest between Fréret and Huang over the study of grammar, so there seems to have been a mutuality of interest between Huang and Montesquieu. For if, at one level, it was Montesquieu who was seeking specific information from Huang, Huang had prepared himself for just such an eventuality by his protracted travels in China before he left, in 1702. And the systematic nature of Montesquieu's questioning might well have given Huang that sense of category and organization about a wide range of formerly inchoate data that would be essential for the grand design of a two-volume work on China he was to develop in 1716.

According to Montesquieu's record, their conversations in 1713 ranged methodically across a wide range of subjects. Montesquieu began by inquiring about the religious systems of China. Huang explained that there were three overlapping systems: Confucianism, Taoism, and Buddhism. Confucians did not believe in the immortality of the soul, though they felt that the vapors from burning sacrificial food did in some way mingle with the vanishing spirits of the deceased, so that during the sacrifice itself those spirits "came to life again deliciously." Buddhists believed in the existence of hell and deemed it improper to take any life, animal or human. Buddhist priests did not marry; the Buddhist goddess of mercy, Guan-yin, was, like Mary, a virgin who bore a child. While not commenting on these Buddhist ideas—was Huang suggesting some parallels with Christianity?—Montesquieu observed to himself that the Confucianists were like Spinozists, making a kind of "world-spirit" (âme du monde) out of their idea of heaven (tien). Huang discussed the horrors of Chinese capital punishment by burning (not in fact practiced during his own time) and by slicing (which was still in vogue), the clothes people wore, their tombs, and their concepts of family property. In a lengthy discussion, Huang presented his views on Chinese language and grammar, Montesquieu perhaps not realizing how much of this came from Huang's studies with Fréret. To illustrate his points, Huang sang a Chinese song to Montesquieu and recited the Our Father in Chinese.

In later conversations, Huang and Montesquieu continued to explore fresh ground. They discussed the place of the Chinese novel in Chinese literature, the problems faced by Western missionaries when living in

Chinese society, the nature and format of the Chinese civil service examination system, and the nature of the Chinese state. Montesquieu was struck by the fact that China had often been fragmented in the past, and understood Huang to say that in some of its earlier guises, China had been a true republic. Claims by the Chinese to greatness in government seemed to Montesquieu typical of their general pride and boastfulness: if China had been such a great nation, how could the Manchus have conquered it so swiftly in the 1640s? Montesquieu was shocked by what he learned about the mutual-responsibility aspects of the Chinese judicial system, which at times led the innocent to be punished along with the guilty. Huang also introduced Montesquieu to certain linguistic peculiarities of Chinese social life: the use of indirection in greetings, and of self-deprecation in all references to oneself and one's own family. Huang made it clear that the Chinese were subjugated and humiliated under the Manchu yoke, and he also discussed the status of women in China and patterns of female deference. The conversations—or at least Montesquieu's record of them—ended with a broad discussion of Chinese history and the dating of China's own great flood and of subsequent eclipses. However confident Montesquieu appears in his cultural and political judgments about China in the *Esprit des lois,* the "Geographica" notes show otherwise: "I believe that the Chinese will absolutely never be understood by us," he wrote.

If Montesquieu helped open Huang's eyes to different ways of thinking about his own society, a very different stimulus came from a group of French merchants who urged Huang to join them in making money from the China trade. The four were all directors of the French Compagnie des Indes, and they proposed to hire Huang as their assistant and interpreter for an eighteen-month period, as they made a determined effort to open up trading contacts in several major Chinese cities. Huang was nervously interested, telling the four that they would have to consult Bignon, the head librarian, and gauge his reaction. Bignon in turn wrote to Pontchartrain, Louis XIV's powerful minister of state and minister of marine affairs, under whose rubric the China trade was included. By February 1714 the discussions were moving briskly, under considerable pressure since the company's ships were just about to sail. Huang's informal journal on the date of February 24 mentions that on that day "Monsieur le Gouverneur Hoang" had "had the grace" to accompany two of the company's directors to see Pontchartrain in person. But this tongue-in-cheek reference was the last that was heard of the idea. Either the ships sailed or Huang could not bear to leave France and his wife.

Perhaps also he feared, not without cause in the tight-money situation of the day, that his stipend, once canceled, might never be restored.

Huang's friend Fréret, too, had come up with another scheme to make money for Huang. Fréret had been impressed by the enormous financial success of the French translation of the Arab tales known as *The Thousand and One Nights,* and he suggested to Huang that "the publication of a Chinese novel might bring him both a profit and a fame that would free him from the discouragement into which the harshness of the times sometimes plunged him." Huang seems to have responded well to the idea, and the two men finished some draft translations of a Ming dynasty literati tale. But they shelved the proposal when Fréret decided the work was at once "too serious and too little amusing" to appeal to the public of the day, since the plot was driven forward only by various "literary disputes" between the protagonists. So instead the two men intensified their work on the projected dictionary, shifting their energies from a dictionary arranged alphabetically by pronunciation of the Chinese words, as initially suggested by Bignon, to one in which the Chinese characters would be arranged by the standard 214 radicals, as Huang had now successfully explained them to Fréret. At Fréret's suggestion, too, Huang began to experiment with transcribing some Chinese passages of prose and poetry, model letters, and examples of ceremonial style.

This intellectually exciting collaboration was interrupted by two dramatic moments in the domestic life of Arcadio Huang and Marie-Claude. The first of these was the decision to leave the cramped room in the Rue Guénégaud and to seek an apartment that would have more room for their newly acquired furniture and better reflect Huang's more exalted status. By April 21 they had found a place on the Rue des Canettes, which ran from the gracious old church of St. Germain des Près to the vast new colonnaded bulk of the church of St. Sulpice. In preparation for the move the couple bought a new bed, a spectacular one this time— four feet wide, with scarlet draperies, feather mattress, pillows embroidered with yellow flowers, and covers of jonquil-colored taffeta. Mother-in-law Regnier brought plumes as a final touch of decoration for the top of the bedposts. Though Huang was often sick, spitting blood again and always tired, and Marie-Claude was often petulant, prone to headaches and pains in her legs, the final move began on July 6 and was completed two weeks later. On the twenty-sixth, Huang summoned the locksmith and had two new locks fitted to their doors. By August there was no more doubt that a second event was to occur: Marie-Claude was pregnant.

Life was tranquil that autumn, though Huang had never imagined such weather. "The weather seems bad all the time," he jotted down on August 24; "this year has been a year of rain." But there were walks, on the few nice days, with Marie-Claude and her parents in the Luxembourg gardens, near their home, or occasionally in the open fields of Les Invalides. Huang joined a syndicate of forty people to buy lottery tickets in bulk, and their new landlady—Mme Bomond—taught Marie-Claude how to ease the aches in her stomach with a concoction of barley and sugar. There was plenty of work for Huang to do, both free-lance translation and the dictionary labors with Fréret.

The routine of their new life together, and the watchful excitement over the forthcoming baby, ended abruptly on the early morning of December 26, 1714, when, without warning, Fréret was committed to the Bastille prison under a secret lettre de cachet. The charge against Fréret was that he had sided with the Jansenist party in France, had helped publish illicit materials on the current religious controversies, and had been especially virulent in his attacks on a *History of France* (by Père Daniel) that was currently considered orthodox. Such a prison sentence on such a charge brought danger to all who were in the condemned man's circle. Huang and his wife must have feared terribly for their future, and for the loss of his job if any breath of such treason clung to Huang himself. A new man was assigned to work with Huang, the scholar Etienne Fourmont, considered a fast-rising "orientalist" in the world of the French Academy, but also a vain, ambitious, and contentious scholar, with whom Huang was never able to form the friendly and harmonious working relationship he had had with Fréret.

In this tense atmosphere, in the spring of 1715, Mme Huang gave birth to a baby daughter at the house on the Rue des Canettes, perhaps in that grand bed with the jonquil-colored sheets of which Huang was so proud. The baby was healthy and, as a neighbor later recalled, "looked quite Chinese, her face and color were just those that distinguish a Chinese from a European." But Mme Huang fell ill at the delivery, developing a fever that swiftly ate away her strength and killed her within a few days. Remembering those awful moments a year later, Huang wrote, it was as though "God had decided, if I may put it that way, to do no more than let me get a glimpse of the wife He had chosen for me, and who was, I have to say, as dear to His heart as she was to mine."

Huang decided that he would not marry again, but would devote his energies to his scholarly work and to raising his little daughter, who was baptized Marie-Claude in memory of her mother. Yet his own health was worsening, his spirits were low, and the work with Fourmont went slowly. Fréret was released from the Bastille in June 1715, but even though he had apparently continued to work away at Chinese while incarcerated, he and Huang did not get together again. Fréret had a host of other intellectual interests, and he plunged into various linguistic and historical works of other cultures with his customary energy, apparently content to let Huang cope with Fourmont as best he could. How much Huang was aware of it at the time, we cannot tell, but it turned out later that Fourmont was bitterly jealous of both Fréret and Huang, and determined to further his own career by claiming their endeavors as his own. Yet the dictionary edged forward through the various radicals and by the autumn of 1716 had reached the "water radical," number 85 out of the 214 that Huang had to cover. Huang and Fourmont also worked at various dialogues, to be used in language teaching as a supplement to the passages of literature already glossed. Sprightly and even amusing, these dealt with the buying and selling of goods, with conversations between literati, even with the racy topic of two scholars discussing the charms of a young singing girl who has just come to their neighborhood.

The old king, Louis XIV, died in 1715, and Huang wrote of Louis's glories with the patriotic pride of a Frenchman. It was the late king's belief in opening the way to China, he wrote, that had been the inspiration of Huang's scholarly life. Now, under the regency, Huang's task had suddenly become clear to him. He would create a great work, in two volumes, that would explain everything about his native land to the French. The first volume would be largely linguistic, a grammar that would illuminate the structure of Chinese language and explain how the written Chinese characters were able to achieve—by different means—the effects made possible in the West by declension, conjugation, and mood. The second volume would introduce French readers to everything they needed to know in order to gain "an exact knowledge of the kingdom of China," a task for which Huang felt himself well suited thanks to the wide travels he had made inside his own country before taking ship for Europe.

It was not to be. Huang felt weaker and weaker as 1716 passed from summer to autumn. He always seemed to be in need of money again, for the rent, for a servant, for food, for Marie Boulle—the wet nurse of little Marie-Claude. He began to drink a great deal of wine, buying it often on credit with money borrowed—in small sums—from local Jewish moneylenders. In an attempt to build up his strength, he made special purchases of fresh eggs and milk, buying these too on credit. He was writing page 1140 of his projected dictionary when the fever caught up with him. For the first time anywhere in this vast work, the languages he had so painstakingly acquired began to blur. French words glided into Italian, Italian into Latin, Latin once more back to French. He wrote one more character, quite neatly, and then just stopped.

On October 1, 1716, Arcadio Huang died, in the Rue des Canettes, leaving Marie-Claude to the mercies of the state and her grandparents. The regent, Philip of Orleans, agreed to pay for the girl's education and upbringing if she lived beyond January 1, 1719. Until then, her grandparents would raise her, drawing on the residue—some four hundred livres—of Huang's small estate. Huang was given a decent burial (costing forty-three livres), and six masses were said for his soul that October. Six more were paid for and promised for sometime in the near future. Huang had hoped, passionately, that at least Marie-Claude would live on, to embody his dream of a merging of China and France that would enable each to understand the other better. But she too died, only a few months after her father. The flicker of light, for this particular dream of a new era between China and the West, was out.

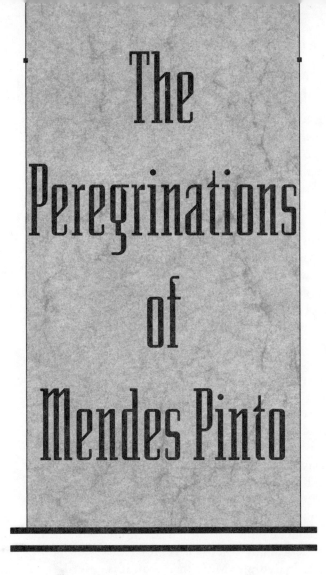

The Peregrinations of Mendes Pinto

Pinto's *Travels*, written in Portugal between 1569 and 1578, is a crazed, dreamy, fascinating, elliptical book. Mendes Pinto lived and traveled extensively in Asia during the years 1537 to 1558, and the *Travels* is his attempt to come to grips with those experiences, and the fantasies and reflections that accompanied them. The huge, rambling manuscript

This essay first appeared in 1990 in the *New York Review of Books*.

was finally published in 1614, thirty-one years after Pinto's death, and enjoyed an immediate success. A fussily emended Spanish edition appeared in 1620, a complete French translation in 1628, and an abbreviated English one in 1653. Pinto's own title for his book was *The Peregrinations*, and that seems to say something different from *Travels*. "Travels" sounds either purposeful or at least touristic, whereas "peregrinations" can begin and end anywhere, can change purpose and goal constantly, or can indeed lack them altogether.

Pinto's book baffled his editors and translators, who were always trying to tidy him up. The Spanish translator tried to give a proper baroque elaboration to the text, while the English translator compiled an elaborate historiographical essay in an attempt to prove Pinto's accuracy. But English readers were not convinced. As Dorothy Osborne wrote to Sir William Temple just after the book's English publication, Pinto's "lyes are as pleasant harmlesse on's as lyes can bee, and in noe great number considering the scope hee has for them." By 1695, in *Love for Love*, the playwright William Congreve could have one of his characters reproach another with the words "Ferdinand Mendez Pinto was but a type of thee, thou liar of the first magnitude."

Pinto has at last found his perfect editor-translator in Rebecca Catz, who sensibly points out that the protracted arguments over Pinto's historicity and veracity have obscured the fact "that Pinto's masterpiece belongs not to history, but to literature, specifically to the genre of satire."[1] Thus "the inconsistencies and improbabilities of the *Travels* are an integral part of its design, a deliberate puzzle." The shades of the various scholars who tried to reconcile Pinto's recorded adventures with the historical calendar should accordingly rest in peace, for Pinto's chronology "is glaringly and daringly inaccurate. More than that, it is absurd."

Freed by Catz's common sense from the need to read Pinto as history, we can instead relax and read Pinto as a fiction that blends the elements of the satirical and the picaresque. Pinto's central goal, Ms. Catz suggests, was to offer a deep and protracted criticism of the actions of the Portuguese in building their overseas empire, and of the Christian crusading ethos that lay behind them. Pinto's critique was thus directed at both the men of war and the men of God involved in the enterprise. Descriptions of Asian beliefs and actions are used to highlight the absurdities and hypocrisy of the Portuguese, something that could hardly be expressed openly by a Portuguese living at home in the later sixteenth century. Again and again, I kept noticing how precisely Pinto was a precursor of Montesquieu and Voltaire, of Defoe and Goldsmith. Yet at the same time, we can see Pinto as narrator in the emerging tradition of the Spanish picaresque novel.

Catz shrewdly draws a parallel between Pinto's relationship with one of his more rascally employers and that of Lazarillo de Tormes (of the 1554 novel) with his fifth master, the seller of papal indulgences. In her words, "since the *picaro* is never quite so corrupt as the society he enters, he has to be taught the tricks of the trade, and in the process much that is underhanded is exposed and analyzed for the reader."

To achieve his satirical goals, Catz believes, Pinto presented his narrative through a single central persona who, however, spoke in four different voices that echo and interact with each other: the four voices are those of the *vir bonus,* the moral and virtuous man who wins our trust by his evident sincerity; the ingénu who wins our sympathy by his naive innocence about the horrors he describes; the hero-patriot, always rushing into the fray against evil; and the picaro who participates in the very evils he condemns.

The structure of Pinto's book is an ungainly one and takes some getting used to. Pinto himself wrote the entire work (his text fills 523 large pages in the current Chicago edition) without any chapter breaks. His posthumous early-seventeenth-century editor divided the book into 226 sections, each with its own descriptive title. These divisions, followed in the original Spanish and French translations, though not in the British, are retained by Catz. But this makes for slightly disjointed reading, since many of the sections are more like vignettes, and the roll of the narrative often spans dozens or even scores of them. According to my reading of this strangely powerful book, it is essentially constructed of ten major, integrated narrative blocks, these ten blocks being enclosed within brief opening and concluding chapters that give some accurate autobiographical detail and present Pinto's views on fate and his own life. The opening lines, especially, are wonderfully effective in giving us the voice of Pinto the narrator, with their mixture of whining, faith, and apparently circumstantial detail:

> Whenever I look back at all the hardship and misfortune I suffered throughout most of my life, I can't help thinking I have good reason to complain of my bad luck, which started about the time I was born and continued through the best years of my life. It seems that misfortune had singled me out above all others for no purpose but to hound me and abuse me, as though it were something to be proud of. As I grew

up in my native land, my life was a constant struggle against poverty and misery, and not without its moments of terror when we barely escaped with our lives. If that were not enough, Fortune saw fit to carry me off to the Indies, where, instead of my lot improving as I had hoped, the hardship and hazards only increased with the passing years.

But on the other hand, when I consider that God always watched over me and brought me safely through all those hazards and hardships, then I find that there is not as much reason to complain about my past misfortune as there is reason to give thanks to the Lord for my present blessings, for he saw fit to preserve my life, so that I could write this awkward, unpolished tale, which I leave as a legacy for my children—because it is intended only for them. I want them to know all about the twenty-one years of difficulty and danger I lived through, in the course of which I was captured thirteen times and sold into slavery seventeen times, in various parts of India, Ethiopia, Arabia Felix, China, Tartary, Macassar, Sumatra, and many other provinces of the archipelago located in the easternmost corner of Asia, which is referred to as "the outer edge of the world" in the geographical works of the Chinese, Siamese, *Gueos*, and Ryukyu, about which I expect to have a lot more to say later on, and in much greater detail.[2]

I had never read Pinto before, having merely seen him referred to as a source in various scholarly works. But with these words I was hooked, and I was determined to follow Pinto wherever he might lead. It is of course typical of Pinto, as I later discovered, that he was not captured thirteen times and sold into slavery seventeen times—or not according to the evidence presented in his own book. He does describe being captured eight times, in various parts of the world, and being sold into slavery seven times, to masters of varying degrees of nastiness, which would be enough for most people. But with characteristic wit he observes of one of those sales that nobody at all wanted to buy him, and he was left sheepishly standing on the auction block unloved, unwashed, and half-starving, "like a sorry old nag put out to pasture."

The world according to Pinto is an unpredictable one, full of violent juxtapositions: insane and sickening cruelties alongside gentleness and concern, accumulation of dizzying fortunes followed at once by the loss of absolutely everything, the crassest of superstitions overlaid with philosophical profundity. Each of the ten narrative blocks pursues all these themes to varying degrees, through the confrontations between Portuguese and native rulers, which is usually (though not always) also a confrontation between Catholicism and Islam. Blame is distributed evenhandedly by Pinto, and the Portuguese are not the only sadists and masters of deceit. But cumulatively they emerge as the worst, because they, with a bemused Pinto always in their midst, are the constants in the book, while the other societies and rulers enter the stage and depart again to the wings in a rhythmic sequence.

Since some readers may be baffled or deterred by the 226 sections into which Pinto's book is divided, it is worth briefly describing the ten main narrative blocks; the blocks are sequential chronologically, so the sequence gives at least some sense of how Pinto spent his many years in the East.

Block one, comprising sections 2–12, is set in the Middle East and Ethiopia, focusing on the search for Prester John's descendants, and on Pinto's life both as slave and as freebooter around Hormuz and Diu. In block two (sections 13–20) Pinto is in Sumatra, involved in the Battak wars; block three (sections 21–37) continues the Sumatra saga with a protracted account of the bitter Aaru-Achin wars. Block four (sections 38–59) is the tale of a different kind of confrontation, as Pinto's piratical employer Antonio de Faria pursues his equally villainous and piratical sworn enemy, the *khoja* Hassim. The long block five (sections 60–116) is a tale both of Pinto's adventures in China and of Antonio de Faria's obsessive quest for a mystical Chinese paradise.

Pinto's "farewell to Peking" ends this section and brings the book to its midpoint and Pinto to his farthest remove from Europe. His slow road home begins as he campaigns with the Tartars, explores Japan and the Ryukyu Islands, and observes the savage Martaban war in Burma, and the convoluted world of Siamese politics. The last major block (sections 200–225) centers on Francis Xavier's mission to Japan, and the saint's miracles, death, and burial. Back home at last in Portugal, deprived by faithless rulers of the rewards that he believed to be his due, Pinto closes his book with a brilliantly composed rhetorical sigh:

> Though I did not get the satisfaction I sought in exchange for so many hardships and services, I realize that it was due more to the workings of divine Providence which ordained it so, for my sins, than to any negligence or fault on the part of whoever, by the will of heaven, had the responsibility for compensating me. For inasmuch as I have always observed in

all the kings of this kingdom (who are the pure source from whence flow all compensations, though at times through channels affected more by favor than by reason) a saintly and grateful zeal and an extremely generous and grandiose desire, not only to reward those who serve them, but also to bestow many favors even on those who do not serve them, from which it is clear that if I and the others as neglected as I have not been compensated for our services, it was merely the fault of the channels and not the source, or rather, it was so ordained by divine justice, in which there can be no error, and which disposes all things as it sees fit and as is best for us.

Therefore, I give many thanks to the King of Heaven, who has seen fit in this manner to carry out his divine will on me, and I am not complaining about the kings of the earth, since I did not deserve any better, for having sinned so deeply.[3]

To separate fact from fiction in all this, to decide what actions Pinto really performed, which ones he saw at first hand, which he heard about from others, which he read about in various travelers' accounts, and which he made up, is an impossible task. Catz gives some good guidelines in her notes, which constitute a heroic attempt to summarize all the various assessments of Pinto that can be found in the various subspecialties of scholarship among which his world is now divided.

From my own narrow perch on the cliff of China studies, I would venture the guess that Pinto never traveled in China at all, though he probably visited Macao, Hainan Island, and possibly Quemoy or some other coastal towns where a little semilegal trading was carried on by enterprising Chinese merchants. But he had certainly read some of the accounts by various Portuguese and Spanish diplomats and missionaries who had the misfortune to be imprisoned by the Chinese[4] and transcribes quite recognizably a few Chinese bureaucratic terms.

Near the end of his book Pinto mentions having a Chinese attendant or male servant at sea with him, which is certainly feasible in light of the prevailing sixteenth-century practices. In an account of a shipwreck in the Ryukyu Islands, he also mentions that he and the other Portuguese had "some women" with them, four of whom subsequently died of terror and exhaustion. Given Pinto's accounts elsewhere in his book of the awful casualness with which Chinese women villagers were seized and carried off by the Portuguese after their coastal raids, these tragic figures might also be real, not fictional.

Some of Pinto's adventures, however, can be authenticated from other sources. He did have various diplomatic and trade assignments in Southeast Asia, and he knew Francis Xavier, the Spanish Jesuit who set up a mission in Japan, and traveled there, returning to Japan as an envoy in 1555 after Xavier's death in 1552 off the China coast. But Pinto, for his own evasive reasons, often did not tell things he could have done, which would greatly have enriched the verisimilitude of his narrative. For instance, he nowhere mentions either that he had accumulated a large fortune in Far Eastern trade by the late 1540s or that he gave much of this money to Xavier in 1551 to build a church in Japan. Nor does Pinto mention that in 1554 he himself joined the Society of Jesus as a lay brother, only to leave the order again in 1557. The fact that in just this period Pinto was both in Goa and at his most devotional helps to explain the moving prose in which he describes the reception of Xavier's corpse in Goa for burial in February 1554. In the recollection of this moment, satire falls silent:

> By this time, as day was breaking, six vessels arrived from the city with forty or fifty men on board who, during the lifetime of the deceased, had been very devoted followers of his, all of them carrying freshly lit candles in their hands, with their slaves carrying tapers. Upon entering the church they all prostrated themselves before the tomb or coffin where he lay and paid him reverence, shedding many tears, and at sunrise they set out for the city.
>
> On the way they saw Diogo Pereira, who was there on a sloop with many people on board carrying lighted torches and tapers, all of whom prostrated themselves face down on the deck as the cutter passed by them. Close behind them, in the same order, were ten or twelve other vessels, so that by the time it reached the pier it must have been accompanied by twenty rowing vessels carrying about 15 Portuguese from China and Malacca, all very rich and respectable people. They were also carrying lighted torches and tapers while their servants, who probably numbered over three hundred, were carrying candles as big as torches, creating altogether a magnificent Christian spectacle that inspired deep devotion in all those who beheld it.[5]

Much of the vigor of Pinto's lengthy narrative derives from the fun he has with style, as he selects a voice for a given character and then lovingly embellishes it. The elaborate rhetoric of the oriental potentate never wearies Pinto, and the jest lies in the very seriousness with which the most fulsome sentiments are expressed. The king of Aaru, for instance, cannot just ask the Portuguese for help in his protracted war with the king of Achin. Instead, he moves to seize the high moral ground before slipping in his profoundly practical request:

> I call upon the almighty God who reigns on high in majesty supreme, with sighs of anguish welling up from the very depths of my soul, to pass judgment in this matter on how proper and just is the petition that I address to both your lordships in the name of my king, loyal vassal of the powerful ruler of all the nations and peoples of India and the land of great Portugal, who has always honored the oath of fealty his ancestors swore to him long ago at the hands of Albuquerque, roaring lion of the ocean waves, who promised us then that as long as the kings of Aaru upheld their oath of loyalty, his king and his successors would assume the obligation to defend us against all our enemies, in keeping with the duty of a powerful liege lord, such as he was. And in view of the fact that we have never violated our oath, I ask your lordships, what reason can you possibly have for refusing to honor your obligation and the word of your king, when you know full well that it is on account of our loyalty to him that the Achinese enemy has set out to destroy us, giving as his reason that my king is as much a Portuguese and a Christian as though he had been born in Portugal? And now when my king turns to you as to true friends, to defend him against this outrage, you refuse him with flimsy excuses, when all it would take to satisfy us and protect our kingdom against these enemies is only about forty or fifty Portuguese soldiers with their muskets and arms to train us and lift our spirits in battle, and four kegs of powder, with a supply of two hundred cannonballs for the culverins.[6]

The king of Achin, in a later negotiation, ends his letter to the king of Aaru (according to Pinto) with the altogether perfect sentence "Written at my grandiose palace in prosperous Achin, on the same day of the arrival of thy ambassador, whom I promptly dismissed, refusing to see or hear any more of him, as he will inform you."[7]

One of Pinto's Portuguese friends, who has been able to drink all opposition under the table, is hoisted aloft an elephant by an ecstatic Burmese mob, and saluted with the memorable chant:

> O ye people, sing joyful praises to the rays that issue from the center of the sun, which is the god that brings forth our rice, for the time has come when you behold in your land a man so holy who, by drinking more than anyone ever born in the world, has brought down the twenty principal heads of our troop. May his fame be spread far and wide forever![8]

Pinto's narrative voice also has an admirable concision at times, and Catz does a fine job of rendering it in English. Here, for instance, are the Portuguese, driven wild by greed, leaving China on a mission to a miraculous kingdom:

> Driven by their hunger for profits, in only two weeks they readied nine junks that were in the harbor at the time, all of them so ill prepared and poorly equipped to sail that some of them were carrying as pilots only the ships' owners, who knew absolutely nothing about the art of navigation. And that was how they departed, all together, on a Sunday morning, against the wind, against the monsoon, against the tide, and against all reason, without a moment's thought for the perils of the sea, but so blind and obstinate in their determination to leave that none of these drawbacks were considered. And I too went along on one of them.[9]

And one would be hard put to do better than this in setting the scene from the local history of Kedah, where a Malay tyrant held sway:

> At the time we arrived in Kedah, the king was in the midst of conducting elaborate funeral services for his father, whom he had stabbed to death in order to marry his mother, who was pregnant with his child. As part of the ceremonies, which were performed with a great deal of pomp and splendor, there was music making, dancing, shouting, screaming, and free meals for the poor who flocked there in great numbers.[10]

One of the many oddities of Pinto's *Travels* is that he almost never speaks to us directly in the first person. Whichever of the four different personae discussed by Catz is doing the observing will relay the speeches of others at great length and with the pretense to absolute literalness and accuracy; but his own speeches and thoughts are summarized as asides, as elliptical exhortations to the reader, or as if being passed on by others. I found only two passages in this long book where Pinto sheds this protection and speaks at us directly in a first-person voice in quotation marks. Since he seems always to have been so aware of what he was doing stylistically, we must assume that he was doing this out of deliberate choice.

The first time Pinto gives us his own words, he is confronting the same tyrannical ruler of Kedah mentioned above. The ruler has just killed Pinto's traveling companion, a Muslim merchant, by the Malay method Pinto calls the *gregoge,* which consists, he tells us, "of sawing a live man to death, starting with the feet, then the hands, the neck, and the chest, all the way down the back to the bottom of the spine." The king, seated on an elephant, shows Pinto his friend's dismembered corpse. Pinto, gibbering with fear, throws himself at the elephant's feet:

> "I beg you, sir," I cried, unable to control the tears, "please take me for your slave instead of having me killed like them, for I swear by my faith as a Christian that I have done nothing to deserve it. And don't forget that I am the nephew of the captain of Malacca, who will gladly pay any amount of money to ransom me. And then there's the *jurupango* in the harbor with all is valuable cargo which is yours for the taking whenever you please."
>
> "Good God, man!" he exclaimed. "What are you saying? Do you think I'm as bad as all that? Now, now, calm yourself, you have nothing to fear. Just sit down and rest a while, for I can see that you are upset. Then after you have regained your composure, I will explain why I ordered the execution of that Moor you brought with you. And I swear by my faith, I would never have done such a thing if he had been a Portuguese, or a Christian, even if he were guilty of murdering one of my sons."[11]

The humor of the grisly situation comes from the juxtaposition of the tyrant's calm logic with Pinto's abject terror, and a point is made about the cowardice that lies behind Portuguese bluster, as well as about the moral ambiguity of the foreign nations they are encountering, pillaging, and sometimes conquering.

The second time Pinto relays his own voice to us comes near the end of the *Travels*. This time the setting is utterly different. Pinto is on a ship with Father Francis Xavier; they have just been attempting to establish the first Christian mission in Japan and are en route to Malacca. Their ship has been hit by a terrible storm, many men have been lost, and everyone is exhausted. In the midst of the dramatic action, Pinto gives us this vignette:

> Then he [Xavier] called me over to the poop deck where he was at the time, looking quite sad as everyone thought, and asked me if I would have a little drinking water heated for him because his stomach was very upset, a request which, for my sins, I could not satisfy, since there was no stove on the *nao*, for it had been thrown overboard the day before when [everything on] the deck had been jettisoned at the beginning of the storm. Then he complained to me that his head was reeling and that he was subject to occasional dizzy spells.
>
> "Little wonder that Your Reverence feels that way," I said to him, "since you have not slept for three nights and it is very likely that you haven't tasted a bite of food either, as one of Duarte da Gama's slaves told me."
>
> "I assure you," he answered, "that I feel sorry for him when I see how disconsolate he is, for all last night, after the sloop was lost, he wept continuously for his nephew, Afonso Calvo, who is on it, along with our other companions."
>
> Then, because I saw the father yawning frequently, I said to him, "Your Reverence, go lie down for a while in my cabin, and perhaps you will get some rest."[12]

Here, Pinto is freed from his terror of the Malay tyrant, and attains, for a rare moment, something approaching a state of grace. I mulled over these two brief passages for many days, comparing their rhetoric, seeking their message, wondering why Pinto had shared his very own voice with us on these two occasions, and these alone. Perhaps there can be no definitive answer, but I can hazard my own guess. Pinto wanted, with all his heart, to let us know two things. That terror can be so overwhelming that we lose all our dignity despite ourselves, and become abject creatures groveling in the dust. Yet when confronted by great goodness, we can, if we reach out sincerely, partake of it. Even Pinto, the rascal, loafer, merchant, coward, pirate, man-at-arms, could console with a few words the holiest man he had met in his life when that man had reached the end of his resources. In these two moments, Pinto has beautifully summarized for us the awfulness and the holiness that were so intertwined in the great historical drama of Portugal's sixteenth-century global explorations.

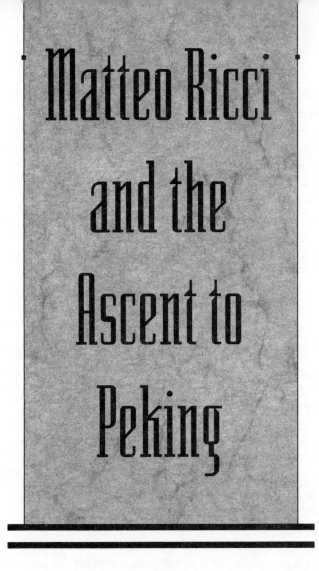

Matteo Ricci and the Ascent to Peking

It took Matteo Ricci (1552–1610) forty-nine years to get to Peking. We cannot tell at exactly which point in his life the desire to get there was sown, but of course the Counter-Reformation world into which he was born was full of dreams for the containment of Protestantism at

This essay first appeared in 1988, in *East Meets West: The Jesuits in China, 1582–1773,* edited by Charles Ronan and Bonnie Oh.

home and the spread of the Catholic faith abroad. Ricci's hometown, Macerata, was in the papal domain, and we can see three nearby geographical loci that may have given wing to his thoughts. One was Loreto, with its powerfully patronized shrine to the Virgin Mary, and its evocation of miracles in her name. A second was Ancona, a port that looked east across the Adriatic and was famous as a center for trade with the Middle East and as a haven for Jews, many of whom had been converted to Christianity. A third was Rome itself, restored to Christian power (if not yet total purity) after the reforms of the Council of Trent and from the time of Pope Pius V onward embarked on ambitious yet phased expansion overseas.

Ricci had initially been meant for a career in law, but he entered the Jesuit order in 1571 and studied for six years in Rome, Florence, and Coimbra before traveling to India in the spring of 1578. While he was a student in Rome, the acting master of novices was Alessandro Valignano (1539–1606), that brilliant and formidable Jesuit churchman from Chieti, who as Visitor to the East was to have such a profound effect on mission work in India, Japan, and China. Valignano's own visions of a purified, expansive, yet loving church may have been passed on to the young Ricci's mind. From Ricci's own pen the only remark we have about early motives is to be found in a letter he wrote to his school friend Giulio Fuligatti, recalling how in Macerata and Rome they had dreamed of missions in the Indies, yet had realized how service could be also as broad at home, for "one needs no thrust of the steel to be a martyr, nor need one embark on a long journey in order to be a pilgrim."[1]

Ricci reached Goa, on the western coast of India, in September 1578. He was to be either there or slightly to the south in Cochin until the spring of 1582, and this period marks his true apprenticeship for the later labors in China. In entering this strange new Indian world, he entered also into a world of doctrinal and strategic problems of exceptional complexity. These included tensions between different religious orders within the church, arguments over the role of the Inquisition, differences between Spain and Portugal (until their union in 1580) and thereafter between both those countries and the papacy, and clashes between strong-willed individuals such as Valignano and Francisco Cabral, S.J. (1528–1609).

Valignano was to prove a central figure in Ricci's Peking journey. Born in 1539, Valignano entered the Jesuit order in 1566. In the Roman college, he studied theology, philosophy, and physics, and mathematics under Clavius (Christoph Clau, S.J., 1538–1612), and by 1571 was appointed acting master of novices. In this role, during the autumn of that same year, he administered the first-year examinations to the young

Matteo Ricci. Valignano then served for a year as rector of the college in Macerata before the general of the Jesuit order, Everard Mercurian, summoned him in 1573 to be Visitor to the missions in India. This order, by the nature of the church's organization at the time, gave the thirty-four-year-old Valignano at one swoop powers equivalent to those of the general himself over all the Jesuit missions from the Cape of Good Hope to Japan.[2] Valignano's assignment was to reinfuse the Asian missions with spiritual ardor, to bring extra manpower to make possible some respite from field work and refreshing of spiritual resources for the missionaries, and to handle the thorny problem of whether to establish separate mission bases in India beyond the Ganges, in the Moluccas, in Malacca, and in Japan.

Valignano had high hopes for success in India, and these were shared by the general, even if it meant upsetting the Portuguese. It is an intriguing index of Mercurian's independence of spirit, as well as of the pressing need for new recruits of high intellectual caliber, that among the thirty-two men the general assigned to Valignano and the additional eight Valignano selected, with his general's agreement for service in the East, were numerous *confessi,* that is, "New Christians" formerly of the Jewish faith. The incumbent Portuguese clerical power holders warned that King Sebastian (r. 1557–78) and his uncle, the Cardinal Infante Dom Henrique, would be sure to object and the Portuguese clerics and *fidalgos* in India who despised the converted Jews would protest vigorously. Valignano doubtless thought that these same senior Portuguese fathers were overharsh in their demands for rigor, discipline, and corporal punishment throughout the Order, improperly claiming this was the true intention of their founder, Ignatius Loyola (1491–1556). Valignano, disagreeing, insisted on the need to follow a road based more on trust and love. The Portuguese, he wrote in a letter of early 1574, "bear on their very features the marks of their inner bitterness. Moroseness and melancholy are everywhere in evidence."[3]

Valignano did surprisingly well with King Sebastian at an audience in January 1574, and this increased his natural optimism. He requested of the king one hundred scudi (and more if necessary) in travel fares for each of the thirty Jesuits, cabins near the stern of every ship with fresh air and storerooms, a special ration of flour so that they could make their own bread rather than subsist on ship's biscuit, and additional funds to pay for those in Lisbon awaiting passage to the East. All this Sebastian granted, with an additional allowance for wine. At last, forty-one missionaries, all filled with zeal by two months of final training, sailed with Valignano in March 1574, reaching Goa in September.[4]

Despite this auspicious beginning, after only a year's residence in Portuguese India, mostly in Goa, Valignano wrote a careful letter painting its future in the darkest hues; he describes a government system so bad that the Jesuits hesitated to hear the confessions of the civil and military officials and depicted a society of badly paid soldiers, poorly armed forts, shabby fleets, and a vilely unfair system of justice.[5]

Two years later, en route to Malacca in 1577, a year before Ricci arrived in Goa, Valignano wrote a new and careful assessment of Indian realities that was as harsh as anything written by the Portuguese. His experience of Indian heat, disease, vice, and lethargy led him to lump the peoples of India with those of Africa as little better than the "brute beasts." He added, "A trait common to all these people (I am not speaking now of the so-called white races of China or Japan) is a lack of distinction and talent. As Aristotle would say, they are born to serve rather than to command."[6] He showed no awareness of or interest in the achievements of Indian culture and philosophy, or the shaping of their millennia-old religions.

Ricci followed a rather similar path. At first, on arriving in Goa, he showed euphoria about the prospects of success in India, stimulated almost certainly by the fact that the great Mughal ruler Akbar (1542–1605) had invited three Jesuits to his court just after Ricci's arrival and had sent a magnificent embassy by sea to visit Goa. Ricci also felt moved by the need to instruct Indians fully in Christian theology and not to treat them as intellectually second-class citizens, as did many of his colleagues.

But within a year or so, Ricci, ravaged by a sickness that forced him to Cochin for recuperation, depressed by the deaths of several friends, chagrined by the low educational level of many of his fellow Catholic religious in India, and baffled and perturbed by what little he could understand of Indian literature and culture, was beginning to sound just like the Visitor. By December 1581, his letters show that he was convinced there was no real hope of converting Akbar and that indeed the only reason that he had invited the Jesuits to his palace was that he had "a certain natural curiosity to learn about new schools of thought" and also wanted to keep in with the Portuguese on account of the civil war he was fighting with his own brother.[7] One of the most dejected-sounding passages Ricci ever wrote, expressing his boredom and frustration, can be found in a letter dated December 1, 1581, to his Jesuit colleague the historian Gian Pietro Maffei (1533–1610):

> All those here known to your reverence are in good health
> and well occupied: only I am here accomplishing nothing, and

have been ill twice this year; I am put to making a formal study of theology because there is nothing else for me to do except to hear an occasional confession. . . . I would gladly bear all the travails that accompany the voyage, and ten times over, just to spend one day with you and my other old friends.[8]

Such nostalgia was not helpful, Ricci knew, and was ungenerous to those in Goa who tried to cheer him up with their love and encouragement; but, he continued to Maffei in a shock of realization, he had "taken on that characteristic of old men who spend all their time praising time past."

As Ricci grew despondent with India, he became excited by Japan, and once again we can see how Valignano anticipated and influenced his views. In a letter from Cochin dated January 18, 1580, to his former theology teacher in Coimbra, Ricci wrote excitedly that the rector of the college in Malacca, along with the military commander Mathias d'Albuquerque, had just arrived in Cochin, bringing copies of the "Annual Letter" of Valignano. In it, Valignano announced the dramatic news of the conversion of the "King of Bungo," lord of "five kingdoms" in Japan. By the thirtieth of the same month, Ricci had elaborated this early enthusiasm into a full-fledged hope that the conversion of this king and his son would be followed not only "by all the kingdoms this man controls, which number five or six, but by the whole of Japan." Ricci had another, more personal reason for praising these successes: one of the missionaries credited with the conversion of twelve thousand souls in Meaco was a Jesuit father from his hometown of Macerata, Giulio Piani (1538–1605), a man from a well-born family, fourteen years Ricci's senior.[9]

And yet, so great are the paradoxes and dissonances of this period, and so complex the forces working on Ricci himself, that just as he began to rejoice at Valignano's Japanese message, Valignano was changing his tune. In 1579, when Ricci from his vantage point in India was reacting with such enthusiasm to the news of the society's triumphs in Japan, Valignano was writing to the general, Everard Mercurian, that it was impossible for the fifty-five Jesuits in Japan (of whom only twenty-three were priests) to handle the spiritual needs of a group of converts now numbering a hundred thousand. The church "was asking too much of her sons"; further, the news of Japanese successes that had been reaching India was quite different from reality. Valignano now realized that the Japanese, whom he had praised in advance as "white" and as "simple pious folk" were in fact "the most dissembling and insincere people to be found anywhere." He felt himself to be "in a state of anxious uncertainty and at his wits' end, at a loss for an answer." He agreed on strictly logical grounds that seminaries for native Japanese youths must be opened and better language schools developed for the Europeans. But "when will we be in a position to ordain native candidates and draw on them for help? I cannot say, nor indeed do I see how this scheme would work."[10]

Japanese cruelty, dignity, depravity, and hypocrisy were so complex that he despaired of analyzing the situation accurately. And even after conversion, the Japanese seemed "tepid" in the faith. Perhaps it were "better to have no Christians than Christians of that type!" A little Christian learning might be a dangerous thing, as Valignano saw in his role as a leader in the Counter-Reformation. Since many Japanese believed that "by invoking the name of Amida (Buddha)" they would be saved, one had to confront the melancholy fact that "their views of justification resembled those of the Lutherans." Thus, tepid congregations led by poorly trained priests might allow Protestantism to flourish.[11]

As Valignano began to grow disillusioned about the Japanese nature and character, he reflected back to the ten months he had spent in Macao during 1577 and 1578. It now seemed to him that it was the Chinese, not the Japanese, who were "the most capable, well-bred people in the entire East."[12] In a long draft section to an essay on the Far East, written in Japan in October 1579, he spelled out the contrasts between Japan and China. Though this whole passage was cut from the essay by Valignano in 1580 and could not have been seen by Ricci, it may serve to illustrate vividly how a sequence was being repeated. In the mid-1570s, euphoria for Japan had succeeded the disappointment with India; by the end of the decade, China, unsullied by personal knowledge, was becoming the focus for euphoria as dejection about Japanese realities deepened. Here are Valignano's words as transcribed by the historian Schütte:

> In China no one can carry weapons; here they invariably go about heavily armed. The Chinese love to see blood flow, and blows are the order of the day; the Japanese never beat their children or servants or blame them or utter a harsh word; they simply use the sword right away and kill without hesitation. The Chinese noblemen and better class citizens live in walled towns, whereas the better class in Japan live in the country. The Chinese wear their hair long like women; here they not only cut theirs short but actually pull it out so that they remain bald-headed. The Chinese go about in long clothes; here they wear short ones and of such a cut that it really seems they do the reverse on purpose. The Chinese are serious in the pursuit of letters and prize learning highly, showing little interest in

arms; the Japanese, on the contrary, pay no regard to learning.

At this point Valignano paused briefly on the topic of diet, noting that
their love of meat and standard fare made the Chinese "like Europeans,"
whereas "one can scarcely describe or imagine" the Japanese meals. He
then attempted to draw some deeper characterological dissonances between
the two peoples:

> The Chinese women are very retiring and modest and are seen
> in public rarely or never; the Japanese enjoy more freedom
> and are looser in their conduct than women anywhere else.
> The Chinese set little store by their priests, the so-called bonzes,
> and pay them no respect, whereas the Japanese have the great-
> est regard and esteem for theirs. The Chinese are very enter-
> prising, lively and alert in their actions and decisions, while
> the people here are the slowest, most indecisive and prolix in
> the world; they can never bring a business affair to a conclu-
> sion, nor can one hope to treat them with any success. The
> Chinese will have no friendly relations nor converse with out-
> siders, while the Japanese are very fond of strangers. The
> Chinese have the best government imaginable and are sticklers
> for ordered ways, while here no order or government pre-
> vails. In short, they behave in a way quite the reverse of the
> Chinese and indeed of any other nation.[13]

When Valignano reached Macao, almost a decade had gone by since the
scandal-ridden period when Cabral and Organtino Gnecchi-Soldo (1532–
1609) had battled over their claims to lead the Jesuit order, and Manuel
Travassos, captain-major of the Great Ships to Nagasaki in 1569 and
1570, had outraged the community by his brutal ways and rough-and-
ready business dealings. In the now tranquil city, Valignano learned
enough about China to realize that intensive language preparation would
be essential before any progress could be made. So despite his greater
current interest in Japan, he had the foresight to order some able Jesuits
to apply themselves at once to Chinese language study. In answer to this
summons, Michele Ruggieri, S.J. (1543–1607), arrived in Macao from
Cochin in 1579. He, in turn, asked that Ricci (with whom he had originally traveled to India and been stationed in Cochin) be ordered to join
him. Ricci left Goa in the spring of 1582 and arrived in Macao on August
7.[14]

A perplexing problem that arises here is why Ricci, sick and exhausted and depressed in India, desperately ill on the rough sea voyage from Goa to Macao, underwent such a change of heart and mind that he could reembark to his ascent with renewed love, tenacity, and skill. His excitement can be seen in a letter to a friend written from Macao at this time, in which he termed the move from India not just a journey but a "leap" (*salto*).[15] It seems that it was the Chinese language that caused his change of heart, but even that is too simple; it was the Chinese language by virtue of its contrast to Greek. This contention, it would seem, can be proved from Ricci's own letters. Writing to Maffei, on November 30, 1580, he mentioned that he had been ordered by his superiors to teach an intensive course of Greek and that he felt he would "never free" himself from this grammar. Although his teaching was interrupted by a serious illness, he was ordered back to Goa to continue his studies after his convalescence in Cochin, and Ricci worried aloud that he did not know if this order would lead him to "end [his] study of this grammar or end [his] life."[16]

If any readers have suffered through schoolboy compulsory Greek as long and unsuccessfully as I did and been as tormented and dejected by the complexity of its grammar as compared with Latin or Romance languages, then they might understand the passion that appeared in Ricci's letter from Macao, dated February 13, 1583, to his old Roman rhetoric teacher Martin Fornari:

> I have recently given myself to the study of the Chinese language and I promise you that it is something quite different from either Greek or German. In speaking it, there is so much ambiguity that there are many words that can signify more than a thousand things, and at times the only difference between one word and another is the way you pitch them high or low in four different tones. Thus when the Chinese are speaking to each other they can be sure to understand—for all the written letters are different from each other. As for these written letters, you would not be able to believe them had you not both seen and used them, as I have done. They have as many letters as there are words and things, so that there are more than seventy thousand of them, every one quite different and complex. If you would like to see examples I can send you one of their books with an explanation appended.
>
> Each word is one syllable, and the fastest way to write them

is to paint them, so they use a brush just like our artists. The greatest advantage of this is all the countries that use these letters can understand each other's correspondence and books, even though the langauges are different. That is not so with our letters.

Ricci then gave the example of the word for "sky" as it might be rendered with a pictogram that could commonly be understood by all cultures, even though one would find totally different pronunciations for that same word in Japan, Siam, and China or in Latin, Greek, and Portuguese. One might not have thought this was very encouraging for the exhausted traveler, but then he delivered his punch line, which emphasizes with admirable concision the contrasts to Greek.

What is of help in all this is that their words have no articles, no cases, no number, no gender, no tense, no mood; they just solve their problems with certain adverbial forms which can be explained very easily.[17]

Ricci's optimism, which had so shortly before led him to hope for the conversion of all India through Akbar, and then all of Japan through Nobunaga, was now centered on the Chinese people. He wrote to Fornari, "We hope for the greatest service to God, since as the Chinese put little trust in their idols it will be an easy thing to persuade them of our Truth if we can deal with them directly."[18] His first view of Chinese bureaucrats in Macao was summed up in a series of images that could be grasped by his readers as relating directly to their own upbringing and experience in Rome, Macerata, or Coimbra: the officials were like gods, their halls large as churches, their benches of office like altars, their hats like those of cardinals; they beat their subjects as commonly as European teachers beat their pupils; their officials werre carried on men's shoulders in a palanquin like the pope; the guards had emblems like the Roman fasces. The one disadvantage of this was an extraordinary severity in their laws which ensured, as Ricci expressed it in 1583, that "they hold their territory so subjugated that no one can raise his head."[19]

Ricci does not seem to have worried about the application of this severity to his own person; indeed, he thirsted for the chance to join his Jesuit colleagues Ruggieri and Francesco Pasio (1554–1612), who had entered China in December 1582. Though these two suffered early setbacks, Ricci was able to enter China in 1583 and to settle at Chao-ch'ing with Ruggieri in the autumn. It is from this time that one can begin to count Ricci's true apostolate in China.[20]

I have used the phrase "the ascent to Peking" to encapsulate my views of the long journey that constituted so much of Ricci's life. In one obvious sense, this was a cartographic ascent, a movement from south to north, as Ricci moved from city to city toward his goal. He had already journeyed from Goa to Malacca and Macao. Now he was to be in Chaoch'ing near Canton from 1583 to 1589; then in northern Kuangtung at Shao-chou from late 1589 to 1595; in Kiangsi province at the city of Nanchang from 1595 to 1598; in Nanking, on the Yangtze River (after a brief but ineffective foray to the edges of Peking), from 1599 to 1600; and finally in full residence in Peking by 1601.[21]

In another sense, the ascent was one into growing linguistic skills as Ricci, a first-year language student at Macao, moved to initial preaching with interpreters' aid and to hearing confessions in 1584; to speaking without an interpreter and reading and writing moderately well (*mediocremente*, as he put it) by 1585; to an initial attempt to translate the *Four Books* (*Ssu-shu*) of the Confucian classics into Latin in 1593; and finally, in 1594, to the first stabs at original composition without the help of other Chinese scholars.[22]

This is a story that has fascinated generations of scholars, and Ricci's activities in each of these Chinese cities, besides being charted in his own journals (edited by Nicolas Trigault, S.J. [1577–1628], and translated by Louis Gallagher, S.J.), have been analyzed by Otto Franke, John Young, Wolfgang Franke, George Harris, and the four Jesuits Pietro Tacchi Venturi, Pasquale D'Elia, George Dunne, and Henri Bernard-Maitre, to name only a few.[23] They have carefully listed the Chinese friends he made, his slow but steady progress in gaining converts despite great difficulties, and his skillful use of scientific and mathematical knowledge to woo members of the Confucian elites to study the beliefs and embrace the faith that lay behind these surface techniques. It is his tact and skill in this missionary work that have won him high and deserved praise.

That saga is not repeated here. Instead, I wish to emphasize other aspects of the final stages of the ascent that have perhaps received less attention. In the first place, it might not be too presumptuous to see in Ricci's eighteen years in China, before he finally settled in Peking, a type of ascent in sensitivity in which he learned to take Chinese values ever more seriously; studied Confucianism so carefully that he could borrow arguments from Confucian texts to counter the theological claims of the Buddhists; gave up the dream of thousands of converts that had enthused him with reference to India, Japan, and China seen from without; and reconciled himself to slow, patient work among an intelligent, skeptical, and often hostile group of scholars. This is the period that saw him move from the first, simple catechism drawn up with Ruggieri, through its increasingly complex revisions, to the final linguistic and intellectual tour de force of his later works of theological argumentation like the *True Meaning of the Lord of Heaven* (*T'ien-chu shih-i*) and the *Ten Essays on the Extraordinary Man* (*Ch'i-jen shih p'ien*).

Despite the bold front that Ricci put on all his endeavors, a detailed reading of his letters through the 1580s and 1590s shows some of the personal and mental anguish that went with the outward successes and apparently deepening devotion. "This sterile land" (*questa sterilità*) he called China in his letter to Fuligatti; to other friends, China was *questa roca* or *un deserto si lontano*, and the Chinese *questa remotissima gente*, among whom he felt "abandoned" or "cast off" (*bottato*). The Chinese marveled, he told his brother Orazio, that he was white-haired and while "not yet advanced in age should already look so old." "They do not know," he added, "that it is they who are the cause of these white hairs [*cani capelli*]."[24]

The passages of Scripture that Ricci cites at intervals in his letters are also reflective, even somber, in their mood and allusions: Genesis 29:15–30, on Jacob's being tricked by Laban and having to work seven more years for Rachel; Genesis 47:1–31, on service to Pharaoh in Egypt; Psalm 126:5–6, on a "time to sow in tears, not bring in the sheaves rejoicing"; 2 Corinthians 11:25–27, on stones and shipwrecks, water and robbers, and betrayal; and Matthew 10:16, on the sheep among wolves.[25]

Intriguing also is one other side of Ricci's ascent, hard to indicate precisely yet reminding us that we must not narrow our historical visions of these men of the Counter-Reformation. Ricci, like so many of the fine scholar-missionaries of his time, had his roots in the intellectual soil of classical Rome and in the reinterpretation of those roots that was central to Renaissance humanism. Images from Dante are not inappropriate here, and perhaps it is not stretching things too far to suggest that in Ricci's Indian years there are elements of the self-knowledge and sorrow that came to Dante in the *Inferno*, while in Ricci's China years one can see elements of the growing wisdom and wonder that came to Dante in the *Purgatorio*. But it is preferable to take the analogy in a different direction and say that it is Dante's wise and constant companion Vergil who also acompanied Ricci through the first two stages of his pilgrimage (as he did Dante, too, before the Latin poet regretfully turned aside from the final climb to Paradise, since being pagan he could venture no farther).

Vergil is taken here to stand for the solace and wisdom of the classical Roman tradition, which was always present at Ricci's side as he made his own slow and difficult ascent. In the *Aeneid,* Vergil describes how Aeneas gets permission to go down to the underworld to see his dead father, Anchises, and is warned by the Cumaean Sybil that "the descent to Avernus is not hard. Throughout every night and every day black Pluto's door stands wide open. But to retrace the steps and escape back to upper airs, that is the task and that is the toil" (6.124–211). It is touching to find that Ricci quoted these lines in a letter of October 12, 1596, written in Nanchang.[26]

Besides the melancholy force of such allusions, Ricci's classical learning shows itself in two ways. First, he attempts to summarize the meaning of China's ethical and philosophical stances in a language that will be intellectually precise to his friends back home in Portugal and Italy. Thus, he talks of the role of rhetoric in the Chinese educational structure, of the *Four Books* as being "in the moral vein of Seneca" or of their moral sentiments forming a pattern of argument comparable to that of Cicero's *Family Epistles.*[27] Expanding out from these Latin examples, he draws too on Greek analogies, comparing elements of Chinese governance to Plato's "speculative Republic" and calling the Mandarins "Epicurean."[28]

Second, he deliberately uses Roman and Latin models to get ideas across to the Chinese, surely because he felt such models would have a greater initial impact than images drawn from the Old or New Testament. At all costs, he had to avoid the blurring in the Chinese mind of Christian principles with those of Buddhism, and so at times he used Latin examples that spoke directly to Neo-Confucian concerns. This can be seen strongly in two of Ricci's works: *Treatise on Friendship* (*Chiao-yu lun*) and *Western Memory Techniques* (*Hsi-kuo chi-fa*). These he wrote in Chinese during 1595 and 1596, as he grew confident of his growing linguistic powers. In the friendship treatise, as D'Elia has so elegantly shown, Cicero, Seneca, Ovid, Plutarch, and Quintilian bear far more of the burden than Augustine, Ambrose, or Chrysostom.[29] And in Ricci's book *Western Memory Techniques,* on which he set much store for eventual influence over the Chinese which would lead to their conversion, he drew almost the whole work from Cicero, Quintilian, Seneca, and above all Pliny's *Natural History,* though of course the attempt to render all this into classical Chinese was Ricci's alone.[30]

In conclusion, let us take leave by considering the ascent that would have lain third in the Counter-Reformation consciousness, immediately after those of Christ Himself and of Dante. This is Petrarch's account of his ascent of Mount Ventoux, written in 1336 during his exile in France. A bond between Ricci and Petrarch can be traced owing to the delightful fact that almost as soon as Ricci reached Peking in 1601, he burst into song. Not with his own voice, indeed, but with his pen; for the Wan-li emperor (r. 1573–1620) was so delighted by the small harpsichord presented to him by Ricci that he ordered the missionary to compose some songs that could be sung by court performers along with the instrument. Ricci obliged, and eight of the songs that he wrote at that imperial summons in 1601 have come down to us. Most of them hark back to Horace's *Odes,* but the third song is different. It tells of a shepherd boy, disconsolate with life on his own mountain, entranced by the vision of a better life on a distant peak that looks far more beautiful. Arriving there after much toil, he finds the new mountain no better than the old one.[31]

"Oh shepherd boy, shepherd boy!" goes Ricci's song, "isn't it better to change yourself than to change your dwelling place? Wherever you go, how can you ever free yourself from your self?" So too had Petrarch progressed, according to his own account, on Mount Ventoux, initially "almost benumbed, overwhelmed by a gale such as [he] had never felt before and by the unusually open and wide view" until he saw the folly of rejoicing in the mountain and its view and turned his "inner eye" toward himself.[32] But Petrarch had not reached this insight unaided. As he tells us in the same essay, his spiritual guide was St. Augustine, whose *Confessions,* consulted for guidance on the mountaintop, fell open to the passage where the bishop writes of men who "go to admire the high mountains" and in doing so "desert themselves." Nor was Augustine alone in Petrarch's thoughts but warred rather with the Roman historian Livy, whose account of Philip of Macedon's mountain climbing had triggered Petrarch's own ascent.

Thus, as Ricci attained his goal in 1601 and settled in Peking, past and present Christianity, China and ancient Rome rolled briefly into one harmonious hymn. He had nine years left until his death in which to draw his Chinese plans to fruition, and he knew with absolute certainty he would never see Europe again. Did he, for a moment, recall another lovely passage from Petrarch's same essay?

> I had better look around and see what I had intended to see
> in coming here. The time to leave was approaching, they said.
> The sun was already setting, and the shadow of the mountain
> was growing longer and longer. Like a man aroused from sleep,
> I turned back and looked toward the west.[33]

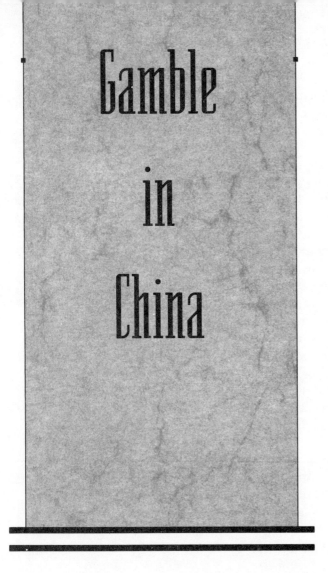

Gamble in China

For those of us tugged constantly by a continuing need to try to understand the dynamics of China's past—and the promise of its future—any witness to lost moods and events is valuable. Sidney D. Gamble is especially helpful since he came at China from three different perspec-

---

This essay first appeared in 1989, in *Sidney D. Gamble's China, 1917–1932*, edited by Nancy Jervis.

tives, out of which he somehow managed to fashion a coherent unity. The three were, first, his deep conviction of the relevance of Christian teaching to China's plight; second, his training in social sciences and economics, which enabled him to accumulate the data that would engender creative changes; and third, his love of photography, which would add the camera's eye to his effort to focus on the crisis of his time.

As if that were not enough to attract our interest, Sidney D. Gamble's four sojourns in China—in 1908, 1917–1919, 1924–27, and 1931–1932— came during times of unusual turmoil, drama, and excitement. The first journey took an eighteen-year-old in 1908 to Ch'ing dynasty Hangchow on a family visit with his parents. Though we know very little of this first visit, Hangchow must have seemed to the travelers a dreamlike vision of timeless China, with its hills, woods, and villas encircling China's most famous scenic lake. And since the Gambles' Hangchow host was himself a serious enthusiast of photography, young Sidney must have had a fine introduction to the opportunities that China offered to the collector of images.

Clear now to historians, but surely shrouded from view at the time, was the fact that the Ch'ing dynasty was doomed, by internal weakness, dissension, and foreign pressures, to a speedy collapse. Both the empress dowager and the reform-minded but politically inept Kuang-hsu emperor died in that same year of 1908, leaving the country's future in the hands of an infant emperor and his Manchu regents. By February 1912, as Sidney entered his last year at Princeton, the Ch'ing emperor was forced to abdicate, and China's fate was left to the untried institutions of a fledgling republic, the politically inexperienced associates of Sun Yat-sen's revolutionary organizations, and the ambitious military commanders scattered across China's provinces.

By 1908 the province of Chekiang, in which Hangchow was located, was a center of radical political activity, in which a host of new Western ideas, including socialism, anarchism, and social Darwinism, were exciting young intellectuals to strike at the foundations of the Ch'ing state, through both the constitutional forms of local provincial assemblies and the extralegal means of inflammatory polemical literature and political assassinations. How little this process could be understood in Chekiang by the local villagers and townspeople, intent on the routines of their own daily lives, has been caught for all time in what is perhaps the greatest of China's modern short stories, "The True Story of Ah Q," written by the Chekiang-born Lu Hsun in 1921.

By the time this subtle yet bitter indictment of the Chinese people's inability to understand the nature of their political and cultural predicament appeared, Sidney Gamble had already made his second sojourn in China, from 1917 to 1919. This journey began with an adventurous photographic expedition in the company of his friends up the Yangtze River, through the rapids above Ichang, to Chungking, in Szechuan province. The excitement of such a journey and the terrible strain on the coolie laborers hauling the heavy boats against the swift currents were later to be indelibly caught by another young American visitor to China, John Hersey, in his novel *A Single Pebble.* Sidney Gamble was then learning to use his camera as well as his words, and his friends recalled how he lugged around his "big, ungainly camera" on all occasions, while Gamble himself, processing his own negatives along the way, as any serious photographer of the time had to do, noted in a diary entry how seventeen full loads of water were needed at a time to develop and wash the film.[1]

It took fifteen chair coolies to carry the small group of travelers and their seventeen pieces of baggage. No Westerners—any more than any Chinese of even modest means—would have thought of tramping the dusty tracks on their own two feet in those days. Surely it is to this trek through Szechuan that the wonderful photo of Sidney D. Gamble belongs, the one showing him perched on his bamboo shoulder chair, a sunproof canopy over his head, a wide-brim hat pulled rakishly down over his sunglasses, his fingers poised above the typewriter balanced on a little stand beside his knees. It is as fine a vision of a Western scholar in action during field work as has survived in any photograph collection.

For Gamble was now a fledgling scholar, and poised to become a fine one. After his graduation from Princeton in 1912, he had worked for a time in California and then entered graduate school at the University of California at Berkeley to study economics. As if anticipating the demands of his future work in China, he not only studied labor and industrial economics but also worked with the California State Commission on Immigration and Housing. Further deepening his understanding of group dynamics and social deprivation, he spent six months on a fellowship working at a reform school for delinquent boys.

Upon finishing his Szechuanese travels, Gamble went to Peking in response to the call of his fellow Princetonian and YMCA activist John Stewart Burgess, '05, who wanted Gamble to make a social survey of the life of the ordinary residents of the city. This information, it was hoped, would both help the YMCA in its day-to-day work and enable the

Princeton men connected with the Y to make responsible suggestions for social reform to the local political leaders.

One problem here was that the political system of China had fallen into a position of near-anarchy since the Ch'ing collapse of 1912. The nominal constitutional assembly in Peking was only a rump group from which most of the once legally elected members had been purged, or else had resigned. The presidents and premiers who followed each other in swift succession often had little or no interest in democratic institutions and were easily manipulated, terrorized, or corrupted by the various generals who, in turn, controlled the various subregions into which north China and Manchuria had fragmented.

It was in 1917, the year of Gamble's return to China, that the gesture of entering the world war in Europe on the Franco-British side had been made by the Chinese government. Some two hundred thousand coolies had been dispatched to Europe to help the Allies with transportation and construction projects, work that would free up able-bodied European troops to be sent to the trenches to face the Germans. In this turbulent European world, members of the YMCA were active, as in China, helping to analyze the Chinese workers' social problems, teaching mass education courses to try to break the hold of the illiteracy in which nearly all such impoverished men were trapped, and introducing elements of Western democratic thought to help them attain greater dignity.

Those governing China had not joined the Allied cause out of altruism; they hoped, by this act, to win support for their attempt to regain all the Chinese territories that had been seized or "leased" by Germany during the previous two decades of aggressive foreign imperialism. Unknown to the Chinese politicians, however, a series of secret agreements that Britain, France, and the United States made with Japan, intended to keep Japan from allying with Germany, had, in effect, promised to Japan the very same territorial and economic privileges that had previously been held by Germany. When this news became apparent in May 1919, thousands of Chinese students and townspeople, in Peking and elsewhere, reacted with furious protests and demonstrations, blaming their political leaders for ineptitude or betrayal and the foreign powers for their deceit and greed. Peking during this period was a stormy, excited place, and Gamble was able, in some unsurpassed photographs, to catch on film the exasperated young people's mood of anger and despair.

While Gamble witnessed these events, he carried on his work at the YMCA—from which he drew no salary, needing none as a descendant of one of the founders of Procter and Gamble—and acceded to Burgess's request that he compile a social survey of Peking. Gamble was fortunate here in that his own training in survey taking and economics coincided with a dramatic growth in enrollment at Peking universities, so large numbers of young Chinese were now interested in learning techniques of Western social science and applying them to the needs of their own society. With the assistance of such students and other helpers, and by his own hard work, Gamble slowly pieced together evidence from the workers in the city that would be tabulated in his first book, written with the assistance of John Stewart Burgess and published in 1921 as *Peking: A Social Survey.*

In his introduction to the book, Gamble made a careful attempt to state his views on the interconnection between the Christian message and the practical problems confronting China. He noted that many non-Christian Chinese were promoting social reforms at the same time that many fervent Christians were preaching God's word but failing to relate it to the needs of the country as a whole. Characteristically, after raising the problem succinctly, Gamble let a young Chinese speaker provide the voice for the rest of the argument:

> The right spirit and attitude are not alone sufficient to trans-
> form the nation. The spirit of love, the general social princi-
> ples of Christianity and even the far-off aim of the kingdom
> are desired by the young, intelligent future leaders of China,
> but they also demand that definite methods and processes be
> used in applying these new principles and realizing these new
> ideals. One young man who recently became a Christian joined
> the church with the belief that it was a group of men and
> women banded together with the purpose of bringing in a
> new social order founded on the principles laid down by Jesus
> Christ. Two months after he was baptized he came to the
> person who had introduced him to the pastor and said, "What
> sort of institution is this that you recommended to me to join?
> I thought you said it was a group of men and women whose
> main business it was to bring in the Kingdom of God in Peking.
> It was with that object that I joined the church. I have been
> there now for two months and have done nothing but listen
> to sermons on Sunday! So far they have given me nothing to
> do!" The lack of a comprehensive Christian social program,
> pioneered by the church, is due not so much to definite neglect

of this important field by the Chinese and Foreign church leaders, as to the lack of accurate scientific knowledge of social conditions and methods of community service. (p. 27)

Gamble's carefully accumulated data on Peking's population—incomes, health, recreation, occupations, and such important matters as police services and orphanage structures—were immediately appreciated by Western reviewers of the book, among them the philosopher John Dewey, just returned from his own extensive residence in Peking. Dewey called Gamble's book "unquestionably the best social survey ever made from the Christian viewpoint in any foreign mission field," praised the range of topics it covered, and termed it "indispensable to further studies of China."

One important feature of the book was the inclusion of fifty photographs taken by Gamble of Peking life and work. These photographs were selected from close to twenty-five hundred in all that he worked on and classified as he wrote the book back in the United States in 1920 and 1921. The photographs were especially impressive for their illumination of social problems: student demonstrators being led away under arrest; blind furniture makers weaving their rush chairs, eyes turned sightlessly inward; girl children recently saved from lives of slavery or prostitution, standing meekly in line, heads lowered, save for two lured by the attraction of Gamble's camera to peer cautiously in his direction; a beggar family of six destitute children and a single parent, where two older boys have obviously shared a single suit of clothes, one confident in the trousers, the other nervously looking sideways out of the picture in an open shirt that fails to shroud his growing genitals; a group of twenty prisoners in a cell fifteen by twenty feet in size, squinting at the sudden rush of light that signifies their jailer's acquiescence in the photographer's presence.

The quality, imaginativeness, technical level, and variety of these photographs deserve to lift Gamble from the ranks of the mere recorder of Chinese life and scenery and to place him among the select few who truly used their cameras to catch the evanescent moment in which a particular face, a gesture, a juxtaposition of elements, comes to be more than itself and to speak for a whole time and culture.

Fine photography already had a distinguished tradition in China. As early as the 1860s Felix Beato and John Thomson set the highest of standards with their portrayals of the tragedies of war and the ranges of Chinese facial types, occupations, and scenery. In the 1870s Saunders and Fisler dominated the Shanghai professional photographic world, as did Griffith in Hong Kong. By the end of the century the empress dowager herself had become an enthusiast of the photographic genre and let herself—often dramatically made up in allegorical or religious guise—be photographed in the company of her favorite eunuchs and retainers. By the 1920s a generation of Chinese photographers had also mastered the genre and moved confidently to begin recording their country.

But Gamble's work stands on its own. In some of his photos—such as the one of the aged Chinese lady aristocrat, with the bound feet in brocade shoes, smoking a cigarette through a long holder as her rimless eyeglasses slide down her nose—Gamble caught an image as arresting as any of those by his greatest successor in China, Henri Cartier-Bresson.

Returning to China in 1924, again under YMCA auspices and now married to Elizabeth Lowe, Sidney D. Gamble plunged once more into the task of analyzing and recording the central elements of Peking life. This time he decided to focus on a smaller group of families and to follow their expenditures more closely. With a team of Chinese assistants to help him, he tracked the daily incomes and expenses of 283 families for an entire year. His classifications, which comprised thirty-seven major categories, were meticulous. He and his researchers related each family's income to its original place of birth and compared wages and consumption per unit, age, sex, occupation (fifty-five categories for men, fourteen for women), food types, clothing, rent, and utilities.

In addition to studying the urban life-styles of Peking families, Gamble had now adapted the more challenging goal of studying Chinese rural life. Some evaluations had already been attempted by Chinese researchers, and an ambitious venture was being developed by John Lossing Buck and his students in the countryside around Nanking. Members of the Chinese Communist party, which had been founded in 1921, were also eager to assess the true nature of rural life and rural suffering, so as to direct their activism toward the areas of greatest effectiveness and need. But Gamble himself at first found the times unpropitious for such a rural survey. China in 1925 was even more perilous than China in 1919—the civil war seemingly more ferocious, the economic demands of the warlords and their troops ever more rapacious. As Gamble noted in a letter of December 16, 1925,

> My own plans for research work in the country have been upset by the war. What with the seizing of carts, extra taxes, etc., the people are very fearful, and would not be at all will-

Sidney D. Gamble with his Smith-Corona, Szechuan province, 1917 (*Credit: Sidney D. Gamble Foundation for China Studies*)

Student protest demonstration in Peking, November 1918 (*Credit: Sidney D. Gamble Foundation for China Studies*)

A beggar family, Summer Palace, Peking (Credit: Sidney D. Gamble Foundation for China Studies)

Temple pilgrim, Miao Feng Shan, 1925 *(Credit: Sidney D. Gamble Foundation for China Studies)*

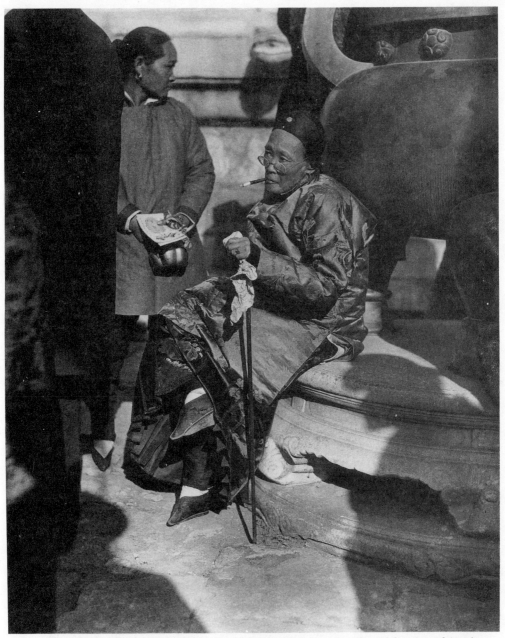

A wealthy dowager, bound feet in brocade shoes, observing the celebration of Armistice Day, Peking, November 1918 *(Credit: Sidney D. Gamble Foundation for China Studies)*

A full-size paper replica of a Model A Ford, with chauffeur, to be ceremonially burned at the funeral of a wealthy Chinese, Peking (*Credit: Sidney D. Gamble Foundation for China Studies*)

ing to give us the information needed for a rural survey. We have been able, however, to get at records in Peking. We have worked out the history of exchange between copper and silver since 1900. We have the figures for wages and the prices of grains and other commodities for the same period and are figuring out the rise and fall of the standard of living of the Peking working man.

So Gamble continued his urban work, but kept such a close eye on local rural realities and the details of warlord politics that his letters through 1925, 1926, and into late 1927, when he ended his third China sojourn, form an important addition to our knowledge of China at the time. Not sympathetic to "the more radical element among the students" (letter of December 16, 1925), Gamble nevertheless discussed their activities and alleged motives with care, and, once again, he was very often there with his camera, catching the street scenes, the faces and gestures of the people. In a careful letter of February 18, 1926, he wrote of the arrival of thousands of wounded warlord troops in Peking and its suburbs, of the absence of doctors and drugs to treat them, of the amputation made necessary for those wounded who, for lack of hospital space, were left to lie out in the bitter cold and suffer frostbite. Was it humanly right, Gamble heard the doctors argue, to amputate both the legs of a wounded man to "save his life," knowing what the life of a legless beggar would be in Peking? And yet, as he observed in a vivid letter of June 1926, these same soldiers, once recovered, or their comrades-in-arms caused agonies in the impoverished countryside around the city:

> The Relief Committee at first planned to sell grain in the principal villages outside the city wall, but this has not been possible as it has been found that even if people could buy the grain the soldiers would take it from them before they got it home. Because of the difficulty in getting food a great many people have had to refugee into the city. The newspapers have reported that as many as 400,000 refugees have come inside the walls, but this is very evidently a big exaggeration. In the refugee camps opened by the various philanthropic organizations they have been caring for about 15,000. Of course a great many more have friends or relatives in the city and are staying with them.
>
> It is almost time for the wheat harvest and recent rains are

tempting many of the refugees to go back to their farms but it looks as though they would not be able to gather much of the grain. In some places the horses of the army have been grazed in the wheat fields. From other villages we hear that the soldiers have demanded scythes so that they can cut the grain for themselves. The soldiers have put signs on some wheat fields saying that the grain must not be disturbed as it is for their use. It looks very much as though the countryside would be faced with famine before fall.

On occasion, Sidney Gamble's testimony echoed and complemented that of some of China's sharpest and most talented observers. An example is the shooting of more than forty student demonstators by warlord troops on March 18, 1926, a massacre that included several of Lu Hsun's own young women students from the Women's Normal College in Peking. Lu Hsun wrote a searingly beautiful elegy for the three young people, so cruelly done to death, but Gamble himself showed how a Westerner's sympathy could also be caught and held. He had an unerring eye for the vivid detail, as in the penultimate sentence of his account in an April 20, 1926, letter:

> The shooting of the students on March 18th was a terrible tragedy. After a meeting in front of the Forbidden City a group marched to the Cabinet office to protest against the ultimatum the foreign powers had given China concerning the closing of the Pei Ho at Taku. Many of them were the more conservative students, though the Kuomintang and the communists were represented in the parade. I passed the crowd on Hata Men Street. They were cheering but were more orderly than many of the demonstrations last May. Just how much the students theatened to use force at the Cabinet office we do not know, but once the guards started firing they kept it up for fifteen or twenty mintues. The soldiers used their bayonets on the wounded and robbed the bodies of the dead. Even glasses were snatched from one of the girls as she was getting out through a back gate. Altogether forty-eight were killed or died of their wounds.

But even in the midst of all this field research, YMCA business, and human tragedy in city and countryside, there was room for family joys.

Almost deadpan, though with deliberate rhetorical effect since the sentence comes shortly after the news of the student deaths and warlord outrages in 1926, Gamble closed the letter of April 20, 1926, with the sentence "Her mother says that the arrival of Catherine Conover Gamble on March 21st is much more important than all this political news."

April and early May 1927, as Gamble noted alliteratively, was a time of "politics, propaganda, panic—rumor, riot, revolution, refugees" (letter of May 13, 1927). Few historians could disagree with this succinct and accurate summary of the period in which the forces of Chiang Kai-shek and his Shanghai allies turned on the Communists and labor unions, killing thousands in the streets; in which the Communists in Hankow tried to unite with a splinter left-leaning group of Chiang's Kuomintang; and in which the troops of the Manchurian warlord Chang Tso-lin broke into the Russian legation area in Peking, seizing all the radical Chinese sheltering there and executing twenty or more after a court-martial trial.

In the Chinese countryside, nevertheless, attempts at mass education and land reform were under way, among the most impressive being the one at Ting Hsien, in Hopei province, south of Peking, directed by James Yen. Gamble found time to visit the area and to write enthusiastically about it in letters home. He was especially struck by the interconnection of mass education with famine relief and could never resist commenting on the bustle, excitement, and energy that always seemed to be such vibrant parts of Chinese life. As he put it in a letter of October 1, 1927,

> The trip to Ting Hsien gave me a fine glimpse of country life as we were able to get into the villages and talk with many of the people. It was the busy season and we found a great many of the farmers irrigating, drawing water from the wells dug with the Famine Relief funds. In some places they use animals, but most of the water was being raised by man and woman power.
>
> In one of the villages they were having a big temple fair. In the country districts there are some religious observances with the temple fairs but for the most part they are for buying and selling. It was a country holiday and crowds came from all around. The village streets were jammed and in the fields all around the merchants were displaying their wares, almost everything used in country life, carts, timber, cattle, brushes, baskets for the wells, grain, wooden benches, cloths, iron ware. The Mass Education people had a big parade of their students,

marching to the village stage where they gave a Mass Education play. I wish I could describe for you the sea of faces that crowded in under the mat shed roof. The people were packed so closely that from the stage they looked like nothing but faces. After the play the secretaries got the people to sing the Mass Education song, words set to a Chinese tune, and going home along the country roads we could hear the people singing the song. The experience of the first year of the country experiment of the Mass Education Association makes me feel that it is going to produce fine results, and I think we can hope for the development of a program that will add much to the life of the rural communities.

Back home in the United States by 1928, Gamble worked steadily with the statistics he had accumulated on the 283 Peking families. The results were published in 1933 in the remarkable study *How Chinese Families Live in Peiping* (Peking had ceased to be China's capital and was renamed Peiping). In the cases of illiterate families, Gamble had employed assistant scribes to help them complete the simple questionnaires he issued, and the results were a fine example of clear sociological analysis, figures, and commentary on the diets of the poor—for instance, the bleak finding that the poorer families could afford no luxuries of any kind, not even vegetables, above a monthly figure of twenty-two cents a month, or fruit of any variety above a monthly total of fifteen cents. In all, Gamble tabulated food alone under an astonishing 310 headings and included detailed figures on clothes, housing, light, weddings and funerals, water, and "miscellaneous," which included the pitifully small outlays made for education, health, travel, objects of household use, and recreation. As in his first book, Gamble included haunting photographs of the highest quality and effectiveness: water sellers hefting their barrows, wayside urban shrines, the paper figures and mock-ups of American-style automobiles now burned to accompany the dead to their final resting places, and Chinese women wailing before the pyramid-like tombs of their deceased family members.

During 1931 and 1932, while the volume was in its final stages, Gamble returned to China for his fourth and last sojourn. Once again, despite the apparent successes of Chiang Kai-shek's regime in uniting the country under his Kuomintang leadership, the outlook was bleak. A Japanese coup d'état in Manchuria led to the fall of the China-leaning regime there and the virtual consolidation of Japanese power. Japanese armed attacks on Shanghai resulted in immense Chinese sacrifices of life, of both troops and civilians. Gamble concentrated on working on details of the rural reforms being attempted at Ting Hsien and on pondering the social and cultural effects of various well-meaning programs. Over the following years, this final visit to China led to three more remarkable studies.

Because of the exigencies of Gamble's own career, family, and the outbreak of World War II, *Ting Hsien: A North China Rural Community* did not appear until 1954. It was a rich and complex study, dealing with family, government, budgets, taxes, irrigation, farm operation, and the local industries in over four hundred rural families. The book included, though less persuasively and prominently than in the earlier urban volumes, a supplement of photographs of local faces, customs, and technology that enriched the study as a whole. In this volume Gamble revealed his endless intellectual curiosity by including a series of literal translations and summaries of the local dramas that gave such life to rural culture. At their most vivid, passages from this book showed a fresh vision of local political self-consciousness among the Chinese.

In 1963, when Gamble was seventy-three years old, he published a much broader study of northern rural China, detailed analyses of no fewer than eleven village communities which he entitled *North China Villages*. Again, the statistical information was full, the narrative lucid and informed, and the small supplement of photographs profoundly effective in its resonance and range: unforgettable were the naked boys and their hogs outside a village shrine, the woman traveler being pushed across country in a wheelbarrow by a tattered coolie, and an old temple pilgrim so deeply lined and worn that in her face one is tempted to read the whole history of China since Gamble's first visit in 1908, imprinted as on a mariner's chart.

Gamble died in 1968, leaving behind his widow, four children and ten—now twelve—grandchildren, along with his four remarkable books. A fifth book, building on elements already presented in the third, was published posthumously in 1970 under the title *Chinese Village Plays from the Ting Hsien Region*. It remains an important addition to our knowledge of traditional Chinese folk culture.

Sidney D. Gamble's findings were open-minded, clear-headed, methodologically intelligent (though not always beyond criticism by scholars of different views), startlingly imaginative, and—when presented in photographic form—vigorous, ebullient, unsentimental, and starkly, yet never cruelly, illustrative of the deep and real suffering that lay at the heart of China's long revolution.

Malraux's Temptation

In his opening paragraph to *The Temptation of the West* (1926), André Malraux gives us all the clues we need in order to get our bearings in this short but dense novel: the book is to be a reverie, dreamed to the throb of engines. To underline this double image, the ship on which

---

This essay first appeared in 1992 as an introduction to the University of Chicago Press edition of André Malraux's *The Temptation of the West*.

Malraux's protagonist "A.D." has embarked for the East is called the *Chambord;* thus, to the "regular pulsing" of the motors, symbol of Western power, is added the evocation of France's days of royal grandeur. For Chambord, the magnificent early-sixteenth-century hunting château of King Francis I, was not only an architectural triumph but also something more—a vivid demonstration of the late Renaissance flair for combining the flamboyant and the geometrical. The reveries, in the same paragraph, artfully run the entire gamut of the stereotypes that the West ascribed in Malraux's time to the "Orient," from "horn-shaped fruits" and palm-framed domes to the restless, frightening armies of the Central Asian hordes.

Just as there can be no engines without some distant factories where the components are machined and assembled, so the reveries themselves do not arise spontaneously, with no outside help. Malraux wants his readers to be clear on that point: "Man, capturing living forms one by one and locking them up in books, has prepared the present condition of my mind."[1] By evoking these unnamed precursors, therefore, Malraux is placing his French narrator A.D. in a cultural context that is narrower than the entire Christian era implied by his name, but still vast. Nineteenth-century France had been awash with reveries of the Middle Eastern "Orient," carried in memoirs, novels, poems, and paintings. By the time Malraux was writing *The Temptation of the West,* in his and the century's early twenties, these oriental images had been joined (and in some cases edged aside, out of the public mind) by new images drawn from China. China, after the Boxer Uprising of 1900 brought avenging Western troops into the heart of Peking and especially after 1912, when the last Manchu emperor of the Qing dynasty abdicated, had become a more open world to the West, one that could be explored with the alleged precision of personal scrutiny.

Because of his passionate concern with the social and political upheavals of the 1920s, 1930s, and 1940s—whether in Vietnam, China, Spain, or in France during World War II—analyses of Malraux often push him forward and ahead of himself in time and in percipience. But in the case of *The Temptation of the West,* written while Malraux was still young and naive, it is surely more helpful to lodge Malraux's views of China among those of his immediate literary predecessors than to see him as a revolutionary visionary.

To my mind, the style and emotions of *The Temptation* seem to be indebted particularly to three of Malraux's older contemporaries—Pierre Loti, Paul Claudel, and Victor Segalen. All three of these men were prolific and popular writers who spent considerable time in China. And all three lived in the hectic day-to-day world of politics and practical life—as Malraux was later to do—as well as in the dreamy terrains of their personal Chinas. "Pierre Loti" (Julien Viaud, 1850–1923) was a marine officer in the French armed forces who saw active duty in China; Paul Claudel (1868–1955) was a diplomat who spent much of the period between 1896 and 1905 stationed as French consul in Fujian; and Victor Segalen (1878–1919) was a physician in the French navy who lived in China for long stretches of time in the years 1906–14.

Pierre Loti's *Les Derniers Jours de Pekin* was one of the most successful books published in early-twentieth-century France, going through fifty printings between 1902 and 1914. The book grew from pieces Loti wrote for the French newspaper *Figaro* while serving with the French anti-Boxer expeditionary force in 1900 and 1901, and its format is, on the surface, a conventional enough example of the adventure memoir. But Loti also brought to his reflections an emotional intensity that transforms his book at times into a downbeat hymn to Chinese exoticism, as we can see through two examples.

For Loti, the city wall of Peking could not just be itself; it had to evoke a mood that stood for China as a whole. And so on its first appearance, Loti describes the wall as being "the color of mourning, of a height [he] had never seen before." It "extended without end, in a solitude that was both naked and gray, like some accursed steppe. It seemed like some extraordinary scene change, carried out with no mechanical sound, no noise from the orchestra, in a silence that was more imposing than any music."[2] Lodged, later, in a billet within an old Chinese mansion where French troops were quartered after the flight of the Qing court following the Boxer defeat, Loti had a second and more sinister experience. As he lay on the huge bed in his ghostly chamber, without touching the elegant postparty supper that servants had laid out for him, he saw the sharp faces and gleaming eyes of rats all around him in the palace walls and ceiling. And long after he had extinguished his light, he could hear the chinking of the porcelain plates as the rats jostled each other in their race to consume his untasted patisserie.[3]

What Loti sought to pass on to his French readers in *Les Derniers Jours* was the sense of loss that came from knowing too much about China, from having penetrated too deeply into a hitherto forbidden terrain, now powerless to resist the assaults of a Western sensibility. Something similar can be found in the works of Paul Claudel, though Claudel presented his view of turn-of-the-century China without recourse to any overt narrative line. Instead, he focused on the images themselves in a series of prose poems through which the Westerner strolls, agape and sometimes aghast, taking in the sights and the smells. Claudel can often serve as a detailed backdrop to the terser phrases of Malraux. Where Malraux, in the first chapter of *The Temptation*, refers without precision to the odors which "disgusted" his shore-strolling passengers, who nevertheless remained "pleased and restless," Claudel provides all the specificity of the experienced night prowler: to him, the smells of a Chinese town are "as strong as an explosive: one smells cooking oil, garlic, animal fat, ashes, opium, urine, excrement, offal."[4]

Like Loti with his wall and his rats, Claudel builds his edifice of words from the fleeting Chinese moment. But he goes further than Loti in edging into a world of universal literary discourse, as Malraux later did with his fictional creation Ling. Here is Claudel's invocation of a religious text in a Confucian temple:

> Here writing possesses this mystery: it speaks. No moment marks its duration, no position. It is the commencement of an ageless sign. No mouth offers it. It exists; and the worshiper, face to face with it, ponders the written name. Solemnly enunciated in the gloom of the shadowy gold of the baldachin, the sign, between the two columns which are covered with mystic windings of the dragon, symbolizes its own silence. The immense red hall seems to be the very color of obscurity, the pillars are hidden, under a scarlet lacquer. Alone in the middle of the temple, before the sacred word, two columns of white granite seem its witness; the very soul, religious and abstract, of the place.[5]

Loti and Claudel could both write with romantic force about the China they experienced or dreamed up. But for the most sensual and violent images of China, surely none of Malraux's contemporaries could match Victor Segalen, who had published his astonishing poetry cycle *Stèles* in 1912, when he was still only twenty-four. Among these poems, numinous and barbaric, one can find the deepest echoes for many of Malraux's images, whether of rogue warriors or of beautiful women. Here one poem from the section "Steles Facing West" must, in its raw and sensual energy, stand as evidence for the rest of Segalen's power:

At Sword Point[6]

We horsemen astride our horses, what do we know
  about sowing? But any field that can be
  plowed by horse hooves, any meadow that
  can be galloped across,

  We have trampled.

We do not stoop to build walls or temples,
  but any town that will burn, with its temples
  and walls,

  We have burnt down.

We honor and cherish our women who are all of
  high rank; but the others, those who can
  be tumbled, spread apart and possessed,

  We have taken.

Our seal is a spearhead; our ceremonial dress,
  armor starred with dew, our silk is woven
  from manes. The other kind, which is softer
  and fetches a price,

  We have sold.

If, in *The Temptation of the West*, Malraux's A.D. places himself, by firm implication, within such a context of Western absorption with China, then Ling, his Chinese other half, firmly rejects both that Western present and the past that the West built on. Among its various meanings, "Ling" in Chinese can be used for "zero," though we cannot be sure that Malraux knew this, or would have cared if he had known. In any case, Ling, by rejecting as transitory A.D.'s minor attempts to construct a "moderate nihilism," does not seem to reject nihilism itself. For Ling is a man on the edge of despair, and his assaults on Western compromise, or its allegedly triumphant assertiveness, are equally damning. He admits to no more than a "hostile curiosity" for Europe and is depressed by the "carefully regulated barbarity" of Europe that blurs the lines separating civilization from law. "Antipathy" is his main emotion when confronted by Western passions. Great art, to Ling, is not "the unfortunate assemblage" that he finds hanging on the walls of the Louvre. Such museums "afford me no pleasure," he tells A.D.; the masters of the past are merely "closeted" there, weary proof that Westerners "prefer the satisfaction of critical judgment to the finer joys of understanding." When there is a Western impact in China, as in the cities of the south, Ling sees it as a sad and shallow one: "The cinema, electricity, mirrors, phonographs, all have seduced us like new breeds of domestic animals. For the people of the cities, Europe will forever be only a mechanized fairyland."[7]

On the surface, Ling's thoughts dominate *The Temptation of the West.* He writes twice as many letters as A.D. (twelve to A.D.'s six) and is always more formal than A.D., responding to each of A.D.'s fraternal "Mon cher ami" greetings with the cool "Cher monsieur." But are we not aware, at all times, that A.D. is setting the pace of the exchanges and pressuring Ling to respond even when Ling is unsure that he wants to? A.D., too, has both the first and the last word in the novel. And while Ling, after a single letter from Marseilles, settles predictably in Paris, A.D. is either on shipboard or unplaced (as in letters 8 and 12) before finally embarking on an agenda and an itinerary that take him through the great cities of China on a northward journey—Canton to Shanghai to Tientsin—an itinerary that implies a purpose, even if that purpose is not made completely clear.

In their protracted debates on aesthetics, history, culture, and the sexes, A.D. and Ling move out of the protective shelter of contemporary images and reevoke an earlier literary tradition that saw its peak in the eighteenth century. The heart of this tradition was the use of images ostensibly drawn from the Orient as a mode for criticizing the shortcomings of the West. By placing the most complex (and even politically dangerous) questions in the mouth of an apparently naive but shrewd oriental interlocutor, the Western authors could say the unsayable in comparative freedom. Montesquieu's *Lettres persanes,* dating from the 1720s, was the most famous French example of this genre, though Montesquieu himself was drawing in his *Lettres* on a rich group of earlier works developing the same idea. But the most powerful of the eighteenth-century fictional dialogues—for literary style, for apparent verisimilitude, and for sophistication of argument—was undoubtedly the Irishman Oliver Goldsmith's *The Citizen of the World,* first published in 1762.

Goldsmith's "Chinese" narrator, Lien Chi Altangi, is presented as an absorbed and occasionally startled skeptic, peering at English religion and politics with the same bemused concentration that he devotes to the prostitutes and fops in London's public gardens. In Goldsmith's structure, Lien Chi does not have a specific English acquaintance to act as his sounding board. His reflections are relayed instead to an old friend in China, heightening the cultural distance by geographical distance and by time of transmission. Malraux, too, remained generally vague about the time lapse in the correspondence between A.D. and Ling, so when a specific indication is given—as in letter 12, where A.D. suddenly mentions that he has been in China for almost two years already—the reader is startled and encouraged to reperuse the letter for evidence that A.D. has used this time to deepen his insights into China. This same temporal indicator could also alert the reader, had he or she the energy, that Ling must have been in Paris for the same length of time. The two friends' overlapping views on the "absurdity" of both fate and their own experiences thus seem more poignant than they did when springing from unfamiliarity with their new environments.

In Malraux's own time, the most debated reprise of Montesquieu's and Goldsmith's "oriental" reflections was the *Letters from a Chinese Official, Being an Eastern View of Western Civilization,* published in London in 1901 and New York in 1903. Though the English scholar Goldsworthy Lowes Dickinson later admitted to being the author, at the time many readers took the eight letters at their documentary face value. William Jennings Bryan was so convinced that the letters were by a Chinese scholar that he published a rebuttal in which he tried to defend the values of Christian home and hearth against the sharp Chinese strictures. Dickinson's "Chinese" observer, in words not unlike Ling's just under two decades later, tried to come to grips with the significance of Chinese culture and its differences from that of the West. As the "Chinese official" explains it in one of his letters, the tragedy of the West is that of a civilization that had lost track of its deeper purposes in the spurious excitement of its current economic and technological power:

> Like the prince in the fable, you seem to have released from his prison the genie of competition, only to find that you are unable to control him. Your legislation for the past hundred years is a perpetual and fruitless effort to regulate the disorders of your economic system. Your poor, your drunk, your incompetent, your sick, your aged, ride you like a nightmare. You have dissolved all human and personal ties, and you endeavor, in vain, to replace them by the impersonal activity of the State. The salient characteristic of your civilization is its irresponsibility. You have liberated forces you cannot control; you are caught yourselves in your own levers and cogs.[8]

Malraux's Ling, after a protracted visit to Rome, writes to A.D. of his "disgust" with the city that both promises and yet hides so much. His experience of the Imperial City has left him shaken and perplexed:

> From Hadrian's palace to the second-hand dealers, whose stalls along the Tiber conceal so much mutilated beauty, to the pastry shops, in which decorated mirrors reflect stone symbols of the Will—all join in making this city, from which you have received your law, the very image of chaos. Time, clinging to the stones, amuses itself by bringing their corroded glory to an extreme of Mediterranean picturesqueness. And occasionally, confronted by this too lucid play of a Western and whimsical time, I mingled my memories of Rome with those of Alexandria: luxury and vulgarity, idols in the morning sun and violent white crowds in immense squares.[9]

Ling's vision of this chaos—at once "European" and "oriental"—reads like an extension of ideas that Dickinson had also explored, though Dickinson chose to present them in the form of his Chinese official's reflections on Jesus, and on the values later espoused in Jesus' name:

> Enunciated, centuries ago, by a mild Oriental enthusiast, unlettered, untravelled, inexperienced, they are remarkable not more for their tender and touching appeal to brotherly love than for their aversion or indifference to all other elements of human excellence. The subject of Augustus and Tiberius lived and died unaware of the history and destinies of imperial Rome; the contemporary of Virgil and of Livy could not read the language in which they wrote. Provincial by birth, mechanic by trade, by temperament a poet and a mystic, he enjoyed in the course of his brief life few opportunities, and he evinced little inclination, to become acquainted with the rudiments of the science whose end is the prosperity of the State.[10]

At the end of his seventh letter, Dickinson's Chinese official writes that he claims no special prowess for himself or his countrymen: "Here are no superhuman virtues, no abnegation of self, no fanatic repudiation of fundamental facts of human nature. But here is a life according to a rational ideal; and here is a belief in that ideal so effective and profound that it has gone far to supersede the use of force."[11] These are among the central thoughts that Malraux's Ling tries to hold on to as he probes the West for its weaknesses and seeks to reassert some confidence in the deeper levels of China's own civilization. It is one of the more ingenious touches in Malraux's novel that Ling's hope is undercut not so much by A.D. as by a Chinese ex-politician named Wang-Loh, whom A.D. meets in Shanghai. In the long conversation, in letter 16, that A.D. records for his friend Ling, the tired and subtle Wang-Loh attacks the modernizing world of the May 4, 1919, student radicals in China as a world of "idiots intoxicated on university nonsense" who had inherited "a revolution made by sick children." Wang-Loh seems at first to echo Ling's ideas on the West when he tells A.D. that China's "best minds" are now "simultaneously won over, yet disgusted by Europe." China was caught up in a "theatre of Anguish," says Wang-Loh, an anguish sprung less from Western threats or internal warfare than from the Confucian structures that once sheltered and enriched her. "Chinese sensibility" was a "work of art." Now it is vanishing unmourned:

> Those of us who are worthy of China's past are disappearing one by one. No one understands any more. . . . Our tragedy is not in the bloody comedians who lead us, nor even in the constellation of death we see every night. If the Empire, with its russet plains, writhes like a wounded beast, what importance have these games of history?[12]

In letter 17, which serves as the climax of Malraux's novel, Ling in Paris shows how deeply he has been affected by Wang-Loh's words as relayed by A.D. Walking through the Paris streets, amid the "calm noises of the city" lit by an early-evening sun, Ling is overcome by the knowledge "that China is going to die." In a reprise to his earlier sharp and hostile remarks on the Louvre, Ling sees that north China has become a "great, bloody museum," "returned to deeds of green bronze," while south and central China live in the superficial newness of a purposeless "revolution." The youths now falsely revered as China's new leaders were busy smashing what remained of their civilization "just as the inexperience of young sailors smashes the sculptured prows of junks."[13]

It is never safe, and often folly, to call any writing "prophetic," but the closing two pages of this last letter of Ling's read now as if they had been designed as an epilogue and benediction to the hopes and fears of China's long revolution and to the millions who died for the future, whether in the antirightist campaigns, in the Great Leap Forward, in the

Cultural Revolution, or under the bullets and tank treads of the People's Liberation Army in June 1989. "What can I tell you?" Ling asks A.D. and us, as he closes. Only that we live in the midst of a "hopeless contradiction," between our acts and our inner lives, answers A.D. on our behalf, a contradiction for which we can say little save that it "prepares us for the metallic realms of the absurd." Separated from the meaning of our inner lives, our minds now can only "revolve emptily," like "a beautiful machine soiled by bloodstains."[14]

Is this soiled machine, we may well ask Malraux, the great ship *Chambord*, which carried us once with all our reveries across the seas to China? As he has throughout the novel, Malraux answers elliptically: "Always, when the day ended, men thought they saw prizes in the darkness." Yet when they reached out for them, they found in their hands "only the last reflections of the dying daylight." It is up to us to decide what to do with this thread of insight as we sail on our way. In the last paragraphs of his novel, Malraux gives us three images from the sea that seem to reinforce the ambiguities we have found in the *Chambord*'s once proud progress. First, the horizon before us now is "naked." Second, even the shore we have left behind shares our melancholy: "From the distance, in the port, a siren howls like a dog off its leash." And, in the closing lines, "the yellow wind cries, as in all those foreign nights when the wide wind echoed around me the proud outcry of the sterile sea."[15]

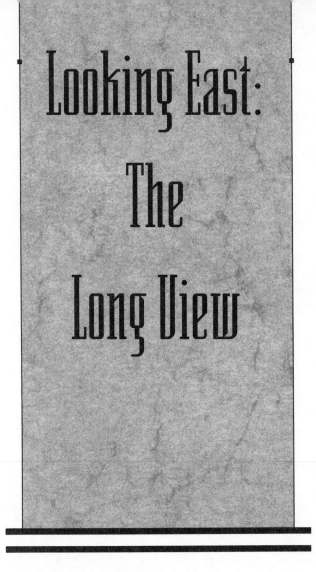

Looking East: The Long View

If we are unclear today about our feelings for China, we should not worry over much. Westerners have been unclear about China since they first began to live there in any numbers and to write about the country at length. The history of our confusion goes back more than

This essay first appeared in 1990, in *Heritage of China: Contemporary Perspectives on Chinese Civilization*, edited by Paul Ropp.

four hundred years: in 1584 the first detailed accounts of China began to appear in the letters home of the Jesuit missionary Matteo Ricci, and Gonzalez de Mendoza's pioneering history appeared a year later. Although Ricci and his other contemporaries were drawing on the preconceptions of earlier generations of travelers to China, the honor of inaugurating a new genre of commentary based on unparalleled firsthand experience nonetheless goes to them.

To the sixteenth-century Westerners, China was large, tough, and well ordered. They never ceased to wonder at the size of the country and the diversity of its products. Few Westerners echoed the hopeful boasts of some early Spaniards—descendants in spirit of the conquistadores—that they could conquer the realm with a few hundred elite troops. The acuter visitors saw that China's cities were walled and those walls were well patrolled, its armies were huge, and its war junks were numerous and well armed. They also saw the magistrates' tough approach toward civil disorder, their rigorous supervision of the civilian population, the terrible savagery of the beatings they were free to inflict on their Chinese subjects, and their control over economic life.

Despite a general view that the first Jesuits were biased in China's favor, I have found no early works in which the dark and light sides did not blend under this early Western gaze. Thus, early Western visitors lyrically described China's ethical system and the ideal of a mandarinate trained through the Confucian classics, selected by examinations, and posted by an absolute emperor to rule benignly over the peaceful countryside. But they also noted the excesses of Buddhist ritual fasting, the magical extravagances of the Taoists, the ever-present evidence of infanticide, the sale of children, and the prevalence of prostitution and male homosexuality. Chinese sophistication in theological debate was remarked upon by many but so was its counterpart of intransigence to the Christian message. The praise of printing and literati culture in China, which seemed to offer great opportunities for the spread of the Christian missionary message, had to be qualified by the melancholy fact that anti-Christian tracts spread swiftly through the cities and countryside.[1]

The fall of the Ming dynasty in 1644 and the course of the Manchu conquest thereafter did not lead to greatly changed perceptions. It became easier, of course, to identify with a man like the K'ang-hsi emperor, who ruled from 1661 to 1722, than it had been with the reclusive Wan-li emperior of the Ming, who never saw or spoke to any missionaries or traders during his long reign, from 1572 to 1620. K'ang-hsi showed consistent curiosity about the West and even affection for several missionaries until he became worried that they were involved with his son's cabals and also grew aware of the papal pretensions to infallibility in matters of faith and spiritual interpretation. In the writings of the later seventeenth century, Jesuits like Bouvet presented K'ang-hsi as a benevolent "sun king" on the model of Louis XIV—not without deliberation, as French funding for the China mission had become a staple for its survival. As Bouvet put it in a letter to King Louis XIV, printed as the preface to his *Histoire de l'empereur de la Chine,*

> The Jesuits, whom Your Majesty sent [to China] some years ago, were astonished to discover at the ends of the earth something that hitherto they had seen only in France: namely, a Prince who, like you, sire, combines a genius that is both sublime and practical with a heart worthy of his empire, who is master of himself and of his subjects and [who is] equally adored by his people and respected by his neighbors. . . . A Prince, in short, uniting in his person most of the great qualities that heroes have, who could be the most accomplished monarch to reign on this earth for a long time were it not that his reign coincided with that of Your Majesty.[2]

But despite such hyperbole, Bouvet's writings, like those of Le Comte who preceded him and Du Halde who followed, were jammed with practical information about Chinese politics and culture. Yet biases also began to appear, especially in the direction of minimizing China's faults so that the tasks of conversion would not appear to be insurmountable. These French writers also dwelt on the ideas that Confucianism somehow presaged the possibilities of a universal morality and that Chinese written ideographs held within them the hope for a universal language that transcended dialects and geography. Both these facets were to be picked up by the alert philosopher Leibniz, along with the binary mathematical structure that lay behind the arrangements of the sixty-four hexagrams in the *Book of Changes* and the hope that China would become a part of a newly internationalized global scientific academy.

For a time Leibniz was also intrigued, as were other scholars well into the eighteenth century, by the figurist position, as it was called; the figurists, far from being alarmed by the great age and comprehensiveness of the Confucian classics, sought to use the contents of those classics to prove the accuracy of the biblical chronology, which was beginning to come under serious question. Their work should be seen in the context of what historians of anthropology describe as the last defense of "monogenic" theories of humankind, which trace all humans back to Noah and eventually to Adam. This monogenic view stood opposed to the mounting interest in "polygenic" theories, which, by allowing for the multifaceted origins of the human race, made possible the downgrading of segments of the human family and the placing of some human groups into a zone of prerationality. Polygenic theories cleared the way for the rise of an allegedly "scientific" justification for racism. By the mid-1730s scholars had begun to do something that would have been literally unthinkable to Ricci: by analyzing the "conic" nature of Chinese heads, they were able to place the Chinese people alongside the Patagonians, the Hottentots, and the American Indians in the category of *Homo monstrosus*, something fundamentally different from the *Homo sapiens* designation that those same scholars claimed for themselves.[3]

The story of Western perceptions of China is so complex in part because at the very time the Jesuits were falling under political suspicion in Europe, coming under attack from both the lay intelligentsia and the Jansenists and also losing any influence they had once had in China—in other words, during the second quarter of the eighteenth century, at the end of the reign of the Yung-cheng emperor and the beginning of the reign of the Ch'ien-lung emperor—the books in which they had analyzed China were reaching the peak of their influence. The Jesuit histories grew in influence in part because they offered firsthand accounts at a time when China was becoming isolationist, restricting trade and travel to a minimum for all foreigners. But this influence was also partly attributable to several French thinkers of the Enlightenment, beginning with Pierre Bayle and continuing through Voltaire, who had seized on the data buried in the Jesuit books—especially the evidence of an ethically moral Chinese society that was also patently non-Christian—to criticize the role that the Catholic church was playing in the European society of the time. Voltaire praised the Chinese in his writings for their "natural deism." Two examples, *Essai sur les moeurs et l'esprit des nations* and *Orphelin de la Chine*, the first a book of world history and the second a stage play, both completed by 1750, illustrate Voltaire's approach to China: in the first he started the history of civilization with the Chinese state and in the other explained how the stony heart of Genghis Khan was softened by the moral purity of the gentle Chinese.

It requires a real effort of the imagination on our part to understand how great the shock must have been to Voltaire's readers when they saw world history start not with biblical chronology but with Chinese time.

Bouvet's equation was reversed with the defiant opening words of the *Essai*, "The empire of China at that time was vaster than that of Charlemagne." Voltaire went on to praise China's laws: "In other countries the laws are used to punish crimes; in China they do more—they reward virtue." As to Confucius, "his morality is as pure, as stern and at the same time as humane as that of Epictetus," and far from being atheists, the Chinese had their own measured view of the realm of heaven: "The great misunderstanding over Chinese rites sprang from our judging their practices in light of ours: we carry the prejudices that spring from our contentious nature to the ends of the world."[4]

This emphasis on the practical and moral force of the Chinese, their potential for raising the quotient of goodness in the world, was still a matter for serious debate in the late eighteenth century. The French physiocrats considered the question in their most influential works. Lord Macartney took it seriously in his journal as he traveled to China for King George III and the East India Company during 1793 and 1794. Benjamin Franklin bought books on China and debated Chinese social organization; he even contemplated sending commissioners to China so that the "young people" of America could study China's aged laws. Thomas Jefferson reflected on the "natural aristocracy" of the Chinese. As if to encapsulate this tradition of admiration, the wealthy Philadelphia merchant Stephen Girard, putting together a fleet to trade with China in 1795, proudly named the four ships *Voltaire, Rousseau, Montesquieu,* and *Helvetius.*[5]

But had Girard read Montesquieu and Rousseau carefully, he would have found profound reservations about the Chinese people and about China's culture and government. Both writers seem to have picked up strands of disillusion with the Chinese that had been growing alongside the admiration from the beginning of the eighteenth century. For example, there is hostility to the Chinese in some of the novels of Defoe and in the memoirs of the formidable English naval commodore George Anson, who visited Canton in the 1740s and found it an awful place, inhabited by a dishonest and craven populace controlled by contemptible officials. In the best-selling account of his voyage, published when he returned to a hero's welcome in England after capturing a Spanish galleon, Anson let all his prejudices show: "Indeed, thus much may undoubtedly be asserted," he wrote, "that in artifice, falsehood, and an attachment to all kinds of lucre, many of the *Chinese* are difficult to be paralleled by any other people; but then the combination of these talents, and the manner in which they are applied in particular emergencies, are often beyond the reach of a Foreigner's penetration." The goal of such passages—and there were many like them—was to cure other European writers of their "very ridiculous prepossessions." Anson particularly labored to correct the mistaken Western view of Chinese morality.

> But we are told by some of the Missionaries, that though the skill of the *Chinese* in science is indeed much inferior to that of the *Europeans*, yet the morality and justice taught and practised by them are most exemplary. And from the description given by some of these good fathers, one should be induced to believe, that the whole Empire was a well-governed affectionate family, where the only contests were, who should exert the most humanity and beneficence: But our preceding relation of the behaviour of the Magistrates, Merchants and Tradesmen at *Canton,* sufficiently refutes these jesuitical fictions. And as to their theories of morality, if we may judge from the specimens exhibited in the works of the Missionaries, we shall find them solely employed in recommending ridiculous attachments to certain immaterial points, instead of discussing the proper criterion of human actions, and regulating the general conduct of mankind to one another, on reasonable and equitable principles. Indeed, the only pretension of the *Chinese* to a more refined morality than their neighbours is founded, not on their integrity or beneficence, but solely on the affected evenness of their demeanor, and their constant attention to suppress all symptoms of passion and violence.[6]

These remarks might be dismissed as the mere rumblings of a naval curmudgeon had they not caught a deeper response in France, where the earlier optimism about China was fading. The most solid critique advanced by Montesquieu, which sprang in part from his ongoing interest in geography, climate, and environmentalism, was that there was something awry in China's so-called laws, which inhibited liberty rather than nurtured it and left the Chinese to be ruled by fear rather than by wisdom. Rousseau, who quarreled with Voltaire on other matters, also disagreed with him over China. Rousseau felt that an analysis of Chinese culture proved the correctness of his insight that education could corrupt rather than ennoble manners, that there was a primitive nobility of character that had to be tended if it was to blossom, and that this capacity had atrophied in China. Nicolas Boulanger echoed the same points in his *Oriental Despotism* of 1763. From these perceptions, it was not a long way to Condorcet's realization that the Chinese were outside the march of human progress, or to Hegel's contentions in the early nineteenth century that China stood outside the development of world history, forever frozen at an earlier stage of the development of the human spirit, prior to the growth of the subjectivity and freedom in which Western cultures now rejoiced. Hegel's words are worth pondering for they demonstrate how far China's ways had been fixed in rigid, abstract systems and how "scientific" the analysis of her backwardness had been made to appear.

> In China the Universal Will immediately commands what the Individual is to do, and the latter complies and obeys with proportionate renunciation of reflection and personal independence. If he does not obey, if he thus virtually separates himself from the Substance of his being, inasmuch as this separation is not mediated by a retreat within a personality of his own, the punishment he undergoes does not affect his subjective and internal, but simply his outward existence. The element of subjectivity is therefore as much wanting to this political totality as the latter is on its side altogether destitute of a foundation in the moral disposition of the subject. For the Substance is simply an individual—the Emperor—whose law constitutes all the disposition. Here we have the One Being of the State supremely dominant—the Substance which, still hard and inflexible, resembles nothing but itself—includes no other element.[7]

There is a good deal of scholarly debate as to exactly what was contributed to Western perceptions of China by the merchants—both European and American—who began to spend long periods of their lives in China as the tributary system sputtered to its end in the late 1820s and 1830s. The record seems mixed: some were entranced, amused, or spoke of the value of their Chinese friendships, but others (like Anson before them) found venality, cruelty, and deceit. However, after 1842, when the Chinese armies had been defeated by the British in the Opium War and the country opened to travel, trade, a Western military presence, and evangelization by both Protestant and Catholic missionaries in large numbers, the very obvious weakness of China bred contempt rather than admiration. If there was any Western sympathy, it was for the individual

Chinese poor rather than for the country as a whole, its government, its ethical system, or its art.

Whatever sincere admiration Americans and Europeans had for Chinese decoration in the eighteenth century, the period of "chinoiserie," when they eagerly bought Chinese furnishings, porcelain, wallpaper, and silks, faded in the ebullient, hard-driving world of the early industrial revolution and the railway age. The world of rococo faded in the glare of Victorian self-esteem. One can pick up many traces of waning Western interest—from the gently dismissive comments of Goethe to his faithful companion Eckermann that the symbol for Chinese culture is the lightness of wicker furniture, or the comments of Charles Dicken's Mr. Pickwick on the impossibilities of a meaningful Chinese morality, down to Ralph Waldo Emerson's analysis of China's fatalism and withdrawal, which he contrasted with the freedom and dynamism he now ascribed to the West. China would have to be "regenerated" by the West, Emerson wrote, if it was to enter the modern world; it had been the "playground of the world's childhood" but now would have to be forced to grow up. Karl Marx concurred in his early writings that touched on China's problems. It would be a long time before China saw the words "liberté, égalité, fraternité" inscribed on the Great Wall, he wrote; indeed, Western imperialism and colonization would contribute to China's historical evolution as they battered down the barriers of isolation that made China a feudal holdout against the spread of capitalism across the world. For it was the spread of capitalism that carried with it the seeds of a new socialist consciousness.[8]

In the later nineteenth century, China was a political problem that was far away and out of mind to most Europeans, except for missionaries still able to be moved by Chinese poverty or the ravages of opium addiction. Americans, however, could not enjoy the luxury of ignoring China: after 1849 they had to face the new and startling problems of rising Chinese immigration into the western United States. As the number of Chinese immigrants rose into the tens of thousands a year and made its presence felt in the building of the western railroads, in the mines, and in the market gardening and fishing industries, the newly perceived threat of a cheap labor force undercutting the gains of the European immigrants became a potent political issue. A racist rhetoric of loathing and fear, with talk of "mongolization," tainted blood, and disease, became a part of political electioneering. Discriminatory legislation in housing, workplace, and school became commonplace. Chinese were killed by mobs in California and Wyoming. They were loathed for their strangeness, their perceived desire to return to their ancestral land rather than to settle and build a better United States, and the appalling conditions of their "China towns," which local legislation had so cruelly helped to create and perpetuate. Chinese immigration to the United States was circumscribed first by legislation in 1881 and 1892 and then, after the trauma of the Boxer risings in 1900, by the final passage of the Exclusion Act of 1908. The restrictive immigration laws levied against the Chinese—and at no other foreign nationals at the time—form a melancholy theme in late-nineteenth-century American history.[9]

We should not be surprised to find that fictional works echoed or even helped to trigger events in the real world. By the 1890s a new genre of anti-Chinese writings had spread into the popular marketplace in the United States. Novels now played on the threat of a Chinese amphibious attack on the coasts of California or, more fearsomely, postulated an alliance of the Chinese in the United States with American Indians and blacks for the purpose of destroying the white population of the continent. Chinatowns became perfect settings for stories of lust, deception, and intrigue. I was amused to discover that in one of these novels, published in 1900, the fiendish crime king of a "tong" syndicate is a Chinese Yale graduate whose racial "shortcomings" obviously transcend the powers of his East Coast Ivy League education to change his nature; but all is not lost for white America, because the villain is destroyed by a Yale classmate just before he can bring his awful plans to fruition. It was a short jump from this kind of caricature to the figure of Fu Manchu seeking world domination, and to his constant frustration at the hands of his white nemesis.[10]

In the post-Boxer Chinese world of the Open Door, the collapsing Ch'ing dynasty, the fledging republic, the warlord period, and the Kuomintang-Communist civil war, Westerners would probably not seek to glean much wisdom from China. Of course, with events such as the First World War, the Bolshevik revolution, the Great Depression, and the rise of nazism, Westerners could hardly congratulate themselves that all was well in their own cultures. And yet, interestingly, the early twentieth century saw the development of a major interest in Chinese studies on the part of Westerners. The pioneering nineteenth-century efforts of James Legge, Thomas Wade, W. A. P. Martin, and S. Wells Williams were followed by the remarkable achievements of Edouard Chavannes and Otto Franke in classical historiography, Arthur Waley in poetry, Osvald Siren in the history of art, H. B. Morse in diplomatic history, and Kenneth Scott Latourette in mission history. Most of us active in the field today owe intellectual debts to this congerie of scholars, and it is hard not to see the dedication of so much of their intellectual energy to China early in this century as being a mark of respect for China's past intellectual richness. (There were, of course, some mischievous and cautionary frauds like Edmund Backhouse, but surely he remains an anomaly.)[11]

My sample list of major scholars in the paragraph above contains a Swede, a Frenchman, a German, an Englishman, and an American, indicating that by the twentieth century the history of Western perceptions of China had become global in scope. Perhaps this internationalization was a result of the telegraph and the growth of daily newspapers that used foreign correspondents, of changes in the world publishing industry, or of the prevalence of voluntary (or politically induced) exile in each other's Western countries. Indeed, there has been in the twentieth century such a proliferation of the modes in which perceptions of China are expressed that I have to abandon chronology and assess these modes in broad categories if I am to make any sense of them.

Such a detailed overview can be built on the accurate, but perhaps limiting, focus of Harold Isaac's influential *Scratches on Our Minds.*[12] Isaacs broke the American perception of China down into the following periods: "benevolence" from 1905 to 1937, "admiration" from 1937 to 1944, "disenchantment" from 1944 to 1949, and "hostility" through the 1950s. This schema makes good sense in describing American reactions to the Kuomintang years, the war of resistance to Japan, the civil war, and the Communist victory. During this period, for the first time, American attitudes were being molded by comprehensive and deliberate political forces—from the efforts of Henry Luce to influence American views of China through his *Time-Life* empire, to the McCarthyites and the Committee of One Million and their attempts to scare Americans out of sympathy for the mainland. I might add that if I were to update Isaacs's schema, I would postulate a period of "reawakened curiosity" from 1970 to 1974, of "guileless fascination" from 1974 to 1979, and of "renewed skepticism" from 1979 through the 1980s. The future will doubtless hold other shifts.

Rather than repeating or expanding on Isaac's formulations for the twentieth century, which would require a survey of all modern histories and political reportage on China, I instead focus briefly on how the most influential purveyors of cross-cultural perceptions in fictional form (which must include films and television in addition to books) have chosen to present the relationships of their protagonists to the Chinese themselves.

The most obvious representation is to focus on the Chinese in China. This approach is, of course, the stuff of most political and historical analysis, and it has produced interesting fictional results. The most influential example has been Pearl Buck's vision of the suffering of China's peasants in their own parched and battered landscape (most famously in *The Good Earth*),[13] although her oddly archaic language seems to root China's contemporary experiences in a timeless zone that has been at the center of so many Western views of China—including Montesquieu's and Hegel's. But other writers drew different lessons from their Chinese actors in Chinese settings. In Judge Dee, Robert van Gulik created a symbol of shrewdness and integrity, overmatching the harshness of his times. In the Kai Lung stories, Ernest Bramah created a hilarious parody of "Confucian" rectitude by trading on every nuance of overblown Chinese vocabulary.[14] In recent years new genres of anti–Cultural Revolution fiction have emerged, ranging from the subtleties of Chen Jo-hsi's stories in *The Execution of Mayor Yin* to the derring-do of *The Coldest Winter of Peking*.[15]

This approach to China should be separated from the very different one that places Western protagonists on Chinese soil with the goal of reaching the Western reader with greater immediacy. (Of course, there is a paradox at work here because the "immediacy" for the Western reader is inevitably once removed from the "reality" of the Chinese psyche.) Such books share at one level the opportunities for reportage caught by many talented Western visitors, including Edgar Snow in *Red Star over China*, Graham Peck in *Two Kinds of Time*, and more recently Simon Leys in *Chinese Shadows* and Vera Schwarcz in *Long Road Home*.[16] The novel and the film, in contrast with reportage, can highlight their central figures and bring the drama into sharper focus: one thinks especially of John Hersey's eager young American engineer sizing up the opportunities for transforming the Yangtze for hydroelectric purposes in *A Single Pebble*,[17] the kidnapped heroine trying to make up her mind about China's war in the film *The Bitter Tea of General Yen*, or the success that James Clavell and Robert S. Elegant had in linking the worlds of Hong Kong and China in either *Taipan* or *Dynasty*.[18] The most magical work in this mode is the novel by the art historian Victor Segalen entitled *René Leys*. Segalen's creation of a brilliant European linguist and decadent illuminates the fading grandeur and internal corruption of the Manchu court.[19] Most books focusing on the Westerner in China end up making him or her appear isolated and frustrated and increase our sense of being unable to bridge the gap between "us" and "them." John Hersey's intriguing novel *The Call* (1985) shows the continuity of this theme.[20]

What, then, of the changes wrought when we transport a lone Chinese into the Western setting? In this case we seek the possibilities for an assimilation of the Chinese that we deny to ourselves. Charlie Chan, bumbling but usually successful, is the reassuring obverse of Fu Manchu because we are ultimately confident of his deference to the whites around him. The kung fu masters, those lonely, peripatetic heroes, fit safely into the individualistic mystique of white Western gunfighters rather than the unsettling image of the Chinatown masses. In its way their intense loneliness is as reassuring as deference because it is firmly rooted in a moralistic code that supports Western society. Similar isolated figures can be placed in Europe or in the ambiguous zones of Malaysia, Singapore, and Hong Kong, as Paul Scott, James Farrell, and Han Suyin have done so well.[21] But the potential to use an individual Chinese figure so as to shock the Western reader into illumination comes best from a Chinese writer of power living in the United States and writing about Chinese values: witness the success of Maxine Hong Kingston and the angry, tongue-tied yet articulate central narrator of *The Woman Warrior*.[22] In this work Western white civilization gets transposed into the world of demons and ghosts that haunted the narrator's own parents.

I have been speaking of works that are in different ways about China and designed to affect our perceptions of its people and culture. But books set in China do not have to be about China: China can also be a device, a foil, as Voltaire knew. Thus, some of the most famous books set in China are really about the author's own politics and should be read and treated as such. I think of two works by André Malraux, *The Conquerors* and *Man's Fate*, in which careful reading shows how rarely the Chinese themselves appear as major actors in the story; the Chinese are present only in statements *about* them made by other mouths.[23] This is even more obviously true in Bertolt Brecht's *Good Woman of Setzuan*, in which China is a backdrop with little precise significance.[24] Those who believe that Brecht had some deeper, realistic purpose for setting his story in China's huge, fertile, landlocked western province in the warlord period may have that belief laid to rest by the fact that Brecht, at the time he was writing, thought Szechwan was a town. Kafka's China, too, is totally cerebral even though exquisitely described. It is a world for phantom explorations of loneliness and time. (These explorations may be seen most vividly in his short story "The Great Wall of China.")[25]

Another extraordinary example of a work that uses China as a device is J. G. Ballard's novel *Empire of the Sun* (1984). Set in the Japanese civilian internment camp in Lunghua, near Shanghai, during·World War II, the novel is mainly a profound and brilliant meditation on suffering and will. The mutual tragedies of the Western internees and the Japanese pilots at the adjacent airfield are seen through the eyes of a starving child, Jim, but the Chinese people appear offstage for the most part, as mobs or as silent, dying figures. Near death in an old football stadium where the Japanese transferred their prisoners and their loot, "Jim lay without moving, as the fires from the burning oil depots at Hongkew played across the stands, lighting the doors of the looted refrigerators, the radiator grilles of the white Cadillacs and the lamps of the plaster nymphs in the box of the Generalissimo." This is a world of nightmare, although it is also a country dominated by the Yangtze, "that vast river barely large enough to draw all the dead of China through its mouth."[26]

Fictional images can drift even farther away from China, reaching a kind of outer limit when authors use characters studying China to present feelings about other matters. Fine books though they are, Western readers will gain little insight into China as a civilization from Joseph Knecht and his search for the tao in Hermann Hesse's *Glass Bead Game* and even less from the crazed and broken China scholar Peter Kien, who burns his house, his Chinese library, and himself in the final immolation that is the climax of Elias Canetti's *Auto da fe*.[27] Despite the apparent particularity of China in these works, here the universalization of human life has become complete.

Such ambiguous or bleak images, however, in no way imply that Westerners will not continue to seek to find themselves through China and to inch toward understanding its remarkable people and their culture. Whatever their limitations, it is not adequate to view the majority of these divergent views as solely reflecting the biases within Western culture or a patronizing and exploitative attitude toward Eastern civilizations. Edward Said, who emphasizes the "cognitive imperialism" of Western scholars in his influential and passionate book *Orientalism*, leaves out too much of the story.[28] There have been so many twists and turns along the way to depicting China during the last four hundred years that no such broad generalizations can hold. And that is as it should be. No one is easy to understand. And the more blurred and multifaceted our perceptions of China become, the closer we may be to that most elusive thing: the truth.

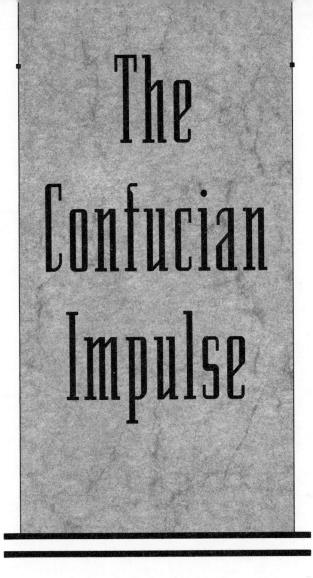

The Confucian Impulse

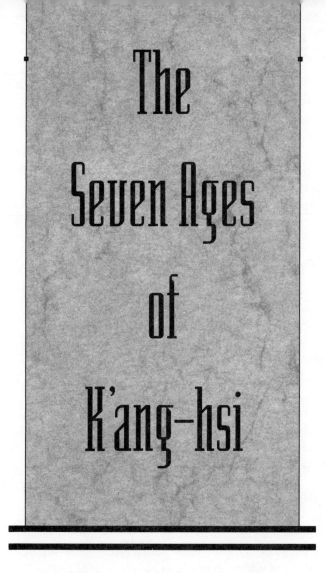

The Seven Ages of K'ang-hsi

In a recent essay entitled "Some Mid-Ch'ing Views of the Monarchy," Harold Kahn announced that he was moving past "the one-dimensional, simple cliché" and "the two-dimensional, complex stereotype" to add a third dimension so that he could show Ch'ien-lung as "a composite figure made up of several images."[1] Talk of three dimensions

This essay first appeared in 1967, in the *Journal of Asian Studies*.

immediately prompts any healthy layman to try to add a fourth: to the three spatial dimensions which are historiographical, perhaps we can add a fourth dimension of time which is more positively historical.

Now that we have learned to look out for stereotypes and distorted images, we can swing back into history and work toward *nien-p'u* (chronological biographies) that would show Chinese emperors, like their subjects, as mortals, trapped in time, as creatures of flesh and blood who had their physical and intellectual limitations and had to function to the best of their abilities within a limited geographical area, using the tools presented to them and such further tools as their imagination might contrive. One simple·way to look at an emperor is through those seven ages of man which Shakespeare so painfully and brilliantly condensed in *As You Like It*,[2] for those ages are universals of the human race rather than the narrow classifications of historians. K'ang-hsi, who was born in 1654, passed through each of the seven ages before he died at sixty-eight, having ruled China for sixty-one years. Let us consider him as a man and emperor.[3]

First, then, "the infant, / Mewling and puking in the nurse's arms." Naturally this infant, Prince Hsüan-yeh, third son of Shun-chih, was institutionally pure Manchu, but the lines of ethnic descent are not clear-cut, since his mother was from the T'ung family that had long lived in Liaotung and served as Ming officials before they became bannermen under Nurhaci.[4] Careful study of this T'ung family lineage might well show that there was plenty of Chinese blood in the young Manchu prince's veins. We may think of him mewling, at least in early childhood, with some justice, since when he was only two years old his father grew infatuated with a concubine and the young prince was raised outside the palace; puking, too, with more than the conventional upsets of infancy, since he was stricken with the smallpox that scarred his face for life. His fortunate recovery helped him to the throne, since he was now considered immune to the dread disease. At least one of his nurses gained materially from holding him in her arms: this was the young lady named Sun, who, on completion of her nursely duties, married the Plain White Banner bondservant Ts'ao Hsi. Later in life K'ang-hsi remembered her with affection, making her husband an honorary president of the Board of Works, granting her the honorific title of first rank *fu-jen*, and using her eldest son, Ts'ao Yin, as a trusted agent in the provinces.[5]

Second, "the whining school-boy, with his satchel, / And shining morning face, creeping like snail / Unwillingly to school." Certainly there was little enough to whine about, according to the official Chinese sources: from the age of four, K'ang-hsi studied joyfully without tiring, they tell us; at five, he had set his ambitions on emulating his imperial father; and at seven, he longed only for peace and prosperity for all his people. K'ang-hsi later assured the scholar Kao Shih-ch'i that he had known how to read when he was four.[6] However, these were not palmy days. In the first place, though K'ang-hsi learned fluent Manchu and good colloquial Chinese, he continued to make mistakes in his Chinese calligraphy—especially in the radicals—until his death.[7] His Chinese education cannot have been too thorough. In the second place, he was but a child in a man's world.

Shun-chih died suddenly in 1661, and K'ang-hsi ascended the throne, but naturally the seven-year-old boy had no power. China was ruled by four Manchu regents, the most powerful of whom was Oboi. It was these regents who produced the "will" of Shun-chih, in which the deceased emperor chastised himself for past errors; startlingly, these errors of the founding emperor were uncommonly like the sins of a "bad last emperor"—infatuation with a concubine, extravagance in private life, failure to employ the worthy (in this case the Manchus), granting of too much power to enunuchs, and the like.[8] It is hard to believe that K'ang-hsi did not resent his father's posthumous humiliation; he did not even long have the assistance of his mother, who as empress dowager would have had considerable influence, since she died in 1663, when he was only nine.

At least he had the satisfactions of "the lover, / Sighing like furnace, with a woful ballad / Made to his mistress' eyebrow,"—a Chinese image indeed, even if K'ang-hsi enjoyed the fruits slightly earlier than implied in Shakespeare's verse. There must have been some lapse of time after his marriage to Empress Hsiao-ch'eng when he was eleven, but his first son, fruit of the union with the concubine née Ma, was born before K'ang-hsi was fifteen.[9] From then on there is ample evidence of the young emperor's prowess. Nor did he restrict himself to the hierarchy of officially selected ladies: the serving maid from the Uya clan, daughter of Colonel Wei-wu, may well have conceived her son, the future emperor Yung-cheng, in rather informal circumstances. The fascinating and auspicious portents accompanying his birth were doubtless more apparent to a later generation of Chinese historians than to palace observers at the time.[10]

Application of Shakespeare's summary blurs at this point; a Chinese emperor was, after all, an unusual being, and K'ang-hsi was called upon to make decisions at an early age. It was not really till the great campaigns against Galdan in the 1690s which he led in person that we can see K'ang-hsi as the soldier "Jealous in honour, sudden and quick in quarrel, / Seeking the bubble reputation / Even in the cannon's mouth," and even then it is only fair to admit that the cannon were on K'ang-hsi's side and that he was never "bearded like the pard." In his early manhood some of the literal accompaniments of soldierhood must be waived. Nevertheless, he had been a hard rider and a good archer since childhood,[11] true to the Manchu heritage, and the speed with which he broke Oboi in 1669 shows his courage and sureness of judgment. The true beginning of the K'ang-hsi reign is 1669, and the next crucial decision came in 1673. In this year, backed by only Mingju, Molo, and Mishan among his senior advisers, he decided to end the power of Wu San-kuei and the other feudatories in southern China, setting off an eight-year civil war which the imperial forces finally won.

These were the years of danger and eventual consolidation. By 1683, in his thirtieth year, K'ang-hsi could say with Confucius, "at thirty I stood firm." Wu San-kuei and the other feudatories were dead and their followers routed, Taiwan had been captured from Coxinga's descendants; as if to prove the point, it was in 1683 that K'ang-hsi set off on his first western tour, and the following year on his first southern tour to Nanking.[12] Yet these were still Manchu years. K'ang-hsi stayed in the banner garrison areas of the cities he visited; his main advisers were Manchus. Only gradually were Chinese scholars such as Kao Shih-ch'i brought into his confidence. Nor was this a time of domestic administrative innovation; K'ang-hsi's main attention was still concentrated on the northern and western borders. For the first half of his reign, until his early forties, K'ang-hsi seems to have fitted the image of an Emperor Wu, a suppressor of domestic unrest and an expander of frontiers.

But *wu* is only the other side of the coin marked *wen;* the soldier yields place to the civil administrator, and once the campaigns were over, K'ang-hsi directed his attention to domestic affairs. This was surely natural sequence, not simply conditioned response, political reality rather than false image. This is the fifth age of Shakespeare's justice "In fair round belly with good capon lin'd, / With eyes severe, and beard of formal cut, / Full of wise saws and modern instances." Here is both the mellowness drawn from a full life and the hardness born of experience. The two aspects can be clearly seen in K'ang-hsi, as he lived and reigned from 1695 to 1715.

First, the mellowness. This was the time of K'ang-hsi's greatest familiarity with the Jesuits; the edict of toleration had followed their negotiation of the Treaty of Nerchinsk and their successful treatment of his fever with quinine. Even Chinese sources report that K'ang-hsi stopped to talk to missionaries on his tours and invited them to his temporary palaces. This was the time of the most leisurely southern tours—four between 1699 and 1707—when the emperor spent days at banquets and watching operas, or in the special gardens and palaces prepared for him by the salt merchants.[13] This was a time when amnesties and tax reductions came easily and the amount of the national *ting* payment was frozen at its 1711 level for the benefit of all future generations; when massive imperial literary compilations were undertaken and a project to remap the empire was launched; and when the great summer palace at Jehol was built. This was the time when worthy and incorruptible officials were plucked from obscurity and raised to the highest offices (with not always fortunate results).[14] Yet moderate corruption could also be tolerated: an official reporting secretly that the governor-general and others were taking 34,500 taels a year illegally from the salt revenues was told by K'ang-hsi to let the matter slide, since "the sum involved is not large, and abolishing it will surely upset the governor-general."[15] This was the time the emperor mediated carefully between Manchus and Chinese, balancing group against group and intervening personally to stop what he believed was Manchu harassment of Chinese officials.[16]

Yet at the same time there was toughness, and there is no point in harping too long on K'ang-hsi's generous and tolerant side. For one thing, there is much evidence to show that from the 1690s onward K'ang-hsi worked systematically to concentrate power in his own hands. Bondservants *(pao-i)* from the imperial household, the descendants of Chinese enslaved before the Manchu conquest, were appointed to key financial positions, as salt censors of Liang-huai with unprecedentedly long tenure, as Canton hoppos, as supervisors of inland customhouses, as copper purchasers, and as grain tribute supervisors, and their activities were carefully checked by the emperor. Bondservants who had originally been appointed as textile commissioners *(chih-tsao)* in Nanking and Soochow were instructed from the late 1690s onward to send confidential reports on the conduct of officials and the financial situation in their areas so that the emperor had a cross-check on the activities of his regular bureaucracy. The system of palace memorials that developed became K'ang-hsi's private information service, bypassing even the Grand Secretariat; the memorials were delivered unopened into the emperor's own hands, endorsed by him in person, and returned by special private couriers to the original memorialists.[17]

The emperor was also quite willing to show his anger in public and in private: the great official Chang P'eng-ko, for example, was made to kneel before all the local officials while K'ang-hsi blasted him for inefficiency in river conservation projects, and the papal legate Maillard de Tournon learned in a few sarcastic sentences that this emperor at least would yield not an inch to the papacy's claims of spiritual power over the Jesuits in China.[18] Many times the emperor praised Ming T'ai-tsu, that formidable centralizing despot of the early Ming.

Finally, however, weakness came. There is no dramatic case to point to, no evil favorite like Ch'ien-lung's minister Ho-shen, rocketed at the age of twenty-six to the pinnacles of power and fortune. There is only a gradual slowing down, a loss of the old clarity and judgment, a loosening of the reins. Predictably, the weakness had physical grounds. The portraits of K'ang-hsi in old age are pitiable proof of the truth in Shakespeare's words: "The sixth age shifts / Into the lean and slipper'd pantaloon, / With spectacles on nose and pouch on side, / His youthful hose well sav'd, a world too wide / For his shrunk shank; and his big manly voice, / Turning again towards childish treble, pipes / And whistles in his sound." K'ang-hsi does not seem to have had the remarkable physical vitality of his grandson Ch'ien-lung; he had been seriously ill both as a child and in his prime, and perhaps his hard life left him prematurely aged. In 1715 he announced in an edict that his right hand was useless and that he was accordingly writing all confidential rescripts with his left hand. Had he suffered a minor stroke? By 1717 his poor health was well enough known for a retired prefect to travel to Jehol and offer him some special medicines—which K'ang-hsi declined to sample. In December 1718 he told Li Hsü that he had not been feeling at all well since the summer, and in 1721 he wrote to Nien Keng-yao that he had recovered somewhat but was still extremely weak.[19] For periods throughout these years the secret memorials received no endorsements; since the emperor let no one but himself read them, how could there be action when he was too sick to read and write? There seems to have been more laxity in the administration generally: there were deficits in *all* provinces, according to K'ang-hsi, but he obviously lacked the energy or will to do much about it. Nor could he stop the perpetual bickering over the question of his heir apparent; despite his repeated warnings, factions inevitably formed around those princes who had the best chances of becoming his successor. There is no doubt that these quarrels were a source of real unhappiness to K'ang-hsi in his declining years, for he had loved his second son, Yin-jeng (his chosen heir), deeply but was forced to bar him from the succession.

Yet his seventh age was mercifully short. Regents could rule for infant emperors, but who could speak for an aging emperor when the "Last scene of all, / That ends this strange eventful history, / Is second childishness, and mere oblivion, / Sans teeth, sans eyes, sans taste, sans everything"? Yung-cheng would have us believe that in these last months of 1722 he was moving gradually and competently into the place his father had earmarked for him; the doctored histories are full of his lengthy policy recommendations, and there is no trace of a rival.[20] Yung-cheng's claims have remained suspect, and it seems probable that he was not his father's choice; but it is unlikely that he hastened his father's death in any sinister way. Yung-cheng was a cautious and patient man, and during the long years of his father's illness he had been carefully laying the groundwork for his succession with the aid of Lungkodo; when death came suddenly to K'ang-hsi in the Peking winter, Yung-cheng moved decisively to clinch his claim.

How can we assess K'ang-hsi? Was he a great emperor? What indeed is a great emperor? Is he a man who rules a great country, or a man who makes a country great? Again, how does one assess greatness in a country, and is it meaningful to assert that one man can bring it about? Greatness in a country, it seems to me, entails vitality and strength and flexibility; a ruler possessed of the same qualities can get an astonishing response, and achieve much, but his country must be ready for him. Circumstances favored K'ang-hsi. The China that he ruled was on the upswing. The horrors accompanying Li Tzu-ch'eng's and Chang Hsien-chung's marauding armies, and the Manchu conquest itself—who can forget reading Wang Hsiu-ch'u's account of the ten-day massacre in Yangchow?[21]—had slashed back population and put large areas out of cultivation. Retrenchment and resettlement, and the resumption of efficient bureaucracy, brought fresh affluence and security. China could absorb the further devastation of deliberately stripped coastal provinces and the eight-year southern rebellion. Government revenues were easy to collect, and even the costs of the great campaigns against Galdan could be met without undue strain. Of course, all was not perfection, and there is no point in glossing over the flaws. There were famines in many provinces in many years, as in Kiangsu in 1708, there was much flooding along the major rivers, there was serious corruption in certain provincial examinations; but these incidents occurred within a favorable context of full emergency granaries, mainly conscientious river conservation work, and an honest examination ethos that allowed complaints to be heard and the guilty punished.

Culturally, too, this was an exciting period. Admittedly, much of the best work was in a sense an art of opposition—one has only to think of painters like Pa-ta Shan-jen and Shih T'ao, or of writers like Wang Fu-chih and Huang Tsung-hsi, but they were allowed to work unmolested. And to counterbalance them were such as the poet Singde and the painter Wang Yüan-ch'i, and the products of the great government-run silk and porcelain works. Interesting things were being said, and fine art produced, as one would expect in a period of consolidation following crises.

I feel that at this time China was a great country. It is possible that K'ang-hsi would have been called a great emperor had he just reigned in such a country for sixty-one years, but the hypothesis is irrelevant, since he brought his own greatness to the task. A lesser man would not have moved so decisively against Oboi, Wu San-kuei, and Galdan, playing for very high stakes after calculating his resources, and winning each time. But besides having the courage to make dangerous decisions and the ability to carry them through, K'ang-hsi was an attractive personality. I am aware how strongly and deliberately the Jesuit historical record draws us to that conclusion, but I am drawn to the same conclusion by the Chinese record.

K'ang-hsi was a man without many affectations, with a sense of humor and a love of the new and the curious. He was capable of genuine friendliness and informality, conscious certainly of his role as emperor—as who would not be—but allowing himself often to appear as a man with human emotions. He inherited some of the quick temper of his father, Shun-chih, but there is no record that he had the same childish tantrums; he could be tough and sardonic at times, but he did not have the sarcastic viciousness of his son Yung-cheng. I feel that in some way he gave a tone to the China he ruled.

The fact that this China was united, wealthy, powerful, aggressive on its frontiers, but capable of flexibility in both domestic and foreign policy was certainly due in part to K'ang-hsi's character and ability. K'ang-hsi's China presents an admirable and essential corrective to the picture of China that we have absorbed from our concentration on nineteenth-century and pre-1949 republican studies. It is the very latest point at which a study of modern China should begin.

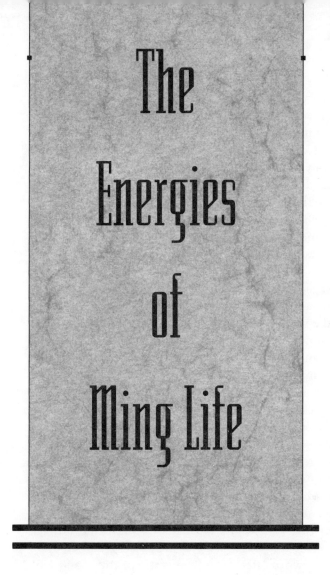

The Energies of Ming Life

Until very recently the great expanse of the Ming dynasty, which ruled in China from 1368 to 1644, was largely uncharted in Western historiography. The dynasty was seen either as having come at the end of a great tradition that had been dominated by the artistic force of the T'ang and Sung or as being a little too early for "modern" Chinese his-

This essay first appeared in 1981, in the *New York Review of Books*.

tory, which could be seen to pick up momentum in the eighteenth century, or even the seventeenth, but certainly not earlier. Furthermore, the "decline of the Ming," a messy and protracted business apparently spanning almost a century, from the 1550s down to the 1640s, was seen as reflecting little credit on China's imperial and bureaucratic institutions.

Ray Huang's unusual and absorbing book *1587, a Year of No Significance*,[1] will hardly raise the declining years of the Ming in the scales of history, but it certainly enriches our consciousness of what went into the pattern of dynastic decline; moreover, his five main characters are beautifully chosen to illuminate a variety of Chinese responses to impending catastrophe.

From his opening page, which describes the background to an imperial audience that never took place, as officials rush around Peking in excitement and puzzled eunuchs and palace guards try to track the sources of the city's excited rumors, Huang shows a mastery of the intricate details of the ritualistic and practical sides of Ming court politics, and an ability to make them comprehensible.

His story is cleverly constructed and deliberately paradoxical. If 1587 is, in the long run, a "year of no significance," it is nevertheless full of incident, and each incident carries promise of future drama. It is the year that the court first hears—from far to the north—an account of the political rise of a Jurchen tribesman named Nurhaci. Though ignored as inconsequential at the time, Nurhaci was to conquer much of southern Manchuria by the time of his death in 1626, and his descendants were to seize the imperial throne and install the Ch'ing dynasty in 1644.

This is also the year that two of the most interesting Ming officials died: Hai Jui, whose biting criticisms of fiscal malpractice and landlord extortions made him a byword later for bureaucratic probity, and Ch'i Chi-kuang, a humane and talented general who built up an effective army in southeast China and ended the endemic piracy there. And it is the year that Shen Shih-hsing, convincingly presented by Huang as a weak, scholarly, intelligent compromiser who could not handle the government he was expected to supervise, became the first grand secretary of the realm.

The relationship between Grand Secretary Shen and the elusive Wan-li emperor is a central part of Huang's story. For Huang, a historian with an awesome knowledge of Ming politics and economy, is absorbed by the historical significance of failure to act. Shunning many historians' concentration on the dramatic moment, the key document, the significant policy shift, he probes for the hypocrisy, boredom, conventionality or fear that prevented the emperor and his senior ministers from ruling. Huang finds partial explanations in the administrative and legal structures of the time, but more importantly in the natural inclination of career bureaucrats—reacting against powerful ministerial predecessors *and* unmanageable, whim-driven emperors—to prevent any new expressions of power:

> With all their talk of the sovereign's responsibility to heaven, the sixteenth-century bureaucrats were actually preventing him from becoming actively involved in the matters brought to the throne for disposal. He was encouraged to be emotionally neutral and personally bland. There was little chance for him to become responsive to state affairs in any functional way. In short, an effort to dehumanize the monarchy was under way, against which the occupant of the throne had no defense. Evidently this milieu first caused the Wan-li emperor, who since childhood had been taught to take rather than give orders, to hesitate to assert himself on the succession issue, and later, when bitter experience enabled him to see the inner mechanism of his court, to feel totally alienated from it.[2]

In counterpoint to this theme Huang develops his fifth and final case study, that of Li Chih. Li, in Huang's reading, is presented as a despondent and less effective Martin Luther, striving to be the conscience of the Confucian literati but deprived of a sympathetic hearing in a society where the weight of the dominant political and family values pressured any individual to "maintain a collective personality." Brilliant but irascible, Li Chih had a miserable personal life, a failed official career, and frustrations as a writer, and Huang's account makes a sad tale. Li's life after 1587 was "futile," Huang says, and he "should have died sooner" than the year 1602, to which he survived.

It is here that those interested in the richness and subtlety of Ming society may take exception to Huang's focus on failure and ineffectiveness and start asking, rightly, whether Li Chih's life does not begin to raise questions that cannot really be absorbed into Ray Huang's model. Li Chih's life (he was born in 1527) is an extraordinary saga, for his own ancestors were traders and converts to Islam, while he himself became a highly individualistic Confucian thinker, deeply influenced by Buddhist ideas; his story presents a different kind of Ming dynasty, one that is alive with acute and excited controversy played out within a world that is economically and socially vibrant.

The German historian Otto Franke was drawn to Li Chih in the 1930s, because Li Chih corresponded with the Jesuit missionary Matteo Ricci; Marxist historians in China seized on Li Chih in the 1960s, when Li's trenchant criticisms of conventional Confucian thinkers were seen to present a possible route to interpreting the hollowness of "bureaucratic-landlord values." In the 1970s historians in the United States grew absorbed in Li's writings on philosophy and in what those works seemed to say about subjectivity; and in 1980 Hok-lam Chan produced a valuable translation and commentary on the current state of Li Chih studies in the People's Republic of China. Now, in his new book, Jean-François Billeter has made the most sophisticated study of Li Chih yet to appear.[3]

It is something more than an aside to point out that Billeter's "Li Zhi" is, of course, the same as Ray Huang's "Li Chih." Zhi is the form required in the pinyin romanization that the Chinese are seeking to make standard usage, and with the exception of Huang's *1587*, which follows the Wade-Giles system, all the other books discussed here employ pinyin. One advantage of this is that when French scholars abandon their own earlier romanization and use pinyin their work is infinitely more accessible to English readers. Unfortunately, we are now in an interim period, where scholars (out of necessity) and general readers (if they choose) are going to have to keep several systems in their heads at once: the great *Dictionary of Ming Biography,* edited by L. Carrington Goodrich and Chao-ying Fang, for instance, is in Wade-Giles, and hence though Li Chih can be traced there at once, Li Zhi will prove elusive to the uninitiated.

Billeter's study, the first of two projected volumes, takes Li Zhi's life up to 1590, the year in which Li published his sardonically entitled *Book to Be Burned (Fen-shu).* Billeter believes that Li's story is important for understanding Chinese society and that it tells us something about ourselves as well—that Li's written work "can enter in some fashion into our experience, and pursue its own movement there." In Li's polemical writings and the melange of ideas and religions that he confronted—Buddhist, Daoist, Muslim, Roman Catholic, Confucian—Billeter sees a way of getting at social and intellectual changes that had been developing in China since the Sung dynasty. Thus he tries to analyze Li not as a man but as a member of the "mandarinate," a class that can be analyzed independently of the "gentry" or "landlord" classes hitherto studied by other historians. Li's life highlights tensions within Confucian society, particularly on the southeast China coast where Li grew up, for there Confucianism as a compulsory ideology helped to destroy the commerce that had enriched the region, and hence made success in the competitive examinations (based on a Confucian curriculum) essential to attaining gainful employment.

Billeter is absorbed by the nature of the "enlightenment" that Li Zhi received in the 1560s, the sense of intellectual strength that this gave to Li, and the relationship between this "symbolic capital" and Li's own class situation at the lower levels of the mandarinate. Li's own relationships with important mentors like He Xinyin and Luo Rufang (and Li's belief that He Xinyin, executed in 1579, had been betrayed in his moment of greatest need by his philosopher friends) are carefully analyzed by Billeter as stages on Li's way to an assessment of the powers of his own self and his own definitions of human nature. In detailing Li Zhi's admiration for Hai Rui (the Hai Jui in Ray Huang's study), Li's quarrels with his erstwhile benefactors the Gengs, and his decision to send his wife and daughter away so that he could enter a more rigorous retreat in the Macheng monastery (the year was 1587), Billeter expands Ray Huang's account and also charts the movement of a restless soul who vowed, at last, "to be dependent on no one," and sought to find his own pure center in a world degraded by dishonesty.

Billeter's book is based on a wide variety of original and newly discovered sources and has many lengthy translations of Li's works. He comments that Li as a writer must be read as Li-the-reader, as a man obsessed with the words of others and his own reactions to them, and always struggling with them. In a letter to a friend Li Zhi wrote,

> When most people write they strive to enter their subject by pushing into it from outside; whereas I am already in there and make sorties to the outside, carrying the battle under the walls of the enemy, rummaging in his supplies, turning his own men and horses against him.[4]

Li committed suicide in jail in 1602, having been accused of improper writings by local gentry-scholars. Billeter feels that this was in large part caused by his proud insistence on his own analytical abilities, by his determination to expose the "dominant illusions" of the mandarinate as false. And he quotes another passage in which Li writes vividly of the pain of being forced to be a writer rather than a reader.

None of those who turned out to have true literary genius
ever started off by intending to write. But their hearts were
filled with such terrible anguish, their throats knotted in such
pain, that they wanted to—yet dared not—spit everything out.
They had so many things to say on the tip of their tongues
without having anyone to whom they could say them that at
last it grew too much, nothing could any longer dam up that
accummulated force.[5]

Once that dam is broken, however, then the writer "abandons himself
to his exaltation, gives vent to his passion, cries out aloud and, tears
streaming down his face, wracked by sobs, gives himself over altogether
to emotion." This is a raw and splendid passage in which Billeter may be
slightly overtranslating—"gives himself over altogether to emotion" (se
livre tout entier à l'émotion) could, from the original Chinese, be equally
well rendered as "was unable to hold himself in." Nevertheless, he presents a magnificent portrait of a man full of intellectual passion.

Li's essay had started as an invocation to the pure emotion that could
be found in certain earlier writings of Chinese fiction, and Billeter reminds
us of Li Zhi's interest in a wide range of works, from the Outlaws of the
Marsh to the Record of the Western Chamber. The heights of this romantic
emotionalism have been acknowledged by generations of Chinese critics
to have been reached by Tang Xianzu in his drama The Peony Pavilion.
Tang was a younger contemporary of Li Zhi (born in 1550), from a
wealthy family, and seemingly headed for a distinguished bureaucratic
career until he chose to devote his energies to writing drama. Like Li,
Tang had been influenced by Luo Rufang and had pursued the meaning
of "pure emotion" in life and in his writings. The two spent some time
together, and Tang wrote to lament Li's death when such lament was
unfashionable and possibly dangerous.[6]

Tang was already writing plays in 1587, though The Peony Pavilion,
his masterpiece, was not finished until 1598. Now fully translated by
Cyril Birch,[7] the play opens yet another perspective into the late Ming
world, one in which passion and propriety both have their strengths and
their purpose. The play is a long story of innocence, love, despair, death,
return from the dead, marriage, and fulfillment. Birch catches the romantic,
bawdy, cheerful qualities of the book, and one reads it with delight. He
is not deterred by the problems that the great erudition of the original
text poses to modern readers. Using the glosses of good current editions

of the play, he explains when essential, but is otherwise content to let the story move ahead, guiding its rhythms by a skillful manipulation of English diction to suggest the range of Chinese attitudes and styles. (Indeed, with the exception of David Hawkes's translation of *Story of the Stone,* the eighteenth-century novel by Cao Xueqin, this is the most delicately tuned translation from the Chinese that I have ever seen.)

Birch has the exuberance needed for Tang Xianzu's work, and without distortion he finds in Tang's cast of minor characters—a mischievous yet shrewd maidservant, a randy yet loyal Daoist nun, a self-important tutor, a drunk and lecherous northern warrior who babbles incomprehensibly—a host of echoes of Shakespearean comedy and Shakespearean diction. Thus the immensely moving story of the two lovers' separation and reunions in both the spiritual and the mortal worlds, which has its own powerful erotic images and to spare, is set in a context that reminds one constantly of the pulse of Ming life beyond the reach of the mandarinate or the court.

This other world, filled with noise and energy, farts and laughter, was of course, part of Ming culture, whether in 1587 or any other year of the Ming period. Elusive in historical texts, banished from classical Chinese essays and poems, the popular culture came to the surface everywhere in fiction, and in the life of Chinese fiction the late Ming was a glorious period. Again, to enter this world one needs guides as well as translators, and here Patrick Hanan gives indispensable aid to those who want to know where to look.

Much more accessible to the general reader than his earlier monograph on Chinese short stories, *The Chinese Vernacular Story*[8] concentrates mainly on the late sixteenth and early seventeenth centuries. Ray Huang, in *1587,* did not ignore this topic altogether—in fact, he has some good remarks on popular literature of the time and on the block printing of pamphlets—and Billeter's references to Li Zhi's interest in fiction have already been mentioned. But it takes the kind of detail Hanan presents here, distilled from voracious reading of story collections and their prefaces, to round out that *"sociologie du mandarinat chinois de la fin des Ming"* which Billeter's subtitle had stated as his subject.

Hanan shows how vernacular fiction emerged through the preoccupations of the dominant Confucian elite. He describes how the idea of a "vernacular" literature grew and what was entailed in the shift away from classical literature. He echoes Li Zhi in seeing how the vernacular serves to criticize the culture's dominant values, and how in its different aspects—

its techniques of narration, its focus and different modes, its styles and sounds—a new effect can be attained that transcends the earlier effects achieved by the written word.

The shift of plots in vernacular fiction from a concern with the thieves and warriors of earlier stories to a concern with the merchants and shop-keepers of the later Ming period already suggests important economic developments within the Ming society. The emerging importance of the narrator's role and the "loosening" of the concept of what constitutes an acceptable story hint at parallel changes in perception. The late Ming figure of Feng Menglong—scholar, adapter, writer, editor, publisher, official, maker of money, admirer of Li Zhi, moralist, and recorder of the ribald—as he emerges from the central chapters of Hanan's book suggests a new kind of focus for our examination of Ming society. That Feng should have the gall to "amend the prosody" of Tang Xianzu's *Peony Pavilion* in a popular edition speaks volumes for Feng's financial ambitions and the size and taste of the public he was trying to reach.[9]

Hanan ends with problems that Huang only hinted at when he mentioned the Jurchen warrior Nurhaci—the fall of the Ming in 1644, and the accession to the throne of those same Jurchen (called now the Qing or Ch'ing, depending on one's romanization). In this new dynastic world, vernacular stories lost their momentum, slid to a rawer eroticism—to a kind of pornography that was divorced from earlier literary conventions—and to escapism, or to careful moral relativity.[10] The withdrawn, bored emperor Wan-li had yielded to new generations of imperial activists, and writers and readers alike withdrew to safer terrain. But the new morality of the Qing state must not blind us to the exuberance and talent of the dynasty that had fallen; these four books attest to the vigor of the culture that was lost.

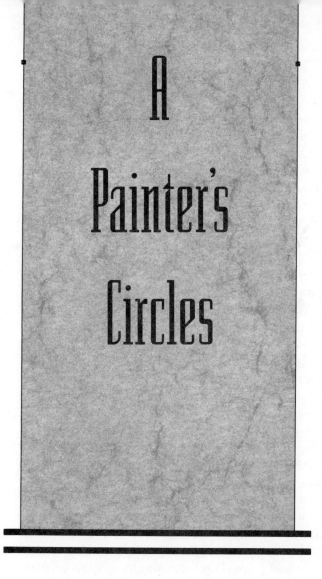

A Painter's Circles

Tao-chi has managed to elude the historians. They have pursued him diligently, because of his eminence as a painter, theorist, and poet, yet all that they have discovered are the approximate dates of his birth and death, the names of a few of his friends, and some of the places that

This essay first appeared in 1967, as an introduction to the University of Michigan Museum of Art catalog *The Painting of Tao-chi*.

he visited or lived in. But even if verified facts are rare, we know that his life spanned one of the most dramatic periods of Chinese history, and it is worth looking at that period a little more closely, in order to show the social and political landscape through which Tao-chi moved. Let us therefore consider three progressively narrowing areas: first, Tao-chi's China; second, Tao-chi's province; third, Tao-chi's circle. That is as far as the historian can go at the moment.

TAO-CHI'S CHINA

Tao-chi lived from 1641 to close to 1720; thus he was born at the very end of the Ming dynasty (1368–1644), grew up in the Shun-chih reign (1644–1661) of the Ch'ing dynasty (1644–1911), and passed the whole of his adult life under the K'ang-hsi emperor (r. 1661–1722).

He was born into a disintegrating world, shadowed by those twin portents of dynastic calamity—internal administrative corruption and external barbarian aggression. The last Ming emperors were unable to put their house in order; at times through idleness, at times deliberately, they had allowed increasing power to fall into the hands of eunuchs and their bureaucratic supporters. The eunuchs have been made the scapegoats for the Ming collapse; in fact, they were as much the symptom as the cause. The increasing centralization of power in imperial China, a continuing process from the Sung, through the Mongol Yüan dynasty, to the Ming, placed a strong burden on the emperor. Only a man of outstanding ability and industry could meet the demands of the highest office, for the emperor was meant to be the supervisor of the entire bureaucracy, director of military strategy and, as Son of Heaven, the mediator between heaven and earth. Not surprisingly, it was a constant temptation to enjoy the perquisites of rule and abandon the responsibilities by delegating them to trusted subordinates. If these subordinates were unscrupulous, there was little that honest and critical members of the bureaucracy could do, since the only ultimate court of appeal was the emperor, and the way to him was blocked. Hence late Ming critics like the members of the Tung-lin and Fu-she academies were generally frustrated, if not doomed.

Internal dissension and corruption in the early seventeenth century meant that Chinese forces could not be effectively marshaled against external threats. The most serious of these threats came from the Manchus northeast of China proper, who had been steadily consolidating their power under two outstanding leaders, Nurhaci (1559–1626) and his son Abahai (1592–1643). When Tao-chi was born, in 1641, the Man-chus had already subdued Korea and sent raiding armies into China; when he was one year old, two of the leading Ming commanders were defeated and joined the Manchus. Many others had already either defected or been recalled and punished on false charges arising from factional quarrels.

The Ming dynasty, however, fell not to the Manchus but to the Shensi bandit Li Tzu-ch'eng, who captured Peking in April 1644. The Ming emperor having committed suicide, the Manchus were able to take advantage of a technical nicety and pose as the avengers of the Ming emperor, the liberators of China from bandit rule. Wu San-kuei, most powerful of the Ming generals, swung to the Manchu side, and in June 1644 the Manchus entered Peking.

Long before this, the Manchus had been employing Chinese with their own forces, organizing defecting Chinese troops into Chinese "banners" on the Manchu military model. The conquest of China was carried through by Manchus and Chinese together; collaboration was the norm, resis-tance occurring only in isolated cities or in those areas that still pro-claimed loyalty to one of the several claimants for the Ming succession. Collaboration brought promotion and rewards; resistance brought ter-rible retribution. Shih K'o-fa, the Ming loyalist scholar-general, deter-mined to hold Yangchow; he refused to surrender, and after a seven-day siege the city fell and the inhabitants were massacred. Later in 1645, after Nanking had fallen, two scholars tried to organize resistance in Chia-ting. Again, defeat was followed by massacre. The simple lesson was not lost to most Chinese, and the Ming cause never showed much sign of reviving, even though there were some like Li Ch'eng-tung who, having defected to the Manchus, defected in turn back to the Ming and died in action. In the 1650s Kwangtung and Kwangsi, the last major bastions of Ming resistance, were captured, and in 1662 the last Ming claimant (who had been pushed slowly west through Kweichow and Yunnan) was exe-cuted near the Burmese border.

From 1644 to Tao-chi's thirtieth birthday, in 1671, there were at least four major shifts in Manchu governmental control, which are probably clearer to historians today than they were to Tao-chi and his friends at the time. The first phase, from 1644 to 1650, was that of the Dorgon regency. Dorgon, uncle to the Shun-chih emperor, acted as regent in name and as emperor in fact. It was his policies that led to the successful conquest of China and to the gradual rehabilitation of the Chinese econ-omy. He kept most of the Ming institutional structure intact and held regular examinations on the old model for the civil service career, an essential gesture to reassure the scholars of the old order that the Manchus would respect their traditions. Sometimes indeed, in his zeal, the dates and places of examinations were announced for areas that had not yet been conquered; this was doubtless an effective propaganda device to offset the darker rumors of Manchu pillage and massacre. Garrisons of Manchu or Chinese banner troops were established in major cities, and Manchus held positions jointly with Chinese in the metropolitan ministries.

The second phase, from 1651 to 1661, was the reign of the Shun-chih emperor in his own right. Dorgon and his supporters had made many enemies, and Dorgon himself was posthumously disgraced. Shun-chih ruled openly as a Chinese rather than as a Manchu emperor. He studied the Chinese language diligently and showed sensitivity to Chinese literature; of an excitable disposition, and physically weak, he tended to be susceptible to outside influences. These influences ranged from the Jesuit Adam Schall von Bell, through the Ch'an priests Hsing-ts'ung and T'ung-hsiu, to the eunuch Wu Liang-fu, and to the concubine Donggo.

It is hard to know how effective Shun-chih was as a ruler; it is possible that China, breathing more peacefully after the conquest, drifted along on the momentum of Dorgon's policies. Certainly, after Shun-chih's death, his actions were severely criticized. This was the third phase, the Oboi regency for the K'ang-hsi emperor, which lasted from 1661 to 1669. The Oboi regency appears to have been a Manchu reaction. Shun-chih was attacked for being infatuated with his concubine, for having given eunuchs too much power (Wu Liang-fu was executed) and, by implication, for having been too lenient to Christians (Schall von Bell was jailed in chains). The Manchus sought a return to their heroic martial virtues.

Oboi himself, however, proved ruthless and corrupt, and in 1669 the young K'ang-hsi emperor had him arrested and thrown in prison, inaugurating the fourth phase, that of his personal rule. Yet it must not be imagined that K'ang-hsi's accession meant immediate peace and stability; not till 1697 were these goals achieved. First, from 1673 to 1681, the emperor was faced by the dangerous rebellion of Wu San-kuei and the other feudatories in the south, a rebellion that proved how tenuous was the Manchu control in that area. Second, from 1688 to 1697, he was involved in difficult fighting with the Eleuth king Galdan in the northwest. Tao-chi was nearly fifty before his country was at rest.

Despite these continuing wars, the splendor of the court was as great as it had ever been. Tao-chi's friends would have observed that the Manchus followed Ming precedents for their imperial processions: elephants in costly trappings, courtiers in special robes, regiments of retainers and guards, accompanied the emperor as he rode in his inlaid and painted carriage to perform the great sacrifices in the temple of heaven. But the Manchus added an extra martial dimension to these ceremonies. It was an elite palace guard of young Manchu noblemen, and well-drilled companies of bondservants, who attended the emperor, rather than the thousands of eunuchs who had milled around a Ming ruler. The elite guards excelled at mounted archery, that nomad specialty requiring strength and skill which had been one of the foundations of Manchu victory. And on annual hunting expeditions north of the Great Wall, thousands of Manchu troops were marshaled in battle array to trap tigers and deer as their emperor rode and shot with them. Ordinary Chinese citizens knew of such Manchu imperial exercises only by word of mouth, but many could see the local garrisons of Manchu troops, the occupying army of alien conquerors, as they rode out to practice archery in central and southern China.

The Manchus worked to preserve their own military skills and their own customs, but they also were influenced and impressed by the Chinese cultural tradition. K'ang-hsi was raised in a Manchu world but was a Chinese ruler in many ways, sensitive to Chinese needs. Often in his long reign, he acted consciously and skillfully as a mediator between warring Manchu and Chinese factions. There is no doubt that he was an outstanding ruler, and should surely be numbered among the great emperors in Chinese history. The varied policies that he used to break internal rebellion, secure and expand the frontiers, and bring internal prosperity were firmly conceived but flexibly executed. This flexibility is an intriguing facet of his character: he was not only willing to experiment, but was also endlessly curious. Jesuits reported him banging cheerfully on a harpsichord when it was presented to him; he learned some Western mathematics to test calendrical theory and agreed to take some quinine when stricken with malarial fever (the medicine, about which the Jesuits knew almost as little as he, worked); in the same kind of way, painting fascinated him.

> The emperor K'ang-hsi often went to the South Library where Wang Yüan-ch'i served as a *kung-feng* (junior official), and ordered him to paint landscapes. There the emperor would lean over the table on which Wang Yüang-ch'i was painting, quite fascinated and unconscious of the passing of time. He

bestowed a poem on the painter which contained the line:
"Your pictures should be shown to the people"; six characters
which Yüan-ch'i carved on a small stone which he used as a
seal in record of the imperial favour. (Osvald Sirén, *Chinese
Painting*, p. 201)

It is therefore not at all surprising that K'ang-hsi, having either seen
some of Tao-chi's paintings or heard about them from scholars at court,
should have invited him to the capital of Peking to paint. From this
invitation stemmed the painting executed jointly by Wang Yüang-ch'i
and Tao-chi, of bamboo and epidendrum, dated 1691 and preserved in
the Palace Collection.

The end of the seventeenth century must have been a fine time for
Tao-chi and his emperor; both men had been profoundly successful, the
one in deepening his artistic sensibilities and perfecting his means of
expression, the other in breaking his internal and external enemies and
bringing an orderly peace to his empire. By the second decade of the
eighteenth century, however, both men had to face the problems brought
on by advancing age. For Tao-chi this may have entailed no more than
reflective inaction, either voluntary or induced by some illness of which
we know nothing. For K'ang-hsi, on the other hand, the times were
more complex: an ailing emperor still *had* to function; there was no
adequate system for the delegation of central authority to subordinates.
Accordingly, the late K'ang-hsi reign was marked by factional infighting
between the emperor's sons and their cliques and by growing corruption
and laxity in both provincial and metropolitan bureaucracies.

The reign of K'ang-hsi's fourth son, Yung-cheng, from 1722 to 1735,
was, as it probably had to be, a period of tough imperial consolidation
and of iron control over the bureaucracy. Tao-chi was dead by this time,
so were his friends, and so was the great period of Ch'ing art. Perhaps
painter and emperor alike had thrived on uncertainty and drawn strength
from the challenges that confronted them. We have no way of knowing.
Without venturing any causal relationship, one may say simply that
eighteenth-century political stability was accompanied by artistic stagnation, whereas the exciting years of the K'ang-hsi reign saw a burst of
artistic energy and originality.

TAO-CHI'S PROVINCE

Westeners have been slow to break Chinese history into provincial or
regional units. The Chinese themselves have long done so, as can be seen

from the mighty corpus of provincial and prefectural gazetteers, thousands of which are still preserved in Western libraries. In the face of China's vastness, the province is a natural focus. Emperors, senior bureaucrats, generals, and foreign diplomats naturally think òf the nation first; but for the mass of people in China, life *was* experienced locally, and Tao-chi was probably no exception.

Although Tao-chi was born in Kwangsi and spent a sizable part of his life traveling, he had a definite base at Yangchou in Kiangsu and spent much time either in Nanking or in Anhwei. He may thus be thought of as a Chiang-nan man, Chiang-nan being the Ch'ing dynasty administrative division that encompassed the present provinces of Kiangsu and Anhwei, in east-central China. Chiang-nan was the heart of early Ch'ing culture, the major source of government wealth through taxation, and the area with the strongest tradition of individual heroism and resistance to the Manchu conquest. It was because of this that K'ang-hsi made no fewer than six major tours to the area, in 1684, 1689, 1699, 1703, 1705, and 1707, in the period between the quelling of the revolt of the Three Feudatories and the onset of old age. During these tours, K'ang-hsi checked on local conditions and met his provincial officials, spending often a week or more in such economic and cultural centers as Suchou, Nanking, and Yangchou. The cities put on festive garb at his coming. Incense burned before every door and bright silken hangings waved over the streets; at night, thousands of colored lanterns shone. The temporary palaces where the emperor stayed were prepared months in advance and filled with costly furnishings and ornaments; operas and lavish banquets were presented nearly every day to the emperor and his entourage. It was not only the officials and scholars who entertained and met K'ang-hsi; salt merchants also built him pleasure gardens, with artificial mountains for him to climb so that he could enjoy the scenery, and mechanical contrivances to keep him amused. It is recorded that K'ang-hsi spent days in the company of Yangchou salt merchants on his tours. Perhaps some of the details on which the Imperial eye rested had been planned by Tao-chi, who is known to have landscaped gardens in Yangchou.

If merchants paid for part of the emperor's diversions, it was still the common people who met the brunt of expenses through the taxes and fees they paid over to the official hierarchy. The officials were omnipresent, and at times no doubt Tao-chi resented them, as everyone outside the hierarchy did. But since he had education, a noble name, and talent, Tao-chi was spared the abuses that were inflicted on the poor and unprotected. He would have known the posts in the Chiang-nan bureaucracy, and at times the incumbents.

Chiang-nan was jointly supervised by a governor-general and two governors. These men stood at the apex of the provincial hierarchy, responsible for maintaining stability in the province and for collecting the annual taxation quotas for forwarding to the capital. In this task, they were aided by two other key officials, the financial commissioner and the judicial commissioner. During Tao-chi's lifetime, only a minority of these officials were ordinary Chinese who had risen through the bureaucracy after passing the civil service examinations. The majority were bannermen, members of the Manchu military establishment which had conquered and then garrisoned China; some were Manchu bannermen, descended from the Manchu clans that had been consolidated by Nurhaci in the north; others were Chinese bannermen, descended from those Chinese who had been captured by the Manchus, or defected to them, either before or during the conquest. The banner organization thus dominated the provincial bureaucracy; naturally, these were the men in whom the Manchu emperors felt most confident in the early years of the Ch'ing, since they were tied to the regime in a special relationship.

Lower in the provincial hierarchy, the Manchus were content to employ a majority of ordinary Chinese officials; indeed, they had to, since there were just not enough talented bannermen to fill all the posts in the empire, and besides the Manchus were committed to a policy of more or less continuing the structure and recruitment policies of the old Ming empire. The important offices here were those of prefect and magistrate. These men controlled the major cities and the surrounding countryside. These administrators were backed by a number of officials in charge of specific areas of governmental concern, such as the salt and grain controllers or the local educational commissioners who supervised the provincial and prefectural school systems. The two broad groupings of banner and other civil service officials may be described as the Banner Elite and the Chinese Official Elite.

These two elites, however, had to work in the closest possible relationship with a third elite, the Local Elite—that is, the group (often called "gentry") that included the wealthy and educated members of local society. Supported by strong clan structures, confident of their importance as the pool from which national talent had to be drawn, and dominating the financial life of their communities through their landholdings, the Local Elite played a prominent part in local government through their charitable and educational work, and were the virtual mediators between the governing elites and the mass of the common people. Their apathy had been a major factor in the Ming collapse; their loyalty was essential to the Ch'ing success.

Members of a fourth elite were particularly strong in Chiang-nan. This was the Imperial Elite, composed of men who drew their power from some special relationship with, or commission from, the emperor. Examples of this group were the Manchu or Chinese bondservants who supervised the customs dues, the salt revenues, and the imperial textile manufactures, in such cities as Yangchou and Nanking. Their occupations were lucrative, and they were often men of culture and patrons of the arts.

A history of Chiang-nan in Tao-chi's time would have to consider all these groups and their interrelationships. Here we may look at a few of them. Governor-general Gali was a Manchu from the plain red banner who directed the province from 1709 to 1712. A man of great abilities, he had had experience in a metropolitan board as a supply officer on the campaigns against Galdan and as governor of Shansi province; yet as Chiang-nan governor-general, he was accused of petty tyranny and gross extortion, and finally dismissed after a protracted and bitter judicial hearing. He eventually committed suicide. Governor-general Chang P'eng-ko, on the other hand, received the *chin-shih* degree, served in the Han-lin Academy, became a famed expert on river conservancy problems, was president of the Board of Civil Office, and ended a long and distinguished life as grand tutor of the heir apparent.

There were similar ranges among governors. Forgotten bannermen contrast with the famous poet and connoisseur Sung Lao, who was an almost impeccable Kiangsu governor for the astonishing span of fourteen years. His Suchou residence was a haven for the scholars of a whole region. Yet scholarship and integrity were themselves no guarantee of success, as can be seen in the career of another erudite Kiangsu governor, Chang Po-hsing, who was finally recalled by K'ang-hsi in the face of overwhelming evidence of incompetence. Members of the Imperial Elite also varied, from Manchu bannermen who worked for one year directing the salt monopoly and then withdrew with their loot, to a bondservant like Ts'ao Yin who became K'ang-hsi's textile commissioner in Nanking, where he established a firm local reputation as a collector of art and a patron of scholars, and also reported secretly to the emperor on the conduct of his official colleagues.

The shifting patterns of such officials, and their friendships within the local elite, must have constantly colored Tao-chi's province. Equally important were natural conditions in the province, for weather affected crops, which affected prices, which affected taxes, which affected officials. The famines of 1708 in Chiang-nan must have touched people of every level, from the peasants who starved to the patrons in the Local

Elite, whether they were landowners who could collect no rent or salt merchants who could not fill their quotas and were plunged into debt. Yangchou, as a center of salt distribution, and a marshaling depot for the grain tribute shipments up the Grand Canal, must have been particularly sensitive to such crises . Tao-chi had made his home in Yangchou, and such things were a part of his life, whatever his public attitude to them might have been.

In Yangchou, too, again despite his own public attitudes, Tao-chi must have been aware of the huge influx of students every three years, as they crammed the city to compete for the *chü-jen* degree; this was the second degree in the examination ladder, success at which entitled a student to travel to Peking and sit for the metropolitan examinations for the *chin-shih* degree, which in turn opened up an official career that might well lead from magistrate to grand secretary. Did he catch some of their excitement and anguish? He certainly could not have missed the events of 1711, when rioting students roamed the streets and abused the examiners for dishonesty. So great was the commotion that K'ang-hsi ordered an investigation, which ended in the execution of several students and several examiners and go-betweens and ruined the careers of two governors and a governor-general.

Any or all of the above incidents and people may have brushed through Tao-chi's life. We think of him as an eccentric and a recluse, and that he was, but he was also a man in his time. For most of his life Chiang-nan was a restless area, although the examination scandal or the local famine were insignificant when compared with the last great attack by Coxinga on Nanking, in 1659, or the threats from the southern feudatories in the 1670s. All come together in determining the province's history and coloring Tao-chi's life. We may generalize that his life was enriched by this turmoil, and go a little further than in the last section to suggest that Tao-chi's art owes some of its greatness to the varieties of experience to which his province subjected him. But we must not forget to add that it was important for him that turmoil occurred in a context of stability; Tao-chi, after all, was free to wander the countryside and draw strength from its mountains and rivers.

TAO-CHI'S CIRCLE

After considering the wider context of Tao-chi's China and Tao-chi's province, it would be logical to proceed to a detailed consideration of Tao-chi himself. Unfortunately, there is not a great deal of information, and what there is has been presented by others. I will not duplicate their labors, but try instead to look at the group around Tao-chi, or at least at those on whom biographical information is available. I will attempt to weigh the basic generalization about Tao-chi: that as a minor member of the defunct Ming ruling house he may be classified with those members of the old regime who opposed the new, and that his friends were Ming loyalists who refused to accommodate to the new order.

Naturally, there is a good deal of support for the generalization. Tao-chi's long and rather ambiguous flirtation with Buddhism linked him clearly with those who chose a religious life to avoid any involvement with the new Manchu state. The very "eccentricity" of his life and his styles of painting and calligraphy may be seen as a type of rebellion, and this rebellion, by association, as a form of political rebellion. A good many of his friends seem to have been Ming loyalists. He was in contact with, or knew personally, the "Three great masters of Lingnan"—Ch'en Kung-yin, Ch'ü Ta-chün, and Liang P'ei-lan. Ch'en Kung-yin's father and his three brothers were all killed fighting the Manchus in the 1640s, but Ch'en fought on with the retreating Ming claimants, lived in retirement after their deaths, and was accused of involvement in the revolt of the three feudatories. Ch'ü Ta-chün also defended the southern Ming court, was involved in a faction supporting Coxinga, and took office under Wu San-kuei in the rebellion. Liang P'ei-lan alone of the three took the examinations and had an official career. But in fact neither Ch'en nor Ch'ü remained a rebel, and in the 1680s they made their peace with the regime that could easily have had them executed, and moved freely in official circles. By knowing them and painting for them, Tao-chi was not doing anything spectacular or even rash.

Tao-chi's two greatest artistic contemporaries, with whom he has often been grouped, were Pa-ta-shan-jen and K'un-ts'an but they seem to have been a good deal more serious about their withdrawal and their Buddhism and more truly eccentric in their personal behavior. Both were older and had experienced the fall of the Ming as adults. Their decisions to retire from the world must have been seriously made; they arrived at them as adults, aware of the significance of what had happened. What was for them a serious decision, however, must be seen more as a gesture when followed by Tao-chi. Three years old at the conquest, he later trod a path that had been cleared for him by others. When he wrote to Pa-ta-shan-jen,

> Your honor and I fell ill on the same day,
> I was only just born when heaven and earth trembled,

Tao-chi was inserting a courteous reference to 1644 rather than a rebellious reminder. He lived as he did because he wanted to, not because of an inner compulsion linked to traditional concepts of dynastic loyalty.

Tao-chi's closest friend, indeed, seems to have led the life of retirement not even out of volition but out of simple necessity. This man was the painter Mei Ch'ing, at whose home in Anhwei Tao-chi often stayed. Mei Ch'ing had successfully taken the *chü-jen* examination in 1654, when he was thirty-one, and thereafter according to his biography "repeatedly tried the metropolitan examinations but never managed to pass them." He was certainly not one of those men who made refusal to take examinations a focus of their anti-Ch'ing sentiment. The two men were friends from 1670 or earlier, so Tao-chi must have known him as he struggled to make a bureaucratic career for himself, and consoled him when he failed. Mei Ch'ing's brother Mei Keng was in the circle of the bondservant Ts'ao Yin and the famous young Manchu poet Singde in the Peking of the 1670s, and later on he became a magistrate. It is not too fanciful to think that Mei Ch'ing and Tao-chi as a young man knew some of the same people, especially since the circle included such eminent scholars as Chu I-tsun and Shih Jun-chang; by the 1690s they *definitely* knew some of them, as we shall see below.

These poets, painters, and scholars of the early Ch'ing lived in general in a small number of major cities and traveled along well-charted routes when they went to sit for an examination or take up an official position. It is quite possible that a surprising number of them either knew each other or had mutual friends. There does not seem to be sufficient evidence in Tao-chi's case to document his circle, but the point can be made by documenting another circle and showing how not only Tao-chi but also several of the major painters of the period fit into it.

The circle I have chosen is that of Ts'ao Yin, for the simple reason that it is the only one that I have studied (in my book *Ts'ao Yin and the K'ang-hsi Emperor, Bondservant and Master*, 1966). Ts'ao Yin is, however, a good case study with which to make my point, since he was not an eminent figure but simply a man of good taste and considerable wealth, who may well have been fairly typical of a large number of upper-class Chinese. Ts'ao Yin had two direct links to Tao-chi, one through the officials and art critic Chou Liang-kung and one through the Manchu connoisseur Po-erh-tu. He also knew Mei Keng, who was presumably in close touch with Tao-chi's friend Mei Ch'ing. Ts'ao Yin knew governor Sung Lao well, and Sung Lao knew and patronized the better Anhwei painters such as Hung-jen and Ch'a Shih-piao. Ts'ao Yin was

close friends with Han T'an in Suchou, and Han T'an knew Wang Hui.
Ts'ao Yin got both Yü Chih-ting and Yün Shou-p'ing to paint in the
scrolls he assembled in honor of his father's memory, and he probably
met them, though he might have acted through an intermediary. Ts'ao
Yin's friend Shih Jun-chang was a friend of Fang I-chih. Chou Liang-
kung, whom Ts'ao Yin had known since childhood, was also friendly
with K'un-ts'an and Kung Hsien. All of the painters mentioned here
were extremely good; many lived in Chiang-nan; Tao-chi probably knew
most of them. Even if he did not, he knew of them and knew their
friends.

This broad circle of which Tao-chi was a part can be shown in diagram
as follows:

Besides Tao-chi's friendship with Mei Ch'ing and Pa-ta-shan-jen, there
is another relationship that would be well worth exploring by any Tao-
chi biographer—namely, that with Po-erh-tu. Po-erh-tu was a Manchu,
a member of the Imperial Clan, his grandfather Tabai having been Nurhaci's sixth son. Po-erh-tu had a minor title as a noble of the imperial
lineage of the tenth rank, third class, and was a competent painter who
led a leisurely life in Peking, since clan members were not permitted to
hold ranks in the regular bureaucracy.

How had the two men met, and what was the significance of that meeting? Presumably, Tao-chi had no cause to admire Po-erh-tu as a painter. One of the Manchu's works was shown in the 1966 Osaka exhibition of five thousand years of Chinese art; it is a simple landscape on two planes, a foreground of hillocks, wintry trees, and a solitary pavillion, and a mountain background with dotted pines (Osaka catalog, p. 56, section 8, painting no. 97). The painting (only a section of this album is shown) seems to be merely a fashionable exercise of precisely that kind on which Tao-chi had turned his back. Such Manchu dabblings could have been useful ammunition for a sarcastic Ming loyalist.

But Tao-chi was not loyalist enough to resist Po-erh-tu's advances, nor eccentric enough to resent his style. After they had met, perhaps in the Peking circles of Ts'ao Yin or Singde through Mei Ch'ing, Tao-chi was offered patronage by Po-erh-tu. He accepted, as most other artists would have done. Tao-chi wrote that he had visited Po-erh-tu's home and gazed with envy on his splendid collection of paintings, which included works by Chou Fang, Chao Meng-fu, and Ch'iu Ying. Probably at the time of the conquest in 1644, Po-erh-tu's father, Baduhai, had been granted the palaces and possessions of some great Ming prince, and the family suddenly found itself placed on a pinnacle with the leading connoisseurs of Chinese art. An open house, kept by a rich man, with such a collection as a focus, would have attracted all but the most intransigent.

Despite his wealth and his Imperial Clan position, Po-erh-tu was no safer from the vagaries of politics than his contemporaries were. He and three of his cousins were disgraced and had their titles removed in 1669, and his uncle Bambursan was condemned to death in the same year. All must have been involved with the losing factions of the Oboi regency. Po-erh-tu and one cousin were reinstated in 1680, but at the same time two other cousins were disgraced. Here the cause must have been their loyalty or lack of it during the Wu San-kuei rebellion. Of the nine members of the younger generation (Po-erh-tu's sons and nephews) on whom details are preserved in the clan genealogy, only four had uneventful careers; all the others were disgraced or dismissed. A noble title clearly did not imply security.

From surviving poems and colophons (printed in Fu Pao-shih, *Shih-t'ao shang-jen nien-p'u*, (pp. 86, 93–94), we know that Po-erh-tu had requested Tao-chi to copy some of his paintings by Ch'iu Ying, and that Tao-chi had done so, taking three years over the job. Furthermore, the copies had been a great success, and Po-erh-tu had shown them to his influential friends at court. Tao-chi made apologies for his inadequacy at figure drawing, writing that he was a good deal happier painting rocks, flowering plants, insects, and fish, but Ts'ao Yin in a colophon on the Ch'iu Ying copy testified to its excellence. Tao-chi may have done this work out of affection for Po-erh-tu, but it is far more likely that he was paid for it in some way, in hospitality or in cash. Similarly, one may assume that further commissions came from friends or Po-erh-tu and Ts'ao Yin, for these men had the money to reward a very small expenditure of effort most handsomely.

Tao-chi started off the poem with which he returned the Ch'iu Ying to Po-erh-tu with these lines:

> The Han palaces rise airy and cool,
> this evening in early autumn,
> Drops of moisture fall soundlessly,
> pale flows the silver river.

In the context of Ming loyalism, where texts were combed for calligraphic conspiracy by zealous Ch'ing officials, this beginning with the character "Han" and a possible reference to weeping may have been intended as a defiant gauntlet, to be hurled by an ethnically pure Han Chinese against his Manchu overlords. It is far more likely, however, to have been a straightforward description of the subject matter of Ch'iu Ying's painting. This little episode is not intended to cast aspersions on Tao-chi's undeniable originality and genius. It is merely a reminder that we should not let generalizations about Ming loyalism and eccentricity totally blur our vision of Tao-chi as a man in society. There is a hoary proverb that may well have touched Tao-chi as often as it has touched us: "He who pays the piper calls the tune."

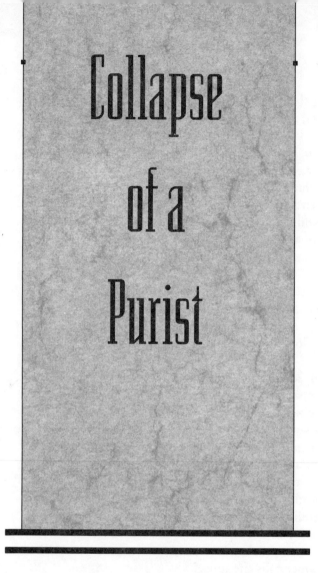

Collapse of a Purist

In the summer of 1714 Chang Po-hsing, the governor of Kiangsu province, shut himself up in the city of Soochow and refused to come out. He would not leave the city to preside over the assizes at Ch'ang-chou; he extended the curfew long into the daylight hours, so business was seriously disrupted; he arrested a group of Shensi hat sellers on the

This essay first appeared in 1968, in the bulletin of the Society for Ch'ing Studies.

grounds that they were conspirators; and he ordered the local officials to call up special constables to protect him. The reason for these actions, according to Chang Po-hsing, was that he was in danger of assassination, either by pirates or by the supporters of the province's former governor-general, the Manchu Gali.

In response to strongly worded secret edicts sent by the puzzled K'ang-hsi emperor, two officials tried to find the true reasons for Chang Po-hsing's odd conduct. "The emperor knows [Chang Po-hsing's] unswerving integrity," wrote Lang T'ing-chi, the director general of grain transport, "so there is no point in my reporting on that. The fact remains that he is extremely suspicious by nature, and concerned with minutiae, so business gets held up badly. In any conversation, if the speaker is extolling someone, then Chang Po-hsing doubts him; if the speaker denigrates someone, then Chang Po-hsing believes him. Consequently, there are rascals who make up completely unfounded stories, baseless rumors, falling in with his wishes in the hopes of gaining his trust." Li Hsü, the textile commissioner of Soochow, developed a similar argument. "I have closely observed the governor; as a general rule, he is extremely suspicious and extremely scared. Being extremely suspicious, whenever something happens, he goes out of his way to find flaws and cannot follow things through to a clear conclusion. Naturally, the innocent get involved, and numerous people are implicated. Being extremely scared, in his heart he's afraid to act and puts an absolute trust in the quite unfounded statements of the meanest people. Being uneasy day and night, his behavior is naturally topsy-turvy."[1]

Chang Po-hsing is famous in Ch'ing biographical compendia as a Neo-Confucian philosopher and as an incorruptible official. Neither quality need be denied to him; but a close examination of the historical record, zeroing in on the fateful summer of 1714, shows at what cost that reputation was bought, and also tells us a good deal about the K'ang-hsi emperor's character.

Born in 1652, Chang Po-hsing was the only son of a wealthy landowner in Honan. He received a rigorous and conventional classical education and became a licentiate at twenty-five and, after failing each examination once, a *chü-jen* in 1681 and a *chin-shih* in 1658. In the palace examination, he placed eightieth in the third grade. In the next fifteen years, he served on three occasions, for rather brief periods, as a secretary with one of the boards or bureaus in Peking. But his preference was clearly for the life of scholarship and contemplation in his native Honan, and it was at his I-jeng home that he spent most of his time. Here he wrote and talked with friends, leaving his study only occasionally to fulfill his obligations as a member of the local elite by helping in irrigation or famine relief works. At such work he was successful, dispensing the family money (his father died in 1695) with a generous hand. He had a large library, over fifteen hundred acres of land, two sons, and three daughters, and now and again someone came to study with him. There is little doubt that he was a happy man.

In 1700, when Chang Po-hsing was forty-eight years old, the director general of river conservancy took note of his local reputation as an upright man and self-made irrigation expert and recommended him for office. Chang Po-hsing strenuously objected, pleading a combination of inexperience and sickness, but was overruled. After two years working on a stretch of the Yellow River, he was promoted to be river intendant at Chi-ning, in Shantung. Though he was not particularly able—he bungled at least two assignments rather badly—there was no doubt as to his integrity and the generosity with which he distributed his own money to the poor in his area. Accordingly, in 1706 he was promoted to the post of judicial commissioner of Kiangsu.

The job was not to his liking. Within the first month, he clashed several times with the governor and offered his resignation. He was not permitted to resign, because the K'ang-hsi emperor was just embarking on a southern tour and there was work for him to do. His relations with his fellow provincial officials were still bad, and he had had little chance to feel his way into his new job, when he was again promoted, this time at the personal insistence of the K'ang-hsi emperor, to the major post of governor of Fukien.

On his southern tours, the K'ang-hsi emperor liked to ask questions for himself, investigate local conditions, and play the role of the benevolent ruler. Virtue would be rewarded, and vice rooted out, by the emperor in person, for the benefit of all. As the emperor made his way south in the spring of 1707, Chang Po-hsing's name cropped up at various times, as an example of the incorruptible official. Yet when the emperor, on reaching Nanking, asked the governor-general and governor to recommend outstanding officials for possible promotion, Chang Po-hsing's name was not among those mentioned. This was the chance for K'ang-hsi to act the Confucian monarch. Summoning Chang Po-hsing to an audience, K'ang-hsi declared, "On my travels in Chiang-nan, I have learned that Chang Po-hsing is regarded as an extremely honest official. Such a reputation is one of the hardest to achieve." According to the biographies, the emperor then asked, "Are there any other officials in

Chiang-nan as good as this Chang?" When told there were none, the emperor replied, "If there are none, how is it that you never recommend him? Accordingly, I personally shall recommend him for promotion. If he proves to be a good official, my people will all know that I am an enlightened ruler; should he prove avaricious or a lawbreaker, then my people may laugh that I am no judge of men." The same day the emperor ordered the Board of Civil Office to appoint Chang Po-hsing to the governorship of Fukien, temporarily vacant due to the death of the previous incumbent.

Reporting for instructions before taking up his new office, Chang Po-hsing was told by his emperor, "Each place has different customs, don't try to change them. Just make sure that your area stays peaceful." Chang Po-hsing replied that though his abilities were small, he would at least be honest in office. K'ang-hsi drily commented that officials always said that; only time would show if Chang Po-hsing could keep to his word. In pursuing his goal of incorruptibility, he must not be hasty in impeaching his fellow officials; only if moral suasion and example failed should they be impeached.

As governor of Fukien, Chang behaved in a proper Confucian manner; he memorialized successfully to have taxes rebated, food prices stabilized, and the quota of *chü-jen* candidates increased. He tightened up the *pao-chia* mutual security system and wrote three versions of the Emperor's Sacred Edict: one embellished with classical allusions for the literati, one illustrated with popular sayings for those of medium intelligence and scholarly ability, and one with memorable jingles for the simple country folk. He collated and published editions of the orthodox philosophers. But in other areas he showed a certain inflexibility, even bigotry, that did not accord with the emperor's instructions: he destroyed the temples on which the locals relied "for death and birth, calamity and good fortune"'; he ordered families to redeem the daughters they had sold off as nuns and to ensure that they got married; he forbade burial practice not in accordance with the rites, although they had long been followed in Fukien; he drew up plans to expel all Catholics from his territory.

Had he chosen to, K'ang-hsi could have seen disobedience in these actions. Instead, he noted them as evidence of Chang Po-hsing's moral uprightness. When the governor of Kiangsu was dismissed for corruption, K'ang-hsi suggested that Chang Po-hsing be appointed to the post, since his undeniable rectitude made him the best candidate for this complex and financially important governorship.

Chang Po-hsing took up office as Kiangsu governor in early 1710, and from the first, things started to go badly. He squabbled with Governor-general Gali over tax rebates, grain distribution, and the contents of joint memorials. The financial affairs of the province were in a considerable tangle, and Chang Po-hsing reopened complex corruption cases which the governor-general had considered satisfactorily closed. In the fall Chang Po-hsing could take no more and requested that he be retired on the grounds of old age and sickness. The emperor turned down the request. Accused by Gali of cowardice for failing to pursue pirates in the area around Shanghai, Chang Po-hsing arrested one of Gali's staff for being a pirate; the arrested man died in prison before trial. In the fall of 1711 the two men clashed again in the examination hall case at Yangchow. K'ang-hsi appointed special commissioners to settle the Gali–Chang Po-hsing mutual impeachments. Though successive commissioners exonerated Gali and found Chang Po-hsing guilty of incompetence and lodging false charges against his superior, the emperor overrode their verdicts, on the grounds that it was the emperor's duty to mediate disputes between Manchus and Chinese and that Chang Po-hsing was a virtuous and honest man. Finally, Gali was withdrawn from the province, while Chang Po-hsing remained in his post as governor.

In late 1713 Chang Po-hsing asked that one of three men in whom he had confidence be appointed financial commissioner of Kiangsu. The request crossed with the emperor's order appointing Mou Ch'in-yüan to the post. Mou was not a friend of Chang's, but had had a respectable official career, and the emperor saw no need to cancel the appointment. Early in 1714 Chang Po-hsing expressed uneasiness and alarm at the enormous number of pirates in his province and requested the emperor to order that every boat in the Yangtze delta area be forced to carry complex registration papers showing that the crew members were engaged in legitimate occupations. By early summer he had shut himself in Soochow for fear of assassination. In July he impeached the newly appointed financial commissioner Mou for hiding pirates in his yamen. The emperor ordered the charge carefully investigated. First Gali's successor as governor-general and then special commissioners appointed by K'ang-hsi found Mou Ch'in-yüan completely innocent of Chang Po-hsing charges, reporting that they could find no evidence that there were pirates around Soochow or that Chang Po-hsing's life was in danger. Each time the emperor reminded the judges about Chang Po-hsing's reputation for honesty and integrity and ordered a fresh investigation. Finally, when the commissioners insisted that Chang deserved death by beheading for having lodged false charges against a senior official, the emperor ordered Chang dismissed, and summoned him to Peking. He agreed to the Board of Civil Office's request that Mou Ch'in-yüan be honorably reinstated, and after a special audience with Chang Po-hsing, K'ang-hsi issued what amounted to a formal apology to his ministers: he found, he said in an edict of December 18, 1715, that Chang Po-hsing "was desperately muddled, and truly not a fit man to hold the office of governor." The emperor finalized Chang's dismissal but called for leniency; Chang was appointed to a minor financial post in Peking.

Chang Po-hsing's closing years were peaceful. He carried out various moderately difficult tasks successfully, continued to write on Neo-Confucian philosophy, was finally made president of the Board of Rites by Yung-cheng, and died in 1725, at the age of seventy-three.

It is a curious life story, and a historical biography of Chang Po-hsing would make interesting reading. But even if the details of piracy on the Yangtze, the cliques around Gali and the other protagonists, Chang Po-hsing's own friends and connections, and the content of his philosophical and other writings were all carefully analyzed, the record would still be unsatisfactory and major enigmas remain. I believe that to understand the life of Chang Po-hsing, and particularly the crisis of 1714, we have to stretch history into the realm of psychiatric studies.

Chang Po-hsing, I would like to suggest, was suffering from the mental illness known as paranoia, and what he did in Soochow in 1714 was to create a paranoid "pseudo-community." Paranoid delusions of discrimination and persecution "develop out of the person's attempt to account for situations and happenings that usually are themselves products of his own asocial behavior, his attitude and his fantasies." Delusion formation is usually started by an unfortunate incident that leads an individual to doubt his own abilities; he becomes primed for certain kinds of happenings and overreacts to unfavorable or danger signs. He then selects from his environment incidents that fit his developing interpretation of the world around him. His delusions are unshakable, well systematized, and highly logical if his basic premise is granted. The paranoid personality is found in those with unrealistic feelings of self-overevaluation, in egocentric and conceited people from highly moralistic and demanding backgrounds. Paranoids have high achievement goals, usually have a high level of intelligence, and show the character triad of orderliness, frugality, and obstinacy.

As paranoia progresses, the individual will mentally organize those around him into "a pseudo-community of attitude and intent," although these people are not in fact united in any common undertaking against him, nor do they carry out the activities for which he blames them and which he fears. Then, in the worlds of the Yale professor of psychiatry Norman Cameron, "the pseudo-community grows until it seems to constitute so grave a threat to the individual's integrity or to his life that, often after clumsy attempts to get at the root of things directly, he bursts into defensive or vengeful activity. This brings out into the open a whole system of organized responses to a supposed functional community of detractors or persecutors which he has been rehearsing in private. The real community, which cannot share in his attitudes and reactions, counters with forcible restraint or retaliation, depending upon whether it recognizes his outburst as illness or wickedness."

The following facts from Chang Po-hsing's biography are suggestive in the light of such an interpretation: he was an only son, puritanical, strictly educated, and concerned with detail; grew confused in the face of complicated problems; failed each major examination once despite his long studies; was consistently reluctant to take up office; first had responsible office when over fifty years old; refused to hire professional assistants (mu-yu) to help him in his new jobs; ran out of money from family sources in 1712; and was backed consistently and emphatically by the K'ang-hsi emperor as being an honest and virtuous man.

A number of other details from the biography are suggestive in the case of his mental breakdown, although Western scholars have been primed to regard them as clichés: he was precocious at book learning, a purist at an early age, did not play with other children, and expressed unusually violent grief when his mother died in his thirteenth year; his father was unusually stern; he always refused to pay the customary fees (bribes if you like) on taking office, punctiliously observed all rites, and had a profound desire to emulate the worthy scholars of the past.

Among the norms of Ch'ing society that should be recalled in considering his breakdown are the special responsibilities and obligations devolving on an only son, the extremely high career expectations held by parents for their children, the complexity of administration at the governorship level, and the need for tact, good interpersonal relations, and the general distribution of customary fees to ease the pangs of high office.

Chang Po-hsing was inexperienced and in his fifties when he took high office. The normal stress was thus heightened in his case, and he grew obsessed with Gali and the pirates, who had caused his first humiliations. To justify and systematize his delusions, he organized the people of Soochow into a pseudo-community of pirates and assassins and chose the financial commissioner Mou Ch'in-yüan as the ringleader to replace the absent Gali. As his terror grew, he embarked on vengeful activity, and because of his high office his charges inevitably involved the emperor himself and demanded a large-scale investigation. In the first confrontation with Gali, in 1712, he had still been in touch with reality; by 1714 he was striking out at a nonexistent target.

A normative career pattern would have saved Chang Po-hsing from these humiliations. Either he would have been dismissed early on for incompetence or he would have learned to make his peace with the system. As it was, the K'ang-hsi emperor in his role of Confucian monarch threw Chang Po-hsing into highly complex situations that his idealized and protracted education had not fitted him to handle. It is amusingly ironic that in suddenly removing Chang Po-hsing from the stressful situation, and letting him devote himself to routine tasks within his range of competence, the K'ang-hsi emperor hit on the one answer that therapists now agree is often successful in the treatment of paranoia.

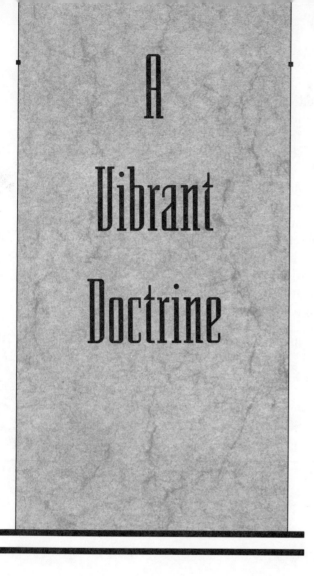

A Vibrant Doctrine

One would be hard pressed, surveying any of the political cultures in human history, to find a parallel for the continuity, longevity, and vitality of Confucianism. This moral and ethical system was given initial shape in the fifth and fourth centuries B.C., drawing on traditions of history and ritual that reached back at least half a millennium before that. It was codified and strengthened in the first two centuries A.D., was

---

This essay first appeared in 1979, in the *New York Review of Books*.

reformulated and reinforced by major philosophers in the twelfth century, and was still vigorous and subtle in the late eighteenth century—an astonishing record. The Confucian theorists offered apparently simple precepts for the relations between man and man, man and ruler, father and son, husband and wife; but they reached at the same time into the most difficult aspects of our relations with the forces of nature, and had much to say about the central problems of ethics and political activism.

Yet for all its remarkable range and complexity, Confucianism is not much studied outside specialized sinological circles. The lack of interest in Confucianism is owing in part to its recent association with a disintegrating polity. Among nineteenth-century Western scholars, as among Chinese nationalist thinkers of the late nineteenth and early twentieth centuries, it was hard to separate Confucians from Confucianism and to see any need to look for subtleties behind the banal façade of the "State Confucianism" that was claimed as their own by the Manchu rulers.

Lu Hsun and other influential Chinese writers of the 1920s associated Confucianism with decay and hypocrisy; Western scholars after World War II modified this view out of a sympathy for China's past culture deeper than that which Chinese iconoclasts could admit to, but even here influential scholar-teachers often viewed any attempts at a *twentieth-century* Confucianism as being either farce or fraud. The late Joseph Levenson of the University of California at Berkeley, for example, tended to dwell on the sense of farce in recent Confucian ideas. He wrote of the earlier-twentieth-century Confucian literati as being "manikins" and raised wry smiles with his images of Yuan Shih-k'ai, Sun Yat-sen's successor in 1912, driving up to the Temple of Heaven in an armored car. But this sense of farce was in turn grafted to a complex ideological schema of Levenson's own, in which he saw the nineteenth-century Confucian world as first made uneasily conscious of itself and then bypassed by the needs and preoccupations of the modernizing and Western-dominated Chinese society.

The late Mary Wright of Yale University saw more fraud in modern Confucian thinking when she analyzed the attempts of Chiang Kai-shek's theorists to take over the nineteenth-century values of the Ch'ing restoration statesmen; she warned Western readers not to be taken in by this attenuated and self-seeking parody of a once fine tradition. Her sense of this fraud was tied to her belief that we must focus clearly on the powerful dislocations and dissonances of republican China in order to understand that China would be shaped only by revolutionary means.

Thus when Confucian values and theories were systematically examined—most imposingly in the remarkable series of volumes edited by Arthur F. Wright in the 1950s and 1960s[1]—they were seen as the values and theories of a vanished civilization, a view only underlined by Levenson's own contributions to those volumes. Most of the historical work on twentieth-century China—if it was concerned at all with problems of ideology—concentrated on problems of Chinese communism, whether in its Comintern antecedents or its "nativist" lineaments. One learned that communism, rooted in social conditions spawned by the disintegration of the old Confucian-bureaucratic social order and by the impact of Western imperialism, was the antithesis of Confucianism.

Two volumes edited by W. Theodore de Bary can be seen as having marked an influential shift in direction.[2] In *Self and Society in Ming Thought* and *The Unfolding of Neo-Confucianism*, de Bary and an impressive list of contributing scholars dug deep into the Confucian ethos, as the contributors to Arthur Wright's volumes had done. Furthermore, by enlisting the philosopher T'ang Chun-i as a contributor to both volumes, de Bary also introduced scholarly readers outside the subfields indicated by the volumes' titles to an important corrective: though T'ang Chun-i's essays were on topics related to the Ming dynasty philosopher Wang Yang-ming (1472–1529), they were also written by a living philosopher-teacher who had no trouble at all—from his base in Hong Kong—in seeing Neo-Confucian thought as both deeply moving and pertinent to his modern needs.

What happened was that many readers now began to see their views of Confucianism as having been too limited; some went further and identified themselves as victims of an emphasis on "modernization" theory that had refused to give adequate attention to traditionalist ideologies in a time of change. Similarly, as familiarity with Chinese communism grew, public attitudes toward Mao's China followed a cycle from hostility to awe, to acceptance, and now to skepticism. It has become less unthinkable to see Chinese communism as connected with the Chinese culture of the past and easier to evaluate Chinese conservatism as being a more lively and variegated force in twentieth-century Chinese life than we had previously allowed.

A further jump in this whole process can be seen from the fact that T'ang Chun-i himself was reassessed—now as a philosopher in his own right rather than as a historian of other philosophers—in an essay written by Hao Chang for Charlotte Furth's stimulating volume on twentieth-century thought, *The Limits of Change*. In his absorbing essay, Chang took as his starting point the philosophical manifesto issued in 1958 by T'ang Chun-i and three other Confucian philosophers in Hong Kong and Taiwan. The date itself is an intriguing reminder that those working in Chinese history have almost certainly subsumed 1958 as standing for the Great Leap Forward in the People's Republic of China and hardly as a momentous year in Confucianist thought.

Chang argued eloquently that this "New" Confucianism was not a mere response to modernization but part of an ongoing and powerful tradition that was responding to a profound crisis of meaning in modern society. Chang disputed Levenson strongly on several counts, especially concerning the effects of emotional humiliations on the Chinese nineteenth- and twentieth-century psyche. Here Chang continued a critical argument already suggested in his book on the late-nineteenth-century reformist Liang Ch'i-ch'ao, a man whose relationship to his own Confucian past was deeply ambiguous—and who had also been previously studied by Levenson. Chang points to the complexity of the New Confucianist formulations and their usages, such as *hsing* ("moral creativity of the human mind") and *jen* ("unimpeded flow of fellow feeling") and elaborates on the religious aspects of these terms. He links T'ang's works of the 1950s sensitively to the Idealist Confucian philosophy of Wang Yang-ming in the sixteenth century and discusses their shared sense of the importance of the view that every man can be a sage. For T'ang that argument, now updated, can show how both democracy and modern science are important for the creation of *jen* in our own time. Yet Chang also points out the sense of frailty that lies at the core of T'ang beliefs:

> In one of his works, T'ang Chun-i tried to drive home the value of Confucianism in this direction by envisaging the absurdity of human life without the guidance of a spiritual-moral ideal. Looking at the enigma of human existence in terms of whither and whence, he compares life to a small isolated light-tower standing in the middle of a vast sea in the night. Just as the light-tower is surrounded by boundless darkness, life beyond its beginning and end is also shrouded in unfathomable mystery.
>
> If the beginning and end of life are seen as arbitrary and absurd, within the life process every phase is riddled with troubles and sufferings. The reason is that life is bound up with all kinds of cravings. Built into every kind of craving, such as the craving for the satisfaction of physical needs, for love, for honor, and even for the realization of lofty ideals and values, are unavoidable disappointments and frustrations. In view of the pervasiveness of sufferings and troubles in the

life-world, it is no wonder that high religions such as Buddhism, Taoism, and Christianity almost all start with pessimistic premises about life.

In T'ang's view, however, Confucianism provides an invaluable source of spiritual support enabling people to face the existential situations of life with equanimity and courage. T'ang's view in this regard found an echo in an observation put forward by Hsu Fu-kuan and strongly supported by Mou Tsung-san, that Confucianism had its origin in a profound sense of sorrow and difficulty that was believed to have pervaded people's outlook on this world in the ancient Chou dynasty.[3]

In an essay in the same volume on T'ang's own philosophical mentor, Hsiung Shih-li, Tu Wei-ming also criticized Levenson's conceptions of the collapse of Confucian value and reaffirmed the complexity and vitality of the tradition even in its twentieth-century guise:

> To study Hsiung Shih-li as embodied in his philosophical treatises is to witness the unfolding of a profound vision, deeply rooted in the Chinese tradition and yet singularly relevant to some of the vital issues of the modern world. . . . Although his ideas have far-reaching implications, they are centered around a single concern: to live authentically as a Confucian thinker amidst depersonalizing forces in contemporary China.[4]

If we draw together these and other passages on contemporary "Confucian" philosophy as given in *The Limits of Change,* we find a number of recurring themes: the profundity of the Confucian vision, and the sense that this vision responds to personal crisis; the need for authenticity, and the strength of negative forces opposing man's ethical endeavors; the recognition of loneliness and sorrow as features of experience and the need for intellectual courage in confronting them.

All of these themes emerge also in Thomas Metzger's difficult, remarkable, and stimulating book, *Escape from Predicament.*[5] The opening sections of this book are dominated by T'ang Chun-i, and it seems to me that Metzger has two main purposes in using T'ang as he does. The first is to set the scene for the practicality of what Metzger is attempting: T'ang "has shown us how one can philosophize in the twentieth century," writes Metzger, and in the second chapter of the study he makes a powerful attempt to underscore the basic elements of T'ang's belief system. These include T'ang's distance from Western ideas of rationality and conflict, his rejection of both Locke and Hume in his quest for a way to avoid the mistake of "keeping static the inherently moving." T'ang's central belief is that "the self participates in a noumenal flow of empathy"—that is, he suggests that the fellow feeling of *jen* I have already mentioned is fundamental to human perception.

T'ang also sees the filial piety of the Confucian tradition not just as a process of deference but as a means of "completing oneself." He sees man as able in a sense to "match heaven" since man partakes of the "godlike" in that "he is the sole existing vehicle of that moral assertion needed to put the world right." Since there is moral decay and corruption in this world, "self-assertion" is necessary to the Confucian; but that self-assertion has little to do with Western individualism—the Confucian rather seeks to "become one in feeling with . . . the heart of benevolence shared by all men." Metzger is obviously deeply interested in, even accepting of, these formulations, though he does refer at intervals, in affectionately critical vein, to T'ang's "Panglossian optimism," to his "pathos of immensity," and to his possessing "the cheerfulness of a kind of metaphysical YMCA."

But the second main purpose that Metzger has in emphasizing T'ang is to enlist him as a major ally in the extraordinarily difficult task of reconstructing the pathos and tension at the heart of the earlier historical Neo-Confucian view of the self and the world; in other words, he sees T'ang as a precursor of his own work and as a stimulant for it. The "predicament" of Metzger's title is that of men trapped in the Confucian "ethos of interdependence," an interdependence between that "godlike power" that T'ang spoke of and an "anxious fear of moral failure"— between, one might say, autonomy and anxiety. Much of Metzger's book is an attempt to identify and analyze that anxiety and sense of failure, an elusive concept at best, but one he pursues with intellectual elegance and tenacity.

Writing of the Confucian idea of *t'ien-ming*—"What heaven has decreed"—Metzger gives a graphic summary of what he is attempting. Here he comments on *t'ien-ming* by relating the concept to the thought of Chu Hsi, the Sung dynasty philosopher (1130–1200) whose commentaries on the Confucian classics made him perhaps the most influential Chinese thinker of the last thousand years:

> Yet although the idea of *t'ien-ming* thus validated the importance of the intervening human will, it also underlined the

predicament within which this will found itself. Since it limited the human capacity to decide the contest between good
and evil, Chu Hsi's statement that "man" can "control heaven
and earth" was at best an oversimplification, an enthusiastic
utterance ignoring the power of "heaven." Heaven existed not
only as a source of moral power, an imperative to use this
power, and an object to be controlled through the use of this
power, it also could thwart the use of whatever moral power
the self was able to muster. Locked into this unending
encounter with something unpredictably elastic and awesomely immense, the self oscillated erratically between the
status of a victim and that of a demigod. The self had immense
capabilities, but they could be exercised only in a slippery
cosmic arena.[6]

Metzger contends that this predicament, which he elsewhere summarizes as "a paradoxical alienation from a constantly accessible truth which
had to be pursued," was not simply the condition in which a few philosophers or reflective politicians found themselves. Rather, he argues, the
sense of predicament was pervasive in China after the eleventh century,
and clichés describing it form the basic "grammar" (Metzger acknowledges Kenneth Burke's influence here) that informs traditional Neo-Confucian discussions. Therefore "what was controversial for Neo-Confucians
was not the fearful predicament they found themselves in but the formulae of enlightenment they advanced to get out of it."

This is a challenging idea, and the very lengthy third chapter of Metzger's book is an erudite and ingenious attempt to marshal enough evidence for the pervasiveness of Confucian clichés throughout Chinese
history and thinking to prove the existence of the predicament. There
are some major assumptions in the historical argument that scholars will
battle over indefinitely. Especially important is Metzger's assumption
that since the collapse of the great Wang An-shih political reforms in the
eleventh century, during the Sung dynasty, a particular kind of hope had
gone out of the Chinese statesman-scholar's world:

The Neo-Confucian sense of predicament is now clear. Whatever the great "revolutions" of Sung society as analyzed by
modern scholars, the "outer" realm of political and economic
affairs had been mostly drained of hope since the disappointment with Wang An-shih's reforms. Perceiving theirs as a

society shaped largely by the selfish pursuit of profit and wrongly designed institutions, Neo-Confucians could labor conscientiously with a spirit of moderate realism but could not hope to realize their classic goal of social oneness, political order, and economic well-being.

Nevertheless determined to pursue this goal, they turned to the "inner" life of moral striving as a prerequisite, but here again, in the eyes of both the Lu-Wang and the Ch'eng-Chu school,* they were confronted by a massive tendency toward moral failure based on inescapable cosmic conditions which they could all too easily sense in their own individual minds. The world, both in its history and in the present, was largely a moral wilderness.[7]

Another of Metzger's assumptions concerns the importance of the sense of fear of moral failure as a motivating force in the traditional Chinese world, the fear that Metzger interestingly links to imagery of water a being both regenerative and able to drown. Another is the pervasiveness of that "perception of rampant evil" that Metzger finds running through Ming and Ch'ing dynasty writings. Metzger sees this sense of pervasive evil as having three important sources in the Confucian tradition of thought: first, the individual's feeling he has made a bad choice, freely arrived at; second, the awareness of the universal weakness of the human will; third, the perception of an "inherently degenerative force" that is "immanent in the very flow of existence and constantly threatening to 'overcome' the self."

Yet another assumption would concern the radical approach to the world of action that Metzger ascribes to Chu Hsi and many later followers. The balances and shifts between this radicalism and the forces of "moderate realism" are very important to Metzger's argument, since they provide a way of linking Neo-Confucianism to Maoism, which he connects with the radical impulses in Confucian thought, and thus let him shift the gears of the argument into the closing sections of the book, in which the escape from the predicament can be discussed.

The sustained detail and intensity of Metzger's argument seems to flag

---

*Abbreviated terms for the two dominant but antagonistic schools of Confucian interpretation in the twelfth to sixteenth centuries.

at this point. The trouble is that he is tackling so many topics at once. He wants to disprove Levenson's views on the discontinuity within the Confucian tradition that marks "modern" China. He wants to refute Max Weber, who failed to see the central tensions born of religious doubt and cosmic anxiety that lay at the heart of Confucianism. He largely rejects Richard Solomon's views that old patterns of psychological "dependency" in Chinese family and political life have been transmitted into current Chinese political culture. He gives short shrift to modern Western academic analysts of Maoism or of Chinese communism more broadly defined. If I may attempt a clumsy summary, Metzger is trying to show that the "radical" wing within the Confucian tradition, having been torn by anguish for so long, found that the coming of the West reawakened a "traditional zeal for total reform." The enthusiasm for realizing moral goals could thus be given its head once more.

This accounts for the burst of radical optimism that has suffused twentieth-century political quests in China and that can be found both in T'ang Chun-i and in the People's Republic, for in both there is a "rising sense of impending solution." The Chinese have long been used to appalling misery and crisis in their country and hence can draw on a tradition that "defined moral action precisely as . . . coping with almost unbearable disasters." If, Metzger points out in conclusion, the hopes are dashed, there will be a return to the earlier sense of "partial moral failure," and hence the old Confucian predicament will reemerge among the senior cadres of the new socialist state. As Maoist imagery yields to the more cautious pronouncements of Teng Hsiao-pingism, we may well watch and wonder.

Confucianism, therefore, breathes as a living force for Metzger across a wide spectrum of time and society; it does not sit tidily within the sphere of conservatism once we see its radical potential, and in the hands of major current thinkers it is certainly neither farce nor fraud.

It is this feeling for the recaptured relevance of Confucianism that gives such a sense of spontaneity to Metzger's work. Indeed, there is more vigor and energy in this book than in any recent contributions to the story of Chinese communism that I can think of; reading it, one gets a feeling that a corner is being turned in Chinese historiography, and even though the goal is not clear, the general direction is: it is a search for enrichment and complexity in a zone where cliché had begun to rule. This is the sort of book that has the density and the originality to push scholars—even reluctantly—in new directions.

The Dialogue of Chinese Science

It will readily be allowed that few historical events were so rich in consequence as the decision taken by certain southern Chinese officials in +1583 to invite into China some of the Jesuit missionaries who were waiting in Macao. It was the first decisive step in the long process of unification of world

This essay first appeared in 1984, in *Isis*.

science in Eastern Asia, and the better mutual understanding
of the great cultures of China and Europe.

These sentences from volume 4 of *Science and Civilisation in China* (pt.
2, p. 436) serve as well as any for the historian of modern China who
seeks to reflect on the impact and usefulness for his own field of Joseph
Needham's immense, learned, and ambitious examination of the entire
pre-seventeenth-century world of Chinese science. The quotation dis-
plays the decisiveness of the moment in the light of a universalistic trend.
Needham again emphasizes the importance of this "fundamental continuity and universality of all science" in the most recent volume of *Science
and Civilisation in China* to appear, *Chemistry and Chemical Technology* (vol. 5, pt. 1, p. xxxviii), just as in volume 2 he opined that China
"merges in the 17th century with the world-wide unity of modern science" (p. 577). Needham also stresses this approach to understanding
how the cultures interacted in volume 3, *Mathematics and the Sciences
of the Heavens and the Earth,* where he writes, "It is vital today that the
world should recognize that 17th-century Europe did not give rise to
essentially 'European' or 'Western' science, but to universally valid world
science, that is to say, 'modern' science as opposed to the ancient and
medieval sciences" (p. 448). In moving towards a synthesis, Needham
invokes the "principle of dynamic equilibrium" of the two famous thinkers Wang Fu-chih (1619–1692) and the "materialistic monism" of Tai
Chen (1724–1777) (vol. 2, pp. 511, 513), while leaving to the realm of
personalities and Jesuit internal politics the burden of explanation for
the fact that "in the early +17th century mathematics and astronomy got
through, in the late +18th century chemistry did not" (vol. 5, pt. 3, p.
221).[1]

This whole concept of a branch of science "getting through" is an
elusive one, and the 1583 date that Needham suggested as marking the
"first decisive step" is worth exploring. It is splendidly characteristic of
Needham's consistent attempt to think things through from a Chinese
perspective that he presents that "decisive step" as being the decision by
"certain southern Chinese officials" to invite the Jesuits into China. Previous generations of Western scholars, of course, would unthinkingly
have given priority to the fact that Jesuits with such-and-such technical
training were waiting on China's borders in Macao to be invited, and
would have explored that amazing fact from the perspectives of religious
and political history. But whichever approach one prefers, that moment
in 1583 which brought the Jesuit Matteo Ricci to Chao-ch'ing, along

with his prism and his clock, is full of resonances. These two rather mundane objects can be seen as constituting crucial elements in the story of early Chinese-Western scientific interchange; yet the more I reflect on them, the more they seem to me to suggest how magisterially the attempt at interchange failed, and why one can argue with some force that China did not enter the world of universally valid modern science in any significant way until the twentieth century.

The long Chinese background to the 1583 clock story has been beautifully told by Needham himself in the clockwork section of volume 4. Needham shows convincingly how the rich history of Chinese horology in the Sung and Yuan dynasties (tenth to fourteenth centuries) gives the lie to Ricci's claim that striking clocks were something "which had never been seen, nor heard, nor even imagined, in Chinese history," even though, given that the great masterpieces of Chinese horology had been deliberately destroyed in the early Ming dynasty (that is, 1368) and the techniques of clock manufacture lost, Ricci's ignorance of China's once great "blaze of horological exuberance" is quite excusable (vol. 4, pt. 2, pp. 210, 298). From the standpoint of comparative history, it is the reason for the attractiveness of the Europeans' clocks at this particular time that matters, and here the reason seems to be the smallness of the clocks. By the late sixteenth century the developments of better springs by European clockmakers had made it possible to reduce certain clocks to a span of two or three inches, and though miniaturization, as in mechanical toys, had been carried to quite a high stage by the Chinese, as Needham also showed, it had never been carried over into the clock-making area. Unfortunately, the size of the clock must be moot for now, since Ricci says only that it was "un horiuolo di rote asai bello" ("a handsome timepiece with cogwheels"), a phrase which his later editor-translators rendered as "a rather elaborate watch."[2]

This initial clockwork gift was followed by more important events in late 1583. At the end of that year Ricci and Michele Ruggieri were settled on the edge of Chao-ch'ing city, under the protection of the prefect Wang P'an, who coveted a clock for himself. Since the Jesuits were desperate for funds to complete construction of their first church, Ruggieri went back to Macao to raise money and buy a clock for Wang P'an, which the latter had promised to pay him for handsomely. Finding Macao a desolate place because the Japanese trading ship on which the fortunes of the little colony depended had not arrived, and unable to raise cash to buy a clock for the prefect, Ruggieri had the happy idea of sending the best clockmaker in Macao to join Ricci in Chao-ch'ing. The man, who agreed to the assignment, was "a black from the Canary Islands who had lived in India" ("un Canarino dall'India, di colore assai negro"), according to Ricci. Eager to speed the work, the prefect made available two Chao-ch'ing metalworking craftsmen to assist the Indian. Thus for a brief moment in China's history Chinese and European-trained craftsmen were both working by mutual agreement on a technical project under the joint supervision of a Westerner and a Chinese scholar without external or imperial interference. This dramatically suggests a model for the development of universal scientific cooperation, but unfortunately the prefect ordered the Indian back to Macao before the work was finished, after angry Chinese anti-Christians made him the scapegoat in a trumped-up child-harassment case. Though Ricci comments that he himself finished the clock and gave it to the prefect, the prefect returned it to him shortly afterwards since no one in his yamen knew how to regulate it ("non lo sapendo ben governare"), and apparently they did not wish to invite Ricci in to do the work.[3] The point here is that though a horological workshop was later established at the Chinese court and staffed by missionaries for nearly two centuries, the concatenation of financial, legal, racial, and religious tensions described here was to bedevil countless attempts at Western-Chinese cooperation from that time to this.

This incident in 1583 can serve to show both how suggestive Needham can be on the subject of horology and how much can still be said on the types of collaboration that might have developed and yet failed. It can be contrasted with the story of the prism. The Jesuits, in describing their clocks as totally "new" to the Chinese, were developing one aspect of the picture of a technologically backward China, but out of a genuine ignorance of prior Chinese achievement. By writing at length about the effect of the prism on the Chinese, however, they were doing something more pervasive and more damaging: they were suggesting levels of Chinese gullibility and backwardness along the lines of the "natives and glass beads" stories that had become common fare for European readers from other contexts of Western exploration and colonization. References to the success that gifts of simple glass prisms had in gaining favors for Jesuit residence from the Chinese bureaucracy are commonplace in Ricci's letters and journal. Although the Chinese had a considerable glass technology of their own and had done fine work on calculating the volumes of solid prisms as early as the Han dynasty, they had not drawn the two levels of technique together and were clearly impressed with the "vitrio triangular di Veneza" brought by Ricci in 1583. They called it, he states, the "precious stone beyond price" ("la pietra pretiosa senza

prezzo").[4] Needham recounts how Joseph Priestley picked up from Trigault's version of Ricci's journal the fact that such prisms might sell to
the Chinese for 500 gold pieces each, but such stories had begun circulating among European traders heading for the Far East even before the
end of the sixteenth century, with who can tell what adverse effects on
their thinking about the Chinese. This tendency to exaggerate could be
traced at length; here one might just mention that Ricci's initial statement that he sold "one glass prism and some other items for twenty
ducats" so as to help build the church in 1583 was amended by his editor
in 1611 so that "the other items" were dropped from the text and the
"ducats" became "gold pieces."[5] The prism story, in other words, was
one tiny element in a vast edifice of European belief that the Chinese
were both rich and incompetent, and its emergence in Needham's same
decisive year of 1583 is a disturbing element that the historian should
confront.

As for the science that did not "get through," the questions that Taoist
iatrochemical tradition raises for a student of modern China are quite
different in type and scope. The richness and complexity of Taoist natural philosophy and scientific experimentation are central themes in
Needham's work, and Nathan Sivin has placed the tradition in a full
Chinese philosophical-cultural context in his contribution to volume 5,
on "the theoretical background of elixir alchemy." In evaluating the
degeneration of the chemical tradition, Needham sees fatal signs of decay
by the late Sung dynasty (that is, the early thirteenth century), which
heralded a general decline into a world of purely "psycho-physiological
alchemy," where concepts were still subtle but corresponded to a "bankruptcy of traditional chemistry." In this reading the last Taoists of major
influence at the court, who attended the emperor Shih-tsung (the Chia-
ching emperor, r. 1521–1567) and quite possibly caused his death, were
mere "charlatans" (see vol. 5, pt. 3, pp. 208, 217–18, 212). The evidence
of this decay can be quite widely seen. Thus in an intriguing poem entitled "Immortality," the great sixteenth-century philosopher Wang Yang-
ming (described by Needham in vol. 2, p. 510, as epitomizing all that
was most anti-research-oriented in the Confucian tradition because of
his "incapacity . . . to grasp the most elementary conceptions of scientific method") placed this later tradition of Taoism in the context of his
own beliefs on the internal powers possessed by each individual. At first
bereft because "lacking pills and money," says Wang, his awareness of
his innate moral knowledge made him see that there was "no need for
oven nor for tripod." A century later, in the 1630s, Sung Ying-hsing,

the compiler of one of China's greatest descriptive treatises, the *T'ien-kung k'ai-wu*, added a supplementary note on "cinnabar silver" as being a mere trick of the magicians" followed only by "the foolish, in their hope to get rich."[6]

Certainly, these examples at one level flesh out Needham's picture of a dying tradition, and yet the evidence suggests that the experimental tradition may have been more vital than we suspect, even if buried in the midst of much absurdity. Once again, Matteo Ricci can serve as our guide. (As an observer in Peking in the early seventeenth century, he surely was not one to inflate Taoist pretensions unnecessarily). Though Ricci is indeed harsh on what he considers the follies of Taoism in pursuing the making of precious metals from mercury and in pursuing immortality from "medicines and exercises," he nevertheless notes with some awe the numbers of their laboratories and the amount of money they put into equipment. And he observes that the numbers of those involved in these practices, far from going down, are steadily increasing among the ranks of the wealthy, the officials in the bureaucracy, and the eunuchs, while the ranks of their teachers swell accordingly.[7] That this tradition was not entirely reduced to "psycho-physiological alchemy" can be seen in greater detail in Ricci's account of his initial meetings with the scholar Ch'ü Ju-kuei (T'ai-su). It is well enough known that Ch'ü came to Ricci because he was obsessed by a passion with alchemy and believed Ricci to be an alchemist; what has not been discussed is that Ch'ü showed all the signs, from their first meetings, of being totally at home in the worlds of technical drawing and the construction of laboratory equipment. As Ricci phrased it in the original draft of his journal, Ch'ü "not only transcribed into his notebooks drawings of all that could be found in ours along with their measurements, his work being in this no way inferior to our own, but he also made many instruments of calculation, such as globes, astrolabes, *quadranti* [could this refer to clock faces?], clocks, magnetic compasses *[bussole]*, and many other fine things—some out of wood, some of brass *[ottone]* and also many out of silver."[8] As Needham himself has reminded us, the most exacting levels of work in wood had already been achieved by China's earlier workers in the indigenous clock-making tradition, and Ch'ü was obviously not one of those whose involvement with alchemical practice had grown restricted to "gentlemanly meditational and discreet physiological *nei tan* [inner alchemy] practices," to use Needham's concise formulation (see vol. 4, pt. 3, p. 499, vol. 5, pt. 3, p. 208). Perhaps a more thorough research into the Ch'ing dynasty schools of Taoism will reveal more skill and vitality than we had expected and help us find some more significant interconnections between late Ming iatrochemical thinking and the appearance of John Fryer's skilled and willing helpers Hua Heng-fang and Hsü Shou in the Chiang-nan arsenal of the later nineteenth century. Needham has already opened the way in his discussions of the "physico-chemical . . . tricks" of eighteenth-century Jesuits like Dominique Parenin, which he rightly deplored, in contrast to the careful thinking of the late Ming theorist Fang I-chih (1611–1671) or the eighteenth-century Chinese Jesuit and scientist Kao Lei-su (ca. 1734–1790) (see vol. 3, pt. 3, pp. 218 and 228). But perhaps, also, this early Taoist-Jesuit episode underlines the impossibility of collaboration unless the underlying Chinese value system was drastically modified, a further blow to the formation of universalistic science.

The importance of so much of Needham's work for historians of later periods lies in his forcing us to pose questions of this kind. He is direct and challenging. In the light of the above representation of Ch'ü Ju-kuei, for example, and bearing in mind that Ch'ü came from one of the most influential and respected literati families of the Soochow area, how should a student of Ch'ing society reflect on Needham's remarks—consistent in tone throughout this vast work—that the contribution of Confucian scholars (*Ju-chia*) to science "was almost wholly negative" while the works of protolegalist thinkers left "no room for science" but "only traditional technology" (vol. 2, pp. 1, 29)? If too much is made of the absolute divergence of the Confucian and Taoist modes of thought concerning nature, there is surely the danger that historians of later China, when Taoism was certainly not in its liveliest intellectual state, will miss those significant levels of scientific thinking that were in fact present. As Needham says of one thirteenth-century Chinese scholar, "one can sense in him the class-distinction between the clerkly administrator familiar with polite literature on the one hand and the quasi-artisanal manual operator on the other" (vol. 5, pt. 3, p. 208). But if we push such thinking too far, we end up full circle with the parodistic view of the later Chinese empire that was held by so many Western visitors—of an effete, impractical elite who would have to be bulldozed into the modern world for their own good.

Needham, of course, has thought this problem through carefully, and one of his most useful discussions of it appears in the recently published *Chemistry and Chemical Technology*, where he reflects on a passage in which Nathan Sivin urges laying aside the core question of "why China never spontaneously experienced the equivalent of our scientific revolution," since it will be both "an utter waste of time, and distracting as well . . . until the Chinese tradition has been adequately comprehended from the inside":

> This formulation might suggest a purely internalist or ideological explanation for the failure of modern natural science to arise in Chinese culture. I don't think that in the last resort we shall be able to appeal primarily to inhibiting factors inherent in the Chinese thought-world considered as an isolated Spenglerian cell. One must always expect that some of these intellectual limiting factors will be identifiable, but for my part I remain sceptical that there are many factors of this kind which could not have been overcome if the social and economic conditions had been favourable for the development of modern science in China. (vol. 5, pt. 4, p. xxxvii)

This line of argument is full of potential pitfalls and of valuable possibilities. On one hand, I am not convinced that in his own published work Needham has really proved his case against the Confucian tradition and in favor of the Taoist one, since the definitions are so slippery. Just to take the case of the northern Sung period, that Needham defines it as a period when Confucian bureaucratic reformers attacked feudal landlords *and* small industrialists, while Taoists linked to those reformers by common antifeudal sentiments acted as "curators and advancers of all kinds of proto-scientific and technological knowledge and practice," suggests the range of argument (vol. 4, pp. 496, 501). Scholars of Sung social, political, and religious history will have to do more work on this period before they can draw any clear inferences. And precisely because Ricci found so much encouragement among the Chinese traditional bureaucratic elite, I am nervous about denigrating the *Ju-chia*'s role in society vis-à-vis any possible breakthroughs in science. Ch'ü Ju-kuei may have derived his especially experimental bent through his work in alchemy, but Ricci's most famous collaborators, Hsü Kuang-ch'i and Li Chih-tsao, who showed profound interest in a wide range of Western science and aided him in such tasks as translating the first books of Euclid into Chinese, held the highest-level *chin-shih* degree, came from well-established elite families in prosperous areas of China, and held senior posts for many years in the regular Ming bureaucracy. Furthermore, Sung Ying-hsing, holder of the *chü-jen* degree and provincial director of Confucian studies, whose *T'ien-kung k'ai-wu* (The creations of nature and man) of 1637 Needham so often refers to, makes this point about general attitude toward knowledge neatly enough in his own preface, in language that could be directed at gentry in any society, not just the Chinese: "There are those who, not being able to distinguish between jujube flowers and pear blossoms, would prefer to indulge in speculations about the water-plants of Ch'u; not knowing the measurements and care of cooking pots, would prefer to discourse emptily on ancient sacrificial vessels of Lü." And Sung adds, sarcastically, "an ambitious scholar will undoubtedly toss this book onto his desk and give it no further thought: it is a work that is in no way concerned with the art of advancement in officialdom."[9] Had he had more money, notes Sung, he would have purchased more artifacts in order to verify some of his statements and assembled a group of friends to go over the book's contents prior to publication. But in general he writes as a well-connected member of a complacent class, a level above Li Shih-chen, perhaps, whose great materia medica the *Pen-ts'ao kang-mu* had appeared in 1593, though Li closed any social gaps by seeing his son through the *chü-jen* exams and his grandson through the *chin-shih*.

On the other hand, when we come to the period of the Ch'ing dynasty, from 1644 to 1912, I grow convinced that there were certain "social and economic conditions" that prevented China from building constructively on the foundations that had been laid—even if very unevenly—in the period following 1583. Yet, perhaps paradoxically, in terms of the major thrust of Needham's argument, I would at least hazard the suggestion that this failure to build was so serious that China cannot be seen as having entered the world of universally valid science during that same long period in any meaningful way. Although such factors are always hard to categorize convincingly or precisely, the social and economic factors can tentatively be grouped under three general headings: those concerning the Manchus, those concerning the geopolitical contexts of the Confucian bureaucracy, and those affecting missionaries in general.

The conquest of China by the Manchus was a protracted process spanning the years 1615–83. During this period new elements of racial tension and political control entered the Chinese state. Because of the timing of certain changes that had taken place in the hierarchical relationships inside Neo-Confucianism during the Ming dynasty, those scholars who had held office under the Ming found themselves forced by ethical norms (as well as, often, by their consciences) to refuse service to the new Manchu Ch'ing dynasty. Such Ming "loyalists" included, of course, many of those who had reached intellectual maturity at just the period of early

Jesuit impact on China, and their careers were interrupted at key moments of influence. Among those interested in the sciences, to whom Needham often refers, one might mention Fang I-chih, Wang Fu-chih, and Ku Yen-wu. The Manchus, because of their role in the Ming demise, were preternaturally determined to be seen as moralistic Confucians. They thus imposed on the population a rigorist interpretation of the synthetic Confucianism of Chu Hsi (that same philosopher who appears in Needham's work—vol. 4, pt. 2, p. 503—taking an abandoned armillary sphere into his own house and trying to reconstruct its water-drive arrangement, without success). This orthodoxy certainly limited the range of texts and interpretation permitted in the civil service examinations. At the same time, because of rapid population growth, these exams became steadily more competitive. The effects of the pervasive jumpiness were widespread, especially in the scrutiny of possibly anti-Manchu works. To give just one example: Needham refers throughout his work to Sung Ying-hsing's remarkable *T'ien-kung k'ai-wu,* at one point terming it "China's greatest technological classic." He notes the surprising fact that this work, well received in 1637 when it first appeared, almost disappeared after 1644 and was preserved in its entirety only in Japan; he concludes, that this may have been because coinage, salt making, and weapon manufacture were all government monopolies (vol. 4, pt. 2, pp. 171–72). In view of the rather widespread circulation of other works dealing with aspects of these three topics, I find this explanation rather unconvincing; more significant, it seems to me, are Sung's fleeting but nevertheless slighting references in his preface to southern Manchuria and Kirin as out-of-the-way and backward areas. Totally unexceptionable under the Ming, the Manchu victories of 1644 made such remarks verge on the treasonous, and it is most unlikely that in the witch-hunting days of the early Ch'ing anyone would take responsibility for reprinting such a work; reprinting became even less likely after the careful Ch'ienlung review of all works for possible antidynastic references, which took place in the 1770s.

It is undeniably true that the early Manchu rulers themselves were to a considerable extent patrons of Western science. The emperor Shunchih was friendly with Adam Schall, as K'ang-hsi was with Ferdinand Verbiest and Joachim Bouvet. But by and large the Manchu emperors kept Jesuit scientists and technicians as court favorites, managed and lodged by the Imperial Household Department, spied on by bondservants and eunuchs. Some important works were published and refinements made in such fields as cartography, mathematics, astronomy, armaments, surveying, and medicine, but because the most talented Jesuit scientists were normally kept hard at work on court-related projects, their workshops were in the inner city of Peking, and the fruits of their labors were stored in the palaces, their work did not have wide influence among the literati in general. In a remarkable section entitled "Palae-otechnic Machinery: Jesuit Novelty and Redundance" in the volume *Physics and Physical Technology,* Needham gives an evaluation of trans-mitted texts and technical drawings and evolves a preliminary balance sheet (vol. 4, pt. 2, pp. 211–28). We find that the result is not impressive for the Jesuit side, and in any case many of the "technical" drawings of European apparatus were inadequately rendered, making interpretation of them problematical to their Chinese contemporaries. In many instances, the Jesuits were forced to work on mechanical trivia used for court diversion or on elaborate paintings kept closeted in the imperial collec-tion: even the grander projects like Ch'ien-lung's magnificent Jesuit-designed summer palaces outside Peking, built in the mid-eighteenth century, were totally restricted to imperial use and thus were far from fulfilling that early dream of Ricci's, first formulated at Chao-ch'ing in 1583 as he supervised the building of his house there, that the elegant proportions and gracious windows of Western architecture would one day reach all Chinese. The Ch'ing palaces became veritable jumble heaps of valuable but little-used Western bric-a-brac, while imperial favorites hoarded literally hundreds of clocks and watches rather than perceiving that the technology behind them should be spread.

What I have termed the "geopolitical contexts" of the Confucian bureaucracy of the time seem to have been equally unhelpful to the gen-eral spread of work in the mechanical or experimental sciences. As his-torians begin to do more work on the Confucian schools, they find everywhere the evidence of lively curiosity, vivid imagination, and gen-uine interest in natural phenomena, so Needham's thought that "inhib-iting factors inherent in the Chinese thought world" were not major factors in the failure of modern science to develop seems as true for the Ch'ing period as he thinks they are for the earlier dynasties. Yet Ch'ing Peking seems to have been a less free place than the same capital under the Ming, and there may have been less chance for experimentation when the last teachers of Taoism were in disarrary and the whole northern city population had been displaced to make room for the great Manchu ban-ner garrisons settled in Peking after 1644. Also, Ch'ing imperial spon-sors worked for themselves, and the carefully watched members of the Manchu royal family (kept in the inner city rather than scattered around the country in great aristocratic estates like their Ming predecessors) never produced protoscientists like the Ming princes Chu Hsiao and Chu Ch'üan, whom Needham discusses so well (vol. 5, pt. 3, pp. 209–11). Although the matter may seem trivial, it occurs to me that the shorter terms in office and the constant reassignment to areas far from one's native place must have made it extraordinarily hard for Ch'ing bureaucrats—who were very often, after all, those with the most money—to develop any kind of facilities for what Needham called their "elaboratories." It may be significant that this lack of development in most fields of sciences was not matched by a lack of interest in mathematics, which, on the contrary, seems to have flourished extraordinarily in the Ch'ing, from the days of Mei Wen-ting and his grandson Mei Ku-ch'eng through to Juan Yuan and Lo Shih-lin. And what, one wonders, were the effects on many levels of scientific experimentation of the combination of recurrent bans on mining by the imperial court and the deforestation of much of eastern and central China, which was reaching crisis proportions by the mid-eighteenth century? Needham has shown the way in his consideration of the technical instrumentation and the developments of furnaces in early Chinese science; obviously, Ch'ing metallurgy, fuel supplies, and the possible shortage of means for scholars to pursue legitimate interests will have to be studied.

In considering the possibly unhelpful ambience of Peking and the concentration of wealth in the cities of the great Chiang-nan triangle bounded by Yangchow, Nanking, and Hangchow, one must take a new look at the effects of the Taiping uprising of 1851–64 on the scientific work that had been under way in the Ch'ing dynasty: it is at least surprising that during the Taiping the fine mathematicians Lo Shih-lin, Tai Hsü, and Hsü Yu-jen were killed or committed suicide while Li Shan-lan (the distinguished collaborator of Alexander Wylie who concluded the work on Euclid first started by Matteo Ricci and Hsü Kuang-ch'i) lost his library in the fighting. After the Taiping, the move of intellectual talent down south to Canton, first begun by Juan Yuan, seems to have accelerated. Here by century's end, in the shadow of Hong Kong, such figures as K'ang Yu-wei and Liang Ch'i-ch'ao were finally to reassess their whole intellectual tradition.

What, finally, of factors affecting the missionaries in general? Here, again, there were important changes from the Ming situation, though church and politics had frequently clashed even then, as Ricci learned when he was forced to leave Peking during Hideyoshi's invasion of Korea in 1598, or as Alfonso Vagnoni did during the bitter persecutions engineered by Shen Ch'üeh in 1617. But in the Ch'ing period, partly because of the imperial attitudes sketched in above, the equation of much of Western science with the Western missionary enterprise became a particularly unfortunate one. Several Jesuits chose to campaign for the Ming dynasty fugitive pretenders after the Manchu victories in 1644; others were imprisoned at the time of the Oboi regency in the 1600s after factional battles over astronomical techniques; others were boxed in by the demands of the papal legate Maillard de Tournon in 1708, while yet others rashly corresponded with the emperor Yung-cheng's brothers, fanning the flames of that tough monarch's always suspicious nature. These political entanglements, particularly the last, led to Christian practices being considered (first informally and then by legal statute) as *hsieh*, or "heterodox," a term applied to the followers of extremist or underground Buddhist and Taoist sects, as well as to practitioners of sexually deviant behavior. In a paradoxical use of older alchemical arguments, eighteenth-century Chinese scholars showed their contempt for Christianity by writing that, under the guise of giving absolution to the dying, Catholic priests removed the eyes of their victims, these eyes being then "mixed with lead and mercury to create silver."[10] It was hard for Chinese scholars to dedicate lives to science associated with such politically dangerous categories, even if the few Jesuits working at the emperor's court kept some semblance of respectability until the dissolution of the order in 1773. Thereafter Catholic missionaries were tarred, along with the Protestants, with the brush of foreign imperialism in China, and the associated moral anguish and damage caused in China by the vast increases of opium sales in the 1800s. One can certainly argue that "world science" as a recognizable concept began to have substance only during the 1850s, when a desperate Manchu leadership, facing rebellion and attack on all points, encouraged Sino-Western cooperation as a means of national reintegration.

All of the above speculations are triggered by Needham's work, which opens up vistas for Ch'ing study few of us had thought of a decade or so ago. How to undertake such study is another matter, for the combination of requisite scientific knowledge with classical Chinese will always be rare and arduously arrived at. Yet I am convinced that true understanding of the last act of the so-called Confucian society will be achieved only when we can get away from the belittlement of their economic roles and technical knowledge that was such a part of the Confucian biographical self-definition, and learn to read more widely in the huge body of materials that coexist with the literary and philosophic writings. Needham shows how rich is this unexploited mass of materials. Again and again, reading his work, my eyes would be drawn to the Chinese characters that accompanied his translations and explanations for the myriad technical and semitechnical terms in which the texts of that tradition are couched. Reading on, I began to dream that perhaps, when Needham's great labor was done, an enterprising publisher would find workers to collate from this sweep of volumes an index-glossary with explanations and cross-references, so that all those trying to embark on similar studies would be able to learn systematically what Needham had learned before them. Thus one would begin to be able to make a truer assessment of whether or not China had indeed entered that dialogue of world science, and if so, when. It would be Needham's finest final gift to the spirit of rational enquiry.

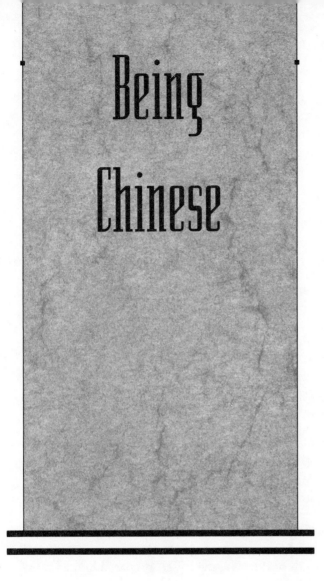

Being Chinese

At once the simplest and the hardest question one can ask if one studies China is "What does it mean to be Chinese?" What kinds of values or cultural factors interconnect with historical experience and shared ethnic origins to bond Chinese together? The question has real immediacy as the multilayered Chinese communities in Hong Kong and Tai-

---

[1] This essay first appeared in 1989, in the *London Review of Books*.

wan, Southeast Asia and Australia, Western Europe and the United States, try to make sense of what the Chinese Communist government did to hundreds of its own young people in June 1989.

In *Qian Mu and the World of Seven Mansions*,[1] Jerry Dennerline offers one of the subtlest, most sensitive and closely reasoned attempts to answer the question that I have ever seen. The fulcrum for his story is the Chinese historian and philosopher Qian Mu (formerly romanized as Ch'ien Mu), who lived in China from his birth in 1895 until the Communist victory of 1949, subsequently settling first in Hong Kong and then in Taiwan. Qian Mu grew up in a village in Jiangsu province—the "Seven Mansions" of the book's title—which was dominated literally, spiritually, and economically by the Qian lineage, its remembered glories, its current wide interests in commerce, and the extent of its landholdings and charitable estates. Intellectually, Qian was of an age group that "looked forward," as Dennerline puts it, to the fall of the Qing dynasty and the end of the old autocracy. But the revolution of 1911 and the Qing abdication of the following year brought not a new era of liberation for the Chinese but the horrors of warlordism, civil war, and Japanese invasion.

Jerry Dennerline does not explore this general historical background in any detail; it is not important to his quest, which is to find out how Qian Mu came to believe what he believed, and how "in the worst of times" Qian managed to hold on to his central values and to try and preserve and reinterpret them for future generations of Chinese. This book, then, is at once intellectual history, to be read with close attention to every nuance in the argument, and local community history rich in vivid detail. Dennerline's previous work, a major study of the Chinese scholars' reactions to the Qing conquest of the Ming in the 1640s in Jiangsu province just south of the Yangtze River, prepared him admirably for the task of reassessing the historical parallels and deep changes in rural Jiangsu two and a half centuries later.[2]

Dennerline had two sets of interviews with Qian in Taiwan in 1983 and 1986, and he also revisited Qian Mu's hometown in the People's Republic, something Qian himself could not do. One of the many joys of this book is the sense it gives of the affection that developed between the aging, blind Chinese scholar and his junior American interlocutor probing always for meaning behind the generalizations, yet also able to share news from the old country with the exile. A moving example comes when Dennerline, groping to find some way of showing how bits of the old value system seem to have survived in the People's Republic tells Qian Mu about an encounter he had in Ganlu (in Wuxi). There Dennerline met a woman worker, crippled since birth, who finally acquired dignity and a small regular income from a new job program designed for the handicapped. When Dennerline asked her what she did with her newfound independence and cash, she looked at him in genuine surprise. She had a family still living, she said, so of course she shared the money with them. "Conjuring up her image in his blindness," Dennerline beautifully phrases it, "Qian Mu tapped the table to express his respect."

The shape of this book is artful without being distracting, based on two modes of organization. One mode is to sandwich the bulk of the text between two key passages of intellectual analysis, the first of which is a summary of Qian Mu's views on Chinese culture and history as presented in an interview with Dennerline; the second, Dennerline's own rephrasing of those views in a way that makes sense to him as a historian. The other main mode is to present three sequential chapters on the world of Seven Mansions. One view is Qian's, from his memoirs and reminiscences. One view is Dennerline's, as a social historian, examining the rural community. And one, Qian's again, is the old scholar's short, affectionate homage to his parents, written long after their deaths, "Reminiscences of My Parents at the Age of Eighty." It was coming across this text that first made Dennerline interested in Qian. By translating it here in its entirety for the first time (it runs to about thirty-five pages), Dennerline makes a real contribution to history, literature, and biography; and by closing, rather than opening the book with the "Reminiscences," he ensures that the reader will have the richest possible context in which to evaluate it.

What I called the "first mode," the presentation of Qian's and Dennerline's views of the shape of Chinese culture and society, is not easy to summarize, as it is already so condensed. But what Qian tried to explain to Dennerline was his view of the way that the Chinese sense of the rites (the *li*) held Chinese culture together. For Qian, the place in which a Chinese grows up, and which he loves deeply, is still no more than local, and so it cannot define national culture. But the scholar who practices that *li* locally, and uses it to give meaning and order to his life within his own community and his own descent group, has within him the power to draw together the worlds of family, rites, and community into a concept that has both a cultural and a national force—that of the "whole people's descent group" *(minzu)*. However carefully Dennerline studied the local community, Qian observed, he would never find culture's broader meaning there.

Dennerline, in his reformulation of similar ideas near the end of the book, takes a different tack, one that springs from his own intellectual fascination with the intricate bonds and structures of Chinese society. Dennerline agrees that the *li* were central to Qian's family world, but they were also full of meaning for the culture as a whole even in their local manifestations. The scholars both enforced and manipulated the concepts of *li* to structure their local communities and their estates so that they could act as a buffer between their localities and the state. The scholars interpreted all local customs as having dignity and meaning in a cultural sense as long as they conformed to the *li*. Thus local variations and all the richness of social and lineage custom that one can regard as Chinese were at the heart of the Chinese state and culture. Any Chinese state seeking in the present decade to revive a sense of Chinese culture which has any internal validity or intellectual coherence must grasp this sense of bonds to the local community and its customs, even as those change with agricultural revolution and rural industrialization.

If that sounds very abstract—and I suppose it does—the fully concrete and engrossing details of Dennerline's second mode make it easy to see what both scholars mean. Qian's initial picture of himself in his community and his national culture is one of an intellectual struggling in a political context whose disintegration is compounded for him by is father's early death. But the sense of the *li* that Qian had received from his father, of the internal order and rhythms of his rural world, with its historical ties across the centuries of Qians, their libraries, and their learning, all gave Qian Mu an inner intellectual strength. He himself could and did rebel, and challenged authority when it was obtuse. But essentially, as both student and teacher (he was teaching in local schools at seventeen, to bring the family extra income), he always sought to reach consensus rather than use physical coercion. And his scholarship was no restricting net, but rather a spur to finding the fullest context of things—the precise taste of pork or the exact sound of wind in the pine trees, to give two of Qian's own examples.

By learning, by thinking, by searching for the inner significance of his cultural legacy, Qian felt ready, at the age of forty-two, to offer his own first major synthesis of his country and its origins. Qian Mu's *Outline History of the Nation*, written in 1937 and 1938, is described by Dennerline as "a monument to national pride," which spanned three thousand years of China's waxing and waning fortunes, of foreign invasion and assimilation, and intellectual evolution. The pattern of this history was all China's, to Qian, and it differed from the West's pattern as a poem differs from a drama. The one develops in a meter from rhyme to rhyme, always by the same rules; the other develops in stages, from act to act, always with a different plot. The one expands to fill a space when it is ordered and disintegrates when it is not. The other progresses from conflict to conflict toward some inevitable tragic conclusion.[3]

China's poems and rhymes could never be understood by Westernized intellectuals who "presumed the universality of the dramatic form."

Some of the ebullience and confidence of Qian Mu as historian must surely have come from the setting and the company in which he wrote the work, a beautiful and secluded temple built beside rushing streams in the mountain countryside of southwest China, near Kunming, with his meals fresh cooked from local produce by a loving, loyal old country woman. And few people can have been odder or apter companions for Qian in his labors than his temple neighbor, a poetry-loving, opium-smoking Taoist monk who made money for his simple pleasures by speculating in soybean futures.

This vision of Qian's raising and writing, which Dennerline calls in his chapter title "To Practice When It Is Timely" in homage to the Confucian view of correct action, is followed by Dennerline's own exploration of Qian's upbringing. Called "The Land of Streams," from the local descriptive term for Qian's home region, this chapter is really a free-standing essay and an immensely skillful and evocative piece of social history. Dennerline's goal is to show the way the *li* functioned in, and ordered, the many lives of Qians and others who lived along "Whistle and Swagger Creek" in the late Qing dynasty. We see how the *li* integrated the nets of social custom, gave coherence and protection to a "little cosmos" in which 42,000 people were struggling for a livelihood on less than ten thousand acres of fertile paddy land. In this little cosmos, centuries of evolution had led to a complex landowning system which separated land into subsoil and surface rights, so those "owning" the right to till did not necessarily (or often) have rights to the subsoil or the ultimate claim to the land itself. Minute social gradations based on such rights, along with multitudes of customary obligations in the spheres of religious ceremonial, or in the playing of music at festivals and weddings, gave every family member status and identity. Charitable estates were one form that had developed as a way of pooling lineage land—freed from all but a fixed state tax—so the less affluent could still get an education and a ration of food. This was the system that enabled Qian Mu to be a scholar after his father's death. And it is as we draw all these myriad pieces together, Dennerline writes, that we can build up the full context in a way that Qian could not do, even had he chosen to. (Qian, for instance, had never seen some of the local genealogical records that Dennerline was able to locate for his research.) And from this indepth study of the Land of Streams, Dennerline came to see that "history was inseparable from value." It was this that gave Qian Mu "his deep respect for China's ordinary people, with their sense of place and the duties attached to it, and for China's country scholars, with their sense of equity and their dedication to achieving it."

In this way, Dennerline sets the scene for his translation of Qian Mu's "Reminiscences on My Parents at the Age of Eighty," written on Taiwan in eight days in 1975, when the author's parents, had they lived, would both have been 110. Some Western readers, used to the steam and tumble of modern biographies, might at first think this bland or evasive, but they would be utterly wrong. Qian Mu is writing in a different genre, with modulations—wondrously caught by Dennerline in his quietly affectionate translation—that illuminate the family world in great depth. Qian Mu here constructed the world of values which he believed had constructed him. It is, above all, a world of loving order, even in terrible times; a world of social value made manifest every day through decorum and deportment and an inner sense of integrity. In other words, a world informed by *li*. That is Qian's message, and perhaps there has never been a lovelier attempt to get it across. It does not matter that Qian's father was sickly and clearly a prey to opium. It does not matter that Qian's mother was illiterate. What mattered to Qian, what was so Chinese, was the way their actions fitted the community and the family, and the way behavior and perception meshed. The Qian males in other parts of the lineage were losing that sense, losing the vision of scholarship and obligation and turning to breeding crickets and flying kites. But for Qian and his father the symbol of meaningful male life was the complete edition of the *Five Confucian Classics*, hand copied by Qian Mu's grandfather and lightly stained with the old man's tears, which was still kept in a family library while Qian Mu was a boy.

The "Reminiscences" were written in twelve short sections, the first eight mainly about Qian Mu's father, the last four about how his mother coped after her husband's early death. The point of the essay, the reason both why Qian Mu wrote it and why Dennerline used it as the centerpiece of his book, is surely that the parents can be understood and described only in the context of their family and their community. To analyze them independently would be meaningless. It is in their social expression of internalized values that they make their mark and leave their name, so years after his father's death Qian Mu still cannot get the local shopkeepers to take his money when he goes to buy necessities. Yet there is nothing sterile or restrictive about this in Qian Mu's eyes, only proof that the world is in order. And the depth of the love was always there, committed and passionate.

The little boy serving the dying father is a theme that occurs in other Chinese memoirs—especially poignant was the philosopher Kang You-wei's description of his father's illness and death some forty years earlier. But Kang's memoir is so tinged with arrogance that it is hard to take. Qian's is about his parents, not himself. Moving laments for revered mothers are also fairly common in Chinese memoirs, but I know of none that has quite the pathos and the brevity of Qian's lament. She died when she was seventy-seven, and her son, forty-eight, was far away from her in Chengdu and unable to be at her side or to carry out proper mourning rites. "I have often reflected," Qian writes, "on how the ancients likened parental love to the light of springtime. Whenever I was with her, I could feel this light in my body. Even a cat or a chicken in the house could feel it."[4] Yet fate did not let them be together much. Qian lamented, "Although my life spans the entire life of the Chinese republic, I spent only three of my adult years in the company of my mother." Across the history of that republic Qian Mu, gently nudged by Dennerline, reaches back to share his values with us. We may not accept or approve of them all, but it is hard to deny that there was something truly worth saying at the center of his being.

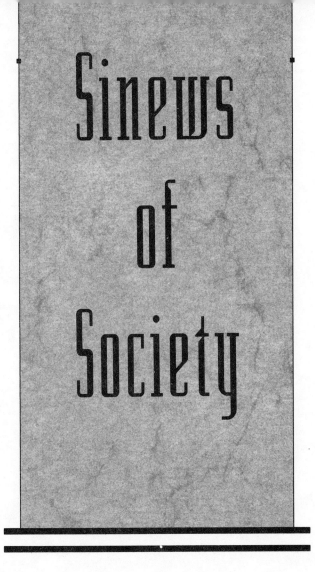

Sinews
of
Society

Food

In an odd and grim essay, written during the reign of Chia-ch'ing (1796–1820), the Ch'ing scholar Kuan T'ung wrote of "The Land of Hunger." In this land no grains grew and no animals lived; there were no fish, no fruit. It was a terrible journey to this land, but the brave of heart could reach it in ten days if they persevered. They would find "an

---

This essay first appeared in 1977, in *Food in Chinese Culture*, edited by K. C. Chang.

open, bright country which looks as if it were a new universe, [where] management falls into disuse and thought comes to a stop" (Hsia, *Gate*, 18–19).[1] It was the land of those who had died of starvation, and for Kuan T'ung there was a moral value in reaching this land if suicide was necessary to preserve one's integrity. But for many Chinese, in the Ch'ing period as before and after, the Land of Hunger was a terrible reality that lay beyond choice; and though this is an essay on food and eating, we cannot in justice pursue that topic unless we are aware of the harsh backdrop of famine or the threat of famine. It was the danger of famine that gave such urgency to agriculture and such joy to eating. The hardship can be traced through the litany of a phrase in the local gazetteers, "In this year people ate each other" *(hsiang shih),* even if this was meant as metaphor. It can also be traced through the diets of the starving as recorded painstakingly by Western observers: flour of ground leaves, sawdust, thistles, cotton seeds, peanut hulls, ground pumice (Peking United International Famine Relief Committee, *Famine*, 13).[2]

THE STAPLE FOODS

That said, we can turn to look at the staple foods that were generally available to the poor during the Ch'ing period. An impressive roster of these foods has been carefully marshaled in the great corpus of local gazetteers. This source of data is varied in scope and quality and awaits systematic analysis by nutritionists, economists, and social historians, but even a quick glance at a provincial gazetteer for a wealthy area, such as the *Chiang-nan t'ung-chih* (gazetteer of the present provinces of Anhwei and Kiangsu) compiled in 1737, during the major era of Ch'ing tranquillity and prosperity, shows the richness of the resources (see chap. 86). Listed in their original order are wheat, rice, pulse, millet, and hemp, and their glutinous, upland, or late-ripening varieties, and the different strains within each variety. Also in the introductory section, dealing with the entire province, are numerous entries under the conventional categories into which food was subdivided at this time: vegetables, fruits, bamboos, grasses, flowering plants, and medicinal plants, as well as animal products, under the categories of feathered or quadruped, followed by fish, crustaceans, and insects. This section is followed by thirty-three pages in which the specialties of every prefecture and county are listed.

Prefectural gazetteers give equally rich information. Thus in the gazetteer for Yunnan-fu compiled in 1696, there are general classifications similar to those for Chiang-nan, but these are then subdivided according to the eleven counties and *chou* in the Yunnan prefectural districts, making it easy to follow a specific product in a given area. We learn that K'un-ming county was apparently the most prosperous, with tea, textile, and mineral productions, but that each of the smaller areas had its special features: grass paper in Fu-ming, hemp in Lo-tz'u, noodles in Ch'eng-kung, honey and winter squash in K'un-yang, and vinegar in Lu-feng. All these Yunnan communities have one shortage in common—not one of them lists any of the tailed animals, be it even sheep, cattle, dogs, or hogs, as being present with any abundance (*Yunnan fu-chih*, 2:1–7).

For the sake of contrast at the prefectural level, one can take the Fu-chou-fu gazetteer of 1754. Here, in rich detail but without separate regional classifications, we find that the ten categories have become twenty, filling forty-nine pages (*Fu-chou fu-chih*, chaps, 25, 26). The extra categories come from a classification much more specialized than those found in the Yunnan gazetteer, and the specialization tells us much about local eating habits: plant fruits (*lo*), such as melons, cucumbers, gourds, and taros, have a complete section, as do bamboos and creepers. Fish are distinguished from other scaled creatures, and both shrubs (*chieh*) and grasses are sorted out from the broader range of plants and trees. Under *shrubs*, for instance, can be found both tea and tobacco. The latter, a note explains, came to China in the Wan-li period, under the name *tan-pa-ku*, and now grows around Fu-chou (ibid., 25:24). This sudden insertion of the name of a foreign plant into the list of Chinese names can be seen again in the vegetable section, where the sweet potato (*fan-shu*) receives a page of commentary to itself (ibid., 25:4). This commentary states that the sweet potato was made widely known in Fukien during the famine year of 1594 by the governor, Chin Hsueh-tseng. Chin's purpose was to teach the locals to grow a crop that would feed them even if the regular grains failed in times of drought, but his action had consequences far beyond localized famine relief. For, as the commentary points out, this was not only a multifaceted plant that could be boiled or ground or fermented and could be fed to old and young as well as to chickens and dogs but also one that would grow in sandy, mountainous, and salty soils, where the regular grains could not take root.

Even the smallest county gazetteers can yield dietary information, either directly or in comparison with others. In the 1673 gazetteer for the poor southern Shantung county of T'an-ch'eng, there are only two pages on local produce (*T'an-ch'eng hsien-chih* 1673, 3:33–34), and there is no discussion of variant strains and nothing on food processing. Yet two things are especially suggestive in this source: first, that no draft or domestic animals are listed, and that the only quadrupeds mentioned are rabbits, two kinds of deer, foxes, and wolves; second, that much the largest section is on medicinal plants, thirty-six kinds being listed in all. The same county's gazetteer for the year 1764 has no more space for food than does its predecessor (*T'an-ch'eng hsien-chih* 1764, 5:33–36); but the deer, wolves, and foxes are gone, and in their place are sheep and cattle, mules, horses, and hogs. The medicinal plants listed have been cut back to nineteen, and even if we have no firm evidence that this was because the early Ch'ing days of epidemics and warfare had spawned a desperate hunt for cures that was now less urgently felt, the change in the edible animal population does suggest a radical change in life-style.[3]

Though the history of the new Western crops in China starts in the late Ming dynasty, it is in the Ch'ing that their revolutionary effects were felt. The crucial importance of the new plants was not that they provided variety for either the poor or the rich (though they did that) but that they allowed a population that had reached the limits of its traditional resources to expand anew. The Ch'ing population explosion—a rise from approximately 150 million persons in the early 1700s to about 450 million by the mid-ninteenth century—was so striking that it must have affected every facet of local life, even though to date scholars have not been able to reconstruct all the elements of that experience. In the course of his studies on the population of China, Ho Ping-ti has come up with some major findings on the effect of these new crops (*Studies*, 183–95).[4] He has demonstrated how maize, sweet potatoes, Irish potatoes, and peanuts all became basic crops in China during the Ch'ing, and how the story of their dissemination is enmeshed with the drama of China's internal colonization.

The sweet potato had became a staple food for the poor in the coastal southeastern provinces by the early eighteenth century; imperial edicts exhorted the people to grow more, and the plant spread west and north. By the end of the eighteenth century, in Ho Ping-ti's estimation, "along the rocky Shantung coast sweet potatoes often accounted for nearly half a year's food for the poor" (ibid., 187). Maize transformed agricultural life in Yunnan, Kweichow, and Szechwan during the early Ch'ing and was a key factor in enabling migrants from the overpopulated Yangtze delta region to farm the hills in the inland Yangtze provinces as well as the high ground in the Han River drainage areas of Shensi and Hupei. In these same areas, by the middle of the Ch'ing, the Irish potato made it possible for still other farmers to find a livelihood in lands that were too poor for maize (ibid., 188). The changes brought by the peanut were less dramatic, but Ho Ping-ti still found them extensive:

> Throughout the last three centuries peanuts have gradually brought about a revolution in the utilization of sandy soils along the lower Yangtze, the lower Yellow River, the southeast coast, particularly Fukien and Kwangtung, and numerous inland rivers and streams. Even within the crowded cropping system of some rice districts, they usually have a place in the rotation because farmers, without knowing the function of the nitrogen-fixing nodules at the roots of the peanut plant, have learned empirically that it helps to preserve soil fertility. (Ibid., 185)

Though accurate figures are impossible to obtain, Ho Ping-ti estimates that the percentage of rice in the national food output may have dropped by about one-half in the period between the late Ming and the 1930s, from about 70 percent to 36 percent. There were also major declines in barley, millet, and sorghum (ibid., 189, 192).

It is not easy to reconstruct local eating habits among the poor either from gazetteers or from specialized population studies, and detailed sources are rare. Fortunately, there were some observers like the magistrate Li Hua-nan, who served in Chekiang (in Hsu-shui Hsien and Yü-yao Hsien) during the 1750s. Li was interested in the local diet, and as he traveled around on business he used to question the locals and jot down his findings.[5] Li does not group the foods in the order customarily followed in the local histories, though he does start his notes with the basic grains and beans. Thereafter he looks at, in turn, pork products, fowl, game, fish, eggs, milk and cheeses, sweet dishes and dumplings, sweet potatoes, mushrooms and squash, ginger, preserved plums, and a variety of vegetables such as garlic and radishes, peanuts, greens, and dates. There is no central theme in this profusion, but certainly Li was deeply interested in the preservation of food rather than in problems of flavor or variety, and we may hazard that this interest was dictated by local realities. When food was rigidly seasonal and in short supply, correct treatment and preparation for storage was essential. The section on flavored sauces made from beans or grains, for instance, has careful instructions on the use of mustard or pepper to keep out insects, the need for cleanliness on the part of the preparer, the cleanliness of the water used, and the rhythms to be followed in opening or closing the storage pots on

sunny or humid days (Li, *Hsing-yüan lu*, 76–78).[6] Similar care is taken
with the storage of eggs: they should be placed in a crock, big ends up,
each covered in a paste composed of 60 to 70 percent reed or charcoal
ash, and 30 to 40 percent earth, with wine and salt added. Water should
not be added to the paste, or the whites would get too tough. These
directions are followed by simple recipes: for boiled eggs and egg rolls,
for eggs with milk, for eggs with grated almond and sugar, and for preparing eggs (chicken, duck, or goose) overnight in a scoured pig's blad-
der (ibid., 31–32b).

This last recipe is a good example of Li's meticulousness in listing all
the ways that the pig can be used in cooking, and again it would seem to
be an obvious reflection of local preoccupations, since pigs were expensive when one earned perhaps one hundred cash a day, and a pound of
pork cost half that (Macartney, *Embassy*, 162, 244, 254).[7] The farmers
had methods for pressing salted pork in a barrel (turning it every five
days for a month) before drying it in the wind, and methods for pressing
strips of pork; the pork fat could be extracted in boiling water and then
preserved with bean sauce; balls were made of pork fat and rolled in egg;
pigs' trotters could be stewed with mushrooms; pigs' intestines were
used in various recipes; the old pigs' meat was softened up enough to
make it edible by repeated boilings followed by soaks in cold water. Li
observed other methods for preserving pork leftovers (which could be
used with chicken as well): the meat was cut in strips, the strips were
notched and salted, and crushed garlic was pressed into the meat, which
was soaked in wine vinegar. The meat was then smoked over bamboo
strips (or supported on metal wires if the peasants had them) and sealed
in a clean jar (Li, *Hsing-yüan lu*, 17–21). Li also described newer crops
like sweet potatoes and peanuts, though he did not single them out for
special attention: he mentions that the sweet potato was peeled, steamed,
and pressed through a rice strainer to remove the fibers, before being
rolled into strips or dried in cake form (ibid., 40); peanuts were boiled,
reboiled in salted water, and then stored in the water they had been
boiled in, or they were drained and stored in pickle juice (ibid., 44).

Even with such detailed local descriptions, it is still hard to make any
interconnections between the availability of food and the eating of that
food. The two variables that remain are the cost of separate items of food
and the amount of money available to the purchaser; and there are naturally so many regional differences and price fluctuations that any kind
of generalization is immensely difficult. We are fortunate, however, to
have for the early Ch'ing period at least one detailed source that gives us

prices for a large number of foods—namely, the "expenses" *(chih-yung)* section of the Imperial Banqueting Court (the *Kuang-lu Ssu*). These prices were fixed in the early eighteenth century and represent a revision down from earlier figures, which had presumably become inflated because of careless spending habits or because of scarcities in the late Ming and early Ch'ing period. The prices apply to Peking and presumably also represent prices for high-quality goods; but at the very least they give us a comparative base between types of staple food costs, which is essential to any informed survey of Ch'ing food (*Kuang-lu ssu tse-li*, 59:1–12).[8] (See table 1.)

This run of figures can be supported by the comments of a late-eighteenth-century visitor. In the notes to his journal concerning his 1793 embassy to China, Lord Macartney gave these prices in copper cash for various articles of food: one pound of mutton or pork, 50; a goose, 500; a fowl, 100; a pound of salt, 35; a pound of rice, 24 (Macartney, *Embassy*, 244). On the basis of his observations, he estimated that a Chinese peasant could live on 50 cash a day; the boatmen who conducted Macartney were paid 80 cash a day; a Chinese foot soldier received 1,600 cash a month, and ten measures of rice (each equivalent to about 130 cash), and his wages accordingly were in the area of 100 cash a day (ibid., 224, 254). Robert Fortune, checking the wages of local tea pickers in the China of the 1850s, found that they received about 150 cash a day, of which about one-third was in currency and two-thirds in food; he felt that, although their food was simple, "the poorest classes in China seem to understand the art of preparing their food much better than the same classes at home." He contrasted their diet favorably with those of his native Scotland, where "the harvest labourer's breakfast consisted of porridge and milk, his dinner of bread and beer, and porridge and milk again for supper" (Fortune, *Resident*, 42–43).[9]

Even if the diet of the poor was adequate, the question of variety is still unanswered. J. MacGowan, late in the Ch'ing period, found that the coolies in north China ate sweet potatoes three times a day, every day, all through the year, and that the only variations came from small amounts of salted turnip, bean curd, and pickled beans (MacGowan, *Sidelights*, 9).[10] A much more sophisticated analysis, by T. P. Meng and Sidney Gamble, taken from the food sellers' account books of the late Ch'ing, also found comparatively little variety in diet, but they were able to give some precise price fluctuations for a number of the staple items of working-class diet in Peking. (See tables 2, 3, and 4. Prices in the tables were computed in dollars at a rate of one dollar to 0.72 taels.)

Table 1: Peking Food Prices, Early Eighteenth Century

	Price in Copper Cash*	Unit
Grain		
Rice	1,300	per *shih* (picul; 133 lbs.)
Millet	1,050	per *shih*
Wheat	1,200	per *shih*
White Beans	1,100	per *shih*
Red Beans	800	per *shih*
Meat, Poultry, Fish		
Pig	2,500	each
Sheep	1,430	each
Goose	520	each
Duck	360	each
Chicken	120	each
Small water duck	60	each
Quail	25	each
Chicken Egg	3.5	each
Pork	50	per *chin* (catty; 1.33 lbs.)
Mutton	60	per *chin*
Dried Fish	300	per *chin*
Venison Strips	120	per *chin*
Pigs' Trotters	28	per *chin*
Pigs' Liver	27	per *chin*
Pigs' Bladder	19	each
Pigs' Intestines	6	each
Fruit		
Orange	50	each
Apple	30	each
Peach	20	each
Pear	15	each
Persimmon	8	each
Betel Nut	5	each
Walnut	1	each
Apricot	3	each
Plum	3	each
Litchi	100	per *chin*
Raisins	80	per *chin*
Fresh Grapes	60	per *chin*
Cherries	60	per *chin*
Fresh Lotus Roots	20	per *chin*
Watermelon Seeds	40	per *chin*

Table 1: Peking Food Prices, Early Eighteenth Century

	Price in Copper Cash*	Unit
Dairy		
Cow's Milk	50	per *chin*
Butter	180	per *chin*
Vegetable Products		
White Honey	150	per *chin*
White Sugar	100	per *chin*
Edible Seaweed	100	per *chin*
Red Honey	80	per *chin*
Pickled Ginger	70	per *chin*
Fresh Ginger	46	per *chin*
Pickled Vegetables	30	per *chin*
Pickled Cucumbers	25	per *chin*
Bean Meal	25	per *chin*
Millet Spirits	21	per *chin*
Rock Soda	20	per *chin*
Soy	12	per *chin*
Vinegar	8	per *chin*
Bean Curd	6	per *chin*

* Assuming 1,000 *li* (cash) to the *liang* (tael)

Other calculations show comparative increases between the late Ch'ing and the early warlord period (see table 5).

One of the other findings of the same investigators was that the monthly fluctuations could be extreme in times of political unrest. White flour, for example, was $5.84 per 100 catties in January 1900; in May it was $5.15; in September, $8.33; in December, $6.94, and in July 1901, back to $5.53 (Meng and Gamble, *Prices*, 11–12). Such figures still do not give exact prices for individual workers' diets during the Ch'ing—the nearest we can get to these is through the study made by L. K. Tao of the poor families in Peking, most of whom were ricksha men with wives who supplemented the tiny family income with sewing or the making of artificial flowers. The list of foods consumed by these families in the 1920s may well still reflect the Ch'ing conditions. Tao found that the foods

Table 2: Flour and Grain, Annual Average Prices—Dollars per 100 Catties

Year	Wheat Flour	Wheat Wholesale	Hsiao Mi Mien	Lao Mi	Bean Flour	Millet Retail	Millet Wholesale	Corn Flour
1900	6.41	—	3.90	6.32	5.55	4.45	—	3.06
1901	5.76	3.71	3.29	4.27	5.26	3.62	2.70	2.14
1902	5.52	3.75	3.84	5.37	5.17	4.00	3.40	2.92
1903	5.77	3.87	4.36	6.01	5.38	4.56	3.74	3.48
1904	5.29	3.33	3.90	5.52	5.08	4.35	3.39	3.11
1905	4.88	3.39	3.80	5.35	4.84	4.25	—	2.87
1906	5.71	3.90	4.08	5.80	5.05	4.50	3.47	3.24
1907	6.32	4.50	4.25	6.25	4.95	4.90	—	3.13
1908	5.75	3.91	4.36	6.11	5.07	5.01	3.57	3.65
1909	5.85	3.98	4.32	6.08	5.29	4.98	3.35	3.25
1910	5.94	4.21	4.26	6.53	5.58	5.01	3.73	3.48
1911	6.77	4.88	4.90	7.33	5.97	5.56	4.34	3.74
1912	6.10	4.37	5.10	7.40	6.60	5.91	4.66	3.97

Source: Meng and Gamble 1926, *Prices*, 28.[11]

Table 3: Pork and Mutton
Annual Average Prices—Dollars per 100 Catties

Year	Pork Average	Maximum	Mutton Minimum	Average
1900	9.45	16.20	11.10	14.00
1901	8.75	18.40	12.30	15.30
1902	10.10	13.80	8.70	10.00
1903	10.40	15.60	8.90	11.30
1904	10.80	—	—	—
1905	10.70	16.00	12.80	14.60
1906	10.70	15.90	11.60	13.80
1907	11.40	18.10	9.80	14.80
1908	11.40	14.10	11.10	12.50
1909	10.80	13.10	8.50	10.50
1910	11.40	13.30	9.00	11.00
1911	11.40	19.40	10.80	14.63
1912	11.20	19.50	9.80	13.10

Source: Meng and Gamble, Prices, 38–39.

purchased by every family were, among the grains, millet, millet flour, hand-milled wheat flour, and coarse corn flour. Other staples were cabbage, sesame oil, salt, soy paste, and vinegar. The only meat bought by all was mutton. The foods bought in some quantity by over 90 percent of the families were rice, buckwheat flour, salted ke-te, sweet potatoes, yellow bean sprouts, garlic, Allium odorum, sesame paste, and shrimp. Peanuts were bought by 89.6 percent (Tao, Livelihood, table 14, pp. 78–79).[12] Expressed in percentages by category, 80 percent of the workers' food expenditures went to cereals, 9.1 percent to vegetables, 6.7 percent to condiments, 3.2 percent to meats, and only 1 percent to all refreshments, including fruit (ibid., table 16, p. 96). There was more variety, however, among mill workers in Shanghai during the same period. They spent only 53.2 percent of their income on cereals, 18.5 percent on legume and vegetable products, 7 percent on meats, 4.4 percent on fish and sea-foods, and 1.9 percent on fruit (Yang and Tao, Study, table 26, p. 51).[13] But even if this was a survival diet, it left little leeway for the other

Table 4: Oils, Salt, Salt Vegetable
Annual Average Prices—Dollars per 100 Catties

Year	Sweet Oil	Peanut Oil	Salt	Salt Turnip
1902	16.00	13.20	2.98	1.11
1903	16.70	13.30	2.98	1.25
1904	16.40	13.60	2.98	1.11
1905	17.40	13.85	2.98	1.25
1906	16.95	13.20	3.62	1.11
1907	18.09	13.85	3.62	1.25
1908	17.50	13.60	3.62	1.25
1909	17.22	13.30	4.45	1.39
1910	18.09	13.60	4.45	1.25
1911	17.85	13.85	4.45	1.39
1912	18.09	15.25	4.17	2.08

Source: Meng and Gamble, *Prices*, 57.

expenses of life. The 230 Shanghai families surveyed spent 0.3 percent on toilet accessories, 0.3 percent on amusements, and 0.2 percent on education (ibid., table 38, p. 68). It is possible that standards were often higher in the Ch'ing countryside and that the rosters of local religious festivals provided both entertainment and dietary variety on a seasonal basis,[14] but there is probably little reason to challenge the assertion made by John Barrow during his visit to China in the Chia-ch'ing reign: that in the assortments of food there was a wider disparity in China between rich and poor than in any other country of the world (cited in Williams, *Kingdom*, 1:772).[15]

THE GOURMETS

Clearly, the many rebellions that occurred during the Ch'ing sprang from a base of rural misery and hunger that was exacerbated by a soaring population living on marginal lands as well as by the serious disruptions of Western imperialism. At the same time, among the gentry there was a sense of cultural pride—of having inherited the accumulated richness

Table 5: Percentage Price and Wage Increases

	1900–1924	1913–1924
Wheat Flour	42	49
Bean and Millet Flour	87	11
Corn Flour	102	59
Rice	14	53
Millet	58	17
Black Beans	150[b]	47
Green Beans	122[a]	44
Bean Flour	40[a]	17
Pork	101	62
Mutton	14	3
Sweet Oil	44[c]	18
Peanut Oil	44[c]	37
Salt	56[c]	7
Salt Turnip	109[c]	4
Wine	31[c]	31
Chiang Yu	40[c]	44
Bean Sauce	37[c]	24
Vinegar	150[c]	118
Cloth	160	51
Coal	16	37
Index Number	80	44
Copper Exchange	264	106
Copper Wages		
Skilled	258[a]	80
Unskilled	232[a]	100
Silver Wages		
Skilled	61	48
Unskilled	27	34
Real Wages		
Skilled	−2	12
Unskilled	−17	8

Source: Meng and Gamble, *Prices*, 71.

[a] 1900 to middle of 1924
[b] 1901–1924
[c] 1902–1924
− = Decrease

of a long and varied past. Here, the culinary arts were treated as a serious matter, as a part of the life of the mind. There was a Tao of food, just as there was a Tao of conduct and one of literary creation. Food, in some form, was taken as a subject by many Ch'ing writers. Often they merely reproduced, or commented briefly on, various older recipe collections; but some, such as Li Yü, Chang Ying, Yü Huai, Wu Ching-tzu, Shen Fu, and Yüan Mei—all significant figures in the history of Ch'ing culture—had strong views, which they expressed forcefully.

An entrance into this world of gourmet sensibilities is provided by Wu Ching-tzu in *The Scholars (Ju-lin wai-shih)*, written during the Ch'ien-lung reign. In this novel, the characters are not defined merely in terms of their appetites and their approach to food; they are presented as being what they eat. The characters of Chou Chin and Wang Hui, for instance, are perfectly caught in this brief paragraph:

> As they were chatting, lights were brought in, and the servants spread the desk with wine, rice, chicken, fish, duck and pork. Wang Hui fell to, without inviting Chou Chin to join him; and when Wang Hui had finished, the monk sent up the teacher's rice with one dish of cabbage and a jug of hot water. When Chou Chin had eaten, they both went to bed. The next day the weather cleared. Wang Hui got up, washed and dressed, bade Chou Chin a casual goodbye and went away in his boat, leaving the schoolroom floor so littered with chicken, duck and fish bones, and melon-seed shells, that it took Chou Chin a whole morning to clear them all away, and the sweeping made him dizzy. (Wu, *Scholars*, 59)[16]

Such a simple contrast, between rectitude and greed, could be carried further into pure parody when discussing the salt merchants—often a butt of the literati—with their solemn talk of trying to find some "hibernating toad" to round off the perfect meal (ibid., 325). The wedding feast given by the pretentious Lu family is another illustration. In this remarkable scene, first a rat falls from the rafters into the bird's-nest soup, and then, as the cook kicks at a dog, one of his shoes flies off and lands squarely upon a dish of pork dumplings and dumplings stuffed with goose fat and sugar (ibid., 168–69). The meal is well and truly ruined, and a social point is firmly made.

This literary representation was one aspect of the intelligentsia's culture tightly enmeshed with gourmet living. Of the many Ch'ing scholars interested in food and its principles, Yüan Mei was probably the most vociferous and the most persuasive. He prefaced his recipe book, *Shih-tan*, with a dozen pages of exhortations and warnings to his contemporaries, phrased as basic premises *(hsü-chih)* of cookery which could not be ignored if the execution was to be successful—the message seems to be directed both to the cook and to the reader as a sensitive eater. The initial principle was to understand the natural properties *(hsien-t'ien)* of a given food (Yüan, *Sui-yüan*, 1).[17] Thus the pork should be thin skinned and fragrant, the chicken in its prime, the carp white of stomach and slender in shape. The search for ideal ingredients meant that the credit for any fine banquet must be divided two ways, with 60 percent going to the cook and 40 percent to the man supervising the marketing *(mai-pan)*. The choice of the condiments was equally important: soys, oils, wines, and vinegars all have their own attributes and defects. Yüan does not retreat here into generalities but gives specific advice (presumably for products in the Nanking area where he was living in the mid-eighteenth century). Thus for oil one should choose the best grade of the Su-chou "Ch'iu-yu"; with vinegar one should guard against those with fine coloration but a flavor not quite sharp enough to provide the true purpose *(pen-chih)* of vinegar. Chen-chiang vinegar suffered from this flaw; the vinegar from Pan-p'u in Kiangsu was undoubtedly the best, with that from P'u-k'ou in Chekiang ranking second (ibid., 16). Washing and cleanliness of the food were also important: obviously, no trace of feather should adhere to the birds' nests, no mud should remain on the sea slugs, and no sand should be left with the sharks' fins; the meat must be without gristle and the venison without any rancid parts, and care must be taken to see that the fishes' gall has not been ruptured so that the flesh is bitter (ibid., 1b–2).

Yüan then proceeded to consider fundamental questions of balance in a given meal. Flavoring must be discriminating and clear, closely allied to the food's nature: the use of wine and water, salt and sauces, separately or in combination, was one focus; the balance of foods in a dish, in terms of blandness, clarity, and richness, was another. It would be folly to put powdered crab *(hsieh-fen)* with the birds' nest, for example, or *Lilium japonicum (pai-ho)* with chicken and pork. Good strong flavors, such as those of eel, turtle, crab, shad *(shih)*, beef, and mutton, should all be left to stand on their own *(tu-shih)* (ibid., 2–3).

These initial sections show the gourmet's approach to the overall strategy of a meal, and in his section on warnings *(chieh)*, a few pages further on, Yüan Mei gives two amusing personal examples of what he considered disastrous meals:

> A good cook cannot with the utmost application produce more than four successful dishes in one day, and even then it is hard for him to give proper attention to every detail; and he certainly won't get through unless everything is in its right place and he is on his feet the whole time. It is no use to give him a lot of assistants; each of them will have his own ideas, and there will be no proper discipline. The more help he gets, the worse the results will be. I once dined with a merchant. There were three successive sets of dishes and sixteen different sweets. Altogether, more than forty kinds of food were served. My host regarded the dinner as an enormous success. But when I got home I was so hungry that I ordered a bowl of plain rice-gruel. From this it may be imagined how little there was, despite this profusion of dishes, that was at all fit to eat.
>
> I always say that chicken, pork, fish and duck are the original geniuses of the board, each with a flavour of its own, each with its distinctive style; whereas sea-slug and swallows-nest (despite their costliness) are commonplace fellows, with no character—in fact, mere hangers-on. I was once asked to a party given by a certain Governor, who gave us plain boiled swallows-nest, served in enormous vases, like flower-pots. It had no taste at all. The other guests were obsequious in their praise of it. But I said: "We are here to eat swallows-nest, not to take delivery of it wholesale." If our host's object was simply to impress, it would have been better to put a hundred pearls into each bowl. Then we should have known that the meal had cost him tens of thousands, without the unpleasantness of being expected to eat what was uneatable. (Ibid., 8b–9; trans. Waley, *Yuan Mei*, 195–96).[18]

A group of Yüan's exhortations are directed firmly to the cook, such as the heat of the fire that should be maintained, the type of utensils, and cleanliness while cooking. He divided fires into two basic categories, *wu-huo* (military heat) for fast frying and *wen-huo* (civil, or literary, heat) for slower cooking. Clams, eggs, chicken, fish—each has the heat that is right for it; the cook must gauge this and not constantly peer into the pot to check the food's progress. If he does so, the water will bubble too much, and the flavor will be lost; the fish will become dead in taste. "Certainly to have a fresh fish and to cause it to become unfresh is a terrible act" (Yüan, *Sui-yüan*, 3; my translation). Also, strong-flavored foods should each be cooked in a separate pot. Some people cook up chicken, duck, pork, and goose in a single pot, and the result is an indistinguishable mass—it's "like chewing wax. I fear that these chickens, pigs, geese, and ducks have souls and will lodge a formal complaint with the god of the underworld" (ibid., 4; my translation). The same principles apply to other utensils: you don't cut bamboo with a knife that has just cut scallions; you don't crush food with a pestle that has just been crushing pepper; nor do you use a dirty dishcloth or cutting board, the flavor of which can linger on the food. The good cook sharpens his knives, uses a clean towel, scrapes down the chopping board, and washes his hands; he keeps tobacco ash, flies, ash from the fire, and his own sweat, all safely away from the food (ibid., 6).

At one point in his cookbook, Yüan Mei criticized a recipe of the earlier Ch'ing writer Li Yü for being "profoundly artificial" *(chiao-jou tsao-tso)* (ibid., 9). This was not just a squabble between gourmets, since Li Yü (Li-weng, 1611–1680) had considerable fame and literary influence. What Yüan objected to in Li seems to have been a kind of over-developed rusticity combined with fancifulness, which led Li to tamper with decent materials, thus violating one of Yüan's basic canons. In his cookbook, Li had criticized meat eaters for being vulgar and wasteful, though he was not a vegetarian; and he recommended meats on the basis of the animal's nature (instead of on the actual flavor and texture of their flesh, as Yüan would have done). Li did not want to discuss eating cattle or dog, since they were friends to humans; chickens he valued because they awoke humans in the morning; geese could be readily eaten, since they were of no use to humans, and fish and shrimp could be eaten with a light heart since they laid so many eggs (Li, *Hsien-ch'ing*, 264–69).[19] Li also rejected scallions and garlic, because of their "foulness" *(wei)* on the breath; he would eat only the tips of chives; and instead of any of these three, he recommended the tender flavor of the rarer, and more fragrant, juniper berry (ibid., 258–59; Lin and Lin, *Gastronomy*, 43).[20] Radishes he rejected because they caused hiccups and fouled the breath, though he accepted pepper because it would liven up a sleepy person and was like "meeting a virtuous man" (Li, *Hsien-ch'ing*, 259). To make the best rice, Li would send his maid to gather the dew from the flowers of the wild rose, the cassia, or the citron and would add this to the water at the last minute; dew from garden roses, however, was too strong in flavor, felt Li, and could not be recommended (ibid., 261; Lin and Lin, *Gastronomy*, 43). With noodles, too, Li sought an extreme purity of taste, though in his concentration on a few light, clear tastes in his noodle recipes he seems to have been nearer to Yüan than in some of his overrefined moments: his method depended on keeping a light broth, with only a touch of soy or vinegar in the water, which would then be poured over the noodles, which had been prepared with a touch of sesame and bamboo shoots, with a flavoring of mushroom or shrimp sauce (Li, *Hsien-ch'ing*, 263).

One modern culinary critic has felt that "there may have been something of the *poseur* in Li" (Lin and Lin, *Gastronomy*, 43). It certainly seems that he allowed his moral biases and his overrefinement to interfere with the pursuit of robust flavors. He also professed a liking for a type of culinary order—"five fragrances in my daily foods, eight flavors when I have guests" (Li, *Hsien-ch'ing*, 263)—which was just the kind of ting that irritated Yüan. It was Yüan's feeling that strict patterns in a dinner were good only in very rare circumstances, like the formal T'ang poetic modes; otherwise, the sixteen dishes, eight platters, four desserts, and so on, of both the regulated Manchu and the Chinese dinner parties became too constricting (Yüan, *Sui-yüan*, 11b–12).

The manner of serving a meal was also of major importance to Yüan, as it was to his wealthy contemporaries. Invitations should be issued at least three days in advance, to allow the meal to be planned properly. If traveling, one must have along some special recipes for foods that could be cooked in a hurry if one had suddenly to give hospitality—fried chicken strips, bean curd and tiny shrimp fish cured in grain spirit *(tsao-yü)*, or fine ham. In serving up the food, one should keep away from overexpensive Ming porcelain, and build up the table simply with a variety of shapes from the finer Ch'ing potteries. Small bowls should be used for the cheaper dishes, fried food should be served on platters, and simmered food should be warmed only in pottery, not in metal (ibid., 46). It was important to use as many expensive ingredients as possible, and as few cheap ones, but it was also important not to cook too much in bulk: half a *chin* (about ten ounces) was the maximum amount of meat that would fry through properly in one pan, Yüan thought, and six ounces the maximum amount of chicken or fish. Other dishes, of course, had to be cooked in bulk if they were to have any real flavor: for broiled white pork you needed at least twenty *chin* (about twenty-six pounds), and for a thick conjee a peck of rice was ideal (ibid., 5b). Dishes must always be cooked and eaten one by one, not piled on the table in profusion, and the cook should utilize as many parts of a given fish or animal as possible (ibid., 9b–10)—here Yüan shared some of the basic frugality of Li Hua-nan. The elegance that such serving could attain has been described by Yüan's contemporary Shen Fu, who talked of the economies worked out by his wife, Yuen:

> Poor scholars, who must of necessity be economical about such things as clothes and food, houses and furniture, can try, nevertheless, to see that their surroundings are clean and in good taste. In order to be economical, the proverb says "act in accordance with circumstances," or "cut one's coat according to one's cloth."
>
> I am very fond of a little wine with my meals but I do not like elaborate food, nor too many dishes at a time. Yuen made a plum flower tray, for which she used six deep white porcelain dishes, about two inches in diameter, arranging five of them about the centre dish in the manner of a five-pointed star. When the box had been painted a light grey, the whole thing looked like a plum blossom, the tray and its cover both having indented-edges, and the cover having a handle like the stem of a flower. When it was placed on the table, the tray looked like a fallen plum blossom, and the lifted cover showed the vegetables served in the petals. One of these trays, with its six different dishes, contains enough for a pleasant meal for two or three close friends. If the dishes are emptied, they can always be refilled for second helpings.
>
> We also made another tray, a round one with a low border, which we found handy for holding our cups, chopsticks, wine pots and such things. These trays could be carried to any place one wished and were easy to remove again afterwards. This is an example of economy in the matter of food. (Shen, Chapters, 70)[21]

Shen Fu emphasized that friendly word games and steady drinking went hand in hand with gourmet eating of the highest order; and though fairly poor, he and his wife were usually able to sit down to perfect dishes of melon, shrimp, vegetables, and fish (ibid., 65). This combination of frugality and refinement was a part of the genre of elegant simplicity much appreciated in mid-Ch'ing China; thus we find Shen Fu, a paramount sensualist, describing the eating of fresh Canton litchis as one of the keenest pleasures of his whole life, and packing up his own stock of crabs steeped in wine, for the journey south that was to give him this pleasure (ibid., 38, 52). And a novel like Ts'ao Hsüeh-ch'in's *Hung-lou meng* is dotted with references to special items of rare food (or perfect specimens of simple food) that brought unusual pleasure: goose foot preserves, for instance, or a soup with chicken skin; junket and mince; a particularly fragrant koumiss; or cypress-smoked, Siamese suckling pig (Ts'ao, *Story*, 192, 195, 370, 376, 519).[22]

The eating habits of one group of Yüan's contemporaries and fellow provincials, the Chinese merchants of Kiangsu and Chekiang who were temporarily residing in Nagasaki, were studied with interest by a Tokugawa official, Nakagawa Shundai. He noted that the basic essentials of daily diet for the merchants were rice and tea, vinegar, soy, pickles, squash, and black beans; their average daily meal was only three or four dishes: for breakfast, some conjee and dried vegetables with pickled cucumber and radishes; and simple dishes of either meat or fish for the noon and evening meals (Nakagawa, *Shinzoku*, 9, 31).[23] But in their meals for guests, they followed a clear ritual of sixteen dishes, including bear's paw, deer tail, sharks' fins, birds' nests, and sea slugs; as well as fried lamb, pigs' trotters "in the Su Tung-p'o style" (a dish which Li Yü had found vulgarized), two kinds of chicken, duck, goose, steamed fish, crab sauce, dried mussels, and fish belly (ibid., 19–24; Li, *Hsien-ch'ing*, 265). In the ten-dish meal, for second-class occasions, the dishes omitted were bear's paw, deer tail, wild chicken, goose, crab, and mussels. The sharks' fins and lamb were further omitted if the meal was a third-class one of eight dishes (Nakagawa, *Shinzoku*, 26).

The Chinese at Nagasaki also drank a good deal of wine, noted Nakagawa (ibid., 9), thus alerting us to another problem in trying to assess the general gourmet eating habits of the Ch'ing. Shen Fu, who was disarmingly frank about such matters, admitted that he got so drunk on his wedding night in 1780 that he passed out even before reaching the nuptial chamber (Shen, *Chapters*, 7). Yüan Mei was quite certain that wine in excess would spoil one's appreciation of the food, but he also had a deep love of good wine and confessed to drinking sixteen cups of an irresistible dark wine made from millet in Li-shui, until his head reeled; on another occasion, a sweet and heavy Su-chou wine led him to take fourteen cups, despite his best intentions (Yüan, *Sui-yüan*, 78).[24] In a delightful passage, he likened wine to the bullies among the people or to the runners in the county yamen: the bullies prove their worth when they chase away more dangerous bandits, and the runners can be useful in getting rid of thieves; so wine is at its most useful when you have a cold or have overeaten. He thought that the wine made in Fen-chou fu,

Shansi, was probably the best, with the kaoliang wine of Shantung second. Such wine could be stored for a decade, till it grew greenish and sweet—just like a bully who has been a bully so long that he's lost his temper and can now be a true friend of yours. Such wine was delicious with pig's head or lamb's tail. Su-chou wines were often inferior, and he thought Shao-hsing wine overrated. There was even a Yang-chou quince (mu-kua) wine which was considered so unworthy that one was vulgarized just by tasting it (shang-k'ou pien-su) (ibid., 78).

It is hard to distinguish the various social and personal functions of heavy drinking, but it was not just a mid-Ch'ing phenomenon. In the K'ang-hsi reign (1662–1722), Han T'an apparently drank himself to death while president of the Board of Rites. Also during this reign, the membership of one drinking club included such worthy scholars as T'ang Pin, Shen Ch'üan, and Chang Ying, and each member had his own special cup inscribed with his name (Liang, Lang-chi, 4:1–2).[25] Earlier in the same reign, Yü Huai described drinking parties that went on in Nanking till all the guests vomited and fell asleep on the ground (Yü, Feast, 95).[26] This was in the brothel quarter, where drinking was naturally heavy, and where courtesans were prized for their abilities to direct, monitor, and participate in heavy drinking games (ibid., 74). But such drinking games were also common in polite society. Shen Fu's wife drank heavily with his new potential concubine (Shen, Chapters, 55–56). P'u Sung-ling has a story of a remarkable drinking game that depended on one's luck in drawing various terms with food and drink radicals out of the text of the Rites of Chou (P'u, Contes, 70).[27] There is enough evidence to suggest that, among the literati, wine and food were firmly intertwined as parts of the good life.

Food blurred with wine, and the wine itself blended into moments of sensual pleasure; and in this epicurean Ch'ing atmosphere, with money and women amply available to men of power and taste, it is not surprising that the vocabularies of food and lust should overlap and blend into a language of sensuality. Shen Fu saw the sixteen-year-old virgin Han-yuan—who became, briefly, the love of both his and his wife's life—as being "sweet and ripe as a melon ready for cutting" (Shen, Chapters, 54). Such similes had been common in male poetry (though perhaps blossoms and flowers and leaves were seen as more appropriate) and had been strongly present in female poetry since at least the eighth century, as we can see from the evocative poems of the prostitute Chao Luan-luan, with her "fresh peeled spring onions," "small cherries," "white melon seeds," and "purple grapes" (Rexroth and Chung, Boat, 26–30);[28] and we need not trouble to compile a list of these from the Ch'ing. But a few brief examples from the *Hung-lou meng* are a proper concern for a study of Ch'ing food and are relevant at this point, since the readers of the novel were presumably the same gourmets we have been discussing: the literate elites, the educated merchant families, and their women, who found satisfaction in taking elegant time off from the classics or their work. Certainly these readers would have found pleasure in Ts'ao Hsüeh-ch'in's imaginative plays upon conventional imagery: "blinds looped and fringed like a prawn's belly" (Ts'ao, *Story*, 359); a little girl with "cheeks as white and fresh as a fresh lychee and a nose as white and shiny as soap made from the whitest goose-fat" (ibid., 89)—even if Ts'ao Hsüeh-ch'in was near self-parody here; and they would have appreciated the young girls of the novel being linked to Pao-yü, the lipstick eater, by images of redness and fruit, with their "apricot" and "peach" quilts and their "strawberry" dresses (ibid., 392, 415, 469).

But the vocabulary of food was able to enrich the language all the more through the complex plot structure of the novel that developed in the Ch'ing. For here the form gave room to a new kind of leisurely exploration of metaphor and to the use of echoes, not of past works in a similar genre, but of past sections of the same work. One way Ts'ao Hsüeh-ch'in developed a subplot was to link it to food or drink. Thus the moving scene in which Pao-yü realizes, for the first time, that his family cannot control everything and that his beloved maid and lover, Aroma, might actually buy her freedom out of bondage comes just after the koumiss he saved for her has been drunk out of spite by Nanny Li. This episode, in turn, is prepared for by Pao-yü's sexual innuendo to Aroma in her own home, when (referring to the koumiss) he whispers, "I've got something nice waiting for you when you get back"; Aroma whispers, "Sh! Do you want them all to hear you?" As she says this, she reaches out and takes the Magic Jade from his neck (ibid., 381–82). David Hawkes, the translator of this novel, has pointed to the sexual role of the Jade in Pao-yü's life, while the koumiss itself was originally a gift from the Imperial Concubine (ibid., 32, n. 8; 376).

A similar type of echo is used to add poignancy to Ch'in Chung's death. In a scene of love and youthful sensuality, Ch'in Chung jokes with the pretty novice, and she ripostes, "I must have honey on my hands" (ibid., 296). And as Ch'in Chung dies, Pao-yü and his servants rush to the bedside "like swarming bees" to gaze at his "waxen" face (ibid., 321). These images of bees and honey are only one fragment of the intricate pattern of oral and anal imagery that Ts'ao Hsüeh-ch'in had woven around the two young boys: they get to know each other while eating (ibid., 179); Ch'in Chung is admitted to the clan school after the extraordinary scene in which an old family servant shouts of the family's filth and has his mouth stuffed with manure as a punishment (ibid., 183–84); the two boys are mocked by schoolfellows with a suggestive jingle about "nice hot cakes" *(hao shao ping)* (ibid., 208);[29] Ch'in Chung's sexual initiation with the novice and with Pao-yü takes place in Wheat-bread Priory ("so-called because of the excellent steamed wheatbread made in its kitchens") (ibid., 294, 299–300); Ch'in Chung's exhaustion after these goings-on is expressed by "loss of appetite" (ibid., 302); and his brief respite from death is ended by choking (ibid., 323).

An equally complex series of ambiguities lies behind one of the few pastoral poems that appear in the *Hung-lou meng*. Nothing could seem much more conventional than this:

The Hopeful Sign

An inn-sign, through the orchards half-discerned,
Promises shelter and a drink well-earned.
Through water-weeds the pond's geese make their way;
Midst elms and mulberry-trees the swallows play.
The garden's chives are ready to prepare;
The scent of young rice perfumes all the air.
When want is banished, as in times like these,
The spinner and the ploughman take their ease.

(Ibid., 370)

But Ts'ao Hsüeh-ch'in does not let his Ch'ing readers rest in that bucolic vision. For, in arriving at the selection of this poem as the decoration for a certain spot in the Imperial Concubine's progress, Pao-yü had cited the lines "A cottage by the water stands / Where sweet the young rice smells," as if to echo the musings of his father, who had just been moved enough by the sight of neat rows of vegetables to declaim that "it awakens the desire to get back to the land, to a life of rural simplicity" (ibid., 334–35). The irony is intense, because Pao-yü is echoing his own earlier thought that came to him when, for the only time in his life, he actually visited a farm, talked to a farm girl, and saw the conditions of life there: only then, says Pao-yü, did he begin to understand the lines "Each grain of rice we ever ate / Cost someone else a drop of sweat" (ibid., 292). Yet Pao-yü remained trapped in his upbringing, with the gourmet tastes he had acquired. For, in his only other visit to a poor family's home, after surveying the carefully arrayed dishes of cakes, dried fruits, and nuts, the best that they could offer to their young master, Pao-yü's maid realized sadly "that there was nothing there which Pao-yü could possibly be expected to eat" (ibid., 381).

THE IMPERIAL LEVEL

At the level of the imperial court, food played many roles. One was the symbolic and sacrificial—the use of food as sacrifice to the gods, with the regulation of those offerings to the minutest detail of vessel and of placement (Ch'in-ting Ta-Ch'ing hui-tien t'u, 1139–437). Here the Ch'ing followed precedent, and there do not seem to have been any significant innovations as far as the Chinese ceremonial usages were concerned. The Manchus did add a new level of ancestral shamanistic religion; and, in their own temples, they added further sacrifices of pigs and grain to placate their own gods—even though the meanings or significance of these gods' names had already been forgotten as early as the Ch'ien-lung reign (Ch'in-ting pa-ch'i t'ung-chih, chaps. 89–93).

The maintenance of food production, of course, was at the center of the court's preoccupations, since it was the taxation on the peasants' surplus that sustained the entire apparatus of empire and bureaucracy; here again, the Ch'ing did not significantly modify earlier policies concerning dike construction and maintenance, emergency grain price stabilization, assessment and collection of taxes, or the shipping northward of the "grain tribute" from the south to feed the capital troops. The most significant shift was in the percentage of the total Ch'ing tax yields that the land tax represented; for, while the amount of land tax did steadily increase during the Ch'ing, the percentage of total revenue that this represented dropped from 73.5 percent during the Ch'ien-lung reign to 35.1 percent by the end of the dynasty—the massive new revenue sources being the maritime customs and the likin (customs charges) (Wang, Taxation, 79–80).[30]

Feeding the court was a massive enough problem, as it had been in all earlier dynasties. Here the Ch'ing slowly moved from reliance on the produce of their own estates and the collection of miscellaneous "tribute" items of local specialties, to a centralized purchasing system operated by the Accounts section of the Imperial Household. In the late Ch'ien-lung reign, this office annually purchased 750,000 piculs of cereals, 400,000 eggs, and 1,000 catties of wine (Chang, "Role," 254),[31] though these enormous quantities represent only a small part of the overall administrative concerns with food. The Imperial Buttery (ch'a shan fang) section of the Imperial Household, as described in the Ch'ing Statutes, is a network of offices for meats, tea and milk, pastries, wines, pickles, and fresh vegetables. A huge staff of cooks and their assistants worked to prepare the daily specifications for persons of varying ranks in the household, from the emperor himself downward in decreasing amounts through the hierarchy of consorts to the princes and princesses (*Ch'in-ting Ta-Ch'ing hui-tien shih-li*, chap. 1192).

There is evidence that, despite their general reputation for extravagance, many of the Ch'ing emperors had in fact quite simple tastes: K'ang-hsi liked fresh meats, simply cooked, fish, and fresh fruit (Spence, *Emperor*, chaps. 1, 4);[32] Kuang-hsü would breakfast lightly on milk, rice gruel, and flat wheat cakes (Der Ling, *Son*, 73).[33] A menu of one of Ch'ien-lung's meals in 1754 sounds delicious, but far from flamboyant (Su, *Dishes*, 16):[34]

Main Course Dishes

A dish of fat chicken, pot-boiled duck, and bean curd, cooked by Chang Erh

A dish of swallows' nests and julienned smoked duck, cooked by Chang Erh

A bowl of clear soup, cooked by Jung Kui

A dish of julienned pot-boiled chicken, cooked by Jung Kui

A dish of smoke fat chicken and Chinese cabbage, cooked by Chang Erh

A dish of salted duck and pork, cooked by Jung Kui

A dish of court-style fried chicken

Pastries

A dish of bamboo-stuffed steamed dumplings
A dish of rice cakes
A dish of rice cakes with honey

Pickles

Served in a ceramic container patterned
with hollyhock flowers

Chinese cabbage pickled in brine
Cucumbers preserved in soy
Pickled eggplant

Rice
Boiled rice

But the personal tastes of the emperor had little to do with the scale of culinary operations or their costs. The regulations were firm about the exact content of all major meals, which were carefully graded in accordance with their level of ritual significance.

The records of the Imperial Banqueting Court *(Kuang-lu Ssu)* were published late in the Ch'ing, and from these we can note some of the variations. There seem to have been six basic grades of Manchu banquets *(Man-hsi)* and five of Chinese *(Han-hsi)*, and a ranking of occupations and offices can be drawn up by observing who got what kind of meal. Senior Mongol princes *(beile)*, for example, got served at the imperial level of Manchu feast, while the Khalka princes ate at the third Manchu level, and the envoys from the Dalai Lama ate at the fifth Manchu level *(Kuang-lu Ssu,* 24:1b, 3;25:1). Foreign tributary missions, whether from Korea, the Ryukyu Islands, or Annam, got sixth-level Manchu food, and it is into this precise slot that we can see the first Western envoys being fitted as they entered China in the Shun-chih and K'ang-hsi reigns. Chinese banquets were similarly graded: first level for compilers of a completed block of the Veritable Records *(Shih-lu),* second level for chief examiners at the palace exams, third level for the guards' officers and physicians in attendance, fifth level for the top three students in the examinations.

The levels of food varied both by volume and by type of food provided, and perhaps also by the number of people seated at a given table, since that is the only way that the quantities provided seem to make sense. Thus at the highest level of Manchu feast, each sitting *(mei-hsi)* had, among other things, 120 *chin* of white wheat flour, 8 *chin* of dried bean flour, 150 hen's eggs, 18 *chin* of white sugar, 4 *chin* of white honey, 6 *chin* of sesame, a variety of dried fruits, and a shifting menu of fresh fruits, according to season (ibid., 43:3–7).[35] For a sixth-level Manchu feast, the quantities were reduced to 20 *chin* of white flour and 2.8 *chin* of white sugar; eggs were dropped altogether, and variety was provided by offering a much wider range of dried fruits than at the upper level *(Kuang-lu Ssu,* 46:1–5). The Manchu meals on the Banqueting Court lists were vegetarian. However, more research is needed before we can decide precisely what Manchu meats were served at which meals, and to which envoys; for the emperor K'ang-hsi declared in 1680 that henceforth the New Year's feasts should be Han-hsi rather than Man-hsi, because of the large number of animals that had to be slaughtered for the latter *(Ta-ch'ing Sheng-tsu Jen Huang-ti Shih-lu,* p. 1513); and when

John Bell visited Peking with the Russian embassy of 1721, he was served large portions of excellent stewed mutton and beef (Bell, *Journey*, 119, 136).[36]

A complete range of meat and fish dishes appears only in the Chinese menus. The Chinese level-one meal included pork and intestines, duck, goose, chicken, and fish, as well as a much wider variety of condiments (*Kuang-lu Ssu*, 47:3b–6); while the Chinese fifth level had pork (though no intestines) and some fish, but substituted mutton for fowl. A note at the end of the source states that chicken had been included in this meal until 1787, when it was dropped from the menu (ibid., 47:15–17). Of considerable interest to a history of Ch'ing cooking might be some of the appended lists in the same source, which give more precise contents for each bowl *(wan)* in the Chinese first-level meal. Each sitting *(hsi)* had thirty-four bowls of main dishes and four plates *(tieh)* of condiments and pickle. To give a few examples, one goose would be shared between three bowls, a whole chicken would be in one bowl, one and eight-tenths chin of pork composed a separate dish, two ounces of edible sea-weed and six ounces of pork were combined for one bowl, five hens' eggs were used in an egg dish, and *pao-tzu* came twelve to a bowl and each one was made with two ounces of white flour and half an ounce (five *ch'ien*) of pork (ibid., 48:1–3).

The logistic data behind each meal were, of course, equally precise: for an upper-level Manchu banquet, eighty *chin* of wood and fifty of charcoal; one set of stoves for each ten *hsi* (with special arrangements for over two hundred); the cooking for every ten *hsi* required four large bowls, a steamer, an open frying pan, metal ladles, a metal roasting pan, a red cloth cover to keep off the flies, and a red oiled cloth for the table. This was not to mention the carrying rods and food boxes, the chopping blocks and benches, the baskets, the strainers of different mesh, the brooms, the skimmers, the buckets, and the scoops (ibid., 43:2–3). Ivory chopsticks were specified for the Chinese meals but not for the Manchu (ibid., 47:3).

This incredible barrage of precise regulation leads us to the last area where food was truly important at the Ch'ing imperial level—namely, the field of compilation and codification. Just as the court collected and compiled its own history and imperial writings, so it had an official corpus of agricultural literature, of which food was an integral part. A basic and approved bibliography was provided in the Ch'ien-lung reign in the form of the commentaries to the immense collection of accepted literature known as the *Ssu-k'u ch'üan-shu*. The references to that work in

A banquet held in the Qing imperial palace for foreign tributary missions (*from Todo Meisho Zue, 1806*)

除日保和殿宴外藩蒙古

Tsung-mu t'i-yao began, predictably enough, with the great sixth-century classic of animal husbandry, the *Ch'i-min yao-shu (Ssu-k'u ch'üan-shu tsung-mu t'i-yao*, 2074). Official data on food and food taxes were organized into the Three Imperial Encyclopedias *(Huang-ch'ao San-t'ung)*, which were designed to be continuations of the great Sung encyclopedic works and were printed during the Ch'ien-lung reign. Virtually the entire history of Chinese food and its eating and production was assembled in the immense compendium the *Ku-chin t'u-shu chi-ch'eng*, which, after the disgrace of its main compiler, appeared in the Yung-cheng reign in type that had been set in the K'ang-hsi period. About fifty *chüan* ("volumes") of this work (the whole has been estimated to have a hundred million characters) are given over to the literature of food and wine, traced down to the early seventeenth century from the earliest references in the books of rituals. There are entire sections on vinegars, wines, honey and sugar, edible oils, meats, rice, poisonous foods, and festival foods, and on the poetry across the ages that celebrated the joys of food *(Ku-chin t'u-shu chi-cheng*, chaps. 257–307). The arts of weaving and plowing were celebrated in new imperial editions (by both K'ang-hsi and Ch'ien-lung) of the Sung *Keng-chih t'u.* Some great Ming works related to food, such as the pharmacopoeia *Pen-ts'ao kang-mu*, were expanded under private auspices during the Ch'ing; others, like the *T'ien-kung k'ai-wu*, which contains valuable data on technology related to food, were never reprinted during the Ch'ing, though a few parts were printed in the *Ku-chin t'u-shu chi-ch'eng.* It would seem that private readers shared with the imperial compilers a comfortable feeling that everything of importance dealing with food and its production had already been said. And the one careful work on agricultural technique that was sponsored and printed by the Ch'ing state, the *Shou-shih t'ung-k'ao*, under the nominal editorship of Ortai and Chang T'ing-yu (in 1742), has been described, by a recent Chinese scholar of agricultural history, as being merely in the class of "orthodox developments of the *Ch'i-min yao-shu* with extensions or annexations" (Shih, *Ch'i-min*, 102–3).[37]

This state of affairs did not change in the nineteenth century. Though, after the suppression of the Taiping Rebellion, the emperors did respond to Western impetus in some ways—for instance, through the development of the Kiang-nan arsenal and of schools with some foreign components, like the T'ung-wen kuan—a desire to broaden or expand domestic agriculture does not seem to have figured high on the list of priorities. Guns and machinery absorbed their attention along with the skills of engineering, physics, chemistry, and mathematics. Among the many books that John Fryer translated for the Kiang-nan arsenal, when he worked for this establishment, between the 1860s and the 1890s, there seem to have been only two related to agriculture: a bibliography of agricultural reference works and a book on agricultural chemistry (Bennett, *Fryer*, 96).[38] Only at the very end of the century did a few "self-strengthening" reformers point to the importance of agriculture in strengthening the nation. In their joint memorial of 1901, Liu K'un-i and Chang Chih-tung noted how few Western works on agriculture had been translated but observed that good, modern Japanese works existed in abundance and should be used by the Chinese (Teng and Fairbank, *Response*, 202).[39] Sun Yat-sen urged attention to scientific agriculture in his manifesto of the *Hsing-chung-hui*, to improve plant and animal husbandry and to save human labor with farm machinery (ibid, 224). Chang Chih-tung probably went further in a practical direction than any other officials, by engaging two American specialists to investigate agricultural conditions in Hupei and by making experimental plantings of new seeds. In 1902 he developed an experimental farm of two thousand mou near Wu-ch'ang (Ayers, *Chang*, 132),[40] and he attempted to make his contemporaries aware that Western food yields per mou were substantially higher than Chinese yields (ibid., 167).

Such probes, however, were still ahead of their time, and Chinese comments on Western food remained vague or flamboyant.[41] Tucked into one of the lists of books that Fryer ordered from England for his own use in 1868 was a request for *Family Cookery* (Bennett, *Fryer*, 76). Whether he planned to introduce some elements of English cuisine to the Chinese, we do not know. Nor do we know if he would have recommended the diet common among treaty port Westerners in Shanghai at the time:

> Begin dinner with rich soup, and a glass of sherry; *then* one or two side dishes with champagne; *then* some beef, mutton, or fowls and bacon, with *more* champagne, or beer; *then* rice and curry and ham; *afterwards* game; *then* pudding, pastry, jelly, custard, or blancmange, and *more* champagne; *then* cheese and salad, and bread and butter, and a glass of port wine; *then* in many cases, oranges, figs, raisins, and walnuts . . . *with* two or three glasses of claret or some other wine. (Fairbank, *Trade*, 160–61)[42]

There seems to have been little meeting of the culinary minds at this time despite the "opening" of China; and William Hunter's wry parody of the Chinese reaction to Western cooking may not have been too far off the mark:

> Judge now what tastes people possess who sit at table and swallow bowls of a fluid, in their outlandish tongue called *Soo-pe,* and next devour the flesh of fish, served in a manner as near as may be to resemble the living fish itself. Dishes of half-raw meat are then placed at various angles of the table; these float in gravy, while from them pieces are cut with swordlike instruments and placed before the guests. . . . Thick pieces of meat being devoured, and the scraps thrown to a multitude of snappish dogs that are allowed to twist about amongst one's legs or lie under the table, while keeping up an incessant growling and fighting, there followed a dish that set fire to our throats, called in the barbarous language of one by my side *Kā-tē,* accompanied with rice which of itself was alone grateful to my taste. Then a green and white substance, the smell of which was overpowering. This I was informed was a compound of sour buffalo milk, baked in the sun, under whose influence it is allowed to remain until it becomes filled with insects, yet, the greener and more lively it is, with the more relish is it eaten. This is called *Che-Sze,* and is accompanied by the drinking of a muddy red fluid which foams up over the tops of the drinking cups, soils one's clothes, and is named *Pe-Urh*—think of that! But no more. (Hunter, *Bits,* 38–39)[43]

Despite these varying levels of Western perception, for the young emperor P'u-i, as the dynasty came to its end, nothing had ostensibly changed in the palace kitchens since the seventeenth century. And even as he lived in seclusion during the first years of the republic, the old, wasteful rituals continued. Processions of eunuchs brought tables of lavish dishes to his presence on his command, each silver dish placed upon a porcelain dish of hot water to keep it warm; but these dishes were never eaten by P'u-i, since he could not bear these heavy meals, which often had been cooked days in advance. The "imperial" meals were returned untasted, to the kitchens, where they were presumably consumed by the palace staff. These procedures raised the emperor's alleged consumption of food to 810 catties of meat and 240 chickens and ducks, every month. In fact, he was eating small, delicious meals specially prepared for him in the imperial consorts' own kitchens. But whatever he ate, of whatever quality or quantity, the eunuchs would always report the emperor's food consumption in terms of that same rustic simplicity which might once have seemed like emulation of peasant virtues but now had become a cruel parody: "Your slave reports to his masters: the Lord of Ten Thousand Years consumed one bowl of old rice viands, one steamed breadroll and a bowl of congee. He consumed it with relish" (Aisin-Gioro, *Emperor*, 43–44).[44]

SERVICE AND DISTRIBUTION

The subject of service and distribution related to food consumption is immense and diffuse, demanding a far-ranging knowledge of social and economic history which this author does not have. But certain aspects of food services during the Ch'ing seem worth considering.

The Ch'ing was a time of flourishing corporate organizations. At the lowest levels, these might consist of small groups of poor families that would pool scarce resources so as to club together for an occasional dinner—even beggars formed such associations to alleviate the regular misery of their existence (Simon, "Note," 12–13, 21).[45] At a wealthier level, there were the powerful associations *(hui-kuan)* composed of merchants and officials from the same province who now found themselves living far from their native place. In their own meeting halls, they could dine on their own foods from common funds and preserve far-off patterns of eating and drinking (Morse, *Gilds*, and Ho, *Chung-kuo*).[46]

Merchant guild organizations frequently specialized in a given area of food production or sale and were in a position to control prices. In Ning-po, for example, Fukienese merchants specialized in dealing in salt, fish, and oranges and also maintained a special section for dealing with sugar products, which could provide seventy days free storage facilities to guild merchants (MacGowan, "Guilds," 138, 142, 146).[47] Shantung merchants in Ning-po were able, for a time, to successfully defend their right to monopolize carriage of pulse and bean cake, even against Western merchants (ibid., 149–50); they gave credit to their members to the tune of forty days on grain sales and fifty days on oils and bean cake—we find the Amoy guild in the same city giving ten days credit on breadstuffs sales (ibid., 147, 150). Wen-chou millers, with a fixed leading group of sixteen millowners, could fix prices for a full month ahead (ibid., 175), while the Ning-po fishmongers' association, with a reserve fund of over $700,000, was able to control virtually every aspect of the fishing business: the boats, weights, quality, and retail outlets (ibid., 171; Jametel,

Chine, pt. 4).[48] Such fishing operations were aided, in turn, by carefully coordinated groups of ice makers who preserved their catches in the summer (Ku, *Ch'ing* 6:4, on ice; Jametel, *Chine*, 195, on Ning-po).[49]

Surviving inscriptions from various Ch'ing commercial groups give us valuable glimpses further into these mutually protective associations—and into the abuses which they either perpetuated or tried to protect themselves against. A number of texts from the city of Su-chou show how the dealers in pork products built their own hall, agreed on fair prices, arranged to prevent the pig slaughterers from taking part of their pay in pork instead of in cash, and finally so abused their power that they had to be publicly reprimanded by the financial commissioner of Kiangsu (Chiang-su po-wu-kuan, *Chiang*, 203–5).[50] Other incidents involved dried-seafood dealers organizing against dishonest brokers; bakeries and tea shops seeking official protection against thugs who took their food; and date merchants getting a guarantee that accurate weights should be used (ibid., 186–89). At least two other associations, that of the soy and bean curd dealers and that of the wine distillers, seem to have successfully defended their claims to have unlicensed competition suppressed or discouraged (ibid., 194–96).

Distribution and carriage of food was, of course, an immense business, involving vast numbers of people. Through surviving merchants' handbooks, it is possible to chart many of the trade routes followed and the important junctions on the way (Wilkinson, *Manuals*).[51] Also, at least for the later part of the Ch'ing, the meticulous work of the clerical staff in the Imperial Maritime Customs allows us to chart at least three different movements of food. A first would be the comparative levels of imports, by product, into a given province: Anhwei, for example, drawing massive amounts of brown sugar from Wu-hu, along with sizable purchases of mushrooms, pepper, and edible seaweed (China Imperial Maritime Customs, *Returns*, 135).[52] A second would be the different levels of goods purchased by different provinces, forwarded under transit passes to the interior: Nan-yang in Honan providing the largest market for brown sugar; Hsiang-yang in Hupei for nutmeg and sugar candy; Chungking, Szechwan, for seaweed, pepper, and cuttlefish; and Ch'ang-sha in Hunan for dried clams (ibid., 91–99). A third would be the exports of foods from China—major sellers, besides tea, being sugar, vermicelli, beans and bean cake, fruit, medicines, preserved vegetables, and rhubarb (ibid., 10). One side of this new entrance into the international food market that must be considered is the fact that Chinese farmers now became dependent on fluctuations of world trade prices. For example, as we can see from a report from Swatow in 1884, the increased beet production by European growers had an almost immediate impact on local Chinese prices (ibid., p. 313).

Among the many areas of retail and distribution that can be observed in the Ch'ing dynasty through surviving sources, we might note at least three major areas: restaurants, itinerant vendors, and cooks. Restaurants and inns, of course, existed at every level of expensiveness and taste in Ch'ing China. Those of eighteenth-century Yang-chou have remained famous and attractive through Li Tou's engaging work *Yang-chou hua-fang lu*. Here are the tourists crowding into the tea shops, famous for their snacks (Li, *Yang-chou*, 1:24b–25);[53] a restaurant that cooks lamb so well that people start queuing at dawn to get a serving (ibid., 9:10b–11); the mansion of a former merchant now made over into a restaurant, famous for its snacks and the beauty of the owner's daughter (ibid., 9–12b); the restaurant where the former pig seller "big-foot Chou" waits on tables, where you can get a fine meal and enough wine to make you drunk for two *ch'ien* and four fen, and where you can also watch cricket fights and fighting birds (ibid., 9:25). There were bars that stocked wine from all over the country and had special wines for every season (ibid., 13:1–2); there were restaurants famous for frogs' legs or for duck or for pigs' trotters in vinegar (ibid., 9:11); and there were others famous simply for good food, served in a beautiful setting by beautiful girls, where scholars could settle for an evening and write poems while they ate and drank (ibid., 15:3a). Famous in Yang-chou, also, were the floating boats that had given Li Tou's collection is name. Those desiring a special dinner could order in advance at a number of restaurants, and once the food had been prepared, it was transferred to one of the floating boats; there the host, with his guests and servants, could eat and relax, while ordering whatever wines they needed from the wine boats that floated nearby in attendance (ibid., 11:3, 16b–17). Many such boats were clearly exceptionally fine restaurants, though others served as meeting places for dallying, or literally as brothels, like those visited by Shen Fu in late-eighteenth-century Canton, which specialized in girls from various provinces (Shen, *Chapters*, 42–45). The latter boats were elaborately furnished with mirrors, beds, curtains, and lamps; at least by the late Ch'ien-lung reign, opium was served with the meals in such floating restaurants (ibid., 44), and by the late nineteenth century, opium smoking was common in Canton and had also spread to major restaurants in Peking (Jametel, *Chine*, 231–32; Jametel, *Pékin*, 251).[54]

In any small town, the inns and restaurants were the centers for social contact and gossip, as can be seen repeatedly in fiction like P'u Sung-ling's short story collection *Liao-chai chih-i* or Wu Ching-tzu's novel *Ju-lin wai-shih*. Buddhist temples also had their great kitchens, where people came to eat at festivals (Li, *Yang-chou*, 4:24b–25). According to one account, such temple kitchens vied for customers and, to enhance the flavor of their vegetarian meals, were not above cooking their noodles in a little chicken broth or having a cloth soaked in chicken fat, with which to touch up a bamboo shoot and mushroom broth (*Ch'ing-pai lei-ch'ao*, vol. 24, no. 56, pp. 47–48). At the level of the rural poor, restaurants and inns were natural social centers but could also be centers of elaborate frauds, as the magistrate Huang Liu-hung noted in the southern Shantung town of T'an-ch'eng; for there peasants coming into town to attend legal proceedings were forced to stay in special inns where their food bills were inflated by handouts to the yamen runners and other attendants. The result could be personal bankruptcy for the unwary (Huang, *Fu-hui,* 127).[55] For other poor people, the network of inns provided meeting places away from the watchful eyes of the state, where uprisings could be planned and weapons and money exchanged (Naquin, *Rising*).[56] Perhaps for this reason, the Ch'ing had, at least on the statute books, elaborate systems of registration for all those staying at inns, and these registers were meant to be turned over at regular intervals to the magistrate's yamen (Huang, *Fu-hui,* 214, 247).

A number of account books kept by travelers in Ch'ing China have recently been found and published by Fang Hao, and they enable us to get some detailed views of Ch'ing food costs. For example, restaurant receipts for the year 1747 in Hsiu-ning show that a sitting *(hsi)* with nine standard dishes cost 9 *ch'ien* (0.9 taels); the price for a sitting with nine large dishes was 1.08 taels (Fang, "Ch'ien-lung," 58);[57] soup for the whole table was 5 *ch'ien* extra. Possibly there were reductions for bulk orders, since an apparently similar dinner of nine standard dishes cost only 7.2 *ch'ien* when an order was placed for eleven sittings at one time. Such restaurants handled large orders, and a receipt has survived from the one referred to above (the Wang Wan-ch'eng kuan on Wan-an Street), showing an order placed for 156 bowls of noodles at 1.2 fen a bowl, for a total cost of 1.872 taels. From a surviving menu of the same restaurant, we know that an eleven-dish meal consisted of mixed cut meats, trotters, venison and dumplings, mussels, sharks' fins and fresh fish dishes, fresh chicken, and preserved eggs (ibid., 59).

For many travelers, however, such prices were prohibitive, and other account books show the care with which prices were compared and coppers doled out along the road: in November 1790, winter bamboo shoots, 30 cash per *chin* in Hang-chou, were up to 32 cash in Su-chou; pork was 80 cash per *chin*, beef 38 cash, mixed meats 72 cash, fish 50 cash, and chickens 115 cash each. In terms of general purchasing power, these foods can be compared with a *chin* of candles, costing 212 cash; a haircut, costing between 30 and 40 cash, depending on the location; or a *chin* of Shao-hsing or Su-chou wine, both priced at 28 cash per *chin* (Fang, "Chien-lung wu-shih-wu," 369).[58] The accounts of six examination students, traveling as a group to Nanking in 1875, enable us to compare some purchases across the span of a century and see that, despite the ravages of the Taiping Rebellion, many prices were remarkably close. Rice, which had cost the 1790 travelers 2.1 taels per picul (shih), had risen to 3.2 taels a picul by 1875; and pork fat, which had been 72 cash per *chin*, was up to 128; but plain pork was up only from 80 cash to 96 in Nanking, and it was still around 80 or as low as 75 in the countryside (Fang, "Kuang-hsü," 289–90).[59]

At the poorer levels, the restaurant network blended into the world of itinerant vendors and peddlers. The restaurants often had little sheds nearby, where a simple meal could be bought or taken home, or a concoction of leftovers from the restaurant's richer customers could be bought for a few cash (*Ch'ing-pai lei-ch'ao*, vol, 47, no. 92, p.12); there were stalls for coolies and for women who came to the coolies' place of work to sell their salted vegetables and rice (ibid., vol. 47, no. 92, p. 1). Even on tiny salaries, one could get something from such vendors: little candies of peanut and sugar or of spun sugar and molasses for one cash (MacGowan, *Sidelights*, 300); pastries for five cash, a slice of dried pork for seven, a bowl of conjee for ten, a full bowl of rice for twenty cash, and one of salt meat for forty (*Ch'ing-pai lei-ch'ao*, vol. 47, no. 92, p. 12). For those without any stoves or fuel, there were hot-water vendors who enabled a family to cook its own hot meal at the lowest possible cost (Yang and Tao, *Standard*, 75).

Paintings and woodblocks give a better sense of the variety than do words: early Ch'ing genre paintings show us a mother and her children buying soft drinks and a scholar tasting one of a large variety of teas. Other woodblock illustrations from downtown Peking in 1717 show an endless variety of stalls and booths and sheds, where the hungry and thirsty could rest a moment and refresh themselves. Many of these vendors had elaborate apparatuses for serving hot food or drinks and functioned as mobile restaurants; they too, like the innkeepers, served as centers for the exchange of news and gossip and also as the potential

Food stalls and restaurants along a Peking street, 1717 (from Wang Yuan-ch'i, ed., Wan Shou Sheng Tien, 1717)

carriers of the messages or weapons of revolt. They were also a prominent part of the festival life of the great cities. From Ku Lu's study of
Su-chou festivals during the Ch'ing, we can see how vendors responded
to the religious and seasonal cycle and, together with other retailers,
combined to enrich the diet of the urban dwellers: announced by written
signs or vendors' cries were the spring cakes of the first month; the green
dumplings (with lotus root) of the third month; the summer wines, sea
scallops, mustard greens, and salt eggs to celebrate summer's coming;
the special, heavy, round dumplings for the dragon-boat festival in the
fifth month; the watermelon at the autumn solstice; the delicate, coiled
cakes of sugar and flour sold at the autumn festival of the weaver and the
cowherd (Ku, *Ch'ing*).[60] As the year ran toward its end, there were the
glutinous rice dumplings with red bean stuffing for the kitchen god's
festival (these dumplings were also believed to soften the feet, so on this
day little girls' feet customarily received their first binding), the lake
crabs of the early winter (when the roe was at its most delicate), as well
as the many specialties prepared for the New Year festivities (ibid., 8:4;
10:3; chap. 12, passim).

But perhaps it is with the cooks that we should leave the last word.
They are not a widely known group, but they could become so abusive,
if attached to official households, that special proclamations had to be
issued to control their behavior around Su-chou (Chiang-su po-wu-kuan,
Chiang-su, 210–11). In Yang-chou their names were remembered with
some of the dishes that made them famous (Li, *Yang-chou*, 11:3). In
Peking a cook, after serving his apprenticeship in Canton, could rise to
own his own restaurant, employing a dozen porters to handle take-out
orders, with an extra four chefs on his own staff just to rent to wealthy
families (Jametel, *Pékin*, 269–72). Cooks from Shantung who had dominated the Ming imperial kitchens with their incomparable skill had yielded
to Manchu cooks, to cooks from Chekiang, and to some from Su-chou,
after Ch'ien-lung had been charmed by central Chinese cooking, and all
these cooks attached their names to their dishes (Su, *Dishes*, 18–19). In
his general cookbook, Yüan Mei had been quite hard on cooks: they
were usually rather petty people *(hsiao-jen)*, he wrote, who had to be
rewarded and punished if they were to be kept up to the mark (Yüan,
Sui-yüan, 13b). But in his literary collection, *Hsiao-ts'ang-shan fang wen
chi*, Yüan Mei included a biography of his own cook Wang Hsiao-yü
which is affectionate and informative. According to Yüan Mei, Wang
had decided to stay on in the Yüan household, despite its comparative
poverty, because he had a demanding and critically acute master who

really cared about food (Waley, *Yuan Mei*, 53). There may be a touch of literary embellishment in Yüan's analysis here and in the summary he gave of Wang's belief that cooking was like medicine—you had to apply your whole heart to the problem of diagnosis, so as to attain the perfect blending and balance (Yüan, *Hsiao-ts'ang*, 7:7).[61] But in his discussion of Wang at work, Yüan gave a fitting epitaph for some of the tastes and joys of Ch'ing cuisine:

> When he first came and asked what was to be the menu for the day, I feared that he had grand ideas, and I explained to him that I came of a family that was far from rich and that we were not in the habit of spending a fortune on every meal. "Very good," he said, laughing, and presently produced a plain vegetable soup which was so good that one went on and on taking it till one really felt one needed nothing more. . . . He insisted on doing all the marketing himself, saying, "I must see things in their natural state before I can decide whether I can apply my art to them." He never made more than six or seven dishes, and if more were asked for, he would not cook them. At the stove, he capered like a sparrow, but never took his eyes off it for a moment, and if when anything was coming to a boil someone called out to him, he took not the slightest notice, and did not even seem to hear. . . . When he said, "The soup is done," the kitchen-boy would rush up the tureen and take it, and if by any chance the boy was slow, Wang would fly into a terrible rage and curse him roundly. . . . I once said to him, "If it were a question of your producing your results when provided with rare and costly ingredients, I could understand your achievements. What astonishes me is that, out of a couple of eggs, you can make a dish that no one else could have made." "The cook who can work only on a large scale must lack daintiness," he replied, "Just as one who can handle common ingredients but fails with rare and costly ones can only be reckoned as a feeble practitioner. Good cooking, however, does not depend on whether the dish is large or small, expensive or economical. If one has the art, then a piece of celery or salted cabbage can be made into a marvellous delicacy; whereas if one has not the art, not all the greatest delicacies and rarities of land, sea or sky are of any avail." (trans. Waley, *Yuan Mei*, 52–53)

Medicine

There has already been an enormous amount of work on American missionary endeavors in nineteenth-century China. Donald Mac-Gillivray's *A Century of Protestant Missions in China, 1807–1907*[1] and *The China Mission Hand-book*[2] survey as much ground as any historian could hope to cover. Kenneth Scott Latourette's lucid synthesis, *A His-*

This essay first appeared in 1974, in *Medicine and Society in China*, edited by John Bowers.

tory of Christian Missions in China,[3] sliced up the chronological and sectarian terrain into manageable plots; and in their *History of Chinese Medicine*[4] K. Chimin Wong (Wang Chi-min) and Wu Lien-teh developed an even sharper chronology for periodization of the Western medical impact and provided an encyclopedic index of nineteenth-century physicians and topics that enables the researcher to roam at will. Apart from these basic works there are an immense number of missionary publications, pamphlets, biographies, surveys, periodicals, and archives, to which have now been added the new files of the China Records Project at the Yale School of Divinity library. As of the summer of 1972 the project had organized 5,120 vertical file folders of correspondence and had received 176 diaries and / or journals; the end of these new acquisitions was nowhere in sight.[5]

What is the value of this mass of material and the pioneer works that it has inspired? It can, of course, be used to compose biographies—hagiographic, dispassionate, or muckraking—of missionaries and physicians, or to recount the trials and vagaries of Western missions, hospitals, and medical schools. But that does not seem to be an urgent task, at least from the standpoint of contemporary studies of China's immediate imperial past. To me the great value of this material is that if we use it in a new way, asking fresh questions, and combine it with data drawn from Chinese sources, we can indeed increase our understanding of society in China.

Accordingly the direction of my interest is along a path that Ralph Croizier followed in his *Traditional Medicine in Modern China,*[6] a path made explicit in his subtitle, *Science, Nationalism, and the Tensions of Cultural Change.* The missionary record, by wittingly or unwittingly pointing to areas of tension and perplexity, can lead us to areas of normative behavior and clarity, much as Chinese legal and medical texts can do, although they often deal with the "abnormal" event. It can add to our knowledge of that society in ways that further our understanding of Joseph Levenson's trilogy, *Confucian China and Its Modern Fate (1958–1965),*[7] and help us to expand the argument, as Croizier has done; at the same time it can increase our sensitivity to the reasons for conflict between Westerners and Chinese late in the Ch'ing dynasty, and lead us to move further along the line of analysis begun by Paul Cohen in his *China and Christianity.*[8]

Since I am not a medical historian and have not made a detailed study of the field, I will limit myself to suggesting some themes that struck me as worthy of further exploration after I had read through medical reports and articles in the *China Medical Missionary Journal,* a sampling of hospital reports, usually in pamphlet form, and biographical memoirs of Western physicians. These materials have been supplemented, on the Chinese side, by the illustrated periodical *Tien-shih chai hua-pao* and the newspaper *Shen-pao,* which provided a general coverage exactly contemporary with the Western medical sources. After this very limited reading I was struck by the complexity of the questions that presented themselves, and what we might be able to learn by trying to answer them.

CHINESE ATTITUDES TOWARD WESTERN MEDICINE

We should perhaps start with the recipient, the Chinese patient. To what internal stresses was he subjected when he sought Western medical help, and what was the relationship between male and female doctors in his eyes? The pregnant wife of a boatman near Canton in the 1880s was unable to give birth, and her midwife gave up in despair. Finally, the neighbors suggested that her husband take her to the Western doctor at the Po-chi Hospital in Canton. This difficult decision he took, but on arrival at the hospital was confronted with another one: since the female doctor was away, could the male doctor examine her? To this again the boatman consented, only to be presented with a third decision: the mother could be saved only if the baby was removed by Caesarean section. Again the boatman agreed. The woman was tied down and given chloroform, a living baby girl was extracted, and the mother was sewn up and allowed to breast-feed after a rest of several days.[9]

For both wife and husband such an experience must have been truly extraordinary. Against what background can it be evaluated? American doctors such as John Thomson in 1893 inveighed against incompetent Chinese midwifery that was "left almost exclusively in the hands of ignorant women"; any moderate complications in delivery often led to lacerations of the vagina and cervix, to uterine rupture, even to the child's arm being torn off in cases of cross-presentation.[10] We must remember, however, that Thomson was deliberately trying to belittle Chinese expertise and, by implication, misrepresented the sophistication or safety of American hospital procedures. To the boatman, at least, the tradition of midwifery he had grown up with did not demand operations with knives, men fingering women, inducing unconsciousness by unknown means, or sewing up bodies with needle and gut.

The question of attitudes of Chinese patients toward Western medical practitioners in nineteenth-century China is an important and unexplored one. Numerous medical missionaries reported, as did Harold Schofield in Shansi during 1881, how their Chinese patients brought them little gifts of eggs, tea, cakes, wine, potatoes, apples, and flour.[11] But perhaps few were as honest as Schofield in reporting how such gratitude was matched by the controlled indifference of local constables and minor officials when he was repeatedly robbed in the same city in 1883, and how his stolen medical instruments were constantly recovered from local pawnshops, until another missionary finally caught the robber and delivered him bound up to the authorities.[12] To take one other example, robbers carved holes in the walls of John G. Kerr's Refuge for the Insane and tied up and robbed his native physician.[13]

Another question is whether Western doctors who provided free medical service were ever able to attain the dignity accorded to Chinese scholar-physicians. Ralph Croizier has written, "The highest prestige belonged to the scholar who practiced medicine purely out of benevolent motives, without any kind of pecuniary reward. . . . The essential thing was that all his treatment was given as a personal favor, or out of charity, never for financial gain."[14]

It seems improbable that Western doctors in nineteenth-century Chinese society could ever have allayed suspicions as to the motives behind their "benevolence"; rather, it is likely that the provision of free services would have engendered fresh antagonisms—either from literati who found yet another of their functions eroded or from Chinese doctors who found their livelihoods threatened. The practice of Chinese medicine was a complex professional task in its own right, and it is difficult to believe that foreign practitioners serving for free would not have upset existing balances. We have bits of evidence pointing to this kind of irritation: some Western doctors recorded how they were constantly called out on fake house calls by "pranksters" and then coldly received;[15] others worked in an uneasy truce with Chinese physicians, as in the case of an 1893 accident victim whose head injuries were treated by a Western physician, the inflammation of his arm by a Chinese.[16] Another doctor was able to make house calls only when he was accompanied by a Chinese patient he had cured and had agreed to "put on native dress."[17] Clearly, assessment of the physician's role needs to take account as much of such variations as of the better-known categories of "venerated doctor" or "victimized outsider."

Separating out local attitudes toward doctors from local attitudes toward missionaries is, of course, an even harder task. Surgical practices led to as many wild rumors as did those about missionary orphanages, however much the doctors denied them.[18] Actual medical practice may indeed have been a great deal less successful than some reports have led us naively to believe. Under the item "chlorodyne," in his *Contributions towards the Materia Medica* of 1871, Frederick Smith sarcastically noted, "Missionaries fond of dabbling in physic would do well to confine their exploits to the use of this single drug, so generally useful and harmless."[19] Parallel warnings might perhaps have been directed at other Western doctors who had ostensibly received a thorough medical training.

It is a question not only of whether doctors who chose to go to China were among the better practitioners in their own countries, which could be verified by examining their rank in the general hierarchy of American or British practice, but of whether their medical training was relevant to the problems encountered in China, a question that Dr. E. Gough asked herself in 1901.[20] We need to consider carefully whether some of the more dramatic medical programs, such as Peter Parker's constant excision of tumors, were medically beneficial in the long run and whether the regular use of opium derivatives in China, compared with their use in Western countries, answered Chinese needs. Thus we find Dr. V. P. Suvoong in Foochow giving a scholar named Hsü, already an opium addict, morphine injections to cure indigestion brought on by eating a surfeit of fresh crabs. While Suvoong observed that this increased Hsü's "faith in Western medicine," such a claim needs assessing, as does the practice of "curing" opium smokers by giving them heavy and regular doses of morphine a common practice among Western doctors in the late nineteenth century.[21]

In some areas, Western approaches to medical problems were clearly both innovative and of considerable benefit. The introduction of disease control and hygienic measures that led to an efficient plague prevention program is discussed by Carl Nathan; here I will look briefly at two other areas, one of which was education of the blind. The report of the Light-Giving School in Canton for the years 1906–10[22] outlines some of the practical and cross-cultural connections involved: the land for the school had to be cheap, so it was low and infertile; to raise the level, the blind girls themselves carried in the soil; they learned to read by means of Miss Garland's system of applying Braille to Mandarin; and they were taught to knit so as to make salable and revenue-raising products. By 1910, at which time boys were enrolled, the pupils were being taught the art of massage on lines developed in the Tokyo School for the Blind and the Deaf, so that they could go out into the world and earn a living.

KERR'S REFUGE FOR THE INSANE

Even more complex, in terms of interaction with society, must have been the issue of treating the insane. Here the pioneer was Kerr, who realized a twenty-five-year-old dream in 1898 when the doors of his Refuge for the Insane opened in Canton. Kerr's declared principles were, first, that insane patients were ill and should not be blamed for their actions; second, that they were in a hospital, not a prison; and, third, that patients must be treated as humans, not beasts. He pledged himself to conduct a course of treatment based on persuasion rather than force, on freedom rather than restraint, and on a healthy outdoor life with a maximum of rest, warm baths, and kindness. He also had the goal of providing patients with gainful employment where possible. Although there were frequent outbreaks of diseases in the hospital because the low-lying land was "a menace to health and life"—in 1907 alone there were outbreaks of diphtheria, beriberi, cholera, malaria, and dysentery—the refuge treated over two hundred male and female patients in a year, claiming "cures" for about 30 percent and "improvements" in 15 percent.[23]

Kerr observed that most of the patients were brought to him in chains,[24] and his descriptions suggest that at that time the insane were often treated as harshly as lepers.[25] But Kerr was a Westerner in a special kind of environment, dealing with a limited range of patients; the true effect of his work can be gauged only after we have studied general Ch'ing practices as reflected in the codes and the whole spectrum of regional or class variants. We do know that the directors of the Canton refuge worked closely with local Chinese officials and that large numbers of patients were referred to the refuge by the local police, who did not know how to handle them; for this, the refuge received an official allowance. Besides patients sent by the police, the refuge handled patients brought by local families, as well as those sent from Hong Kong and Wei-hai-wei by the British authorities.

We get flashes of evidence that show other potentially fruitful fields of inquiry. Scholars have made an attempt, for example, to compare the mental stresses involved in the Chinese mastery of Western culture with those placed on Chinese by their own, demanding examination system. Among the patients in the Canton refuge in 1909, we find a Chinese graduate of Columbia University who had been in the diplomatic service in the United States and Germany;[26] similar cases might be available for study.

In later years the refuge categorized patients according to symptoms, and if we could trace the way the definitions of these categories shifted over time, the figures for later periods might illuminate some of the problems endemic in Ch'ing society. In 1916, for example, of 276 "insane" patients in Canton, ninety men and thirty-one women were classified as having dementia praecox and forty-seven men and thirty-seven women as being manic depressive; by contrast, other cases were very few; seven suffering from alcoholic psychosis, three from senile dementia, and one from involutional melancholia.[27]

PHARMACEUTICAL ADVERTISEMENTS

Western medicine, like other fields of specialization, could be abused or misrepresented. Dr. Philip Cousland wrote in 1901 of the "ex–house boys, ex–hospital coolies, ex–school boys" who peddled medicines or advertised themselves as "practitioners of Western medicine."[28] As early as the T'ung-chih regime (1862–74), the pages of the newspaper *Shen-pao* were full of advertisements for medicines and cures. Based on a combination of Western commercial and medical practices and Chinese techniques of salesmanship, these advertisements are themselves an important source for study. Incorporating text and advertisements, we find in 1872 at least four categories:

1. The medicine is good because it is linked to traditional Chinese practices—as in the case of a medicine labeled "Pills for bloody stool or piles, good for men and women, old and young, safe for pregnant women, too, 500 *wen* per dose"; or because of the age of the formula it is offered as a public service—the ancient printing blocks have just been discovered, as in the case of an "eye-bath."[29]

2. The medicine is good because it has been handed down from generation to generation within a single family—"For cholera, vomiting, dysentery, and intestinal problems. Not good for pregnant women. Ho family private prescription."[30]

3. The medicine is good because it comes from heaven—"This prescription was chosen by Lü Tsu, Taoist patriarch of alchemy, via planchette, *chi-t'an*, and so comes from the Celestial Ministry of Medicine, *T'ien-i-yüan*. The Taoist Ma received this heavenly edict."[31]

4. The medicine is good because it is Western—"White powder to cure fever, invented by a Western doctor, first tried in America, all Westerners take it, sold in bottles at three *yüan*."[32]

By 1883, in a single issue of *Shen-pao* we can find more than a dozen medical advertisements, among them powders to keep the skin smooth, medicines to end indigestion, cures for coughs and wheezing, mouth-washes, and teeth cleaners. Some give interesting insights into the society. One is to make women with bound feet "be like a lotus," since it helps contract the foot muscles and squeeze the foot sharper without pain, at 56 *wen* a bottle; at 70 *wen* it comes with a lotion to cure foot rot. One practitioner, "just arrived in Shanghai from Hunan," uses religious charms, *fu*, to end difficult or unusual diseases, be they external or internal, without knife or acupuncture. He is staying in a hotel south of the foreign cemetery, and charges only 168 *wen* if you bring incense and candles. There is a remedy for epilepsy, as sold in Paris drugstores, which the French Dr. Lin worked on for twenty years; it can be bought at the British hospital for 5 *yüan* a bottle.[33]

Other advertisements speak of eye medicine from Japan, alerting Western historians to Japanese influences on China during the Kuang-hsü reign, which they have so far largely neglected; of restoratives for men; and of specialists in female diseases.[34] The text also gives hospital appeals and warns of Chinese doctors who refuse to go on house calls and so cause the death of certain patients.[35]

Another intriguing area of interaction between Chinese and Western society and medicine is that of cures of opium addiction. While some studies have been made of the establishment of anti-opium refuges, often directed by Western doctors and occasionally supported by local officials,[36] no systematic use has been made of Chinese records to examine this problem. A brief survey, again of advertisements in *Shen-pao*, suggests the following paradox: while Chinese hostility to opium smoking grew strong, and foreigners were blamed for bringing it to China, the prestige of Western medicine was high enough to ensure that most claims for anti-opium remedies emphasized their Western origins. Thus in 1872 we find a "foreign white powder to stop opium smoking and prevent you starting again,"[37] while the *Shen-pao* office offered for sale a bottle of twenty-four pills for 5 *ch'ien* (silver) made "specially by an English doctor to deal with the problem—better than all the other anti-opium remedies."[38] At the same time the Lao-te-chi drugstore claimed it had the only pills, "newly arrived, guaranteed, exclusive," all others being "fish-eyes posing as pearls."[39]

By the 1880s, however, perhaps reflecting the fact that a rural market was now being added to the treaty port market, large foreign firms such as Watson's, which specialized in anti-opium prescriptions,[40] were being jostled by a variety of Chinese products. A Kwangtung firm with a branch in Shanghai guaranteed cures and asked heaven to cease protecting it if any opium paste or ash was in its mixture. One shop offered "three-fragrance medicine" to cure a ten-year addiction in forty days; another offered to let you continue to smoke opium, mixed with its prescription, so that "be you retiring scholar or rich merchant, as you smoke you will stop."[41] One advertisement was for a book sponsored by a prince, a member of the imperial clan, and a Shanghai taotai: so good are the formulae in the book that the "accumulated oils of the opium will come out through the pores in the skin."[42]

Chinese merchants battled with Westerners for dominance of the anti-opium remedy market, just as Chinese opium growers from the 1870s onward began to compete seriously with Westerners for domestic opium sales.[43] We have neglected to study the Chinese side of the case in both areas.

ADAPTATION OF WESTERNERS

Similarly, in the area of cultural adaptability, we have constantly studied Chinese adaptation of western method and paid little attention to Western adaptation of Chinese methods. While some Westerners were content to decry the absence of sanitation, decent drugs, and common sense among the Chinese, others began to study the enormous corpus of Chinese materia medica and to standardize Western translations of Chinese medical terms. The initially limited goal of these projects is shown graphically in the preface to Smith's materia medica in 1871, in which he "hoped that for the purposes of travellers, military camps or gunboats in the interior, and Mission Hospitals, as well as Coolie-depots of Chinese residents in foreign countries, this work will have some practical value, in suggesting the best available remedies, or substitutes for foreign drugs dictated by necessity or economy."[44]

Other doctors began to show considerable ingenuity. H. W. Boone developed a special "ambulance" that could be slung between two bearers and used to carry poor patients, sheltered from rain or cold, in difficult terrain; the contrivance cost only $10.50 (Mexican) to construct.[45] William Wilson, isolated in west China, adapted a local condensing apparatus to make his own alcoholic spirits and nitrous ether, roasted local gypsum as a substitute for plaster of Paris, and made absorbent wool by boiling the local cotton wool in half an ounce of carbonate of soda and drying it in the sun. Struck by the fact that the most prevalent local complaint was scabies, that his patients were Moslems, and that the sulfur ointment he had been trained to use contained lard that was unacceptable to them, Wilson used local sulfur and lime to make his own unguent.[46]

These different themes, or aspects of them, have to be considered if we are to have a systematic study of the role of medicine and medical personnel in the community. Such a study must in turn be rooted in the context of traditional Chinese medical practice and literature. We need to read Western missionary and medical sources in the light of Chinese historiography, and to keep perspective by taking into account the slow process of medical professionalization in the West and the exaggerated or misinformed claims that have often been made. We will then have a reasonable background against which to assess even such apparently absurd items as that in *Tien-shih-chai hua-pao* describing a remarkable European gentleman in New York who was given to eating glass and magnets, gasoline and candle wax, sulfuric acid and mercury—a diet that made smoke come out of his mouth.[47] Even here we might not be so far from reality as we might think; the man may have been some kind of performer, not unlike one of William Lockhart's Chinese patients who had been a successful practitioner of the hook-and-needle trick until he made a mistake and ended up with six needles piercing his esophagus in different directions. After five days of intense pain, and despite Lockhart's ingenious attempted remedies, the juggler, who was also an opium addict, died.[48] If something so apparently extraordinary could have a mundane explanation, then we must remember the converse as we read in the same periodical the brief account of some senior Chinese officials in Shanghai who supported the introduction of smallpox vaccination; when the doctor who had done the vaccinations left, the group retained another doctor to set up a clinic in the British concession and give free vaccinations.[49] The historical background to such a brief transaction is extremely complex.

The pioneer role of young Chinese women doctors such as Ida Kahn and Mary Stone has also not been explored. Chinese women with unbound feet, they graduated from the University of Michigan Medical School and in 1896 returned to Kiukiang, where they opened a free clinic. While contemporary Western sources record that they were apparently well received both by the local people and by the local Chinese doctors, since we do not know the professional level of the latter, we cannot readily gauge the level of acceptance.[50] Nor can we tell, without more research, whether the fact that the women were Chinese helped such local acceptance of their Western skills as there was.

The question is a large one: the treatment by Chinese of Chinese Christian converts in the 1900s may be just one line of a difficult equation in which we must be sophisticated about considering *types* of foreign learning, *sex* of the *recipient,* and *nature* of the occupation (translator, comprador, student, doctor, and so on). This line of inquiry could lead to an even less understood area, that of racial intermarriage. One intriguing example from Chungking early in the twentieth century is that of a German doctor who married his Chinese maid and who was boycotted by both the Chinese and the Western communities.[51]

These questions, like that of adoption, have been almost totally unexplored. Perhaps a start could be made by following through on Chinese students successfully trained in China by Western doctors. Leads to this end are provided by tables such as the one compiled by James Boyd Neal, and printed in the 1898 edition of *The China Medical Missionary Journal* (table 1). These students were also learning some medical techniques through the journal, which had announced in its inaugural editorial in 1887, "We spend our lives among a strange people, uncongenial to us in their ways."[52] Such medical education must be seen in terms of the Chinese educational environment, where, presumably because of prudery, we find detailed illustrations of the penis and testicles removed even from imperial editions of anatomical texts,[53] and where curious doctors had to study the human viscera on the execution grounds or in animal equivalencies, because of the prohibitions against dissections.[54]

Given the richness of the sources, the accumulation of examples could continue indefinitely; I hope I have provided enough here to show the range and variety of problems and interactions.

KERR'S GUIDEBOOK TO CANTON

In conclusion, we might consider the varied elements that made up the medical community in China, even if an understanding of how they interacted demands knowledge that I do not have. Westerners in China did not usually look at communities from this perspective. John Kerr lived and worked for a long time in Canton, and when he wrote a guidebook to the city, he included information on many kinds of medical institutions.[55] There were major medicine shops and pharmacies grouped along Tseung-lan Street; in the Poon family mansion in the seventeenth ward, there was a "native dispensary and club" developed at a cost of $60,000, whose current expenses were met with real estate income; it had three doctors giving free care, a coffin supply, a free school, and a

Table 1: Chinese Students Trained in Western Medicine (Late Nineteenth Century)

Location	Physician	Number Trained	Number in Mission Employ	Number in Private Practice	Men Now in Training	Women Now in Training	Total Already Trained and Now in Training	Years Required
Canton	Kerr	79	Not known	Not known	18	6	103	3 or 4
Tientsin–Viceroy's Hospital	Houston	—	—	—	26	—	26	—
Soochow	Park	9	5	3	10	6	25	5
Hangchow	Main	12	7	5	8	3	23	5
Hongkong	Thomson	7	—	7	12	—	19	5
Foochow	Whitney	14	2	10	3	—	17	5
Chingchowfu	Watson	16	8	5*	None	None	16	—
Foochow	Masters	6	2	4	—	9	15	6
Moukden	Christie	9	2	7	6	—	15	5
†Chinanfu	Neal	10	3	7	5	—	15	4
Peking	Curtiss	4	2	2	9	—	13	4
P.otingfu	Atterbury	13	—	13	None	None	13	6
Foochow	Goddard	4‡	None	None	—	6	10	6
Nanking	Stuart	4	1	2§	5	—	9	5
Changchow	Fahmy	3	—	3	6	—	9	5
Chungking	McCartney	3	3	—	5	—	8	5
Sioke	Otte	4	—	4	4	—	8	5
Kinhwa	Barchot	2	1	1	4	—	6	5
Kakchieh	Scott	3	3	—	3	—	6	4
Ch'aochowfu	Cousland	—	—	—	4	—	4	5

Eng-chhun	Cross	—	—	—	4	—	4	5
Pingtu	Randle	1	—	—	3	1	4	4
Chinchow	Brauder	—	—	1	2	1	4	4
Chentu	Kilborn	—	—	—	3	—	3	4
Miscellaneous		65	22	41	21	1	87	—
	15 places in all	268	61	115	161	33	462	

* Three dead.
† Dr. Johnson of Ichowfu assisted in the training of one class of five students.
‡ All dead.
§ One dead.
Source: James Boyd Deal, in *China Medical Missionary Journal* 12 (1898).

dental office; Mary Fulton's hospital for women was on To P'o Street, as was the Roman Catholic orphanage, staffed by Chinese nurses; in the northern suburbs was the "City of the Dead," where coffins were deposited for a $10 fee and a monthly rental until the omens were propitious or a good burial site was found; after fanning the god in the Temple of the God of Medicine the worshipers would take the fans home to fan the suffering patients in their own families; the massive Po-chi Hospital, were Sun Yat-sen studied, established by Parker and developed by Kerr, had 300 inpatient beds by 1904, and spread over eleven buildings in the southern suburbs; the home for old men; the foundling hospital, established in 1698, for 300 children, with one wet nurse for every four infants; the Yung-sheng Temple, with its own depository for coffins and altars for worship; the home for old women; an enormous home for the blind with 500 rooms, each holding four inmates, who begged and made handicrafts to supplement their allowance of 6 *mace* a day; the nearby leper community; another coffin depository; the Protestant cemetery; and the cemetery for criminals. In Honam were the major coffin makers; the Temple for Mothers and Children, with the twenty deities who guarded each stage of childhood; the large Jen-chai "Native Hospital"; the customs opium godown; the mission houses of the American Scandinavian Mission and the United Brethren in Christ; the foreigners' cemetery; and the Hospital for the Insane.[56]

This was the late Ch'ing world, which me must investigate if we are to begin to understand either the Western medical endeavor or China's response to it: a multifaceted, overlapping, and ambiguous world, as rich in echoes of the past as in the variety of the present, as rich in present variety as in dreams of the future.

Taxes

Among the great and enduring questions in the study of Chinese history are these: In an agricultural country of such extraordinary size, how was the land farmed and what were the patterns of ownership and tenancy? How was the rural revenue extracted from the farms and apportioned to the different sectors of the imperial bureaucracy? What

This essay first appeared in 1986, in the *New York Review of Books*.

was the ideology that served as the country's social bond, and what was the relation to the state of the scholars who created that ideology? The scale of these questions and the span of China's history make definitive answers elusive; but the recent appearance of three remarkably fine books by Madeleine Zelin, Philip Huang, and Benjamin Elman certainly takes us a major step forward in our attempts to find explanations.[1]

The fact that all three books concentrate on eighteenth-century China—Zelin's entirely so, Huang's to a significant extent, and Elman's in great measure—testifies to an important change that has taken place in the recent historiography of China. In studies of late imperial China, at least those written in America, there have been several broad shifts in emphasis over the last forty years. The first important field of research was that of nineteenth-century Chinese reactions to the pressures of Western trade, warfare, and technology. By the later 1960s, though there were still important studies of nineteenth-century history, the attention of many scholars moved to the specifics of the 1911 revolution, which brought down the Ch'ing dynasty, and to the era of warlordism and emerging Communist organizations that followed.

By the later 1970s a significant number of able young scholars were turning backward. They were beginning to explore the history of the later Ming dynasty, the reasons for that dynasty's collapse in 1644, and the reactions of the intelligentsia to life under the successor Ch'ing dynasty in the second half of the seventeenth century. In the mid-1980s we suddenly reached a new stage, one in which we began to get a sense of eighteenth-century China as a whole.

Each of the three new studies considered here makes a clearly stated point which is of considerable polemical importance for understanding the shape of Chinese history and which is designed to stop us from giving undue weight to the place of Western imperialism in China's recent history. Madeleine Zelin, in *The Magistrate's Tael*, suggests that the failure in the late eighteenth century to maintain the impetus of earlier financial reforms proves that the economic disasters of the nineteenth century—seen by other historians as crucial precursors of revolution in the twentieth century—were in fact mere sequels to a pattern fixed a century earlier.

Philip Huang's study of the peasant economy of north China, after a careful examination of land tenure in the eighteenth century, concludes that patterns making rural labor a semiproletariat, the development of managerial farms, and the dangerous overreliance on certain specialized cash crops such as cotton long antedated the impact of the world market on China. Hence these cannot be seen just as recent phenomena trigger-ing revolutionary tensions.

In his analysis of the shift "from philosophy to philology," Benjamin Elman finds that the eighteenth-century Confucian scholars conducting "evidential research" had themselves begun the systematic unraveling of classical Confucian beliefs that is often attributed to nineteenth-century Chinese scholars reeling under the impact of the military and technolog-ical superiority of the West.

One should add that all three of these studies not only show a remark-able grasp of Chinese archival materials and difficult printed sources but are also deeply grounded in the works of contemporary Japanese schol-ars on late imperial China. (For those whose Japanese is less than fluent, two new publications offer a large sampling of recent Japanese scholar-ship in English translation, so readers can gauge for themselves how use-ful, varied, meticulous, and often combative current Japanese research can be.)[2]

The magistrate's "tael" of the title of Madeleine Zelin's study refers to the exchange unit of one ounce of silver that was used during the Ch'ing dynasty as the official currency for paying tax assessments. The "magis-trate" was the official in charge of county administration, whose duty it was to supervise the collection of local taxes from the landowners in his jurisdiction. There were some fourteen hundred counties in the 1730s, and their magistrates were the crucial link in the chain that drew a per-centage of the profits of China's farms to the treasuries of the court in Peking. Most magistrates had passed the highest levels of China's state examinations system, so they may be considered learned men, at least in the intricacies of Confucian textual history, even if they did not neces-sarily have much financial or administrative experience before taking office.

Zelin concentrates on the period of the emperor Yung-cheng, who ruled China from 1723 to 1735. Like other scholars before her, she sees Yung-cheng as a talented and vigorous imperial reformer, with a passion for administrative detail and efficiency; she has little to say about the emperor himself, but she goes far beyond those scholars in her financial analysis, since she was able to make extensive use of the financial archives of the period that are stored partly in the Palace Museum collection in Taipei and partly in the Number One Historical Archives in Peking. The result is a meticulous and, to the specialist, wholly engrossing study of the interconnections between imperial decision making and the rural rev-enue collection system.

Far from accepting any clichés about a stagnant China, Zelin writes that we "must learn to look at China in the late-imperial period as a dynamic state, struggling to devise its own formula for rational and efficient bureaucratic rule." She finds evidence for this dynamism in the relationship between the emperor Yung-cheng and financial specialists like T'ien Wen-ching, and their decision to work out a system that would impose a standard surcharge on the basic land tax.

Though this may not sound dramatic to us today, Zelin argues persuasively that it had the greatest importance in the 1720s. What was at issue was the creation of a workable tax base for China's separate provinces, so that they would have sums of money available to pay adequate salaries to the magistrates and to undertake important local work projects for irrigation, land improvement, communications, and education. By retaining this money in the provinces, peasant proprietors would be spared myriad special levies and illegal exactions, while local administrators would be freed from the delays and dishonesty of the centralized bureaucracy, and be able to devise imaginative and independent programs which—cumulatively—would strengthen the country as a whole.

The changes were carried through most effectively in the northern and northwestern provinces, particularly Shansi, Honan, Chihli, and Shensi; here the landholdings were on a small scale and tax collection and supervision were relatively simple. In the southwest, and on the southeast coast, things were more difficult: the provinces had low tax bases to begin with, and a number of special costs to bear, including the pacification of aboriginal populations and the maintenance of coastal defense. And especially in Kiangnan—comprising the two east Yangtze provinces of Kiangsu and Anhwei, traditionally the richest area of China and one with powerfully entrenched landlord special interests—the emperor and his staff ran into virtually insuperable problems of local resistance.

In *The Magistrate's Tael* Zelin describes the types of resistance and the efforts of the imperial squad of over seventy skilled bureaucrats to push through fair reforms. Her chapter on these matters is a splendid example of sustained investigative scholarship, as she leads the reader into the realms of proxy and overlapping registrations, manipulation of famine rice and timber sales, clerical embezzlement, false flood reports, secretly coded tax record books, juggled receipt stubs, and crooked mortgage documents. (It should be assigned reading for anyone seeking to reform tax systems today.)

In her conclusion to this chapter, which sets the scene for the failure of the tax reforms later in the eighteenth century, Zelin notes that the Ch'ing reformers could never have got their way "without a vastly expanded bureaucracy capable of supplanting the informal networks of local power." This the society could neither tolerate nor afford. By the end of the eighteenth century in China, "rational fiscal administration was dead, and informal networks of funding once again became the hall-mark of the Chinese bureaucracy," though now the population was over 300 million, and the fragmentation of peasant holdings and the commer-cialization of the economy were proceeding apace.

Philip Huang's analysis of the peasant economy enlarges on this story and gives it a rather different emphasis. Like Zelin, Huang sees major changes occurring in eighteenth-century China, most importantly in the development of a growing distance between the rich peasant managerial farms that hired labor, on the one hand, and, on the other, the poor peasants and agricultural workers who sold their labor. Huang sets his changes against the background of a growing population, inheritance that was divisible, changing crop patterns, and selective development of commercial farming, particularly of cotton. He concludes that there is "no question that the small peasant economy of North China underwent dynamic change long before China's contact with the modern world economy."

In several ways Huang's analysis is richer than Zelin's since he con-centrates on a far longer period and goes into immense detail about a number of rural communities in north China—specifically in Hebei province and western Shandong. (Huang prefers the new "pin-yin" romanization. These provinces were originally rendered as Hopeh and Shantung.)

He was able to extract such detailed information by an ingenious use of sources. Starting with the extremely thorough surveys made under the auspices of the Japanese South Manchurian Railway Company between 1935 and 1942 (the "Mantetsu surveys"), Huang compiled data on thirty-three villages which could be classified into seven different categories according to their levels of commercialization. He then received permis-sion to go to several of the same communities in the early 1980s, to study the land-use patterns under the People's Republic, and to interview peas-ants about the details of past landholding and cropping patterns. In the Ch'ing dynasty archives in Peking he examined the cases presented before the Board of Punishments involving homicides related to land use and tenancy for the region during the eighteenth century (most especially during 1736, 1737, and 1796) as well as the Baodi (Paoti) county punish-ment office archives as these related to problems of rural tax collection between 1800 and 1911.

Huang's book is extraordinarily rich, and I believe it to be the best sustained study of rural north China yet written. He is interested in a great many theories concerning peasant production and entrepreneurship, and he leads us through the technical literature on these topics with clarity and fairness. He evokes the ecological setting of the region from dry upland to marshy lowland, noting the wells, the irrigation works, the patterns of settlement, and the strength (or lack of it) of lineages. He analyzes the effectiveness of labor use on managerial farms in the 1930s, and then backtracks to study the development of such farms in the early Ch'ing dynasty, the relationship of "hired worker-serfs" on great estates to freeholders, and the class composition of the landholding class as a whole. He looks at the steady growth of tenancy, the parceling out of holdings, the social relations between small landlord and landowning agricultural workers, the development of sharecropping contracts, and the contrasts in efficiency between managerial farms and small family farms. Central to this analysis is his careful study of human and animal productivity, in an agricultural environment where—as Huang illustrates in detail—one laborer's daily wages were precisely equal to the cost of one day's donkey fodder.

The survival of millions of uneconomical, even below-subsistence, tiny farms into the 1930s leads Huang to pose some of his most searching questions on the interconnections of farming with local handicrafts and partial commercialization, the hiring out of labor in the busiest seasons, at the very time when, of course, it was needed on its own farm, and the downward spiral that resulted from such practices when the farmers also became disastrously linked to a depression-prone world economy with violent price fluctuations in certain cash crops. Huang summarizes the process in one of his many succinct and effective formulations:

> The combined workings of population pressure and social stratification on a stagnant peasant economy thus resulted in a tenacious system that was particularly vicious in human terms. Poor peasants came to be locked into a dual dependence on family farming and hiring out, unable to do one without the other, and compelled to accept below-subsistence incomes from both. Their cheap labor, in turn, propped up a nonproductive landlordism and a stagnant managerial agriculture. Poor peasants, more than anyone else in the rural society, had to labor under the mutually reinforcing pressures of overpopulation and unequal social relations.

A good part of Huang's discussion also concerns the relations of the village and the state; here he sees considerably more isolation and insularity than most recent analysts of rural China have tended to do, and he also notes how the post-Ch'ing state tried to penetrate below the county level, but only succeeded on an extensive scale after the revolution in 1949.

Did this "success" bring great change? In general welfare, yes, but, as Huang points out, his central finding concerns the "formation over several centuries of a poor-peasant economy and society under the twin pressures of involution and social stratification, without the relief of dynamic economic growth." As a consequence, the shape of collectivization in the People's Republic was more predetermined than we might have realized. The Communist production brigades and teams, like the old, desperate farms, were units "of both production and consumption, which under severe subsistence pressures will tolerate agricultural involution [that is, retrogression in productivity] to an extent unthinkable for a capitalist enterprise. Like the family farm, the collective does not fire its surplus labor."

One might add, parenthetically, that Huang's work has not lost topicality with the promulgation of new reforms in the People's Republic which are abolishing much of the collective farming system. To the contrary, his work will be essential background reading to understanding what choices the Chinese now really have, and what the greatest dangers confronting them are. As he shows in chapter 10 of *The Peasant Economy*, many of the achievements in the People's Republic are the result of new developments made possible by the scale of socialist investment, especially in state-financed irrigation works that allowed for more vegetable growing and intercropping, the drainage and regrading of waterlogged land previously restricted only to sorghum growing, tractors that allowed faster plowing and sowing and thus altered the small work-to-land ratios of earlier times, and state hog-raising policies that boosted fertilizer supplies. The challenge will be to see if newly entrepreneurial farmers can build on these foundations a pattern of prosperity that does not drive new generations of workers back onto the downward slope of subsistence farms and forced sale of their own labor.

In discussing the "underdevelopment" of managerial farming in Ch'ing China, Huang suggests that the wealthier Chinese had generally understood that even the most successful farming could lead to only limited profits and that the big money was to be made either in commerce and loan operations or especially by passing the state examinations and entering the imperial bureaucracy. Landowning as a source of ultimate wealth was quite different from managerial farming for one's own sake, and "in this upper tier, a family needed to secure an office only once in several generations to be able to own land on a scale unthinkable for the average managerial farmer."

That this gives an excessively rosy picture of Ch'ing bureaucratic life is, I think, convincingly shown by Zelin's analysis of the difficulty of getting adequate salaries in the provincial bureaucracy, by the unstable conditions of rural office holding, and by the constant risks of dismissal or fines for actual or alleged incompetence. Huang's view also suggests a continuity in the intellectual world of the bureaucracy and in the Confucian components of the state examination.

In fact, as Benjamin Elman expertly demonstrates in *From Philosophy to Philology,* the eighteenth-century intellectual world of Ch'ing China was a turbulent place in which major shifts were occurring. In particular, Confucian scholars were beginning to use the "exact sciences" of linguistics, philology, and mathematics to analyze their own cultural past, especially the works of the Confucian inheritance from which they drew the premises of ethical government.

Reading Elman's admirably lucid analysis of eighteenth-century intellectual trends in the light of Zelin's and Huang's studies is instructive, for the three books together give us a fine survey of the ways that land-tenure relationships and imperial attempts to modify the entrenched powers of local gentry accompanied the search for certainty in scholarship. Ch'ing scholars felt betrayed by the immediate past, when the Ming dynasty had collapsed in the face of domestic rebellions and Manchu attacks; they sought reasons for that collapse not just in the military, economic, and political spheres, but also in those of morality and philosophy. They concluded that Confucian scholarship had lapsed into empty speculation on metaphysical issues; and they sought, through the careful examination of early texts, calligraphy, and archaeological remains, to get a sharper grasp of Confucius' original intentions.

In pursuing this research, they went back behind the Sung dynasty (A.D. 960–1279) commentaries and analyses (which had dominated early Ch'ing thought) to the later Han period (A.D. 25–220) and eventually to the earlier Han (202 B.C.–A.D. 9), edging ever nearer to what they thought were true Confucian origins. In doing so, they brought all their skills to bear on evaluating the Confucian canon: as early as the 1690s certain key "Confucian" texts had been proved forgeries, and by the mid-eighteenth century the body of Confucian wisdom was being treated as history, and history itself was being tightened in definition. "The writing of history is the recording of the facts," as Wang Ming-sheng put it in 1787. "Overall, the goal is simply to ascertain the truth. Besides the facts, what more can one ask for?"

Elman speculates on the effects that Chinese knowledge of Western science and mathematics (derived mainly from the writings of Jesuit missionaries) might have had on this belief that new kinds of certainty were possible in scholarship, and he quotes the Ch'ing historian Ch'ien Ta-hsin's revealing comment that "in ancient times, no one could be a Confucian who did not know mathematics," whereas later generations "usually denigrated those who were good mathematicians as petty technicians." By default this left the field to Westerners, wrote Ch'ien, for in their computations there would not be "the most minute discrepancy." Just as Huang leaves us thinking about Deng Xiaoping's dismantling of China's recent collectivization, so Elman forces us to reflect on the new "seeking truth through facts" that is allegedly at the center of China's new pragmatism and modified Marxism.

Elman places his eighteenth-century thinkers in a richly evoked setting. In a series of deft and original chapters, we are told not only what they thought but also how and where they thought: about their academies and schooling, their economic backgrounds (many were from merchant stock), their libraries and their diaries, and their social conventions. We also learn how books were printed and by whom, and the arguments for use of movable type as opposed to xylography on wood blocks. In a useful corrective to accepted beliefs about printing, Elman points out that in China movable type was the more expensive option— woodblocks could be stored easily, and small runs of a given item printed as needed, whereas with movable type one had to gauge the needed print run accurately and face the high costs of dismantling and reordering the type. But the destruction of so many sets of the woodblocks in the major foreign and civil wars of the mid-nineteenth century was one of the reasons for the decline of the research centers of the literati in Kiangnan and the shift to new centers in the south, such as Changsha and Canton.

Historians of science have long since explained to us how shifts appear in fields of knowledge and how new "paradigms" are slowly formed from a number of apparently disconnected investigations, so eventually what seemed to be "anomalous" becomes the expected. My guess is that we are now witnessing something similar in Western studies of eighteenth-century China,[3] as China's last great period of independent growth and strength is assessed afresh, free from hindsight that ties indigenous developments either to foreign imperialism or to Maoist ideas of the necessity of rural revolution.

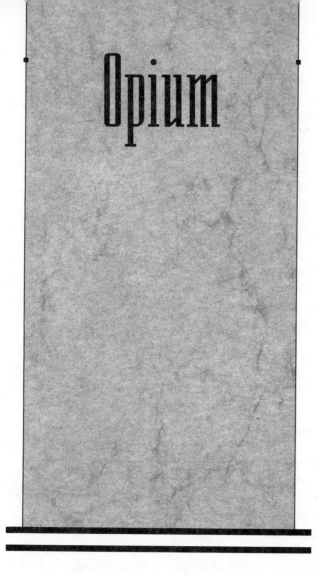

Opium

Opium addiction in Ch'ing China is a large subject.[1] At one level, it is a story of international trade, warfare, and diplomacy. At another level, it concerns the psychic needs or the demoralization of individual Chinese, and the local economic arrangements that were made to grow

This essay first appeared in 1975, in *Conflict and Control in Late Imperial China*, edited by Frederic Wakeman and Carolyn Grant.

and to distribute the prepared opium. At yet another level, it concerns the most complex interactions between Western powers and individual Chinese: the triumph of trading interests over morality and the collapse of older agricultural ideals; the linkage of "evil" with "the foreigner"; the growth of special interest groups such as Canton merchants, Triads, Shansi bankers, and Parsee firms; shifts in Chinese taxation patterns; and the final shattering of images of the emperor as paternal protector.

To date most studies on opium in China have focused on the areas of international commerce and diplomacy.[2] Here I attempt to widen the area of debate by developing certain themes that show opium smoking as a phenomenon that radically affected all levels of Chinese society. Furthermore, I have attempted to marshal the data in certain categories that will encourage two areas of comparative study: first, opium addiction as a problem of deviance and control in Ch'ing China, and second, opium addiction as an economic and social problem that can be compared with drug dependencies in other cultures. The categories I have tried to isolate are consumption, prohibition, distribution, and economic function.

One other category, that of motivation, should have a section for itself; only the data are extraordinarily elusive. Opium was highly regarded in China, both as a medicinal drug (which checked diarrhea and served as a febrifuge)[3] and as an aphrodisiac.[4] Therefore, people might become addicted either because they took opium intensively during an illness—for instance, in the great cholera epidemic of 1821[5]—or because they had vigor, leisure, and money and wanted to make the best of it.[6]

Such general considerations aside, it is obvious that different occupational and economic groups had different motivations, but in many cases one can only guess what these might have been. For the eunuchs and members of the imperial clan, there was a boring life in sheltered circumstances, without the possibilities of release that political power had given them in other times—for instance, the late Ming for eunuchs or early Ch'ing for the Manchu nobles.[7] Soldiers, whether banner or green standard, faced similar elements of boredom, compounded by a routine life and their being barred from release through trade or other gainful employ; furthermore, the officers were unlikely to use the opium-addicted soldier in crucial combat situations.[8] For Chinese literati, mu-yu (private secretaries), and officials, opium provided a relief from career frustrations and stresses generated within the family;[9] it may also, for Chinese humiliated by their positions under barbarian conquerors, have been a surrogate for withdrawal, a form of eremetism in one's own home. If such a proposition has any validity, things must have been even more depressing after 1842, when the Manchu overlords were themselves humiliated. This may explain why a man like the famous translator of Western political theory Yen Fu became an addict.[10] Merchants sometimes smoked because they believed opium sharpened their wits and helped them to drive shrewder business deals with their competitors.[11] They and other wealthy Chinese also took and offered opium to guests after dinner parties as a social gesture.[12] Students took opium during their key state examinations, thinking that it helped them to do better.[13]

Sometimes the explanations for addiction are rather tortuous; thus, the *Gazetteer of Amoy* reported that many rich Chinese encouraged their sons to stay at home and smoke opium rather than indulge in debauchery or gambling.[14] This motive, with an additional social twist, was sufficiently accepted to provide the theme for the first feature film made by a Chinese production company, *Wronged Ghosts,* shot by the Huei Hsi company in 1916. The synopsis of the film begins, "A wealthy miser has a son who is enthusiastic about public welfare and gives money generously to relieve the poor. His father fears that the family fortune will be wasted in the son's hands, and he persuades the son to start smoking opium, hoping that this will keep him idle and at home."[15]

For the rich, or those with some surplus cash, the rewards held out by opium must have been sharper perception, greater social ease, removal from present worries, and a pleasing distortion of time sequences; unfortunately, there is no literature in praise of opium that can match the euphoric compendia on tobacco written by eighteenth-century Chinese.[16]

Those who ate regularly and well did not show physical deterioration resulting from their addiction;[17] but for the poor, addiction was a serious health hazard (even though, ironically, it was often first taken for health reasons), since scarce cash resources were used to purchase opium rather than food. The rewards for the poor were a blurring of the pains of prolonged labor, and an increase in work capacity over short periods of time.[18] Thus there was heavy addiction among coolies and chair bearers,[19] boatmen who had to work their boats upstream, and stonecutters working outside in cold weather.[20] The last Chinese to become addicted seem to have been the peasants, though as they grew more opium crops the incidence of heavy opium smoking rose, and by 1902 one could find entire rural communities that were in desperate straits because addiction had become almost total.[21]

By the late Ch'ing, it seems, no major occupational group was without its addicts. We can give individuality to some of these forgotten opium smokers by describing them in terms of their relationships: they were

Ch'en Tu-hsiu's grandfather, Kuo Mo-jo's brother, Feng Yü-hsiang's parents, Hu Shih's stepbrother, Ch'ü Ch'iu-pai's father, Lu Hsun's father.*[22] Others survive only in fiction—the lean servants in Pa Chin's *The Family* who told their stories to Chieh-hui while the little boy, rapt, watched the light of the opium lamps play over their faces.[23]

We cannot tell why they all smoked; but we can, at least, begin to sketch in the story of why the opium was available to them.

CONSUMPTION

The habit of opium smoking in China was an offshoot and development of tobacco smoking. Tobacco reached the Fukien coast sometime late in the Wan-li reign (1573–1619)[24] and was first transplanted in the Shih-ma area of Chang-chou.[25] Tobacco grew so luxuriantly in China that it rapidly became an important domestic cash crop, dashing the Portuguese hopes for developing an oriental outlet for their Brazilian tobacco.[26] By the K'ang-hsi reign, tobacco smoking was a national Chinese habit; Shih-ma and other brand names were inscribed on the shop signs of hundreds of tobacco retail stores in downtown Peking,[27] and large fields of tobacco were growing just outside the city walls.[28]

The earliest Chinese reference that I have found to the fact that opium, too, could be smoked is a comment by the Ming dynasty scholar Chang Ju-lin (who died in 1626) that appears in the *Gazetteer of Macao.* Appended to a note on snuff he has this remark: "There is also opium (*ya-p'ien-yen*); in a raw state it looks like mud, but it can be treated so that it's smokable. There's a prohibition against selling it."[29] The delight taken by Chang Ju-lin and his family in the widest range of sensual delights is well known,[30] and they would be worthy candidates for the mixed honor of being China's first opium smokers. There is evidence that Chinese in Jakarta were smoking opium as early as 1617, and Chinese in Batavia were dealing in opium and tobacco mixtures in 1671.[31] More detailed records on opium smoking appear in the 1690s, when the Dutch physi-

---

*This roster shows the extraordinary prevalence of addiction among the families of major figures in twentieth-century China: Ch'en was dean of Peking University and cofounder of the Chinese Communist party, Kuo a leading romantic poet, Feng one of the most powerful warlords, Hu China's leading philosopher, Ch'u the first Chinese journalist in the Soviet Union and later secretary-general of the Chinese Communist party, and Lu China's greatest modern short story writer and essayist. Pa Chin's *Family* was China's most popular novel in the 1930s.

cian Engelbert Kaempfer was in Java and noticed shops that sold pipefuls of opium mixed with tobacco to passersby.[32] Opium smoking may have been introduced to Taiwan by the Dutch when they controlled the island early in the seventeenth century, but again the first careful description comes only much later—in a comment given by the Ch'ing dynasty official Lan Ting-yuan in 1724, after he had returned from the campaign against Chu I-kuei.[33]

Lan described opium smoking as being a harmful trap, set by the barbarians in Taiwan to ensnare Han Chinese: neophytes were given free meals and free opium at first but, once hooked, were made to pay. Addiction was common in Taiwan, and smoking had been widespread in Amoy for over ten years. Lan gave no details about smoking methods, save that the opium was "heated in a copper pot and smoked through a pipe like a short club." But Huang Shu-ching, who recorded his impressions after returning from a stint as Taiwan inspecting censor in 1723, wrote that the opium, after being mixed with plants and boiled in a copper pan, was added to tobacco and smoked through a bamboo tube filled with coir fibers.[34]

None of these sources sheds much light on the smokers or gives exact details as to what was being smoked. Lan and Huang merely noted that those who smoked were either the criminal or the gullible, while Chang Ju-lin did not say who was smoking. Nor is the first detailed prohibition of opium smoking, which appeared in 1729, much help on this point; it merely refers in general terms to the seduction with opium of minors from worthy families (liang-chia tzu-ti) as being particularly reprehensible.[35]

This 1729 prohibition struck at distributors but not at smokers, and it does not seem to have been strongly enforced; so we may assume, though we cannot prove, a gradual spreading of opium and tobacco smoking throughout the eighteenth century. The French merchant Charles de Constant discussed the widespread smoking of opium mixed with tobacco in the Canton of the 1780s,[36] and the British traveler Clarke Abel in 1816 described the smoking of opium imbedded in tobacco, or of tobacco steeped in opium solution, as being common "in all parts of the Empire."[37]

The vagueness of these data has led to an understandable imprecision about who was smoking what and when; it has even led some students to reject the data altogether. Thus Ch'en Ch'i-yuan, reviewing some evidence from 1729, concluded that the officials could not have known what they were talking about, since opium is not smoked with tobacco.[38] The problem is solved if we realize that two different types of opium derivative are under consideration. Until the late eighteenth century most

Chinese were smoking madak, not pure opium. Madak is crude opium that has been dissolved in water, boiled and strained, boiled a second time till it reaches a syrupy consistency, and then mixed with shredded leaves preparatory to smoking. It is smoked in a regular pipe, like tobacco, and yields about 0.2 percent of morphia by volume.[39] Huang Shu-ching had partly understood this process in 1723, when he wrote that the crude opium was mixed with *ma* and *ko* leaves and then cooked.[40] His testimony is not decisive, but it is backed independently by the Dutchman Valentyn, who saw madak being smoked in Java in 1726.[41] The smoking of madak, or of tobacco dipped in opium solution, can be seen as the connecting point between tobacco and opium proper. The moderate pleasures of madak—perhaps equivalent to taking a few inhalations of marijuana—were rejected by many smokers when they discovered the smoking of pure opium. When properly refined and aged, a unit of smokable extract (chandu) yields between 9 and 10 percent of morphia.[42]

The 1760s has been suggested as the time when the smoking of pure opium began in China, and the date is a plausible one, though there seems no way of definitely proving when *ya-p'ien yen* came to refer to unadulterated opium.[43] It was in the 1770s that Charles de Constant observed that the Chinese had suddenly developed "une passion pour ce narcotique qui passe toute croyance,"[44] and perhaps this new passion— echoed by a quadruple rise in imports, from around 1,000 chests in 1773 to 4,000 chests per annum in 1790[45]—was the result of encounters with the stronger drug. Nevertheless, the demand was not yet immense, since it was in 1782 that Warren Hastings dispatched the *Nonsuch* with 1,000 chests of Patna opium and found almost no buyers at Canton, being forced to sell to Sinqua at only $210 a chest.[46]

There is an extremely detailed passage on opium smoking in Chao Hsueh-min's continuation of the *Pen-ts'ao kang-mu;* the preface to this is dated 1765, so here we have a rare source of Ch'ien-lung reign opium practices from the Chinese viewpoint. Though the author gives the nod to previous writers by saying the opium is mixed with tobacco and smoked, it is obvious from his description that he is describing pure opium:

> When you're going to smoke you must get a group of people together, and take it in turns. Place a mat on the *k'ang** and

---

*The *k'ang* was a raised platform, heated from below, on which Chinese families slept in the cold northern winters.

> have everyone recline on it; put the lighted lamp in the middle
> and smoke *(hsi)*, from a hundred to several hundred puffs.
> The smoking pipe is a tube of bamboo, eight or nine *fen* in
> diameter, filled with coir fiber and hair. Bind each end firmly
> with silver bands, and at one end open a hole the size of your
> little finger. Mold some clay into the shape of a gourd, hollow
> it out, dry it in an oven, and push it into the little hole on the
> top of this gourd. You take only a little bit of the opium, and
> it is all used in one inhalation. It makes a gurgling sound.[47]

Apart from the fact that one person could not make a hundred inhalations, and that the text does not say how the opium is heated over the
lamp before inhalation, this is a full enough description to leave no doubt
that pure opium is the substance being smoked, not some tobacco mixture or madak.

The dissemination of opium smoking, however widespread, did not
rouse the Ch'ing emperors to action until it became noticeable at court
in the early nineteenth century; thereafter, the interplay of memorials
and edicts enables us to trace the spread of addiction through the bureaucracy in some detail. By 1813 there were a number of opium smokers
among the palace guard officers *(shih-wei)*, and Chia-ch'ing suspected
that eunuchs were smoking as well.[48] He was posthumously proved right,
in a sensational investigation conducted by the directors of the Imperial
Household in December 1831. The directors found that a large number
of senior eunuchs were opium addicts and that some of them had been
smoking for twenty or thirty years; also, they sometimes smoked with
Manchu members of the imperial clan.[49] But the wide range of smokers
had already been graphically described in a remarkable memorial written
four months earlier by Lu Yin-p'u (grand secretary and concurrently
president of the Board of Justice) together with six other board presidents and vice-presidents. Tracing the origins of opium smoking to corrupt secretaries and merchants, the memorialists found that it had spread
from them to the sons of great families and rich city merchants, and from
them to the common people. "At the present time, there are opium
smokers in all the provinces, with special concentration in the various
yamens; we estimate that among governors-general and their subordinates, and at every level of both civil and military officialdom, those who
do *not* smoke opium are few indeed."[50]

In 1832 it was finally proved beyond doubt that opium addiction in
certain parts of the army had become so serious that the troops were

incapable of combat. After investigating the reasons why the troops of the Liang-Kuang governor-general, Li Hung-pin, had been roundly defeated by the Yao rebels in the area of Lien-chou (in northwest Kwangtung, near the Hunan and Kwangsi borders), the Manchu imperial commissioner, Hsi-en, concluded, "Six thousand combat troops were sent [from Kwangtung], but they were not used to the mountains; and many of the troops from all the coastal garrisons were opium smokers, and it was difficult to get any vigorous response from them."[51]

The extent of these revelations alarmed Tao-kuang and many senior officials, and from this time onward the opium debates developed in intensity, reaching an initial climax in the legalization versus prohibition arguments in 1836. The most graphic account of widespread opium smoking appears in Chu Tsun's memorial of that year. Chu Tsun attacked the arguments made by Hsu Nai-chi and his friends in Juan Yuan's Canton academy—they wanted legalization for the common people and prohibition for scholars, officials, and soldiers[52]—as being hopelessly impractical, since there was no way to control private smoking unless the ban was total. Chu Tsun analyzed the smoking population as follows: "The great majority of those who at present smoke opium are the relatives and dependents of the officers of government, whose example has extended the practice to the mercantile classes, and has gradually contaminated the inferior officers, the military, and the scholars. Those who do not smoke are the common people of the villages and hamlets."[53]

The spread of opium to the common people can be gauged through three different groups of sources: import figures, analyses of domestic production, and the guesses of informed observers.

Imports—of Bengal, Malwa, and Turkish opium—stayed within the 4,000- to 5,000-chest mark until 1820. During the 1820s they hovered around the 10,000-chest mark, with a sharp upward jump in 1828, to 18,000.[54] They had passed the 20,000-chest mark by 1832, and reached 40,000 by 1839.[55] The steady climb continued, to 76,000 chests in 1865 and 81,000 in 1884.[56] There followed a slow drop until the 1900s, when imports stabilized around 50,000 chests.[57] This imported opium was smoked mainly by the rich, who found it to be of better quality than the domestic—in both flavor and strength.[58]

Chinese domestic production of opium has been traced back to the T'ang dynasty, and the poppy seems to have flourished in western China, particularly in Yunnan, Szechwan, and Kansu.[59] By the early Ch'ing we find that the gazetteers of Kweichow and Fukien also listed Ying-su poppy among their plants, though they did not elaborate on production methods or uses.[60] Hsu Nai-chi, in 1836, pointed to domestic production in Kwangtung, Fukien and eastern parts of Chekiang, as well as Yunnan.[61] Trying to back up his legalization arguments, Hsu noted that domestic Chinese opium was milder than foreign, and hence addiction could be more easily eliminated; he drew a parallel with the tobacco plant, showing how, after domestic prohibitions were relaxed, the native, gentle Chinese tobacco ousted its harsh, dizzying Philippine competitors. Unfortunately, Hsu's argument had little weight, since wealthy opium smokers wanted strength, not mildness. As Chang Lu, certainly the most widely known doctor and medical writer of the K'ang-hsi reign, had written in 1705, the domestic opium can still cure some maladies but "its strength is less and it is not so efficacious" as the foreign.[62] Presumably, the same strength differential held true through the 1840s, when domestic poppy cultivation spread to Kwangsi, Hunan, and Hupei as well.[63] The British diplomat Thomas Wade estimated Kwangtung domestic opium production at between 8,000 and 10,000 piculs in 1847, noting that it sold well locally and was often mixed with other types: "It resembles Patna in smell, is not equal to Bengal in strength. . . . When two years old it is preferred by some smokers to any foreign drug." On the other hand, Fukien opium, said Wade, "is weak in quality, coarse in flavor, and is not produced in qualities sufficient to compete with the foreign article."[64] The price of this inferior domestic product was, however, only $250 a picul, whereas Hsu Nai-chi had listed the imports at $800 per picul for Wu-t'u (Bengal opium), $600 for White Skin (Bombay), and $400 for Red Skin (Madras).[65]

Since Kwangtung was not the area where the great opium fields were to be found, we can guess that western Chinese production was already several times this 8,000-picul level, and internal prices were often lower than $250. In this case, Chinese production and consumption almost certainly exceeded the estimates made by the British consuls in 1847[66]— and were vastly greater than the estimates made by Hart's Imperial Maritime Customs survey of 1863.[67] It would seem probable that this domestic production, though initially spurred by a desire to cash in on the available market among the wealthy, came to cater mainly to Chinese workers—especially the coolie laborers, chair bearers, and boatmen who seem to have become addicted on a massive scale by the 1870s.[68] Besides its low price—in Kansu, Indian opium could cost ten times as much as the local product[69]—Chinese domestic opium had the additional advantage that it could be smoked more often in residue than Indian.[70] Chinese workers were also willing to accept opium that had been repeatedly adulterated—not only with husks or pods from the poppies but also with pork fat, sesamum seed cake, willow shoots, and thistle juice, according to an observer in Manchuria.[71] Though richer Chinese had long smoked blends of domestic and Indian, they seem to have swung to pure domestic opium out of desperation; thus the prolonged famine around the Chefoo area from 1875 to 1878 forced the wealthy city dwellers faced with shrinking rents to smoke domestic opium. They got used to it and never changed back, with the result that Indian sales slumped in the area.[72] This process was accelerated as Chinese producers grew wiser on the question of quality control, and their wealthy buyers grew more numerous.[73]

Smoking among the peasantry, we may again estimate, probably began on a massive scale during the 1870s, when domestic production was increasing so rapidly. That the growing of opium does indeed encourage the growers themselves to smoke has been proved for a later period of Chinese history. J. L. Buck, an American scholar who comprehensively analyzed Chinese rural life in the 1920s and 1930s, found that peasants came to consume about a quarter of their own opium production themselves.[74] And though high yields depended on moderately favorable weather conditions, there were plenty of advantages in growing opium poppy as a cash crop. It would yield at least twice the cash of an average cereal crop on a given acreage;[75] it could be planted in the tenth month and harvested in the third, when nothing else would grow; it could survive on very poor soil, as long as there was a reasonable amount of fertilizer; it could be interspersed with food crops such as beans or potatoes, or planted in alternate rows with tobacco.[76] Winter growing was especially profitable to tenants holding lands on metayer tenure—that is, paying the landlord a fixed percentage of the yield of the *summer* crop.[77] Furthermore, though techniques for gathering poppy juice were labor-intensive, they were very simple.

Increasingly, opium poppies began to be grown on good soil. By comparing Baron von Richthoven's 1872 surveys with W. D. Spence's in 1882, we can see how the poppy had come down from the hills to the valleys in southwest China.[78] Robert Hart tried to estimate addiction on the basis of a ratio between population and known production, and came up with a figure of just under 1 percent.[79] But most observers found this far too low—Chang Chih-tung insisted that smokers made up 80 percent of the population in Shansi cities and 60 percent in the countryside,[80] (though Tseng Kuo-ch'üan thought rural smoking was even greater than urban).[81] Kansu observers also came up with an 80 percent figure.[82]

Accurate figures are unobtainable, but a sensible one seems to be that of a 10 percent smoking population, which James Legge arrived at as he jolted on his mule cart through the Shantung poppy fields en route to Confucius' tomb.[83] Legge's guess can in turn be modified by the separate estimate of the experienced Dr. William Lockhart, who also estimated a 10 percent opium-smoking population but who felt that only 3 to 5 percent of the Chinese were smoking "in excess."[84] This would give an 1890 figure of somewhere around fifteen million opium addicts in China; if they smoked about one-third of an ounce a day, or seven pounds a year— which local observers found common[85]—this means that around 105 million pounds were required each year. Hence the estimate that, in the 1880s, 850,000 acres of land in Szechwan were producing 177,000 piculs (23.5 million pounds) per year at an average of 50 ounces per mou seems not unreasonable.[86] Feasibility cross-checks may be made to more accurate studies in the twentieth century: 29,750 mou of land under opium poppy in the Kunming district of Yunnan;[87] 23,000 piculs from the Fuchou district of Szechwan alone;[88] around a million mou under poppy cultivation in Shansi;[89] and half a million mou and a million and a half smokers in Shensi.[90] A general estimate for turn-of-the-century interregional trade in domestic production yielded these figures: rice, 100 million taels; salt, 100 million taels; opium, 130 million taels.[91] Undeniably, opium was being smoked in China on a gigantic scale.

PROHIBITION

Much of the legal history of opium prohibition in Ch'ing China revolved around the search for a precedent. Tobacco prohibition might seem to have been a logical point from which to build—but even the tobacco prohibitions were vague in formulation and execution.

Abahai (Ch'ing T'ai-tsung) discussed the tobacco problem at some length in 1635 and noted some of its ambiguities. Certainly it was wrong, he said, for officers to forbid all smoking in their offices and then to smoke at will in their own homes; but that did not mean that a good example was absolutely essential, and that the lower orders necessarily aped the ways of their betters. In any case, Abahai continued, he was going to ban smoking for one reason, and one only: smokers were ignoring their retainers' wretched condition and using what money they had to buy tobacco, and he found this inexcusable.[92] The argument here was clearly one relating to military morale. In 1638 two Manchu generals collected and publicly burned all the tobacco that they found in the western section of Mukden. Strict penalties against sellers and smokers were both promulgated and implemented in 1641; but that same year the attempt at suppression was abandoned. Henceforth planting for one's own use was to be legal, and a fair price of three *ch'ien* per catty *(chin)* was fixed.[93] In partial explanation of this turnabout, Abahai stated that the prohibition had proved unenforceable, and also that tobacco smoking was a minor crime compared with the neglect of archery. It was to this latter that the Manchus should apply themselves.[94]

The Koreans had known tobacco since the 1620s, calling it "smoke-tea" *(yen-ch'a)* or "smoke-wine" *(yen-chiu)*; believing that it gave the power to foretell the future, and noting its habit-forming qualities, they also termed it "magical herb" *(yao-ts'ao)*.[95] The Chinese believed, too, that it had strong powers and was useful in quelling disease. In his authoritative medical treatise *Ching-yueh ch'üan-shu* (Complete medical works), the Ming scholar Chang Chieh-pin observed that tobacco smoking had saved troops in Yunnan from malaria and that this had increased its popularity.[96] The late Ming tobacco prohibitions in 1637 and 1640 seem to have been initially promulgated because it was believed tobacco was helping the Manchu military cause: "Those who hawk clandestinely tobacco, and sell it to foreigners, shall, no matter the quantity sold, be decapitated," and "the people beyond the [northern] border are subject to diseases caused by extreme cold, and cannot be cured without tobacco."[97] The Ming withdrew these prohibitions because the morale of their own troops was suffering without tobacco.[98] K'ang-hsi had smoked as a child but issued a prohibition in 1676 against smoking in the palace areas; his motive here was fear of fire, not moral uplift.[99] The prohibition, clearly not very effective, was rephrased in 1684. K'ang-hsi now stated that since his grandmother feared the possibility of fires in the palace, people should not smoke carelessly.[100]

These were not useful precedents, and when Yung-cheng was apprised of the opium-smoking problem and tried to stop it, his legal advisers had to look elsewhere in the Ch'ing code. The first opium prohibitions in Chinese history, formulated between 1729 and 1731, reflected this uncertainty.[101] Opium dealers were to be sentenced, in accordance with the law for those handling forbidden goods, to a month in the cangue and military banishment; those who opened opium dens and seduced the worthy were to be sentenced, in accordance with the law for teachers of heterodox religions, to strangulation after the assizes; soldiers and runners abusing the new laws and engaging in extortion were to be punished proportionately in accordance with the laws on bribery in connection with unlawful objects *(wang-fa)*. Further prohibitions in 1730 were directed specifically against those using Taiwan as a base for opium dealing—they were to be punished and sent back to their native places.[102] Perhaps because of a general feeling that it was the distributors who were the problem, the penalties for smokers and planters were not so serious—they were to receive one hundred blows in accordance with laws for violating an imperial decree.

Some isolated attempts were made to tighten and coordinate the laws against smoking as a whole. Grand Secretary Fang Pao submitted proposals for banning tobacco planting in 1736, and Chang Jo-chen, financial commissioner of Shansi, tried the same tactic in 1751. According at least to later Ch'ing legal opinion, legislation against both dry-tobacco smoking and water-pipe smoking was a sine qua non for successful opium prohibition, and the failure of the ministries to back up either Fang or Chang made the spread of opium inevitable.[103]

A further confusing element was that throughout this period opium in small amounts was coming into China on a fixed tariff as a medicinal drug; the tax was two *ch'ien* per ten *chin* in 1589, and the assessment was raised to three *ch'ien* in 1686.[104] In the late K'ang-hsi reign, as we have seen, it was also being smoked in some quantities, mixed with tobacco. The only detailed account of a prosecution case that I have been able to find for this period[105]—involving an opium seller named Ch'en Yuan in Ch'ang-chou fu, Fukien, in August 1729—shows the complexities of enforcing the law. There was no easy way to have opium *(ya-p'ien)* freely available as a medicinal drug while forbidding the sale of *ya-p'ien-yen*, or "opium ready for smoking," since the one was directly linked to the other, separated only by a process of further refining. Ch'en Yuan, who had sold some opium to a prefectural stool pigeon, was sentenced by the prefect under the terms of the new law to the cangue and military banishment. This sentence was overthrown by the governor, who defended Ch'en's right to sell opium as a medicinal drug, and Yung-cheng agreed that the governor was right in so doing. Both governor and emperor agreed further, however, that the overzealous prefect should not be punished, lest the ignorant common people think that the "prohibitions against opium for smoking have been relaxed."

If these laws were hard to interpret and enforce in China, they were nevertheless taken seriously by foreign traders at this time, as is shown by an alarmist order issued to commanders of East India Company ships in June 1733 by members of the council:

On board the *Windham* June 16th

It having been a usual thing heretofore, for shipps bound from Fort St. George, to carry ophium with them for sale to China, & not knowing but that there might be some of that commodity now on board your ship design'd for the same markett, we think it our Duty (lest you should be a Stranger to itt) to acquaint you with the late severe laws enacted by the Emperour of China for ye prohibition of Ophium, the penalty, should any be seiz'd on board your Ship, being no less than ye confiscation of Ship & Cargoes to the Emperour, as well as death to the person who should dare offer to buy it of you; upon these considerations therefore, & the more effectually to prevent any such like misfortune attending of us, you are hereby required to take the best measures you possibly can, by a strict enquiry & search in your ship, to be well informed whether there be any such thing on board or not, & in case there be, that you then take effectual care to have it removed out of your Ship before you leave Malacca, since upon no consideration whatsoever, you are neither to carry, nor suffer any of it to be carry'd in your Ship to China, as you will answer the contrary to the Honble Company at your peril.[106]

After 1729 there seems to have been no further development in anti-opium legislation until the Chia-ch'ing reign (1796–1820), so the Ch'ien-lung reign saw the domestic spread of smoking and the increased boldness of foreign traders. Even the well-known early Chia-ch'ing prohibitions, though they included sections on domestic growing, were directed mainly at foreign merchants bringing opium from India.[107] It was not until 1813 (Chia-ch'ing 18) that the Chinese seriously tackled the problem of tightening their internal laws to cope with the mounting foreign trade and smuggling of opium.

The Board of Justice in 1813 noted that though precedents (for example, in 1729) existed for punishing dealers and owners of opium dens, the law against purchasers and smokers had never been specifically clarified in the Ch'ing code and they had been punished with a hundred blows in accordance with the laws for violating an imperial decree. It was now time to tighten up the law and to distinguish between officials and common people. [108] The new penalties for opium smokers were to be as follows: guards, officers, and officials would receive punishment of a hundred blows, plus dismissal and two months in the cangue; soldiers and commoners would receive a hundred blows, plus one month in the cangue. Dealers and den owners should be punished as before, but more care should be taken to try to separate ringleaders from their subordinates. Chia-ch'ing agreed to these proposals, adding that he had also heard rumors that eunuchs in his own palaces were smoking; if they were discovered, they would be sent as slaves to Heilungkiang after two months in the cangue.

This attempt to handle opium smoking under the laws for "violating an imperial decree," with extra penalties attached, must have proved quite inadequate, an apparent exception being Juan Yuan's arrest of sixteen Macao dealers in 1821.[109] A further flurry of legislation came in 1830 following the memorial by the censor Shao Cheng-hu on the extent of domestic opium planting and sales.[110] Henceforth, domestic growers and refiners were to be handled in accordance with the old laws on dealers. Local headmen who took bribes were to be punished on the same scale as the principal offenders. New provisions were that those growing opium poppy were to have the plants torn up and their land confiscated by the government. However, Tao-kuang was very skeptical about this provision, since he castigated Juan Yuan for daring to suggest that local opium could be successfully rooted up.[111] Also the senior provincial officials were to order their subordinates to carry out meticulous cross-checks at the village level and to procure annual affidavits that local areas were clear. Regulations incorporating new refinements were added in 1831: manufacturers of opium pipes and other smoking equipment were to suffer military banishment, in accordance with the laws against those making gambling utensils, and boatmen or landlords who leased space for smoking would be banished or beaten like those who leased rooms to gamblers; parents whose children dealt in opium or smoked it would get forty blows, in accordance with the laws against "parents who cannot stop their children from stealing."[112] In the same year of 1831 a new dimension was added to existing penalties: in the future all accused smokers would receive the standard penalties as long as they named the dealers and those dealers were arrested, in line with the laws covering gamblers who named those who supplied their equipment; failure to name and catch the dealers would lead the smoker to be treated as if he himself were a dealer.[113]

Officials in the Board of Justice struggled to make these laws work, and cases have survived which show how they argued over the special problems raised by opium addiction. In the case of the P'an brothers in Kwangtung in 1827, for example, where the younger brother was an opium dealer who involved his elder brother and other outsiders in his deals, the board corresponded at length with the Kwangtung governor on the correctness of ascribing blame to the elder brother in accordance with normal legal practice.[114] The argument centered on the problem of whether opium dealing constituted "direct injury to the person," and was continued by the Board of Justice and the governor of Anhwei in 1831; the conclusion was that opium sellers were like sellers of gambling equipment in that they did not deliberately seek to do harm but only wanted profit.[115] In another ruling, however, it was specifically stated that an opium seller should not be treated leniently, even if "his parents were very old and he were the only male descendant."[116]

The increasing complexity and severity of these laws—new categories were added and finer distinctions drawn in 1839, 1850, and 1870[117]—did not make them any more effective as a means of control. Nor did the smokers respond to an additional law that promised them pardon if they gave themselves up.[118] Contemporary Ch'ing officials were fully aware of the difficulties behind enforcement. Ho Ch'ang-ling pointed out that the opium smokers were simply not dissuaded by punitive legislation: they grew their opium locally and smoked it themselves not because they were evil but just because they were weak, like drinkers or lechers. Also, smoking could be done in secret: the severer the penalties, the more secret the smoking, so it got harder and harder to catch the smokers—their main danger was from blackmail or other harassment.[119]

The levels that this blackmail and harassment had reached long before the Opium War is clearly shown in a case reported in late 1831 by Ch'ü Yung, a circuit censor with special responsibility for northern Peking who had proved expert at rounding up preparers of raw opium.[120] A certain Wen Cho-chiao had purchased a post in the banqueting court and brought a supply of opium with him when he moved from Kwangtung to Peking. Wen's cook, aware that his master was smoking, told two ward runners, and they in turn told a local constable. This group, together with some other servants, climbed over the wall of Wen's residence one night and caught him smoking with two friends. They locked up the three smokers, impounded two and a half boxes of opium and three pipes, and the constable Wang San blackmailed Wen for 1,000 taels. Wen handed over 25 taels in cash (of which 15 were immediately passed on to the cook) and gave a promissory note for the rest. Later on, a friend told Wen to refuse to pay: but the constable and his friends came back with reinforcements and forced Wen to disgorge 600 taels. The opium was distributed among the various accomplices. Nobody reported the case to the authorities.

Such a case suggests the prevalence of both dishonesty and fear and gives real force to the arguments of men like Chu Tsun. Chu was passionately against any legislation that might leave opium available—for example, to commoners—while making it prohibited for officials. In his words (made more eloquent by the *Chinese Repository* translation of January 1837):

> And if the officers, the scholars, and the military smoke the drug in the quiet of their own families, by what means is this to be discovered or prevented? Should an officer be unable to restrain himself, shall then his clerks, his followers, his domestic servants, have it in their power to make his failing their plaything, and by the knowledge of his secret to hold his situation at their disposal? We dread falsehood and bribery, and yet we would thus widen the door to admit them. We are anxious to prevent the amassing of wealth by unlawful means, and yet by this policy we would ourselves increase opportunities for doing so. A father, in such a case, would no longer be able to reprove his son, an elder brother to restrain his junior, nor a master to rule his own household. Will not this policy, then, be every way calculated to stir up strife? Or if happily the thing should not run to this extreme, the consequences will yet be equally bad: secret enticement and mutual connivance will ensue, until the very commonness of the practice shall render it no longer a subject of surprise.[121]

What Chu Tsun wanted—and in this desire he was at one with Hsu Nai-chi and Lin Tse-hsu—was consistency in the law, for without it there could be no control system that was enforceable. But what began to emerge after 1842, and became the norm after 1860, was a legal patchwork: the sporadic punishment of opium offenders in the midst of legalized foreign opium imports and accelerating domestic production.[122] Examples taken from the *Peking Gazette* during the 1870s and 1880s show the range of opium offenses punished, and often the *nature* of the offense hints graphically enough at the types of abuse that were commonplace.

An imperial clan member is punished for both living in and operating an opium den in northern Peking;[123] a musketry instructor in the Foochow arsenal kills his servant for breaking his opium pipe;[124] a Kiangsu magistrate is banished for *selling* opium;[125] a eunuch is beheaded for opium smoking in the palace *and* operating an opium den *(yen-kuan)* inside the Imperial Equipage Department;[126] the correctors of a batch of *chü-jen* examination papers are addicts;[127] a boy is condemned to death by slicing for providing his mother with opium—he had apparently thought that she wanted to smoke but she used it to commit suicide, thus making him guilty of "wilfully causing a mother's death";[128] a sedan chair carrier operates his own den and has connections with a military officer;[129] two others are accused of smuggling opium on their own patrol vessel;[130] a *chü-jen* has the nerve to prosecute some rowdies for breaking up an opium den which he *himself* owned and operated;[131] and most poignant historically, perhaps, among random cases of officials dismissed for being addicts[132] we find the name of the Wuhu taotai, son of the once prestigious treaty negotiator Ch'i-shan.[133]

The ambiguity and inconsistency of the law in such cases made the spread of addiction and distribution patterns quite uncontrollable.

DISTRIBUTION

The more widely opium was smoked, the more complex the distribution network must have been, but it is not easy to locate the network's various components. The following analysis, which concentrates on *Chinese* distributors, is therefore, both episodic and sporadic.

As early as 1674 a Chinese merchant named Bonsiqua was buying substantial quantities of opium from the Dutch in Batavia; he had trouble disposing of it, and it was eventually sold at public auction.[134] Only three years later the Dutch signed a new treaty with the Mataram prince of Java, and one of the objects of this treaty was to check the bulk trade that Chinese merchants had built up in cloth and opium.[135] I do not know whether Bonsiqua or these merchants had contacts with Taiwan customers or not, but a Batavia–Taiwan–Amoy route is certainly feasible. Also, early opium sales areas were often identical with tobacco areas, and already established tobacco transport and marketing patterns may have been utilized for distribution of madak. Ch'en Yuan, the man convicted and then pardoned in the 1729 case already discussed, had obtained his opium from a merchant in Kwangtung he was unable (or unwilling) to name; he traded orange cakes he had brought from Fukien for the opium, and himself carried the opium back to Ch'ang-chou fu. He sold it as a medicine in his store.[136]

Chang Hsin-pao has described how, in the early nineteenth century, the brokerage houses *(yao-k'ou)* of Chinese partners in the Canton area would pay to pick up the opium from the foreign receiving ships anchored offshore.[137] The *yao-k'ou* sold to brokers who followed certain set routes—westward to Chao-ch'ing, and thence to Kwangsi and Kweichow; northward to Lo-ch'ang and Nan-hsiung for shipping to Hunan and Kiangsi; and eastward via Ch'ao-chou to Fukien.[138] The latter was the route taken by Ch'en Yuan.

This analysis can be extended through the testimony of Feng Tsan-ch'in, a Kwangsi-born censor in Hu-kuang[139] who was deeply interested in distribution methods in the Canton area and made a detailed report on them in 1831.[140] The large brokerage houses *(ta yao-k'ou)*, said Feng, were collaborating with local criminals who took advantage of two inter-locking fears: the foreign merchants' fear of landing on Chinese soil, and the Chinese merchants' fear of putting out to sea. The criminals set up so-called money-changing shops which they used to monopolize the opium trade; it was in these shops that Chinese merchants met with the West-erners and signed a contract for the deal. The shops were located either in the thirteen factories or in Lien-hsing Street, and from these bases the criminals sent out their boats—"fast crabs" with three masts, fifty or sixty oars, iron nets to protect them from cannonballs, and a capacity of several hundred piculs. They were so swift that the local slang for them was "glued-on wings" *(ch'a-i);* but many patrol boats would not catch them even if they could, since they were all in league together, and the trade took place openly by daylight. In such places as Amoy, Tientsin, Hainan, and southwest Kwangtung, there was no need for the "fast crab" boats, though even here merchants had to work through the *yao-k'ou* brokers, and the same brokers had bases in other cities of Kwangtung and thus controlled distribution beyond the provincial borders. Once the opium had moved inland, it was handled by other criminals and yamen clerks through local brokerage houses *(hsiao yao-k'ou)* and sold in small amounts at the local markets.

Other memorialists in 1831 filled out this picture a bit more. In Shan-tung the opium was ferried to deserted parts of the shore, far from har-bors or garrisons, by shallow-draft lighters *(po-ch'uan)*, and sold for distribution right there at the water's edge.[141] In Kweichow it was enter-ing along the established trade routes from Kwangtung and being sold by local merchants who were private operators, since there were as yet no opium dens *(yen-kuan)* in the area.[142] The Kwangsi governor simi-larly denied any knowledge of local production, claiming that opium was found only in certain prefectures bordering the West River, where merchants brought it in from Kwangtung.[143] The governor-general of

Szechwan admitted that there were many smokers and some domestic production in his area, and noted that "when there are so many smokers there must be many distributors." His proposal was to check at customs points and defiles on the established trade routes and to concentrate on certain key interprovincial junctions: K'uei-chou-fu, for the Kwangtung and Chekiang traffic; Ning-yuan-fu, for the Yunnan traffic; Kuang-yuan-fu, for Hupei; and so on.[144]

In Peking itself distribution had become fairly complex, as can be seen from three examples of police raids conducted during the late summer of 1831.[145] Wang Erh ran his opium business from his own house near the Hsuan-wu gate, where he also kept dice and a set of account books; the latter he managed to burn before the raid. Chiao Ssu operated out of the hostel for merchants from Fu-shun, in Szechwan (Fu-shun *k'o-tien*), and also had dice, dominoes, and other equipment for gambling. Hsiao Shen sold his opium in the Kwangtung Provincial Hostel (Yueh-tung *hui-kuan*). All three distributors had an ample supply of bags (*tai*, perhaps used for take-away orders), copper pots, and other equipment for heating and smoking opium. All three seem to have performed the same role of buying the crude opium and selling it in smokable form *(mai-t'u mai-yen)*; they claimed that their source was either seagoing vessels at Tientsin or the sales section for Cantonese goods *(Kuang-huo tan-shang)*, but none of the three would identify their sources of supply by name.

We have already noted that by 1831 the Ch'ing were trying without success, to force smokers to reveal the names of their distributors; in this case we see how small-scale distributors similarly defended their wholesalers from exposure. The lengths to which a smoker might go in order to throw officials and police off his tracks can be seen from the testimony the eunuch Chang Chin-fu made to investigating officials of the Imperial Household:

> At first the opium that we used was bought in small quantities directly from the Moslem Chu Ta. Then I learned that when the sea vessels came into Tientsin the opium prices got lower, so I asked K'o-k'o-ssu-pu-k'u for a loan of 100 string of local cash and I also sold my mule cart for cash. I took [my servant] Ch'in Pao-ch'üan with me to Tientsin, and got Ch'in Pao-ch'üan's old friend Yang Hui-yuan to act as an agent and buy 160 ounces of opium from Chang Erh for 240 strings of cash. I gave Yang a commission of three strings and 800 *wen*.[146]

In this particular case careful investigative work by the censors and a rather full confession led to the discovery of a certain sequence: smoker to B to C to distributor. But the distributor himself was only a small-time dealer, and as we saw in the case of the three Peking distributors the trail often went no farther than to these minor intermediaries. The rounding up of distributors depended to a large extent on local agencies—the police magistrates, their assistants, and the constables. When the constables themselves were involved in blackmailing smokers and in selling opium, as they were in the 1831 blackmail case, even the most admirable laws would not work.

Any final analysis of opium distribution would have to include a full section on police activities and procedures. Here we may draw some cases from the *Peking Gazette* to show the dimensions of the problem, both in Peking and in the provinces. Local opium distribution might be dominated by groups of deserters from the army who would use "foreign pistols" to fight off police.[147] An opium shop might be owned by a member of the imperial clan.[148] Even those constables on the rolls were not paid their full wages,[149] and local citizens were growing so jumpy that they would fire their guns at random through the night.[150] Smuggling of goods over city walls involved so many people that the police were "afraid to interfere";[151] on one occasion members of an entire police patrol were robbed of their sheepskin coats as they went about their duties in winter.[152] It seems likely that when the police did get up the evidence or the courage for a raid, they struck only at the small dealers.

In the latter part of the nineteenth century, the distribution of opium took place in a three-tiered system, in what looks like a logical extension of the two-tiered brokerage house system described by Feng Tsan-ch'in. These were, first, the big wholesale dealers; second, the large-scale retailers; third, the local sellers.

The big wholesalers bought in bulk both from the British and from domestic growers. R. E. Bredon in 1887 thought that this group was dominated by men from Swatow and Ningpo.[153] They were men of great wealth, and we can contrast the vast resources at their disposal with the scanty funds generally made available for "self-strengthening" or other enterprises. Thus in 1881 Li Hung-chang memorialized that a syndicate headed by the Cantonese merchant Ho Hsien-ch'ih wanted to corner the entire Indian opium stocks through a company Ho would head in Hong Kong; they offered the Ch'ing government at least three million taels in additional annual taxation, in return for sole distribution rights in Chinese ports. Ho was going to capitalize the company initially at $Mex 20,000,000. As Li Hung-chang commented,

> I've heard that Ho Hsien-ch'ih and the others are very rich, and have long been doing business in the Kwangtung and Hong Kong area. They understand both Chinese and foreign business methods. Other rich merchants have heard of this and want to put up capital and get stock; they all know that a company with a monopoly of the opium trade is bound to make a profit, and not to fail, so it's not hard to raise capital.[154]

Li himself sent the taotai Ma to Calcutta, to negotiate directly with Lord Ripon.[155] His plan was to combine some kind of Chinese monopoly with a graded decrease in imports, spread over twenty or thirty years, until the trade stopped entirely.[156] Even if the scale of such deals was exceptional, there were regular opium fairs in major cities where half a million taels or more would change hands.[157] These wholesalers affected opium trade on a provincial scale; the Chekiang governor noted in 1887 that though there was plenty of opium growing in his province, it did not cross the provincial boundaries, because there were "no large merchants to undertake its export."[158] Sung Ts'ai, the comprador for Sassoon's in Chinkiang, sold one and a half million taels of opium in 1875 alone.[159] One would assume that these men were above police harassment and that even officials handled them carefully.

The large-scale retailers, who may be seen as descendants of the earlier small brokerage houses, were those who kept the retail shops (t'u-tien) and joined the local opium dealers' guilds (t'u-pang).[160] They also refined the raw opium by boiling off the impurities so that it was ready for smoking, a process that involved simple equipment but a fairly sophisticated knowledge of relative yields and prices—as we can see from a table on Tientsin preparation drawn up for Robert Hart—since 100 catties Malwa would yield 70 catties boiled, with a price shift from 506 to 567 taels, whereas 100 catties of local opium would yield 50 to 60 catties boiled, involving a shift from 285 taels to anywhere between 304 and 364 taels.[161] This refining process could not be done in secret (as Ch'ing officials had noted well before the Opium War), since the smell was so strong and since the treacly yen was much harder to transport than the raw t'u;[162] so these retailers clearly operated with official connivance.

These large-scale retailers may have sold some stocks to wealthy purchasers for use in their homes, but probably their main customers were the two chief groups of local sellers: the owners of opium divans and the itinerant merchants. These men sold opium in lots of a few cash, for smoking on the spot. The number of divans in any city was very high by the late Ch'ing: one observer counted 170 in Tientsin;[163] one guessed at over 1,000 in Hangchow;[164] in Lanchow, Kansu, there were "five stalls in one street, within fifty yards from the shops";[165] in Chungking there were 1,230 opium shops of various kinds.[166] Ratios of population to number of divans suggest either that one divan catered to very few people or else that the divans in large towns catered to large numbers of out-of-town visitors. Thus Chefoo had an estimated 132 dens for a population of 32,500, while Wenchow served a population of 80,000 with 1,130.[167] Sometimes a city was subject to reforming zeal; thus Ting Jih-ch'ang's anti-opium proclamations in 1869 led to the closing of 3,700 opium shops and dens in Soochow, according to Young J. Allen; but, as Kuo Sung-t'ao noted, such urban prohibitions had absolutely no effect on the countryside, where business continued as usual.[168]

Along all major transportation routes there were stalls or booths where opium could be bought; a detailed study of the tea export routes showed opium constantly available, like tobacco.[169] The coolies would often stop for about an hour after each three hours' work for a smoke of opium and a rest.[170] Here, also, they could buy some opium to carry if they knew there would be no chance to smoke along the next stage of their journey: either little balls of opium, bits of which could be broken off and chewed;[171] or some smokable extract that could be carried in a little cup at the belt and licked off the finger;[172] or even, perhaps, one of the concentrated tablets which Westerners had thoughtfully provided as an aid to withdrawal from addiction. Dr. William Gould was surprised, in Swatow, at how quickly his 50,000 morphia tablets sold,[173] and duty-free morphia—known as "Jesus opium" because it was often sold by Chinese Christians—became a major import in the late Ch'ing.[174]

Itinerant vendors also did a brisk business at annual fairs and festivals, setting up their booths near the temples in advance of the festivities and then selling to the holiday crowds that came in from the countryside.[175] This would have been a good way to widen the market, as those in high spirits with loose cash in their pockets (for probably the only time in the year) might well contract a habit that would last a lifetime.

ECONOMIC FUNCTION

For at least the last fifty years of the nineteenth century, opium played an important role in the Chinese economy, in three major areas: it served as a substitute for money, it helped local officials meet taxation quotas, and it helped finance the self-strengthening program.

Both British and American merchants saw, after the Opium War, how useful opium would be as a medium of exchange in the *interior* of China; and though they themselves were still restricted to the treaty ports, they sent their compradors inland with large stocks of opium that could be exchanged for upcountry tea or Soochow silk.[176] Ahee, for example, was entrusted with $440,065 of specie and opium by Jardine's in 1855.[177] Similarly, in the Taiping-induced financial crisis at Shanghai in the early 1850s, it was the Western companies with large opium stocks that were able to exploit the tea market most successfully.[178]

Noncomprador Chinese were equally quick to see the advantages of opium as a substitute for cash. One of these was its light weight. In a number of homicide cases in the later Ch'ing, we find that travelers were often murdered because their boatmen or bearers had guessed from the heaviness of their baggage that they were carrying silver bullion.[179] Though opium, of course, was worth less by unit of weight than silver, it was far lighter than a copper cash equivalent, and its bulk and weight distribution might confuse the bearer. For this or other reasons, it was early used by small shopkeepers in Hong Kong to remit funds to the mainland,[180] and it was commonly used as currency in western China; even students traveling to Peking for the examinations would take opium with them to pay their expenses along the way.[181] Others used it as a temporary investment to increase their earnings. Thus, at the lowliest economic level, coolies who had pulled barges up the Yangtze would load up with opium in Szechwan and then carry it on foot through the mountains and sell it to dealers in Hupei (or sometimes carry it on a commission basis).[182] At a more sophisticated financial level, the expectant prefect Wu Shu-heng in Szechwan in 1881, asked by the financial commissioner to take 30,000 taels to Hupei, invested the money in opium, in hopes of reselling it at a profit when he reached his destination. As he could find a local market for only 37 of his 168 piculs of opium, he asked the Hupei governor to sell the rest for him at Hankow.[183]

Opium revenue was a boon to harried magistrates trying to fill their tax quotas. Especially after the great rebellions of the mid-nineteenth century, the magistrate's position was extremely precarious. Where agricultural production had slumped while quotas remained unchanged, the magistrate would run the risk of serious local unrest—and hence of losing his job—if he tried to squeeze more from the conventional agricultural sector. Tso Tsung-t'ang reported three magistrates and one deputy magistrate accepting fees from local poppy growers in return for exempting their fields from uprooting in 1874,[184] and a local censor found matters even worse in Shansi, where only two prefects in the whole province did anything to check growing. Everywhere else, people and officials were linked by the desire to make money from opium.[185] Some of the officials who "levied opium taxes without authorization"[186] had been formally approached by the local people. For instance, on taking up his new office, one magistrate was visited by the local farmers and gentry and given a lump sum (of unspecified size); a few months later he was given 1,163 taels in cash and opium worth 3,000 taels. The agreement seems to have been that he would receive a percentage of the yield.[187] On another occasion, it was the local military officer who was bribed not to report 2,500 mou of opium fields.[188]

The general trouble, as the Shansi governor Pao Yuan-shen analyzed it, was that opium had now become "routine"; local officials both needed the revenue and were unwilling to irritate the people they governed by attacking "one of the prevailing customs of the day."[189] (Kuo Sung-t'ao, incidentally, mocked Pao for the inefficiency of his suppression moves, which made Pao the butt of jokes in Peking. According to Kuo, people would simply pull up a few poppies along the roadside when they heard that one of Pao's inspectors was coming; apart from that, they took no notice of the prohibitions.)[190] In Kiangnan, Governor-general Shen Pao-chen echoed Pao's sentiments: opium, once regarded as a deadly poison, was now treated as if it were tea or rice,[191] though Shen continued to dismiss officials in his own jurisdiction who were opium smokers.[192] That taxes for opium growing were quite public in some areas can be seen from the example of Ning-hsia. In 1878 the local inhabitants kept their best land for opium, saying that otherwise they could not pay their taxes; and the prefect refused to send grain relief to Shensi, because half his land was now under opium and he had no grain surplus.[193]

Taxes on local growth, tacit acceptance of local growth, and bribery to permit local growth all took place in the context of the traditional tax system and the traditional bureaucracy. Quite the opposite was true with likin,* where one had a new tax, levied in a new way, to be applied to new purposes. Proposals for taxing opium had predated the Opium War. They were revived in 1853, when a censor suggested a rate of 40 taels for

---

* "Likin" was a new tax levied on the transport of goods inside China.

each imported chest.[194] In 1856 a collection of 12 taels per chest was started by the taotai in Shanghai, and in 1857 the same rate was levied in Ningpo. The 1858 tariff agreements between Britain and China settled on an import duty of 30 taels per picul; opium had to be sold by the importer at the port and could be transported inland only by Chinese as Chinese property.[195] Inland taxation on opium in transit was a difficult question for both the Chinese and the British, and it remained a separate problem in the inclusive import-duty debates—where the British 7.5 percent and the Chinese 12.5 percent had ended up with a 10 percent compromise that was never implemented.[196] In the original Chefoo convention, opium was granted treatment "different from that affecting other imports," since each provincial government was to be free to assess its own likin rates and collect them from the Chinese distributors. Debate continued on this question through the 1870s and 1880s. Tso Tsung-t'ang wanted a uniform rate of 120 taels per picul; Li Hung-chang swung between 60 and 90 taels; Thomas Wade suggested raising import rates to 45 taels and thought 40 taels would then be a generous likin assessment. The final ratified agreement of 1885 was for retention of 30 taels as import duty and a payment of 80 taels likin, which would exempt the opium from all further inland taxation.[197] On an annual import rate of 50,000 chests, this would yield 5,500,000 taels to the Chinese government.

In 1881, writing to the secretary of the Anti-Opium Society, Li Hung-chang stated, "Opium is a subject in the discussion of which England and China can never meet on common ground; China views the whole question from a moral standpoint, England from a fiscal."[198] But in fact it was the very complexity of the fiscal role that opium revenue played in late Ch'ing China's economy that made suppression so difficult. We can note a progression in the practical experience of several great officials: Chang Chih-tung in 1884 was most eloquently pleading to banish all opium from Shansi; in 1890 he was reorganizing the taxes on Hupei opium, in 1899 he was raising them, and in 1904 he was still discussing the use of funds from Hupei-processed opium for the purchase of foreign weapons.[199] Tso Tsung-t'ang had been savagely efficient in attacking smokers in Kansu and Shensi in the early Kuang-hsu reign; by 1881 he was talking of raising taxes on local opium to discourage smoking.[200] Tseng Kuo-ch'üan had been a powerful opium suppressor in Shansi; in Kiangnan by 1887 he was discussing uses of opium revenue in the handling of Shanghai affairs.[201]

Li Hung-chang's memorials yield the richest evidence. There, between 1862 and 1889, we find opium taxes used to make up deficits in the merchants' taxes—Tientsin opium for Chihli defense, Tientsin opium taxes to pay for Peking police, Tsingtao opium to pay for new patrol boats, coal for the cruiser *Chen-hai* to be bought with opium funds, opium to pay off interest on foreign loans to the new armies, and so on.[202]

Most of this revenue was doubtless import tax revenue collected at port of entry, but in some cases likin is specified, and one censor insisted that almost all local likin revenues came from domestic opium.[203] A survey of the *Peking Gazette* yields several examples of likin on both locally produced and foreign opium in transit, which show how tightly bound to opium revenues some self-strengthening and modernizing enterprises were. In 1877 the Kwangtung governor-general reported that sixteen gunboats were being built at the Canton arsenal; the cost to date of 96,860 taels plus the 4,148 taels a month in wages and sundries was all drawn from opium likin revenue.[204] The same work was continuing in 1880, on a base revenue from opium likin of 110,000 taels per annum (the total collected was 230,000, of which 120,000 was sent to court as a "subsidy").[205] In 1887 the governor of Taiwan, Liu Ming-ch'uan, was given Takow and Tamsui opium likin revenues to meet his naval and military expenses.[206] In the same year the Szechwan arsenal drew 67,771 taels from opium likin, which were used to make machinery, guns, cartridges, and percussion caps.[207]

Opium became such a major component in overall likin receipts that shifts in distribution patterns or changes in legal enforcement procedures could have wide-ranging fiscal repercussions. The case of Honan in 1870 illustrates this. In that year the governor reported that nearly all wholesale dealers were now based in Yü-chou, which had had no likin office since the Taiping days; the lesser dealers in Shen-chou, Ho-nai-hsien, and Ch'ing-hua-chen, who had "compounded" for the payments, were going broke for lack of business, whereas Yü-chou had "several scores of new firms." Opium was a key part of likin, and most of it originally came from the produce of Shensi and Kansu. Tso Tsung-t'ang's prohibitions of opium in northwest China had upset the conventional opium trade patterns; it was now Szechwan opium that was flowing into Honan, and new branch stations were needed to catch the new revenue. Teng-chou was a key town at which to tap the Hu-kuang and Honan shipments.[208] After approval had been granted, the governor set up his new stations as well as smaller substations to "inspect the opium duty certificates" and stop "the adoption of circuitous routes" by tax-evading merchants.[209]

Such reports as this must have been studied by the Board of Revenue, for in 1887 they tried to standardize domestic opium likin on a fixed-payment plan—as foreign opium had been standardized at 80 taels in the 1885 agreements—deciding on a rate of 45 taels per picul. Just as harsh tax collection in times of dearth led peasants to riot, so did increased opium taxes lead to discontent. News of the higher likin rate caused a mob led by a military graduate to sack the magistrate's yamen at Yuan-ch'ü in Shansi.[210] Two years later, at Hsiangshan, near Ningpo, two local growers and an opium seller joined forces to whip up a crowd on market day and sack the magistrate's yamen and destroy the three new likin barriers that had driven up local opium prices.[211] (The rioters may have had a point, in that such opium-likin stations seem to have been prone to rather extraordinary graft—furthermore, at least one corrupt likin station was run by an expectant magistrate, which suggests that this may have developed as a new and lucrative post that could be used to relieve bureaucratic unemployment.)[212]

The revenue potentials of native opium grew more and more tantalizing to the Ch'ing. In 1891, through a system of official dues which were to replace likin, the central government started to collect opium revenue itself.[213] In 1896, when the twenty million taels of annual Imperial Maritime Customs revenue was already 80 percent pledged to cover foreign loans, they approached Robert Hart. The Board of Revenue asked Hart on May 16 if he would take over all collections on inland native opium.[214] In mid-June they renewed the offer. Hart, who had hoped for such an offer since 1894,[215] wrote to Campbell,

> I have again been asked to take *Native Opium* in hand and consented; but it will be no easy job for it extends our work over all China, will be disliked by officials and people and will take years to getting into anything like efficient condition. As I said before—if I had only twenty years more work in me, or, better if I was twenty years younger, I might now look forward to doing something big and being really useful: so far all I have done has been to keep the customs on its legs and go on widening its base at every chance and so securing stability—now I might build, but "hélas!" that's for other men to do.[216]

Hart started work on an opium taxation memo, but the president of the Board of Revenue "funked it," according to Hart, on June 24.[217] Hart expressed his disappointment in a letter dated July 4, 1897, after the board had drafted its own plans:

> The *Hu-pu* stole my "thunder" and instead of giving me the *Native Opium* have directed the provincials themselves to deal with it: ordering them at once to collect Tls. 20,000,000 annually on chests 330,000—I had promised that result in *thirty* years time! Of course my plan is spoiled, and their experiment will fail.[218]

No satisfactory system had been developed by 1906, when the mutual accords with Britain on a 10 percent per annum suppression rate were made.

We can see from the foregoing discussion that in seeking to eradicate opium addiction the Ch'ing state had to deal with a formidable array of vested interests. The damage that opium growing caused to Chinese agriculture and to peasant and urban morale has long been known to us; but we should also entertain the hypothesis that these vested interests— criminals, poor peasants, coolies, merchants, and officials—may have been so resistant to suppression just because opium had provided fluid capital and fresh revenue sources in a stagnating domestic economy. Only when moral outrage transcended these special interests could a successful suppression campaign commence. This moral outrage was coordinated by tough senior officials like Hsi-liang[219] who were not afraid to use military force against Chinese growers; and it was encouraged by the British, who had clearly lost their dominating position in the Chinese opium market and, with new types of investments in China and new sources of revenue for India, were willing to be reciprocally gracious.[220]

The considerable success of the opium suppression campaigns between 1906 and 1915 points up the force of emergent Chinese nationalism and the recovery of a sense of social purpose,[221] just as the fall back into massive addiction between 1915 and 1945 points to the premature frustration of that nationalism and sense of purpose.[222] The success of the Communist suppression campaign reaffirms the cycle.[223] As a sequence, these events seem to indicate that in ending opium addiction psychological factors are more important than physiological ones.

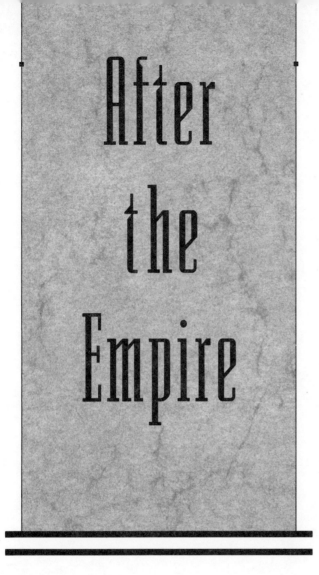

After the Empire

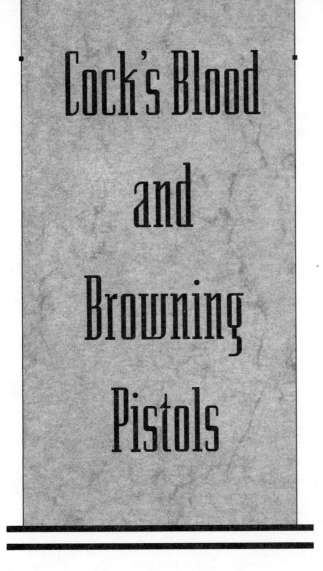

Cock's Blood
and
Browning
Pistols

During the play-off matches for the intercollegiate east China soccer title in the early 1920s, passions ran high. The president of Shanghai's prestigious Communications University was no less a soccer fan than anyone else, but he was also a rigorously trained and didactic Confucian scholar who demanded that his students observe the highest standards of

---

This essay first appeared in 1991, in the *New York Review of Books*.

deportment. He lectured them on ethics for an hour every single school day. There was no question of his being in the stands with the fans, especially not in the long traditional scholar's gown which he insisted on wearing for all university functions. Instead he had a telephone line installed, running from the soccer field to his presidential office. Kept informed of all goals scored by his own or the rival teams, he could cheer wildly or weep at the outcome in dignified seclusion. After the game was over, he would emerge once more into the public eye, in order to praise or castigate his team.

Nearly a decade later, in the spring of 1930, a north China villager, with the chafed and roughened fingers of the peasants who had added rug making to their other agricultural labors, graduated from the Rockefeller Foundation–funded Peking Union Medical College. Sent to work in a north China rural community, where a smallpox epidemic was ravaging the local populace, he decided to carry out a vaccination campaign. The supplies that he had been so expertly trained to use were simply not available. Accordingly, to administer the vaccine he gave his health workers sewing-machine needles, which they disinfected in wads of cotton soaked with Chinese brandy. By these means 21,605 local people were vaccinated, and indubitably many lives were saved.

The day-by-day business of what we often term "modernization" is inevitably full of paradoxes and adaptations such as these. They seem especially numerous in China, where the processes of economic growth and intellectual change were stymied or deflected by the warlordism, civil war, and foreign invasion that wracked the country from 1916 to 1949. They have been central, too, to the People's Republic of China, in which extraordinarily diverse policies have veered from total rejection of the West to an uncritical acceptance of almost everything Western. Leaders such as Mao Zedong, the "Gang of Four," and Deng Xiaoping have had little sense of how to proceed and how to channel these uncertain forces. The modernization of the Chinese army overlapped with the visionary and ultimately chaotic experimentation of the Great Leap Forward. President Nixon was invited to China when the xenophobic Cultural Revolution was still in full swing. Deng Xiaoping threw open his country to the West and condoned or ordered both the campaigns against "Spiritual Pollution" and the mass killing of civilians seeking democratic change in Peking during 1989.

The crisis now facing the leaders of the People's Republic has several overlapping components that appear to be intractable. Prominent among these are the problems of changing traditional rural patterns of life in ways that can benefit both the state and the local farmers; the attempts to organize urban workers so that they can live peaceably and work profitably in the impoverished cities; the need to encourage a modern managerial and entrepreneurial elite within a centrally controlled economy; the task of introducing China's brightest students and intellectuals to the techniques and ideas of the West without turning them against their own government and society; and the need to check the violent antisocial impulses that threaten to tear apart local communities and seriously disrupt the economic and social life of the nation as a whole. It is a sign of the energy and verve of Chinese studies in the West at the moment that five impressive new books, each based on extensive research, illuminate these matters from the perspective of the 1920s and early 1930s. Such a long view gives us a sense of how others tried to deal with the problems that the Communist leaders are now confronting.

The extent and complexity of non-Communist attempts at land reform in the 1920s and 1930s have been among the better-kept secrets in the People's Republic, where for obvious reasons the innovations and successes (as they were declared to be) of the land redistribution of the early 1950s were held up as the signal achievement of the Communist party itself. In fact, as Charles Hayford shows in his absorbing study of the liberal reformer James Yen,[1] primary attempts at land reform began during the pre-Communist period of the Chinese republic and were based in many ways on theories of mass education and of urban uplift, as these had been practiced for decades in the West, especially by groups such as the YMCA.

Yen was born in 1893 (the same year as Mao Zedong) to an educated family in northern Sichuan and made his way through local schools, which taught him the Chinese classics, to a modernizing missionary-run school in a nearby city, to a small college in Hong Kong, and thence to Yale, where he graduated in the class of 1918. Both in China and in Hong Kong, James Yen's world had already become one strongly influenced by Christianity and the strenuous religious image projected by the YMCA. "Confucius would have been a 'Y' man," a Chinese of the time observed, and the idealistic Protestant students to whom Yen became closest at Yale reinforced this message, as did the members of the Huie family, whom James met in New York. The head of this clan, Huie Chin, was the minister of the Chinatown Presbyterian Church, who had married a red-haired Irishwoman from Brooklyn.

The careers of this couple's nine children are neatly summarized in a couple of Hayford's paragraphs. Six of the Huie children were girls, and all married activist Chinese students studying in America. James's marriage (in 1921) to Alice Huie, a swimming champion and graduate of the Columbia Teachers' College Physical Education Department, was long and happy, ending with her death in 1980. As Hayford observes, this remarkable family formed "an important intersection in a network of Christians which reached across the Pacific" and was part of a chain that linked young Christian Chinese to many well-to-do young Americans, classmates or the friends of friends within their elite schools.

Yen returned to China via France, where he served with the YMCA among the more than one hundred thousand Chinese laborers who had been recruited by the British in World War I to help them with the digging of trenches, the unloading of transport ships, and the preparation of base areas behind the front lines. Hired as noncombatants, the Chinese at times got caught in the cross fire and were occasionally deliberately attacked by German planes or artillery. But their main function was to release more British men for active service. Among these uneducated and homesick Chinese, Yen found a ready audience for his offers to write letters home, for the simple reading primers he distributed among them, and for the few social services the Y could provide; in return, he absorbed a knowledge of the poor people of China for which there had been little room in his own previous education. From France, Yen traveled back to the United States, taking an M.A. degree from Princeton in history and politics and meanwhile strengthening his many contacts and friendships in the United States. After another stay in Sichuan, where he was an active leader of the mass literacy campaigns then under way, Yen was transferred to Peking, where he had a similar part in the mass education movement there. By 1926, he was hard at work with rural reform in Ting-hsien county in north China.

James Yen and the Chinese reformers who worked with him in the county were, in Hayford's apt words, "Trans-Pacific Liberals," but this did not mean they were "passive victims of foreign influence." They were, rather, "active adapters and creative developers of cosmopolitan ideas." In this they were not unlike the young Mao Zedong, and like Mao they "addressed the problem of how political power and China's culture could be used to build a modern nation. Each combined respect for China's traditions with a contempt for the educated elite who defined Chinese culture in selfish literary terms." Endeavoring to deal with "factors as diverse as modern ideas of nationalistic patriotism, new techniques of popular mobilization, the germ theory of disease, and the spread of flush toilets," their dedicated hard work and their pragmatism were intermingled with a "pastoral" conception of politics.

The attempts made at widespread change by these hardworking reformers—aided often by Western advisers, philanthropists, and co-workers and by the new techniques of social analysis and planning offered by the developing field of sociology—were truly broad. Their efforts, described by Hayford, are instructive not only for their intrinsic interest but also because they give one a sense of how daunting the task was, especially when one reflects that all this energy was concentrated on only a part of one county, as opposed to the nationwide attempts to be made by the Communists in the early 1950s. But many of the tasks and issues were the same and have endured or reemerged at the present day: the breeding of better livestock strains, the development of an efficient rural water-pumping system, the pooling of economic resources through cooperative associations, the building of an effective rural school system, the supervision of better cotton growing, development of commercial fruit farming, improvement of agricultural tools, increased availability of fertilizer, the curbing of insect-carried plant diseases, and the introduction of local health-care facilities.

When Yen's imaginative friend H. Y. Yao traveled with his sewing-machine needles and his Chinese brandy-soaked cotton wads to check the spread of smallpox, he did so as part of Yen's program in Ting-hsien. Yao and his fellow health workers also led fly-killing campaigns and hygiene classes and helped diminish the devastating extent of postnatal tetanus by teaching midwives not to smear the babies' severed umbilical cords with mud. Under the guidance of another extraordinary figure, the Peking- and Harvard-trained physician C. C. Ch'en, Ting-hsien reformers worked at a major plan to "deprofessionalize" the practice of Western medicine in China, by preventing the emergence of separate specialties of preventive and curative medicine. Instead, they worked to make the most of the available health-care resources by developing a three-tiered system of health-care delivery.

At the lowest level, they trained village health workers, chosen from among the local farmers, who were "fortified with brief training and armed with a simple first aid box." The first aid boxes, made available to each village at a cost of three dollars, contained eye ointment and calo-mel, castor oil and aspirin, scissors, bandages, vaccination equipment, and disinfectant. Above these local health workers was a second tier of health stations in market towns, run by a doctor and a nurse, with lay helpers. Hospital beds were concentrated at the top tier, in district health centers, where other doctors were backed by dentists, pharmacists, laboratory assistants, and sanitation staff. Birth control, however, remained an intractable problem at all levels, and they reluctantly decided it would have to follow after basic changes in economic growth and education, instead of preceding and encouraging them.

Had all these interconnected experiments and initiatives been able to spread peacefully and effectively, China's modern history would certainly have been vastly different. But they did not spread, and Hayford tells us cogently and carefully why they did not: there were problems of ideology, of national versus local politics, of nationalist impulses versus Christian ones. The government officials who took an interest in reforms wanted to impose them from the top downward. There were too few trained people to provide leadership in the villages. Foreign funding often went to inept government agencies rather than to local reformers; there was a shortage of money and a shortage of will. Banditry, world depression, local corruption, Japanese aggression, all undermined the hopeful initiatives, which collapsed altogether during World War II. After the war, despite much goodwill, energetic fund-raising, and the emergence of promising new groups like the Joint Commission on Rural Reconstruction, little could be done to check the Nationalist collapse.

As the Communists consolidated their hold over China in 1949, James Yen, his wife, and their two daughters left for an apartment he had maintained on West End Avenue in New York. After a time in the United States, James Yen worked in the Philippines for the rest of his long life. But all three of his sons insisted on staying in China to help build the new society. The three young men made an agreement with their sisters: after one year in the People's Republic they would sent a snapshot to New York. If the three brothers were shown as seated, all was well. If one or the other were standing, they were in trouble, and the sisters should not try to return. The snapshot arrived as promised: it showed all three brothers standing. The youngest of the three subsequently committed suicide.

Even though reforms like those attempted by James Yen and his associates in Ting-hsien brought a measure of heightened local prosperity along with better health standards, they could never begin to solve the huge problems of rural poverty; and throughout the 1920s and 1930s there was always a steady migration away from the north China countryside, either to southern Manchuria, or other regions where seasonal farm labor was needed, or else into the larger cities where jobs might be available in transport industries, in factories, or in construction. For those who were truly desperate, one line of work was almost always available, that of the rickshaw coolie. Slotted between the long protruding shafts of the rickshaw, his passenger seated comfortably behind in a padded seat slung between the rickshaw's two rubber tires, the rickshaw puller represented human labor in one of its lowest and most apparently debased forms: desperately dodging cars and mule carts, his legs pumping down the road through dust or mud, his breath rasping in his throat and his heart pounding.

Yet though he was often perceived as the prototype of the desperate country hick adrift in the big city, the rickshaw puller also became, as David Strand shows in *Rickshaw Beijing*,[2] the model of the street-smart operator. Though often desperately poor, the rickshaw pullers had their own culture and their own style of life. Able either to use the newly paved roads of China's modernizing cities or to slip down narrow alleyways, where no car or cart could penetrate, they learned swiftly to hunt out customers, to bargain, and to exploit the interlocking worlds of the streets, the restaurants, the theaters, and the brothels. They became, in Strand's words, the performers of "social dramas" and the partners in a "politics of the streets," with their own camaraderie and their own cult of insolence.

Perhaps more than any other city dwellers, they learned to explore the new phenomenon of "public space" that had entered into Chinese urban life along with the twentieth century, a space somewhere between the previously exclusive zones of private life and official administration. In a world in which all sorts of new regularities were demanded, in which streetcars had to proceed on fixed tracks, passengers had to pay their fares, automobiles had to stick to one side of the paved roads, trains had to follow schedules, tariffs of charges had to be adhered to, the rickshaw puller had his own flexible sphere in which he was free to bargain, work his own hours, and break any rules as long as the police weren't watching him. (Some police, indeed, whose salaries were also desperately low, and often in arrears as various Peking governments succumbed to fresh warlord conquests, moonlighted as rickshaw pullers themselves.)

In *Rickshaw Beijing* David Strand takes us into a part of urban China in the 1920s that we have not seen before and provides an admirable addition to the studies of the urban work force in such cities as Shanghai and Tianjin that have recently appeared. But because Strand deals with workers in a very volatile line of work, in which injury or even death were commonplace, upward social mobility was almost impossible, and hostile confrontations with police were constant, he comes close to showing us the city as potential anarchy. He describes for us a limbo or netherworld that in the 1920s, as today, the Chinese urban administration watched over with constant anxiety—a world largely unregulated, untraceable, with its own rules and codes and networks that had little to do with those of the state.

In the 1920s, Strand shows, rickshaw pullers were a constantly visible part of Peking's population of 1,100,000. There were about 60,000 pullers, who represented almost one-sixth of the city's working males between the ages of sixteen and fifty. (Occasionally, women disguised themselves as men to get work as rickshaw pullers, and sometimes two or even three children squeezed between the shafts to try and perform the work of one adult.) They were tied in an intimate economic and social relationship to the garage owners who rented out the rickshaws to them by the day and who sometimes offered shelter overnight in the garages or provided emergency food and drink. More important, the pullers had relations with other members of the working class that make it hard to fit them into conventional economic categories. Certainly, "worker solidarity" was far from their thoughts, either with other laborers or even with their fellow pullers, who were often their rivals. Their enemies included mule cart drivers, automobile chauffeurs, and increasingly during the twenties the drivers and conductors of the new city streetcar and bus services. More than a few workers died in the clashes between the rickshaw pullers and their competitors.

The Communist party tried early on to organize the rickshaw pullers, but even if one could persuade them not to abruptly leave talks about the union in order to pick up a fare down the street, it was hard to convince them of the benefits of union organization. Rickshaw pullers tended to be loners, and instead of improving their lot, a strike was more likely to force potential customers on to other forms of public transport. Nor would a rickshaw strike have the immediate consequences of a strike by the other desperately poor denizens of Peking—night-soil collectors, for instance, could have an immediate impact by ceasing their rounds, as could water carriers; coffin makers would quickly have an impact too, especially in hot weather, as could shoemakers and tent sewers, at least when a military campaign was under way.

Nevertheless, in times of national humiliation rickshaw pullers might refuse to pull Japanese or British customers. When interviewed by inquisitive students, they could present articulate views of what "revolution" meant in their eyes, and by the late 1920s many thousands of the pullers had begun to seek union protection. When goaded beyond their limits, they could flare into sudden and alarming violence.

One such episode took place on October 22, 1929, when for a long night the rickshaw pullers virtually controlled the city. The story of how they came to do so is complex, involving tensions with a militant street-car union, arguments among leaders of the fledgling rickshaw union, and anger caused by college students, who hired rickshaws to pull them long distances back to campus and then ran inside to sanctuary without paying, leaving the gatekeepers to beat up the pullers when they tried to invade the campus. The members of "aristocratic" unions such as the telephone and postal workers, and those in the electric power companies, were often unsympathetic to the rickshaw pullers and increased their sense of isolation. The rickshaw pullers started to order passengers out of the streetcars in the afternoon of October 22; soon they were smashing the passenger shelters, breaking streetcar windows, and cutting power lines. Then they started to derail streetcars and to block the streets, until the services were brought to a complete halt. The police carefully stayed away, as the pullers wrecked or destroyed sixty out of the ninety streetcars then operating.

Late at night army units moved in, firing blank rounds and laying about them with rifle butts; only then did the pullers slowly retire from the fray. Many of those returning to the original flash point of the riot found that their rickshaws had been stolen while they were away. No one was killed, but two hundred pullers were arrested; four of the leaders were subsequently shot by firing squad, and thirty-five were jailed. As Strand rightly says, this was the largest outbreak of unauthorized urban violence in Peking between the Boxer Rising of 1900 and the Tiananmen incidents of 1976 and 1989. The warlord troops and police of the chaotic 1920s can be seen to have exercised a discipline and restraint that eluded their latter-day successors, the rulers of the People's Republic.

Such parallels are worth making, and reflecting on, if we are to try to make sense of the People's Republic and come to a realistic assessment of its successes and failures. Marie-Claire Bergère is especially candid about the need to reconsider the previously accepted Marxist categories in the field of modern Chinese history if we are to understand it. As she notes in her introduction to *The Golden Age of the Chinese Bourgeoisie,*[3] her book originated as a dissertation for the *doctorat d'état* in France. Conceived along Marxist lines with the help of Marxist academic advisers, it was to be part of a three-part investigation of the basic class categories of the Chinese state: the bourgeoisie, the proletariat, and the peasantry. The Chinese bourgeoisie itself, following received Marxist wisdom, was divided into three distinct groups:

> the "comprador bourgeoisie" under foreign influence, the "bureaucratic bourgeoisie" linked to a reactionary political apparatus and, finally, the "national bourgeoisie," the only group that had worked for the progress and modernization of the country.

Only years after she had finished her research for her thesis, and the world and China had changed, did Bergère come back to the topic. Why, she asked herself, did Deng Xiaoping, in opening China to the West, seem to be relying on so many children of the old bourgeoisie, descendants of millionaires like the Rongs, once known as the "Rockefellers of China"? Where had these people really come from, she wondered, and what had their history been like? A completely revised version of her book was published in France in 1986 and has now been excellently translated by Janet Lloyd. It appears in the series on capitalism as a world system under the direction of a group at the Fernand Braudel Center at the State University of New York in Binghamton, and at the Maison des Sciences de l'homme in Paris.

As she reconsidered her original work, Bergère concluded that the Marxist categories of comprador, bureaucratic, and nationalistic bourgeoisie had no historical basis. The Chinese bourgeoisie had emerged from a changing imperial Chinese society in which the state, although it could not control economic organizations and growth, initially "did manage to control the social transformations connected with that growth." Despite these restrictions, a "cosmopolitan and entrepreneurial China" emerged as the Western powers enforced the newly devised "treaty port" system of fixed tariffs, foreign residence and investment, and missionary activity, both on China's coast and along the major inland waterways.

The Qing state tried to persuade overseas Chinese entrepreneurs to invest in their homeland; in doing so, they contributed to the growth of a new urban, commercial intelligentsia. But such investment and the accompanying growth depended to a considerable extent on foreign firms and employees. The more Bergère looked into the subject, the more the idea of a "nationalist" bourgeoisie faded away. She found "that, strictly speaking, there were no Chinese businesses independent of the foreigners in the treaty ports in the early years of the twentieth century." The more telling distinction to be made was "between the relative economic and cultural alienation [from other Chinese traders and investors] of the modernised urban elite groups and their more or less unanimous nationalistic aspirations."

Furthermore, the overthrow of the last Qing emperor in 1911–12 was not, in any sense, a "bourgeois revolution," as Marxist interpretation insisted. True, "an urban elite connected with modern business," participated in the overthrow, but the basic work of ending the imperial system came from "high-ranking officials, landowners, military officers and the heads of secret societies and armed bands." This was of crucial importance to later-twentieth-century China, since the apparent acceptance of aspects of democracy, constitutionalism, and nationalism by such powerful groups did not alter their underlying social conservatism. "Freedom" in China continued to be "not defined so much in terms of the individual but rather in opposition to the authoritarianism of central government. So it is not surprising if the local elite groups regarded the establishment of their own power as a triumph for democracy."

The Golden Age of the Chinese Bourgeoisie is an important book, but the dates in its subtitle—1911–1937—are misleading. This subtitle suggests that the Chinese bourgeoisie was somehow flourishing until the onslaught of the full Japanese invasion of China after 1937. This, in turn, implies that the decade of Chiang Kai-shek's rule from Nanking, between 1927 and 1937, was a prosperous period for the Chinese bourgeoisie, which implies in turn that Chiang Kai-shek's downfall was somehow a tragedy for the flourishing bourgeoisie. In fact, Bergère's book shows that this "golden age" lasted until 1927, not 1937. Only an epilogue of 25 pages, coming at the end of 270 pages of text, deals with the 1927–37 period, and that epilogue shows that Chiang helped to end the growth of the bourgeoisie by reasserting bureaucratic state control over their activities. This reimposition of state power, Bergère writes, was more important to the fate of the bourgeoisie than even the Communist victory of 1949. Why, then, is there a fairly consistent view in the West, and inside China, that Chiang Kai-shek heavily favored the bourgeoisie and encouraged their growth? There were indeed, as Bergère cites, some valid ambiguities, and some real difficulties in determining what the dominant social forces were under the Nanking regime:

> But the misunderstandings also seem to have been deliberately fostered by the Chinese themselves—by communist theorists anxious to make developments in China conform with Marxist schematas, who have sought to establish the existence of a

bourgeois phase, never mind whether it was comprador, bureaucratic or feudal, and above all by the government of Chiang Kai-shek, which was skilled at presenting the image of itself that most favoured its interests, the image most likely to win sympathy and financial aid from the West. Just as Mao Zedong's China was able to dangle before the eyes of the leftists and radicals of a Western world in a state of crisis the image of a society still pure, frugal and fraternal, Chiang Kai-shek's China tried to convince and win over the democrats of Europe and America by exaggerating its bourgeois character. In both cases, the success achieved by these manipulations gives some idea of the degree of our own ignorance as far as China is concerned. (p. 274)

The true golden age of the Chinese bourgeoisie, in Bergère's view, was between 1910 and 1920, when the collapse of the old Qing state, the weakness of the ensuing republican leadership, and the enforced removal of the Western imperialist powers from China following World War I, led to a period of "spontaneous capitalism" and "import substitution." Foreign businessmen were called away to active duty; the prices of materials like tungsten increased more than threefold; shipping costs to London from Shanghai went up twenty-five times, and weak local and national bureaucracies were unable to collect taxes. As a result, China's industrial growth rate between 1912 and 1920 averaged 13.8 percent. Bergère gives rich accounts of various groups of Chinese entrepreneurs during this time, concentrating on mechanical engineers and on cotton mill owners. She concludes that, in line with her earlier analysis of the "revolution" of 1911–12, the apparent "modernity" of this bourgeoisie was

> not based on a break with tradition but on its ability to make tradition serve new objectives. It was Chinese urban society itself that rose to the challenge of modernization and it did so according to its own terms. . . .

This initial "golden" period was followed by what Bergère calls the "bid for liberalism" on the part of bourgeois business leaders between 1920 and 1923, the occasion for this initiative being the instabilities caused by the emerging warlord regimes. The threat of the warlords' instability prompted the bourgeoisie to try to establish new organizations that would defend their newly won local liberties—but this did not mean they were seeking to defend individual liberties. Their attempts to establish some kind of "provincial federation" were merely designed to end the long-standing and vicious cycle by which free enterprise had been accompanied by civil disorder, and political order accompanied by economic exploitation.

The growth of merchant militias, chambers of commerce, and other industrialists' and producers' associations was a part of this process, which attained a peak of sorts in June 1923, when the Shanghai Chamber of Commerce set up the seventy-member "Committee of People's Government" and declared the city's "independence." The committee collapsed by August in the face of military and foreign pressures, and no little public ridicule. During the next four years, between 1923 and 1927, the bourgeoisie in Canton and Shanghai tried to adjust to the new centralizing politics of Sun Yat-sen and Chiang Kai-shek, a politics that included the mounting of the Northern Expedition to bring about national reunification, and the suppression of the radical peasant and workers' movements, along with the attempted annihilation of Chiang's erstwhile ally—the Communist party. In yielding up its bases of economic power to Chiang Kai-shek, Bergère concludes, the bourgeoisie was not "betraying the proletariat." It was merely betraying itself. "By abdicating its political autonomy, the bourgeoisie laid itself at the mercy of the State power that it had itself helped to restore."

Bergère mentions in passing the close interconnections between the newly prospering capitalists and the Chinese "modernist avant-garde," connections that

> were developed on a family and friendly level, were manifest in the diverse careers pursued by the various members of a single family, sometimes within a single lifetime, and were an integral part of the structure of Chinese society.

As an example, Bergère cites the Zhang family of central China, where one brother became China's most powerful banker, one a leading philosopher, and their sister the wife of China's best-known romantic poet. But as Wen-hsin Yeh shows in her new study, *The Alienated Academy*,[4] this "modernist avant-garde" was itself far from united and far from happy. One of the most important and original contributions of her richly documented study is that it shows the deep intellectual and social divisions that lay at the heart of China's emerging university world. Especially valuable are Yeh's analyses of the profoundly conservative thinking of many leaders of the public universities, in contrast to those at the smaller private universities that were often dominated by progressive "May Fourth movement" figures, who in different ways had set their sights on the twin goals of "Science and Democracy" proclaimed by the movement's leaders in 1919.

A good example of university conservatism can be found in the thinking of Tang Weizhi, the president of Communications University (formerly Nanyang School of Technology), whose passionate but private involvement in his school's soccer matches we noted above. President Tang, born in 1865, was a former scholar of the Qing dynasty's prestigious Hanlin Academy for Advanced Confucian Studies, and a leading interpreter of the *Book of Changes*. He believed that his school (over which he presided from 1907 to 1921) should not only teach modern engineering at the highest levels but also support traditional Chinese cultural values. Students had to pass a series of rigorous examinations based on the lengthy daily lectures he gave on ethics; waivers of tuition within the university were granted solely on the basis of performance in these exams. While other schools might celebrate commencement with a performance of a play of Shakespeare to prove their cosmopolitanism, President Tang celebrated Confucius' birthday instead, with all his faculty and students taking part in a full and formal ceremony. He also insisted on holding an examination in Chinese for the entire school on the anniversary of the old Confucian state examinations (which had been abolished in 1905). Tang himself acted as the proctor on this occasion. Dismayed by radical currents that reached into even his school by 1920, Tang resigned his presidency in order to found the Institute for the Study of National Learning; here he continued to instill purist Confucian principles into a new student generation during the entire Nanking decade.

The values expressed by President Tang in no way vanished with his resignation. Indeed, as Yeh shows in detail, a kind of Neo-Confucian revivalism, often linked to classical phonology, gained ground in the later twenties and thirties. Such studies in universities "provided the foundation of a highly historicist culturalism that rejected foreign elements both on grounds of systemic incompatibility and of adulterated genealogy." Administrators even more purist than President Tang posed linguistic examination questions that could be carefully answered only by wordplay that subtly denigrated leading May Fourth intellectuals like Hu Shi. Trendiness or unpopularity was not the issue here; purity was. "As elitist scholiasts," writes Yeh, "the classicists felt no compulsion to enlarge their academic constituency."

The "alienation" that Yeh ascribes in her title to Chinese academic life derived in part from frustrating and formula-ridden experiences like these, but also from the impracticality of many of the more "modern" schools, where the English language was considered more important than Chinese, radical politics were the order of the day, and yet no clear-cut system for getting students jobs in the upper economic echelons of society had been established. As many as 15 percent of the new college graduates could not find work, and the proportion was much higher in the humanities. Either warlord troops or, after 1929, the Guomindang Nationalist party often brutally intruded in university life. In some of the more elite private universities, there was a general hedonism, a pursuit of romantic love and of social conformity to a supposedly chic code of Western behavior. In one of the many fascinating pictures in Yeh's study, we see a 1931 cartoon of a young naked Chinese university student with bobbed hair, wearing only black high-heeled shoes, reclining with her bottom in an oversize cocktail glass, while she plays on the saxophone. Even in the private schools, continual tuition hikes and special charges for every conceivable cause—library use, late arrival on campus, makeup examinations, building construction, "damage deposits," lab equipment, musical instruments, sports, medical care—gave the university a mercenary aura and undermined student morale.

In the public universities most students were poor, and food and living conditions were atrocious. Regular complaints and protests only brought more state harassment. Students had to wear standard uniforms, follow Guomindang party rules on campus, attend compulsory courses on the infallibility of Sun Yat-sen's "Three Principles of the People," sing national songs, and undergo compulsory training for military or nursing service. Though this was still far from the political domination over the universities that prevailed during the People's Republic, Yeh reminds us that in the Nanking decade, "what the appearance of conformity and rituals of compliance on college campuses reflected was a profound penetration of state power into university administration and student life." These changes affected private and public schools alike, apart from a few missionary schools run by stubborn foreigners who successfully managed to avoid being browbeaten.

By the late 1930s, Yeh shows, the academy had become impoverished and humiliated, with little chance left of exerting influence on the nation's life. Nevertheless, some intellectuals and teachers refused to give up. Near the end of her study, Yeh quotes at length from Zhu Guangqian—the leading Chinese scholar of aesthetic theory during the 1920s and early 1930s—who sought the path to a new constructive regeneration of the Chinese spirit. He wanted to broaden the idea of self-cultivation within

society—through developing the "inner landscape" of every citizen—
though this demanded that the Chinese in turn be able "to nurture enough
sensitivity and to exercise sufficient self-discipline to participate in the
community of aesthetic insight." The great strength of Confucius, wrote
Zhu, had been his "unyielding resolve to pursue his moral vision despite
a sense of futility." More quietly pessimistic, but still hopeful that some
form of meaningful action could be found, was Hu Shi, the veteran of
the early May Fourth movement battles over the place of a "new culture"
and of "Science and Democracy" in China. Yeh quotes Hu Shi at his
most moving, in a passage written in 1930, suitably enough in the introduction to a book on human rights:

> A parrot used to rest on the top of Mt. Jituo. One day the
> mountain caught fire. The parrot, seeing the fire at a distance,
> dipped its feathers in the ocean, flew over the mountain, and
> sprinkled drops of water into the fire. The deity said to the
> parrot: "Your attempt is admirable. But how much difference
> can you possibly make?" The parrot replied: "This mountain
> once gave me a spot to rest. I cannot bear to see it it being
> reduced to ashes." (p. 276)

The metaphor of the reduction of the mountain to ashes suggests, with
a terrifying precision, the state of a China in which all social and political
controls have finally eroded, and where only untamed violence rages. It
was this specter that Communist leaders invoked in 1989 when denounc-
ing the democracy movement and defining the protests as inchoate and
rebellious actions led by hoodlums (even though the original demands
of the students had in fact been to meet with their government's leaders
and their most radical demand was for more freedom to publish). The
Guomindang in the 1930s had repeatedly invoked similar fears in its
attempts to rally the nation behind its attempts to eradicate Communists, just as the Qing dynasty had previously invoked similar arguments
to warn its people against the nascent revolutionary and republican
movement led by Sun Yat-sen.

The fear of the social chaos that lay below the surface of apparent
order was not an idle one either in the late nineteenth century or in the
late 1920s, as is amply demonstrated in Phil Billingsley's harrowing study,
Bandits in Republican China,[5] a carefully documented guidebook to a
hellish world, complete with an astoundingly erudite and bone-chilling
eight-page appendix entitled "Selected List of Bandit Slang." "Plucking
flowers" was the term for kidnapping women and children. "Wrapping

the tablet" meant eliminating a rival gang. Bullets were called "white rice." "Fire carriers" were those who led night attacks. "Eaters of two dumplings" were the scavenging gangs that picked up the leavings that the main bandit force happened to leave behind. "Wearing colors" or being "gaily dressed" was to be wounded; to "hang up a sheep" was to capture a middling wealthy man; a rich one was a "fat duck." To get "an earthly ticket" was to capture a woman (a "twofive" was a virgin woman captive). To "release" a captive meant to kill him, to "burn the ticket" meant to kill or maim a captive with fire, whereas "clipping the ticket" meant cutting off an ear or a finger. "Having fun" was to fight; "slapping bean curd," to beat someone on the buttocks.

Like Charles Hayford and Marie-Claire Bergère, Phil Billingsley worked for almost two decades to refine his subject and prepare his research for publication. In many ways his topic is the most elusive of all, but it is one that we need to know about if we are to understand the growing pains of modern China. Billingsley is not sentimental about the bandit forces he analyzes, nor does he overestimate their leaders' goals and intelligence. But he does show convincingly how they sprang from the social dislocation of the times, how they flourished in regions where state supervision was extremely weak. He is also well informed on how the Communist party sought either to co-opt or to recruit the bandit gangs into their own program of social revolution, and how—whether one is talking of Communists or Nationalists—"the state's implicit acceptance of the transformation of bandit gangs into armed protection groups, like the routinization of the Mafia in Al Capone's Chicago, was the most obvious example of the consequence of the 'overworld' and the 'underworld' in China."

In his analysis of what he calls "fierce democracy," moreover, Billingsley gives an absorbing account of how gangs were created and organized in republican China. Qualities of natural leadership, the ability to command respect and to act as "surrogate family," courage and intelligence, local ties, physical strength, cunning, sometimes even youth, when combined with extraordinary quick wits—any or all of these factors could push a man (and occasionally a woman) to the top of a gang, which could number anywhere from tens to thousands of followers. Once formed, the bandit gang had a fairly rigid hierarchy, which echoed the obedience and loyalty structures of the family and of the state. Nevertheless, Billingsley writes, the "appointment of new leaders was essentially democratic, based upon achievement and acknowledged ability." On one occasion, at least, the leadership of a gang was offered to a captured American doctor, H. J. Howard, whose height of six feet plus, membership in the Freemasons, training as a doctor, knowledge of Chinese, and fearlessness at the moment of capture all led his captors to elect him their chief. He did not accept.

The Western world got an awestruck view of this bandit universe—and Billingsley some of his best sources—when in May 1923 an unusually daring gang in Shandong province hijacked the entire Tianjin-to-Pukou passenger express train, kidnapping over three hundred passengers for ransom, including thirty Westerners, several of them Americans. (The incident later became the inspiration for the film *Shanghai Express*, starring Marlene Dietrich.) Most of the captives were released for a ransom sum of $85,000—the money, ironically, being supplied by a confidant of Chiang Kai-shek, who also happened to be one of Shanghai's leading racketeers in the gambling, prostitution, and heroin trades. Most of the bandits were then incorporated into regular army units, as they had requested, and their leaders received commissions.

In one of the most vivid of the many incidents recorded by Billingsley, in November 1911 three young anti-Qing revolutionaries set off into the mountains of western Henan province to try to recruit the members of a particularly notorious bandit gang to their revolutionary cause. Having studied up on the gang's "dark language" (that is, private slang) and been received into the bandits' base camp, the young men lectured the bandits on their revolutionary goals. They were given a feast of duck, chicken, pork, and mutton, washed down with abundant liquor. One of the young revolutionaries, named Wu, ritually prostrated himself before an elderly woman named Guan, mother of a bandit murdered the summer before, and indicated his desire to join the revolution together with her, "overthrow the corrupt officials and local tyrants, and carry out the Way on behalf of Heaven." The following day all met before the same old lady and signed an oath of brotherhood, sealing the oath by pouring a freshly killed cock's blood into a bowl of wine, from which they all drank. As Billingsley observes, at the end of this remarkable meeting, "when the ceremony was over, Old Mother Guan presented Wu with the Browning pistol that her son had treasured when he was alive."

The cock's blood and the Browning pistol draw us back full circle to the soccer stadium and the Confucian gown, to the Chinese brandy swabs and the smallpox vaccine. Each of these five books reminds us of the traditional elements lying at the heart of the new, and of the paradoxes that have lain side by side during China's long struggle to achieve a modern transformation.

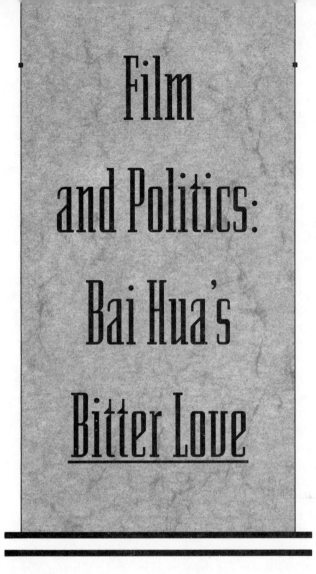

Film and Politics: Bai Hua's Bitter Love

The difficulty of gaining a precise focus on China's long revolution grows with each passing year. If one defines a revolution as the transformation, in varying degrees, of a society's basic cultural impulses, economic life, and structures of government—then China has been involved in revolution for more than eighty years. Such a duration has

---

This previously unpublished essay is based on a lecture delivered in 1982.

the effect of making the word "revolution" appear almost meaningless; accordingly, rather than throw out the word altogether, we might attempt instead to view the history of modern China as a series of revolutions, a series in which the events of 1949 and afterward are merely a part, not the total watershed that they have commonly been held to be.

There are almost infinite ways of charting the sequences that dominate this revolutionary process. One interpretation can be found in Lao She's play *Teahouse (Chaguan)*, first published in 1958. Lao She was a remarkable figure—a Manchu, a scholar of classical Chinese, an instructor at SOAS, a lover of Dickens—who lived through the Second World War in China, spent the late 1940s in the United States, and returned in 1950 to the fledgling People's Republic of China, where he met fame, fortune, and a violent, untimely death. In *Teahouse* he chose a characteristically idiosyncratic way of presenting China's revolutionary course— linking each moment of profound potential change to a parallel moment of profound political repression.

The three acts of the play are set in 1898, 1917, and 1947. In the first of these years, the Qing dynasty chose to strike down the Confucian reformers who were attempting to guide the Guangxu emperor in the direction of institutional, economic, and educational change. Kang Youwei's younger brother and Tan Sitong were executed, while Kang himself and his leading disciple, Liang Qichao, were forced into exile. In 1917, after Yuan Shikai's death, militarists moved toward a second imperial restoration, shattering the last hopes for a constitutionally valid republic in China (which had already been crucially weakened by the assassination of Song Jiaoren and the banning of the Guomindang as a political party) and opening the way to the protracted era of warlordism in China. The third year stands more loosely for the period in which Chiang Kaishek, following the assassination of Wen Yiduo and the failure of the Marshall mission, chose to concentrate his energies on confronting the Communists in Manchuria while crushing all domestic dissension, signally failing to make the kind of political concessions or economic reforms that might have won the intellectuals and the business classes over to his side.[1] The shape of Lao She's play and its essential open-endedness left hovering in the air the question of a fourth act, one that would be set in the audience's mind in 1957, as Communist leaders and the internal security forces in China chose to convert the "Hundred Flowers" movement into an "antirightist" campaign.

The structure of Lao She's drama seems to me to contain a fundamental historical insight concerning the major stages of China's revolution:

namely, that there were three such stages in the half century before 1949 and that they can be identified as the search for a viable constitutional monarchy, the search for a viable republic, and the search for a coherent nationalism. To these three phases in the history of modern China, one could add three separate periods of equally dramatic change, or attempted change, within the People's Republic, giving us a six-part analytic structure for the period 1898–1982.

In phase one, from 1898 to 1910, there was a revolutionary attempt to transform the world's longest tradition of imperial rule. The attempt was rooted in the overlapping pressures from foreign imperialism, internal tensions both intellectual and economic, and the ambiguous status of the Manchu ruling house itself in Han Chinese society. Proposals for change included sending imperial commissioners to Europe to study the constitutional monarchies, transforming the educational system and the recruitment of bureaucrats, and restructuring the whole notion of governmental participation through local councils and provincial assemblies. The failure of the attempt, through a combination of internal military and gentry resistance, overseas Chinese opposition, and Manchu incompetence, does not lessen its drama or scope.

Following the failure of efforts at constitutional monarchy, the second phase, from 1910 to 1920, concentrated on establishing a republican government. Here the absolute rejection (instead of the modification) of the more than two millennia of imperial history paralleled in depth and fury the French Revolution, which was a pervasive model at the time. With additional stimuli from studies of democratic institutions in the United States and of socialist theories filtered through Japan, this decade saw the fall of the Qing, China's first broad-based elections, Chinese participation in the First World War, and the May Fourth movement. The wide array of practical and theoretical questioning of the basic structures of government that surfaced during this period could not, however, prevail against the negative forces of political assassination, military intransigence, China's lack of any prior history of democratic institutions, Yuan Shikai's own attempts at imperial restoration, and the venality of Peking politicians.

A third phase, dominated by the search for a coherent nationalist ideology, can be identified as falling between 1921 and 1947, though the extraordinary complexity of the period and the development of the struggle between the Guomindang and the Communists make a precise delineation difficult. Nevertheless the fact remains that both parties decided during this period to accept the failure of the republic's institutions and to move against warlordism and foreign imperialism with an ideologically indoctrinated army controlled by a democratic-centralist party. Once again, this constituted a quite radical shift in Chinese politics, during a period dominated by such markers as the Communist party's agreement with Sun Yat-sen, the May Thirtieth movement, the Jiangxi soviet declaration of war against the Japanese, and the Xian agreements of 1936–37.

The years between 1947 and 1957 mark a fourth phase, in which the Communists, first in Manchuria and north China and then across the whole country and in Tibet, sought a radical reorganization of China's economic foundations. The massive change they sought included the nationalization of domestic industry, the expulsion of foreigners, the expropriation of foreign assets, the obliteration of the landlord class, the distribution of land titles to poor peasants and landless laborers, the overhaul of the army after the Korean War, the restructuring of the bureaucracy, and the shift to pro-Soviet and anti-U.S. policies. But we may contrast this fourth phase with yet a fifth, which might be termed the attempt at a radical transformation of human nature, extending (with interruptions) from 1957 to 1974. This period saw remarkable attempts to deepen and intensify the already formidable changes of the earlier period by means of the full collectivization of agriculture, the assaults on individual psychology and family behavior in the Great Leap Forward, the development of the People's Liberation Army into a leading interpreter of the thought of Mao Zedong, the search for revolutionary criteria governing entrance to the fruits of higher education, the revitalization of the Communist party from within, and the rejection of the Soviet Union, added to that of the United States, in China's quest for a newly pure culture as free from foreign as from feudal influences.

Though it is not precisely clear when this fifth phase ended—one could suggest various dates between 1971 and 1976—it seems safe to say that there followed a sixth phase, from 1977 to 1981, in which the revolutionary goal shifted to the rapid technological transformation of Chinese society. The chief means for rapid change in this period included the large-scale importation of Japanese, American, and European managerial and technological skills, the centralized and concerted assault on the problem of population growth, dramatic shifts in incentive patterns for Chinese workers and for foreign investors, the overseas education of a Chinese technological elite, and the upgrading of communications networks. Doubts about the possibility of such speedy change seem to have set in during 1981, if not before, and to have become widespread by 1982.

Bai Hua's filmscript *Bitter Love (Ku Lian)*, completed in the spring of 1979, offers an ideal marker for this moment of transition into the moral ambiguities of the 1980s.[2] Bai Hua, in 1979 a fifty-year-old writer and director of the Tianjin propaganda department, had apparently recovered from criticism of his overly frank writings during the Great Leap Forward, and during the late 1970s flourished in a bureaucratic career that led to his appointment as vice-chairman of the Tianjin Revolutionary Committee in 1977.[3] He was made one of the featured speakers at the Fourth National Congress of Writers and Artists, which met in early November 1979. In his address to this group, which had already heard the remarkable speech of the recently rehabilitated novelist and short story writer Ding Ling, as well as the formulaic remarks of Deng Xiaoping, Bai Hua praised those "comrades and comrades-in-arms [who] have left us forever. We can still remember how they hoped and fought as we did. They left behind for us their hopes and struggle." He referred to "the past 50 years," in which

> our great nation, under the leadership of the CCP, used its blood—which flowed like a turbulent river—to open a road to national survival, wakening us from a state of feudalism and ignorance. Precisely because more and more people were awakening, we had more and more fighters, won ever greater victories in battle and built a great people's republic. Our motherland has had a bright and beautiful morning. In the morning, we were sober and made great sacrifices to achieve our goal. At that time our Party was fully confident and had inexhaustible power. All the people responded to its calls. This was because the Party took root among the people.[4]

Then, switching more specifically to the Gang of Four period, he discussed the people who "distorted scientific Marxism-Leninism and rigidly turned it into a religion":

> They deified the revolutionary leader by making use of the dictatorship and the mass movement. Most people did not dare oppose and doubt this deification. Even today, when we oppose modern fetishes and advocate science, we can still see

scenes which resemble those before the revolution of 1911 where anyone who smashed an idol was surrounded and beaten to death. Martyr Zhang Zhixin died in this way. Her blood awakened more and more people. However, there are still some people who obstinately stick to their wrong course and some who feign devoutness for private reasons. Those who obstinately stick to their wrong course are pitiful. Those who feign devoutness are hateful like the silkworm. We must vigorously bite off the cocoon we have built around ourselves. Only by so doing can we get fresh air and sunlight and have the space for our survival and growth.[5]

Bai Hua noted that China was "an innocent and honest nation," yet a "gullible" one. To help it to self-awareness, writers would have "to restore the minimum function of literature and art in reflecting social life"; they should refuse to "eulogize the state of ignorance for which we have made a great national sacrifice" and reject the newly looming world in which "hypocrites are safe and the honest are in danger." In his peroration, he appealed for democracy, unity, and what he called "the minimum conditions for writers and artists" and "a show of concern for the training of young writers." He ended the speech, which was fully reported in the *People's Daily* for November 13, 1979, with an appeal for a "breakthrough."[6]

Bai Hua's working script for *Ku Lian,* which has luckily been preserved, is a maze of overlapping flashbacks, designed to illuminate the life and political fate of his hero. This intricacy must certainly have made the film hard to follow, but Bai Hua is meticulous in providing chronological signposts throughout the work that orient the reader or viewer. He also gives lengthy, often reflective stage directions; it is therefore quite easy to reconstruct the script so that it offers a coherent chronological survey of the life of the protagonist, Ling Chenguang. This exercise seems to me worth undertaking in order to get a sense of the patterning of the Chinese revolutionary experience that Bai Hua intended to share with a wider world.

Ling Chenguang is presented as having been born in a small town in a mountainous area of China, around 1925; the population of the region is mainly Miao, and Ling is shown to be living happily among these "minority peoples." We gather the levels of his parents' education and sophistication from the fact that his father plays "the organ" (*fengqin* in the original Chinese) and his mother teaches children's art. Ling himself loves to watch the local potters, impoverished yet creative, who form little votive statues to be used in local Buddhist shrines. He often plays truant from school in order to watch them at work.

The first phase of Ling Chenguang's shift from childhood innocence to political maturation is presented by Bai Hua as occurring in 1937 or 1938, when young Ling leaves home after his father's death to seek his fortune in the world. As the twelve-year-old boy strides down the road with his bundle on his back, he encounters refugee students fleeing from the advancing Japanese armies. One group of young women, in their panic, struggle with each other to clamber aboard "an almost new Dodge truck" that stops for them, even though the driver (one assumes he is in the Guomindang army, though this is not specified), "fat-headed, big-eared," taunts them with sexual banter and threats. All that the boy Ling can do, as the driver roars off with the girls aboard, is "stare fixedly, with grief and fright at the dust rising from the highway."[7]

Four years later, however, he can take a slightly more active stance, though he remains largely a spectator rather than a participant. Now growing into manhood, Ling has discovered powers as a painter, and he lives in contented poverty developing his new skills. He has found his first love, too, a young woman called Juan-juan; the girls' mother plays Chopin and her father, once a scientist in the West, has returned to China to help his nation in its need, only to be rejected. Ling finds friendship in this sensitive family, just as he finds spiritual solace and scholarly encouragement in the local Buddhist monastery. The senior monk there leads him a step on the way to enlightenment, for when Ling asks why the Buddha image in the shrine is black, the monk replies, "The incense from devout men and women has blackened him. . . . My child, in the mortal world the consequences of affairs frequently turn out contrary to the best of intentions."[8] Despite his happiness, Ling makes the crucial decision to leave this aesthetic haven and to seek continued meaning in the outer world.

In phase three of his life, he finds that meaning in both suffering and love. Conscripted into the Nationalist army by press-gang methods, handcuffed, shackled, and beaten, he escapes and finds shelter with a group of boat people. Their gentle yet courageous care of Ling contrasts with the violence of the world he has left, but Ling again decides he must travel on and leave the boat girl Lu-niang, with whom he has fallen in love. "In a man's life voyage," intones an offstage voice, "everyone has many ports and harbors that he is reluctant to leave but has to leave."[9]

It is only between 1947 and 1948 that Ling reaches his full political maturity. Now in his early twenties, he throws himself into the socialist struggles of his time. The scene is the Shanghai Bund, and Ling is one of the masses who chant, "Down with hunger! Down with Civil War! Down with persecutions!" His brilliance as an artist is now dedicated to the radical cause, as he produces streams of woodcuts "showing hungry people either stretching out rice bowls or holding weapons and sticks, their eyes spurting flames of fury";[10] Ling himself distributes the woodcuts in leaflet form to the Shanghai crowds and to those jamming the harbor in search of escape to the West. Even more courageously, he paints revolutionary pictures high on buildings for all to see. Fired at by police, sheltered once again by boat people (including his beloved Lu-niang of World War II days), Ling finally takes refuge on an ocean liner tied up at the dock. To his horror, as police patrol the waterfront, the boat raises anchor and glides out to sea. Ling has no escape. He has become, unwillingly, an "overseas Chinese."

In a brief but powerful interlude that follows, Bai Hua gives us a vision of Ling's success. The stage direction in his script reads: "An American seacoast city toward the end of the forties. In brilliant sunshine, rows and rows of multi-storied houses, white as snow. On the bathing beach, thousands of men and women sunbathing, many-colored sunshades like multicolored mushrooms." Ling himself is famous. A "modern art gallery," attended by a "stream of elegantly dressed people," holds a one-man show of his work. And here comes Ling, in his black limousine: "Dressed in a trim foreign suit and wearing a pair of sunglasses, Chenguang steps out of the car. At first we hardly recognize him, with his small well-trimmed beard and a big pipe between his lips."[11] And it is from this fame, this latest idyll, that the boat girl Lu-niang comes to rescue him. How she ever reached America is not made clear, but her message is simple: China, the new People's Republic, needs them both. After Ling has seduced her in his sensual American haven, they return together on board the SS *Sainte Jeanne d'Arc*. Their first and only child, a girl, is born on shipboard but, as they discover to their excitement, within China's territorial waters.

Chronologically, we switch now to Bai Hua's vision of People's Republic history. China welcomes Ling, his bride, and their child. The 1950s are presented as a time of joy, peace, and fulfillment. Ling paints with brilliance and enthusiasm, for now he serves his country and not just himself. He and Lu-niang teach the Young Pioneers, the party members of the future. The most vivid cinematic images are of tiny birds wheeling over fields of green grass, and of fireworks ascending above the

Tianan Men. "New China," calls out an offscreen voice, "what a wonderful beginning you had."[12]

The dream that has become reality is shattered by the Cultural Revolution—a Buddha grown dark because "the incense burned by faithful men and women has stained him black." This reprise of Ling's childhood memories of temple happiness is now transposed to a Beijing street, "full of people waving the *Quotations of Chairman Mao*, all those devout and artless faces fired by a feverish fanaticism."[13] Ling and his family are now doomed. In the last decade of his life, political maturation has become political nightmare as he is evicted from his home, has his health ruined by forced labor, watches his friends die and his beloved daughter leave China for the West, is denied the solace of his art, and is finally forced to flee to the marshes after being identified by the police in his final "revolutionary" act—the posting, on a Peking wall, of a portrait of the third-century B.C. hero of liberty, the poet-statesman Qu Yuan. In the now famous conclusion of the film, Ling meets his death on a snowy plain, his errant footsteps forming a giant semicircle which his own corpse, a black dot on the white land, transforms into a giant question mark.

One is hardly surprised that the film made from this script, which was released and then withdrawn in 1980,[14] drew criticism from "responsible persons." It was not just that the Cultural Revolution was painted in unrelievedly dark colors—that was being done by hundreds of other writers now that open war had been declared on the Gang of Four. Nor that the period *after* the autumn of 1976 could rate no more than a question mark in Bai Hua's estimation. Nor even that the overseas Chinese were being warned off China just as the government was trying to woo them back as tourists, sympathizers, and potential investors. But what was especially troubling was that the Communist party of China itself was allowed no positive role in Bai Hua's presentation of the pre-1949 development of the revolution, and precious little after that: no mention of the Long March; no mention of Yan'an; no mention of a single Communist leader in a position of constructive authority; no mention of the party as vanguard in leading either peasants or workers.

What is even more surprising is that it took a good deal of time for the criticism of the film to develop and to find an outlet. In the event, it was the army that took the lead. Though Bai Hua's career had been mainly in the Tianjin propaganda department (he had been deputy director there as early as 1958, and, as we have seen, was serving as director in 1979),[15] he also apparently had ties with "the P.L.A. Wuhan units" in some capacity.[16] After an initial criticism on April 20, 1981, the *Jiefangjun Bao*

(*Liberation Army Daily*) of May 15, 1981, carried a major critique by Zhang Chenghuan, entitled "The Issues and Lessons of 'Bitter love.' "* Long excerpts from this attack were aired over Shanghai radio on May 17.[17]

Zhang criticized Bai Hua for representing an erroneous trend within overall bourgeois liberalization and for having been influenced by those who "wanted to see the whole country plunged into chaos [and] openly slandered socialism as going against human nature and paying no attention to human rights."[18] Zhang charged that Bai had described the "new," post-1949 China as "modern feudalism" and "said with certainty that it was even worse than the feudalism before the 1911 revolution"; he had failed to separate his criticisms of the "bunch of scum"—Lin Biao and the Gang of Four—from his criticisms of the motherland generally; he failed to identify the "different intrinsic characteristics" of socialism and capitalism; and he failed to realize that Mao Zedong's "merits are primary and his mistakes secondary."[19] Referring to a speech Bai Hua made in 1979, Zhang Chenghuan observed,

> The author has said that without a breakthrough there can be no literature. The courageous spirit of making a breakthrough is something that should not generally be criticized. However, the question is what kind of a breakthrough is it, what is to be broken through and where is the breakthrough directed. Is it not true that some people have suggested they want to break through the four basic principles? Such a breakthrough will inevitably lead to a deviation from the four basic principles and even to the direct opposite of the four principles. This situation has presented itself in some localities or some works. It has been found in "Bitter Love." This is something that should require us to think three times over.[20]

There was obviously some doubt in mid-1981 as to how to proceed against Bai Hua. One "literary paper" was quoted on Shanghai radio as saying of Bai Hua that "rumors circulating about his whereabouts after

---

*In some translated sources, *ku lian* is rendered as "bitter love"; in others, as "unrequited love."

his film script had been criticized were 'totally absurd' ";[21] the *Hebei Daily* criticized Bai Hua and noted that others "managed to benefit society by going to settle in the countryside";[22] in early June, officials at *People's Daily* apparently rejected a request from *Jiefangjun Bao* that they run the army critique in their own newspaper.[23] Bai Hua was also one of thirty-five writers given writing awards on May 23; and on July 17 Deng Xiaoping observed that "no campaigns" were necessary.[24] An upbeat interview with Bai Hua in *Ta Kung Pao (Da gong bao)* that same July reported that Bai Hua was "escaping the summer heat" at Beidaihe and writing both a new filmscript, *The Meng Qiao Bridge*, and a stage play, *The Golden Lance of King Wu;* Bai Hua stated that he was not worried by all the criticism in the press, because "the leadership of the army unit he is attached to showed him great concern." In association with the director Peng Ning, he was rewriting the *Bitter Love* script as reshooting proceeded in the Changchun studios, though Bai Hua concluded, "Further editing is still required."[25]

Deng Xiaoping's July stand was modified, however, in a lengthy speech by Hu Yaobang at the end of August 1981. Although Hu upheld a moderate stance by stating that criticism of Bai Hua's script must be "handled well," he emphasized that *Bitter Love* was "not good for the people and socialism and therefore should be criticized," and that it was "not an isolated matter" and represented "a wrong tendency."[26] *Beijing Review* commented on the case in some detail in September and October, urging readers not to think that all this signaled a return to the days of the Cultural Revolution.[27]

Bai Hua wrote his own lengthy letter of apology and thanks to the literary and military journals *Wenyi Bao* and *Jiefangjun Bao* in early December, and it was given national coverage in *People's Daily* on the twenty-fourth. In the letter, Bai Hua stated that when he first read the criticisms he "harbored resentment" and "lacked a modest 'pleased to hear that' attitude"; but the party had expressed such love for him that it constituted a "gigantic heat-wave"; Bai Hua acknowledged that he had wrongly "associated, and even equated, the fate of intellectuals since the feudal society of Qu Yuan with the unjust treatment suffered as a result of Leftist mistakes committed by the Party in its policies." Now he could feel in the depth of his heart the "great contributions of Comrade Mao Zedong," and he had learned afresh that the lessons of the Yan'an forum on literature and art were "still of universal guiding significance today."[28] On December 27, 1981, Hu Yaobang met with film delegates in Beijing and told them that Bai Hua had "recognized his error and made a self-criticism," adding, "This is good, and the question is closed satisfactorily."[29]

One can never totally isolate a case like this. The criticisms and self-criticisms of Bai Hua should be seen in the context of those directed at the poet Sun Jingxuan, and indeed it was Sun who, in his own self-criticisms, was to make the most complex and original criticisms of Bai Hua. Sun Jingxuan's long poem "A Phantom Is Wandering over the Vast Land of China," datelined Chengdu, December 1980, was published in the literary magazine *Chang'an* in January 1981.[30] Like Bai Hua's work, it had also aroused vehement criticism because of its strongly expressed views concerning the tenacity of feudalism in the People's Republic. To correct his thinking, the party sent Sun to examine the flooded areas of Sichuan province and the construction sites of the huge Gezhou Dam, on the Yangze River. When he returned, he wrote two lengthy essays. The first, for *Sichuan Ribao* (published November 11, 1981), was a paean of praise to the Communist party and China's workers. Sun contrasted Gezhou and the practical world of farmers and construction workers with the effete intellectual world he had drifted into:

> Here you can neither find idlers who talk volubly in tea houses, flirt their palm-leaf fans nor any sightseers who grow long hair, wear outlandish clothes, and swagger through the streets. Here, you know nothing about boredom, empty lives, sentiments and sighs. All the constructors have a deep love for the great project of Gezhouba and call themselves "people of Gezhouba." They are proud of this title.[31]

Sun's second essay, which appeared in *Wenyi Bao* in late November 1981, was a transcription of his speech to a Sichuan provincial CCP committee addressing "problems of the ideological front." In this, Sun was careful to draw Bai Hua into his own critique by name:

> This erroneous work was not written accidentally, neither was it an individual case. It was created under a specific historical and social background. After the 10 chaotic years, the CCP Central Committee brought order out of chaos, emancipated the mind and launched discussions on "practice is the sole criterion of testing truth." The ideological front was unprecedentedly active, and all fronts scored significant results.

However, historical dialectics shows us that with the emancipation of mind, at the turning point of history and with every social change, it is inevitable that dragons and fish are jumbled together and the good and the bad are mixed. All kinds of ideas and sayings, including bourgeois liberalization ideology which deviates from socialism and the party's leadership, would emerge. This is a very common historical and social phenomenon. Some said: Comrade Bai Hua's "Unrequited Love" [i.e., "Bitter Love"] was the representative work of this erroneous trend. In my opinion, besides "Unrequited Love," there are other works which are negative, unhealthy and poisonous. Although my poem "A Phantom Is Wandering Over the Vast Land of China" and "Unrequited Love" are not exactly identical, they share some common features. Both of them are products of bourgeois liberalization, which represented the erroneous social trend at that time. Over the past few years, having experienced the 10 chaotic years, like many other middle-aged and young writers, I tried to sum up the experiences and lessons learned from history. I attempted to investigate and analyze the historical, social and ideological roots of the mistake; in other words, I did not take the Marxist-Leninist view as my guiding ideology, I indulged myself in fantasy. As a result, I was trapped by bourgeois ideology and followed the capitalist path. This is indeed a profound lesson. In the past few years, there were sayings such as "the emancipation of mind has no limits," and "discard all taboos." It was exactly in these areas that I made mistakes. I did not draw a clear line of demarcation, but set emancipation of mind against the four basic principles.[32]

Sun himself said in a memorable sentence, "When I started my journey to Gezhou Dam, my hair was long and I was full of melancholy." By implication, this was also the condition of Bai Hua and of other errant writers of the day, and Sun quoted several lines from his own "Phantom" poem, to draw the other intellectuals into his context:

> Originally, we thought that we were masters of our lives,
> And we could live happily in our own land.
> But, we are actually nothing but screws
> Which are firmly screwed to the steel machine.

> We are but figures in statistics,
> Or black and white chessmen on a board game.
> Even though we are made of flesh and blood,
> And have brains to think,
> We cannot express our feelings and ideas. . . .[33]

In his self-criticism, Sun continued,

> It was obvious that what I advocated in this poem was totally
> based on the theories of human nature and human rights.
> So-called human rights and human values were publicly advo-
> cated. At present, a certain trend of thought is popular among
> some middle-aged and young authors, including myself. We
> blindly worship the theories of Western "existentialism," and
> discuss so-called human values and human rights with keen
> pleasure. We advocate the liberation of the individual and
> consider it in vogue. As a matter of fact, these things are but
> some outmoded stuff, reprints of humanitarianism advocated
> in the West several centuries ago. They are nothing new.[34]

These comments by the poet Sun Jingxuan seem to me particularly
valuable for highlighting the problems inherent both in Bai Hua's presentation of his view of China's revolutionary history and in the Chinese
Communist leadership's attempts to criticize him effectively. How well
can one sustain the charge that the works of Bai Hua and others in the
period 1979–81 represented "some outmoded stuff, reprints of humani-
tarianism advocated in the West several centuries ago" and contained
"nothing new"?

There are two ways to come at this from the standpoint of intellectual
history. In the first aspect, we can say, "Yes, there are deeply ingrained
Western humanistic ideas in Bai Hua's *Bitter Love*." But in saying this
we are not asserting that Bai Hua drew these ideas from Western sources
in any direct way. We must read *Bitter Love* as a text influenced most
deeply by Bai Hua's own partly Westernized Chinese predecessors—
men from within the May Fourth generation of writers who played such
a key role in China's cultural transformation between 1918 and 1948.
The echoes are everywhere in Bai Hua's script, and here we can merely
point to them without knowing which are deliberate and which coinci-
dental. In his role as activist-painter, loving father, critic of Chiang Kai-
shek's conscription procedures, and exponent of Qu Yuan, Ling Chen-

guang recalls the great poet-painter-scholar Wen Yiduo, killed by rightist assassins in Kunming in 1946. Ling's decision in 1949 to leave what is surely San Francisco, his spurt of creative energy in the 1950s, and his subsequent Cultural Revolutionary fate are close images of Lao She's own later life. Quite apart from the elements of criticism in Bai Hua's later paralleling of the incense-blackened Buddha with the cult of Mao, the earlier phase of Ling's aesthetic admiration of Buddhism revives memories of two sides to the intellectual movements of the 1920s: the romantic poet Xu Zhimo's exquisite poems to the Buddhist Temple of Heaven's Stillness (the Tienningsi) as escape and fulfillment, and the link of Buddhist compassion with Marxist social criticism as exemplified in the thought of Qu Qiubai. And the episodes of bucolic harmony among the Miao and the boat people of southern China could have come straight from the more sentimental early writings of Shen Congwen.[35]

But to emphasize this aspect of indebtedness to, or echoes from, an earlier generation of partly Westernized Chinese gets us nowhere near the deeper levels of Chinese culture that are embedded in the script. It is this second aspect that makes *Bitter Love* a richer text than any of its Communist critics would ever dare suggest. Once again, in pointing to some of these echoes, we leave unanswered the problems of indirect, direct, or unconscious influence. Let us just say that Ling as rustic fugitive, conversing with a fugitive historian and a fugitive poet, is deeply rooted in the Chinese tradition of "eremetical" withdrawal, a tradition in which the intellectual as fisherman or as woodcutter waits out a time of troubles in the wilderness. Bai Hua's scenes remind one especially of the closing act of Kong Shangren's great drama of the 1690s, *The Peach Blossom Fan (Taohua shan),* which presents Ming loyalists who live in hiding from their new Manchu masters. A more obvious reprise of Ling's desolate marsh is the marsh in *Water Margin,* where the gregarious gang of Song dynasty rebels holds out against the state; this antecedent highlights the double tragedy of Ling's aloneness, for there is little glamour in solitary flight. The Qu Yuan imagery, too, which runs through Bai Hua's script, is *not* a distortion, as some of the critics implied, but reflects the image of Qu Yuan as it developed in the Han dynasty; this image symbolizes critical courage and independent artistic achievement, subject to change over time, but never losing its magic and its force. Even the geese that fly overhead so often in the film, in the V formation that is described in Bai Hua's stage directions as resembling the character for humanity itself, *ren,* have historical resonances that eluded the army critics in *Jiefangjun Bao.* For from the very earliest times in classical Chinese poetry, flying geese have symbolized the frontier, their annual migrations leading poets' thoughts to lonely or distant lands. In a discussion of overseas Chinese, Bai Hua's geese have as strong an evocative power as similar images did in the border poems of the famous Tang poet Wang Wei.

We might conclude with the richest echo of all, both mischievous and direct, which Bai Hua placed at the crucial moment in his story of *Bitter Love*. As Ling and his family sit in the tiny, dark room to which they were banished in 1966, they are overjoyed to receive visitors in the persons of Xie Qiushan and his wife. Xie, a poet who wrote for overseas Chinese newspapers in the United States, had returned, like Ling, to his homeland in 1949 on board the *Sainte Jeanne d'Arc;* now, like Ling's, his sacrifice has been rejected, and their joy turns to sorrow as he speaks. "We have both been promoted!" says Xie, "You should congratulate us!" And to Ling's unspoken question he replies, "From the proverbial monsters and demons we have been raised and promoted to '7 May' fighters. I have to go to the land of Chu, she has to go to the land of Lu."[36] Chu is the southern kingdom where Qu Yuan lived and wrote in the third century B.C.; Lu is the eastern kingdom where Confucius taught in the fifth century before our era. There is nothing here of ideas "advocated in the West several centuries ago," and the joke is that indeed at the same time these references "are nothing new." These places and their dual symbolisms are as old as any we can find in historical Chinese culture. It is by the ways we reinterpret our own past, Bai Hua is saying, that we state most clearly our commitment to the future.

Tiananmen

Tiananmen Square, where so many of the impassioned events of the spring of 1989 unfolded, is the most emotionally and historically charged urban space in China.[1] Tiananmen itself—"the Gate of Heavenly Peace"—is of great antiquity and great beauty. It is at once the entryway into the inner vastnesses of the Forbidden City, and the exit

This essay first appeared in 1990, in *Children of the Dragon*, by Human Rights in China.

from that imperial and bureaucratic world into the zones of public space and revolutionary memory. In the ninety-acre square in front of it stand the massive monument to China's revolutionary martyrs and the mausoleum honoring the embalmed remains of Mao Zedong. On either side of the square are the huge buildings that house the National People's Congress and the museums of revolutionary history. To the east and west run some of Beijing's busiest boulevards, with their government offices and big hotels, and off these arteries lie a maze of narrower streets and alleys filled with the hubbub of stores and small restaurants. To create a rough parallel in modern American life, one might imagine Times Square in New York expanded to a space ten city blocks long and four wide, with the White House at the northern end and the Lincoln Memorial at the southern end.

The original version of the Tiananmen that we see now was built in the 1420s, when an emperor of the ruling Ming dynasty (which controlled China from 1368 to 1644) moved the capital from Nanjing, on the Yangzi River, to Beijing. The city built on the orders of the Ming emperors comprised two segments. The inner segment, housing the emperor himself and his many consorts and children and the main audience halls—what is now called the Forbidden City—was protected by a wall twenty-two feet high, thirty feet thick, and two and a quarter miles around. This inner palace complex was itself completely surrounded by a second palace and temple complex—the "Imperial City"—where the emperors' more distant relatives and the offices of many administrative bureaus were housed. This Imperial City covered almost two square miles, and was enclosed within a wall eighteen feet high and six and a half miles in circumference. Outside the Imperial City were the residences of the bureaucrats and their families, and of the shopkeepers and citizens of Beijing. This whole area of close to twelve square miles was protected in its turn by a third set of walls, sixty-two feet thick at the base, forty-one feet high, and about eleven and a half miles in circumference. It was a colossal concept, beautifully executed.

The Tiananmen Gate itself was the central entrance to the Imperial City, situated on a geometrically precise axis that led north between the main ancestral temples to the Wumen, or "Meridian Gate," which guarded the Forbidden City, and south to the outer lines of defense. According to the cosmological and geomantic descriptions offered to the Ming emperor by a Chinese scholar involved in the planning, the Imperial and Forbidden City structure was a macrocosm of the human body. The Forbidden City represented the viscera and intestines, and points on the outer defensive perimeter walls the head, shoulders, hands, and feet. In this schema the Tiananmen represented the protective tissue around the heart, and the avenue that led to the gate formed the lungs.

The Ming emperors and their Qing successors (who ruled China from 1644 to 1912)—guided in part by this symbolic vision, but also affected by practical administrative criteria—gave to Tiananmen a significant role in the rituals of royal governance. Edicts that had been issued by the emperor within his Forbidden City audience chambers were carried on elaborate trays, protected by yellow umbrellas, through the Meridian Gate and down the long avenue between the ancestral altars to the platform above the main arches of Tiananmen. There, as the officials of the relevant ministries knelt by the little stream that runs under its five marble bridges to the south of Tiananmen, a court official declaimed the edicts aloud. Then the edicts were ceremoniously lowered to the waiting officials, for copying and distribution around the country.

Under the Ming and Qing rulers, there was no open Tiananmen Square, as there is today. Instead, the space between the gate and the residential building and defensive walls to the south was composed of an unusually shaped T-form walled courtyard. At each end of the top of the T, and at its base, were triple archways providing passage through the wall for those approaching Tiananmen. The T-shaped courtyard was itself built on a fairly massive scale, the top of the T being 1,250 feet from east to west and 575 feet wide. The stem of the T was almost half a mile long, and 330 feet wide. Fitted into the two spaces on each side of the walled courtyard were clustered the neatly aligned rows of offices assigned to various ministries, military bureaus, and other government agencies. There was thus no Changan Boulevard running on a west–east axis in front of Tiananmen, as there is today, the boulevard down which the tanks rolled on their mission of death in June 1989. Instead, the two gates that led to the open courtyard were known as the "left" and "right" Changan gates.

The symbolism of Tiananmen Gate and its role in central rule could be seen in many other elements: from the mythical animals decorating the roof whose task was to protect the inner palaces from fire to the great ornamental stone pillars that stand in front of and behind the gate, each topped by a mythical animal in a swirl of clouds. These animals watched over the rulers' conduct, those to the north observing their deportment in the palace and those to the south observing how the rulers treated their people. Originally, according to chronicles, such pillars were made of wood, and any Chinese who chose to could carve his criticisms of his ruler into the wood, and the ruler was duty-bound to read it.

Tiananmen and its front courtyard were thus initially symbolic, ritualistic, and bureaucratic spaces. They became a public space only at moments of grave national crisis. One such moment occurred in 1644, when Li Zicheng, a peasant rebel from the western province of Shaanxi, seized the city of Beijing. The gates of the Forbidden City were opened to his troops by traitors within the Ming court, and the last of the Ming emperors committed suicide in the imperial garden to the north of the palace. It is alleged—though the story does not sound entirely likely—that as he rode his horse up to Tiananmen, Li fired an arrow at the character for *Tian*, "Heaven," painted above the gate, shouting that if he hit it his dynasty would be invincible. He missed (tourist guides would show the arrow hole to the curious as late as the 1930s), and the dynasty Li attempted to found was in fact toppled the same year by invading Manchus from the northeast, who established their Qing dynasty in his place. Whatever the truth about Li's arrow, it is certain that in heavy fighting in Beijing during 1644 Tiananmen was badly damaged, perhaps almost destroyed. The gateway that we see now, with its five archways and elaborate superstructure, is a reconstructed version, completed in 1651.

The next intruders into Forbidden City space—apart from a handful of rebels who managed to penetrate one of the gates in 1813—were foreigners. British and French troops, who fought their way to Beijing in 1860 in order to force the Qing emperor to allow their diplomatic personnel residence in the capital, bivouacked near the gate and briefly considered burning the whole Forbidden City to the ground in retaliation for the murder of some of their negotiators by the Qing. But having decided to preserve the city, they marched to the northwest suburbs of Beijing and burned the emperor's exquisite summer palace complex instead.

Once the Qing emperor capitulated to their demands, the foreign powers established a "legation quarter" for their diplomatic staffs, just to the southeast of Tiananmen, on an area of land stretching one mile from east to west and about half a mile north to south. When the antiforeign and anti-Christian rebels known as the Boxers rose in 1900, it was in this area of the city that they besieged the foreigners for a tense seven weeks of heavy fighting; the siege, actively encouraged by the Qing's redoubtable Empress Dowager Cixi, was lifted only when a joint expeditionary force of foreign troops fought its way through to Beijing from the coast of Tianjin. The office complex south of Tiananmen sustained heavy damage, and several of the ministries were burned down. The Qing court fled the city for the northwest as the allied armies entered the city. This time the Western troops forced their way through Tiananmen into the Forbidden City, which was used for a time as the allied headquarters. The space in front of Tiananmen became an assembly area for foreign troops and their horses. The beginnings of what now constitutes the southeastern portions of Tiananmen Square may have been first cleared at this time, and to prevent any resumption of such a siege threat the foreign powers not only erected a wall and dug a dry moat around the whole legation area but also cleared a field of fire outside their walls, to prevent any surprise attacks or infiltration. In addition, the Western powers demanded and obtained permission to patrol those portions of the forty-one-foot high Chinese city walls that might have given the Qing a line of fire into the legation area.

The Qing dynasty collapsed in1912, fatally weakened by a series of provincial Chinese rebellions, and China became a republic, albeit a weak and troubled one. Sun Yat-sen, who had been fighting the Qing since the late 1890s in hopes of establishing a constitutional republic, was named the provisional president in January 1912. He tried to establish Nanjing as China's new capital, as it had been in the early Ming. But he was outmaneuvered by the tough and politically astute former Qing general Yuan Shikai, who insisted that Beijing—where most of the troops loyal to Yuan were stationed—remain the capital. Yuan was so much more powerful militarily than Sun that Sun agreed to have Yuan named provisional president of the new republic in his place. Recognizing the symbolic importance of Tiananmen as the focus of central power, Yuan ordered his troops massed in front of the gate and received them there in massive parades at the time of his inauguration.

The boy emperor Puyi, who had been forced to abdicate in early 1912, was allowed to stay on with his family, retainers, and eunuchs, in the northern part of the Forbidden City, along with most of the Qing palace treasures. The area between Tiananmen and the first courtyards north of the Meridian Gate (Wumen) was, however, nationalized, and became the seat for some government offices and museums. The Tiananmen courtyard figured in two other major public events at this time. One was the funeral of Yuan Shikai, who died in 1916 after a humiliating rebuff by provincial generals and politicians when he tried to name himself emperor instead of president. Despite this fiasco, the funeral was a grand event, a true public spectacle. The other was more bizarre, the attempt by a Manchu-loyalist general named Zhang Xun to restore the abdicated boy emperor Puyi, now aged eleven, to the throne. For a few days Zhang's troops occupied the square and the Forbidden City, and the old imperial dragon flags flew once again. But after Zhang's defeat by armies loyal to the republic, new restrictions were placed on Puyi, and he was finally expelled from the palace in 1924. At this point the whole Forbidden City area was nationalized and turned into tourist sites, staff offices, and museums. The courtyard now became a truly public square.

In this period the city of Beijing underwent changes that were of great importance in shifting the symbolic significance of Tiananmen Square. Though the shift was gradual, the square slowly emerged as a natural forum for rallies and debates over national policy. Part of the reason for this was that the area round the square was becoming a political and educational hub. The new Department of Justice was located on the west side, and the new Parliament just farther west beyond the department. The area was the site of a host of universities and colleges, on which ambitious Chinese young men and women focused their career hopes after the demise of the old imperial system. The three main campus units of Beijing University (Beida)—those for literature, science, and law—were all just to the east of the Forbidden City, an easy walk to the square. More than a dozen other colleges were clustered near the square, mainly to its west, including several schools and colleges for women, and the prestigious Qinghua College, where many students developed their English-language skills before going off to the United States to study.

Students and townspeople had gathered in the square in 1917 to celebrate the defeat of the attempted restoration of Puyi, and Tiananmen itself was draped with republican flags. But the rally and demonstration that had the greatest impact on this period of Chinese history was that of May 4, 1919. On that day three thousand student representatives from thirteen area universities and colleges gathered in the square to protest the disastrous terms of the Treaty of Versailles. By those terms the victorious Allied powers, celebrating Germany's defeat, granted several former German concessions in China to the Japanese, who had signed secret agreements with those powers prior to joining their side in the war. The Chinese were outraged. They had also had joined the Allies in the war and sent more than one hundred thousand laborers to Europe to work in the trenches, docks, and supply lines of the British and French forces. Now the Chinese were crudely rebuffed.

The protests begun on May 4 inaugurated a new phase of nationalist consciousness in China and fixed firmly in the nation's mind the idea of the square as a political focal point. For the demonstrators, despite what they believed was their patriotic message, were harried by Chinese police and foreign-legation guards, and several were arrested; one of the arrested died from his injuries. Small-scale in the light of the demonstrations of 1989, the protests of May 4, 1919 nevertheless roused the nation's conscience, and the date was then adopted to describe the entire "May Fourth movement" as Chinese scholars, scientists, writers, and artists struggled to explore new ways of strengthening China and incorporating the twin forces of science and democracy into the life of their society and government. Linked in its turn to a study of the plight of China's workers and peasants, and to the theoretical and organizational arguments of Marxism-Leninism, the May Fourth movement directly influenced the growth of the Chinese Communist party, which convened its first congress in 1921.

If 1919 marked Tiananmen Square's inauguration as a fully public and antigovernmental space, it was 1925 and 1926 that saw its true coming of age as a site for massive demonstrations, and its true baptism of fire. These were terrible years in the history of the Chinese republic. The Beijing government was corrupt and ineffective, the pawn of a succession of militarists or warlords. Other warlords controlled sections of China, sometimes whole provinces, sometimes scattered cities or stretches of countryside. Foreign economic and political exploitation of China continued unabated, with Japanese assaults on China's territory—especially in Manchuria—growing ever more determined. In the south, at Canton, Sun Yat-sen and Chiang Kai-shek were struggling to put together a new revolutionary government, allied with the Communists, that would enable them to reunify the country by force of arms. Antiforeign outrage reached a new peak on May 30, 1925, in Shanghai, after British police killed forty or more Chinese demonstrators taking part in a major rally; the inhabitants of Beijing responded with a vast sympathy rally of their own, and Tiananmen Square was their naturally chosen location. Now the crowd that assembled represented a wide range of occupations and used many of the organizational and propaganda devices that were to be such a central part of the 1989 protests in Beijing. The 100,000 or more Chinese who gathered in front of Tiananmen on June 10, 1925, included not only many students and intellectuals but also carpenters, shoemakers, pawnbrokers, blacksmiths, and barbers. Chambers of commerce sent their delegations, as did teachers' associations and agricultural associations. A public rostrum in front of the gate was covered with the slogans of the day: "Abolish Unequal Treaties," "Boycott English and Japanese Products," "Down with the Great Powers." Five other platforms in different parts of the square were assigned to different occupational groups. Paper banners with political slogans fluttered from the trees—for the square had still the feel of a public park rather than that of the vast sterile space it is today—and other slogans were scrawled in black ink or charcoal on adjacent building walls. Local philanthropic societies served tea, and soft-drink sellers offered their sodas free to thirsty demonstrators. Student pickets kept order, and the police and troops kept their distance.

But as demonstration followed demonstration that fall and winter, the patience of local authorities faded. Police attempted to prevent organized demonstrators from reaching the square. Municipal authorities actually tried to shrink the public space by planting more trees and removing areas of pavement. Clashes between police, students, and the troops of regional warlords became more common. At last, on March 18, 1926, the anticipated violence on the part of the authorities erupted. A fresh crowd of six thousand or more, drawn mainly from student and labor groups, met at Tiananmen to protest the warlord government's spineless acceptance of new Japanese demands. After emotional speeches, the crowd moved off toward the cabinet office of the Beijing-based government. Regular troops opened fire on the crowd, without attempting to disperse it first, and at least fifty demonstrators were killed and two hundred or more wounded. It was the first such massacre in China's history, but it would not be the last. "Lies written in ink can never disguise Facts written in blood," cried out China's best-known writer, Lu Xun, several of whose students were among the dead. "Blood debts must be repaid in kind; the longer the delay, the greater the interest."

The importance of Tiananmen Square as a public space diminished for a while after 1928, for Chiang Kai-shek's troops and their allies, launching a successful northern expedition from their Canton base, nominally united the country in that year and declared Nanjing the nation's capital, as Sun Yat-sen had hoped to do fifteen years before. Beijing, now renamed Beiping, lost its central role, and as government bureaus relocated to Nanjing, student protests in Tiananmen lost much of their former significance, although Sun Yat-sen's portrait was hung now over the central arch of Tiananmen. An exception was the demonstration held on December 9, 1935, when students and citizens met in the square to protest Chiang Kai-shek's continued appeasement of Japan. Police in the city, who had tried to prevent the demonstration by blocking the gates into the square, used violence against the students and sought to quench their ardor by turning fire hoses on them in the near-freezing weather. Though the impact was not as great as that of May 4, 1919, or March 18, 1926, the "December Ninthers," as they were swiftly dubbed by the public, did become a potent symbol of anti-Japanese resistance to the country as a whole.

Beijing lost many of its students after 1938, when Japan's full-scale invasion of China led to the retreat of Chiang's armies deep inland to the west, in Sichuan province, where a new university in exile was founded. The Communists, for their part, now led by Mao Zedong, established their own base in Shaanxi and attracted many radical students there. The Japanese decorated the Tiananmen gate and square with colored lights, held various pro-Japanese rallies there, and reviewed the troops of their puppet allies. In 1943 they closed down the legation quarter and converted it to other uses. In 1945, with Japan's defeat and the return of the students from the southwest, the square again became the focus for rallies. These now tended to be against Chiang Kai-shek and to be led by radicals, for the Communists and the Nationalists were locked in a civil war for control of their country's destiny.

Mao Zedong and the Communist party re-created Tiananmen as both a public and an official space. As the Communist victory became a reality in late September 1949, Mao convened a series of meetings in Beiping to consider the country's future course, though there was never any doubt that he intended the country to follow the orders of the Communists. To underline this point, the front of Tiananmen was bedecked with two giant photographs, facing out across the square—one of Mao Zedong himself and one of his leading general, Zhu De, the builder of the Red Army and its finest leader during the long years of guerrilla fighting. On September 30, Mao led the delegates who had been attending the political planning meetings out into the walled square. At a spot half a mile south of Tiananmen, they broke ground for the "Monument to the People's Heroes," which was to arise on the central axis between the palace gates. And on October 1, 1949, Mao chose the platform above Tiananmen Gate in the city now renamed Beijing to declare the founding of the new People's Republic of China in front of cheering crowds.

Tiananmen now became the Communist government's preeminent public space. But as the scale of parades grew more grandiose and daily traffic congestion worse, the left and right Changan archways to the top of the square interfered with the required pomp and circumstance. "After two years of heated debates," according to one of the Chinese architects who worked on the project, "the citizens of Peking [Beijing] agreed that these gateways were a serious obstacle to the development of the capital," and they were pulled down in August 1952. The removal of the gateways allowed larger crowds to circulate and more massive military equipment to pass in review, but the space was still enclosed by the other retaining walls of the original T-shaped design. Finally, in 1958, all those walls were torn down, along with the buildings sheltered behind them. The square was vastly extended, to cover a space of over forty hectares (roughly 99 acres), a size that would allow one million people at a time to assemble there. Two huge buildings were constructed on opposite sides of the square to house the National People's Congress and the museums of the revolution. That same year of 1958, the ornate monolith to the martyrs of China's century or more of revolutionary struggle was completed, as the new square's centerpiece. For May Day rallies and October First anniversaries, Mao and all the central Communist leaders would stand upon Tiananmen Gate, gazing out over their people in the square, while another ten thousand or so officials and invited guests crowded the reviewing stands just below them, along the wall of the former Imperial City. In 1966, as Mao launched the cataclysmic Cultural Revolution, first hundreds of thousands and then as many as a million of the so-called Red Guards marched in serried ranks before him, cheering and waving the red book of his selected speeches, as they dedicated themselves to lives of "revolutionary purity" in his name. Fired up by such rallies, Red Guards fanned out across the city, and thence across the country, to root out any of those in power who had ties to the old order or could be accused of "bureaucratism" or lack of revolutionary zeal. Among those seized, dismissed, maltreated, and publicly humiliated was Deng Xiaoping. The din of those rallies must have reverberated in Deng's ears in 1989, above the calls for democracy and the chanting of slogans and pop music from the students' loudspeakers in the square.

The Chinese Communist government's remodeling of the square and its dedication of the site to political rallies in favor of its leadership, seemed to move the space further away from being the open political forum it had provided between 1919 and 1949. Moreover, the government in the first years of the People's Republic moved almost all of the student's colleges and universities to the outskirts of Beijing. The alleged reasons for these moves were practical ones, based on the need for space and facilities. But if the government wanted to preserve the square for itself, it certainly made the task easier by placing Beida, Qinghua, and the other prestigious schools in the far northwest of the city. From there it is four hours on foot or more than one hour by bicycle to the center of Tiananmen square; there is no subway link, and the only bus service is erratic and requires several changes.

Slowly, almost indefinably, however, something began to erode the government's control of the public space of Tiananmen. The erosion began in 1976, after Premier Zhou Enlai's death, as thousands of demonstrators and mourners assembled on their own, without government approval, to voice their disillusionment with their leaders. Though the government reclaimed the square to hold solemn rallies and funeral ceremonies for Mao, who died in late 1976, the people had relaid their claim to it. The square was further expanded to house an elaborate new mausoleum for Mao to the south of the revolutionary monument—seemingly a declaration that this was the intractable center of the government's power. And yet the square also became a beacon of opposition. In 1978 and 1979 groups gathered there to hear discussions of new ideas concerning democracy and the arts, initially triggered by writings posted along the stretch of "Democracy Wall" on the edge of the Forbidden City. In 1986 and 1987 they gathered to show solidarity with their fellow students and others protesting the party's refusal to allow valid elections or any other meaningful discussions of the nation's shaky course. In 1989, in April, they moved to Tiananmen again, to mourn the death of Hu Yaobang, who they believed had been sympathetic to ideas for change and reform. Tiananmen became the people's space in a way it had never been before.

Until June 4.

Poetry and Physics: The Spirits of Opposition

Once I goosestepped across the square
my head shaved bare
the better to seek the sun
but in that season of madness
seeing the cold-faced goats on the other side
of the fence I changed direction.

These essays first appeared in 1990 (Bei Dao) and 1991 (Fang Lizhi), in the *New York Times Book Review*.

Thus did Bei Dao, then a young Red Guard—he was born in 1949, the year of the founding of the People's Republic—gaze with sudden awareness at his once venerated leaders and change direction with a vengeance. By 1974 Bei Dao had finished the first draft of his emotionally powerful novella, *Waves,* and begun the sequence of poems that made him the guiding voice for young Chinese in that stillborn "democracy movement" of 1976–79. Most of those calling out to Deng Xiaoping to change the country's direction and let them keep their first taste of freedom knew Bei Dao's poem "The Answer" by heart:

> Debasement is the password of the base,
> Nobility the epitaph of the noble.
> See how the gilded sky is covered
> With the drifting twisted shadows of the dead.

And the poetry, fiction, and essays published in the magazine *Today* (*Jintian*), which Bei Dao edited with his friend the poet Mang Ke, for a short time gave that truncated movement some of its truest voices.

Bonnie S. McDougall, an expert on modern Chinese literature and history, was one of the first Western scholars to see the brilliance of Bei Dao, and over the past few years she has worked tenaciously to bring his work to a wider audience, publishing her translation of his work in a variety of journals and formats. Now the two volumes of Bei Dao's poetry and short stories, in fluent and colloquial translations by McDougall and Susette Ternent Cooke, allow people who do not read Chinese to gauge the full range of Bei Dao's work, and also to appreciate his hauntingly sad imagery.[1]

Bei Dao uses words as if he were fighting for his life with them. "We are / children lost in an airport / wanting to burst into tears," he tells us in "Daydream." "Don't ask our ages," he tells us in another poem, "like fish in cold storage we are fast asleep," In "Space" the silence and the cold are helplessly conjoined:

> We sit in a circle
> around a dead stove
> not knowing what is above.

At one of the many levels of meaning, we know, "what is above" is a government that constantly seeks to smother such voices, and Bei Dao, whose works were sometimes tolerated but also publicly condemned in the 1980s, is currently in exile abroad.

Bonnie McDougall also knows "what is above" for Bei Dao and his fellows at the ideological level, for her own earlier researches focused on the celebrated "Yan'an forum on literature and art" of 1942, when Mao Zedong laid down his interpretations of what were to be the "correct" modes of literary expression for the intellectuals, who henceforth were to "serve the people." This background knowledge of hers and her awareness of the frustrations of so many Chinese writers in the four decades following Yan'an give her almost an insider's knowledge of the insistent difficulties that lay in Bei Dao's way as he struggled to find words that had not been cheapened by politics, that could still carry the pure emotional freight of the heart.

As she finely expresses it in her introduction to "The August Sleep-walker," "Bei Dao's early poetry is a revelation of the self inhabiting two unreal universes: a dream world of love, tranquillity and normality, that should exist but does not, and a nightmare of cruelty, terror and hatred, that should not exist but does. To depict both of these worlds, the poet was obliged to create a new poetic idiom that was simultaneously a protective camouflage and an appropriate vehicle for 'un-reality.' "

McDougall seems to have just the right pitch to relay Bei Dao's songs, whether they are wistfully joyful, as in "The Red Sailboat:"

> If the earth is sealed in ice
> let us face the warm current
> and head for the sea . . .
> we seek only a calm voyage
> you with your long floating hair
> I with my arms raised high.

or unbearably sad:

> We are not guiltless
> long ago we became accomplices
> of the history in the mirror, waiting for the day
> to be deposited in lava
> and turn into a cold spring
> to meet the darkness once again.

In Bei Dao's short stories, collected in *Waves*, the images are often equally powerful, but now the form lets Bei Dao explore his own self and his own society with more leisure. "In the Ruins" is set amid the tumbled pilasters and carvings of the old Qing imperial Summer Palace, built for the emperor Qianlong at the apogee of his power in the mid-eighteenth century and destroyed by invading British troops, on Lord Elgin's orders, in 1860. But Bei Dao does not even bother to remind his readers of these specific historical facts, so perfectly poised to make a neat reminder about the wasteful excesses of the old "feudal" order, or the dark designs and deeds of Western imperialism. Instead, he focuses on the confrontation between a politically disgraced intellectual contemplating suicide among the ruins and an eight-year-old peasant girl out gathering grass for her rabbits, who watches him gravely as he makes his preparations to hang himself. It is the girl who stops him from dying—by remarking briefly, and without emotion, that her own father has just been beaten to death by the men of his own village. This sudden, violent, irrational death in a terrible way gives a meaning to the would-be suicide's own dissolving life.

Bei Dao's vision is not totally despairing, although he has seen and heard about much that might justify such an attitude. But it is certainly dark, and the flashes of light that cut through the haze of anguished memory seem at times too frail to make up for all the loss. At their best, his stories are almost unbearably poignant. In "The Homecoming Stranger," a father returns home to his family after twenty years in political labor camps. Almost totally unable to communicate after his years of lonely suffering, the man at the story's end gives to his daughter the one thing of beauty he has been able to make in hell—a necklace he painstakingly assembled for her over the years, made entirely of the colored, broken handles of discarded toothbrushes.

The 130-page novella *Waves,* which gives the volume its title, is Bei Dao's most ambitious work; it was initially drafted in 1974, revised in 1976, and revised again in 1979 for his own journal, *Today.* Like many of Bei Dao's stories, it is about people who insist on believing in love, even when society and those around them make such belief seem folly. But it also introduces the underside of Chinese society in the 1970s, the crooks and thugs who manage to add an extra level of despair to those Chinese already harried or driven almost mad by the state. Bei Dao is an imagist, and the varied characters in *Waves* circle and swoop around one another in unpredictable rhythms; their lives intersect without premeditation. Stories are pieced together out of fragments; decisions are made, unmade, deferred.

To the novella's hero, Yang Xun, it is Xiao Ling, the girl he loves, who is "a glistening wave" in the generally "black ocean," while the stars above are "countless drops of flying foam." But the waves of the collection's title, and the water images that course through all of Bei Dao's work to date, are more than this romantic vision; they are relentless forces as well, unthinking yet oddly enticing, bringing us out of our ordinary lives. As Bei Dao puts it in what I feel to be one of his most astonishing and beautiful poems,

> He doesn't have a boat ticket
> how can he go on board
> the clanking of the anchor chain
> disturbs the night here . . .
>
> when the waves tower up
> glittering indeterminately, the eyes of the dead
> float up from the ocean depths
>
> he doesn't have a boat ticket.

This is the Bei Dao who has found a way to speak to all of us, the Bei Dao who learned to assimilate the terrible truth, as he tells us in "Comet," that "what is hard to imagine / is not darkness but dawn."

* * *

Fang Lizhi, the Chinese dissident, likes sometimes to present himself as the very model of the absent-minded intellectual, a man so wrapped up in his own thoughts that he has little consciousness of the world around him. In middle school, he tells us in *Bringing Down the Great Wall*,[2] a moving collection of his essays, interviews, and speeches, "I was so absorbed with the daydreams that my teachers aroused in me there that at times I would walk right into utility poles on the side of the road." But he at once adds a gloss to his fairly conventional metaphor, one that shows the mischievous and pragmatic side of his character: "So hard did I bump into them, in fact, that I can still remember the numbers that were written on those poles." It is not the pain he wants us to know he remembers but the numbers.

As one of China's leading scientists, first in astrophysics and later in cosmology, Fang is very good indeed both at dreaming and at remembering the numbers. But as an incorrigible freethinker, who has seen with mounting anguish the hopeless state into which Chinese society is drifting, Mr. Fang also has become an accomplished expert at deliberately walking into immovable objects—in this case, the hard-liners in the upper echelons of the Communist party's political and educational bureaucracies.

Fang Lizhi is now one of China's best-known dissidents. He was accused by the Chinese government of being one of the ringleaders of the huge spring 1989 demonstrations in Tiananmen Square; and, after the mass slaughter of civilians in Beijing on June 4 by the People's Liberation Army, he and his wife sought shelter in the U.S. embassy. Allowed to leave the country in the summer of 1990, he has since received academic sanctuary at Cambridge University and at Princeton.

Fang's popularity and notoriety have been due in part to his visibility: as an internationally prominent scientist and the vice-president of the important University of Science and Technology, at Hefei, in Anhui province, he was at the forefront of those trying to train China's youth to participate successfully in the front ranks of the international scientific community. Fang has also gotten attention because he has been through a lot: he was purged and deprived of his Communist party membership in the antirightist campaign of 1957 for his outspoken critique of the sterility of Communist party discussions; he was rehabilitated in 1978, after the Cultural Revolution; he was deprived once more of his party membership in early 1987, as the hard-liners struck back against the late 1986 student demonstrations; and he brought the government's anger down on himself again in January 1989 when he appealed to the party to release Wei Jingsheng, the foremost protester of China's long-crushed democracy movement of 1978, who had by then spent ten years in jail. But, above all, Fang Lizhi has been listened to because he is witty, passionate, tenacious, and articulate. Students have loved his speeches; whether he had prepared carefully or spoke off the cuff, he could hold an audience in the palm of his hand.

The rhythms of Fang's life as a highly visible protester against his government's stupidity, greed, and cruelty have inevitably led to his being compared to Andrei Sakharov in the Soviet Union and to Václav Havel in Czechoslovakia. But in various interviews Fang has always dodged all parallels with Sakharov and has explicitly rejected those to Mr. Havel. He emphatically denies that he is a political leader and insists that he does not want to be one. It is one of the weaknesses of China, he explains, that the Chinese reject one leader only to submit themselves to another. It would be far better, he says, for the Chinese "to learn that democracy requires a confrontation of ideas and not a leader who says one thing and everybody follows. . . . If the Chinese people are expecting the appearance of a hero, it had better not be me. This expectation in itself is very unhealthy."

In *Bringing Down the Great Wall*, James H. Williams, a scholar on

science and technology in China, and a few of his colleagues have compiled and translated an admirably comprehensive selection of Fang Lizhi's
written and spoken words, focusing on his works since 1979 and ending
with some of the pieces he wrote after being allowed to leave China in
1990. Fang's writings are divided into sections corresponding to what
they see as four sides of his nature: the cosmologist, the cosmopolitan,
the democrat, and the dissident. The translations are fluent, and the
introductions to each section, along with Orville Schell's long introduction to the book as a whole, are intelligent and pertinent. The Fang Lizhi
who is thus introduced to us is humane in an immediately accessible
way: decent, courageous, sometimes evasive, sometimes sarcastic, urbane
yet emotional, a socialist and an elitist, opinionated and impatient of
official cant.

Readers today are likely to have trouble remembering just how
"unsayable" so many of Fang Lizhi's thoughts were in the contexts in
which he uttered them. His courage is thus not obvious to an outsider.
The fervor of the students' responses came from the fact that they had
never heard such words before, certainly not from a senior figure in the
establishment. As Fang says in a beautiful essay, "The End of Forgetting
History," this does not mean such things had not ever been said in China—
they had been said spiritedly in 1957 and in 1978—but the Chinese state
had erased them from the record, replacing the vanished voices with a
void that could be filled only with whispers.

In the mid-1980s, as Fang hit his stride as a social critic, a host of other
Chinese were also trying to give their own versions of truth, not just in
essays and speeches but also in films and paintings, novels and poems.
But whereas most of them chose to be indirect to some extent, there was
little that was indirect about Fang. He suggested to his audiences that
the best global parallels for China were to be found in the zealotry of
Iran, the economic stagnation of Poland, and the terrible poverty of Chad;
he told them that "Marxism has become ossified," that the government's
habit of continually shifting its policies was "an infantile way of running
an economy," and that the philosophical pronouncements from the Office
of National Dialectics in the Chinese Academy of Social Science merely
perpetuated "the image of a Chinaman with a long pigtail, clad in a Western
suit."

During the 1980s, Deng Xiaoping and the Chinese Communist party
were trying to make people subscribe to the "Four Upholds": the socialist road, the dictatorship of the proletariat, Communist party leadership,
and the leading role of "Marxism-Leninism-Mao Zedong Thought." Fang

countered these by saying that he believed a university should have its own four upholds: "a spirit of science, democracy, creativity, and independence." Told by a reporter that his four upholds might be seen as "a little dangerous," Fang replied that perhaps he could clarify things by relating his four upholds to what the government's four really referred to—namely, superstition, dictatorship, conservatism, and dependency. To give some idea of Fang's bravado, this particular speech was delivered to about three thousand students and faculty at Tongzhi University, in Shanghai, in November 1986.

Commentators on China's various democracy movements, those of 1978, 1986, or 1989, have stated that there never seems to be any content to Chinese discussions of democracy and that this makes the whole movement seem elusive. Fang, however, has offered frequent, crisp, and intelligent analyses of what he means by democracy—definitions that even those comfortably raised within such democracies might find hard to improve upon. Democracy, Fang told his Chinese audiences, means genuine pluralism rather than personalized attacks on the opposition; it means controlling corruption through public scrutiny and accountability; it means upholding the right to complain about injustice of all kinds; it means supporting the fundamental idea of shared human rights; it means government responsibility to its citizens; it means not relying on informers and not taking punitive action on the basis of casual suspicions; and it means refusing to quote as wisdom the observations of political leaders who know nothing.

Chinese and foreign journalists and Fang's student audiences have often asked how such values might be introduced into China. Fang has no easy answers. Perhaps change can come from within even if the external structures of government remain the same, he suggests, illustrating his point by using the words of a homely traditional Chinese metaphor: "In front of the shop the sheeps' head keeps dangling, but inside the shop sells dog meat." But, he says, before that happens the people must make it clear to the party that they want change. And that will not be easy, since the Chinese, unsure about what to do, are "like a swarm of headless flies, buzzing around in every direction."

But Fang suggests two ways out of this box. First, it is possible that the government, faced with the strength and determination of the democracy movement in China and abroad, might be forced to change constructively, "just as a bandit gives in when he meets a stronger force." Secondly, it is possible that current global changes themselves might force the issue: "The greenhouse effect, the population explosion, are issues that cannot be solved without a global solution. If China cannot catch up with the rest of the world, the world will make China catch up with it."

Fang Lizhi may reject comparisons between himself and Andrei Sakharov or Václav Havel, but others will continue to make those comparisons for him. As James Williams succinctly puts it in his introduction to one of the sections of this moving and intelligently orchestrated collection, Fang's great skill is that, "like Sakharov in the Soviet Union, he used the prestige of science to ferry ideas from beyond the margins of political permissibility into the general discourse on reform." We might supplement that comment with an idea that Havel expressed in his books *Disturbing the Peace* and *Letters to Olga:* in the grim world of Communist dictatorship, where optimism seems too facile an idea, there is always a deeper force, something we can term "hope." Hope to Havel is the power that enables us to keep alive the belief that one day things will again make sense. This making sense of experience is one of the things that gives us courage as we pursue what Havel calls our "entirely obscure task" on this planet. Fang, this book shows, has the mental strength to keep that hope alive and to maintain the faith that one day all that he, his contemporaries and his country have gone through during the last half century will somehow make sense. On the day that happens, the Great Wall will truly come down.

Teachers

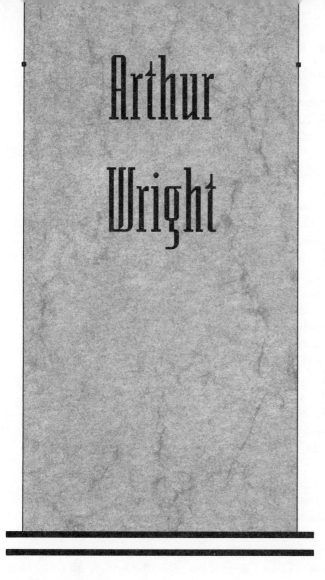

Arthur Wright

Arthur Wright (1913–1976) was studying in Peking when the Japanese bombed Pearl Harbor; and in the weeks that followed he concentrated on finishing a careful review of a recent Japanese contribution to Buddhist studies. The book was *Ryūmon sekkutsu no kenkyū* (A study of the Buddhist cave-temples at Lung-men, Honan), by an assemblage

This previously unpublished essay was written in 1976 and 1977.

of Japanese research scholars, one of whom was Professor Tsukamoto Zenryū; Arthur had lived in Kyoto between September 1940 and May 1941 and had studied with Professor Tsukamoto—who was also a priest of the Myōsenji—laying the groundwork for his study "Biography and Hagiography: Hui Chiao's Lives of Eminent Monks." It was Arthur's conclusion that though the new study did not supersede the Lung-men sections of Edouard Chavannes's *Mission archéologique dans la Chine septentrionale,* it had nevertheless "earned a permanent place beside Chavannes in the libraries of all scholars interested in the scientific study of Chinese art, Buddhism and cultural history." Arthur also wrote that Professor Tsukamoto's "long training in the Buddhist clergy and in Buddhist studies, plus thorough scientific discipline and clarity of thought have given us what will long stand as a fundamental study of its kind. It is the type of essay which Western scholars have thus far been unable to produce."[1] In these few sentences we find encapsulated many of the historical values and attitudes toward the field that dominated Arthur's professional career: that cultural history—however broadly conceived—still was to be "scientifically studied"; that art and Buddhism were a part of that cultural history; that clarity of expression was essential to good history; that French sinology had occupied a dominating place in the world arena but that Japanese scholarship was now opening up crucial new areas of investigation.

As far as one can now reconstruct the sequence, Arthur came to Chinese studies through Buddhism; he came to Buddhism through aesthetic preoccupations; and those preoccupations were themselves grounded in a prior concern with problems of generalization in European history. This last, which seems a rather precocious starting point, was due largely to the influence of Albert Léon Guérard, author of *The Life and Death of an Ideal: France in the Classical Age* (1928) who taught Arthur during his junior and senior years at Stanford University. Before working with Guérard, Arthur had been struggling to understand Giordano Bruno's attitudes to the society that first hounded and then killed him—in a bibliographical note to a later essay, Arthur wryly referred to this stage of his work as follows: "Wright, Arthur F., *Giordano Bruno, a Synopsis of his Life, etc.,* unpublished masterpiece, Stanford University, Calif., 1933."[2] With Professor Guérard's encouragement, Arthur began to drive his thoughts much more rigorously against the problems of individual will and social environment in history. First, he tackled the literary tradition in an essay entitled "Balzac and the Historical Spirit," concentrating on Balzac's refusal to believe in progress and attempting to trace the roots of his "confidence in the past and its institutions," which, Arthur felt, Balzac portrayed "with remarkable objectivity, not with the colorlessness which is called objectivity today, but with the burning fire of individual genius." In the autumn and winter of 1934, again for Guérard, Arthur pursued these topics in a more ambitious essay entitled "Merezhkovsky and Napoleon, or Mystery, History, Theory and Nonsense." Anyone who was later Arthur's student, or whose essays were edited by him, would recognize the mind at work here—the closeness of the reading, the impatience with pretension, the groping for precision of expression, and the final boldness of judgment once confidence was felt to be justified.

Again encouraged by Guérard, Arthur considered revising this piece for publication. In his notes for the Merezhkovsky revision, Arthur projected four main sections: first, the idea of the legend "in its most extreme form," in this case the ideas of "superman," of man as "divine," with an aside on "the Sun-god" as a concept; second, the author of the latest phase of the legend in his roles as man, as artist, as philosopher; third, the aesthetic ideal behind the writing; and fourth, a study of the "alterations" which made this particular treatment "a blending of new and older elements of the aesthetic ideal."[3]

Yet, as these interests developed, Arthur was increasingly drawn to the study of Chinese Buddhism. His interest was presumably sparked by a visit to the Far East with his parents when he was sixteen (an interest that they do not seem to have shared directly, since the voluminous family photograph albums of this period have only a handful of snapshots of Asia—the Summer Palace gateway, the Kamakura Buddha—amid the tide of snapshots of family houses, cars, the family business, and the scenic spots and hotels of travels across America). On this journey Arthur acquired a massive Chinese seal, the impressions from which he used as the bookplate of a few selected titles. The earliest of those I have seen is in Raphael Petrucci's *Chinese Painters*, with an introduction by Lawrence Binyon, which had been published in New York in 1920. Arthur's inscription is dated May 1933. If he had already been reading some Chinese history, he could not have failed to be struck by the difference of weight attached to Buddhism by historians and by historians of art. Buddhism was often barely mentioned in historical surveys, yet here was Petrucci viewing the rarefied conventions of the later Han and going onto say, "This refinement, arising from the exhaustion of a world which even thus retained a certain primitive ruggedness, was succeeded by a stupendous movement which followed in the wake of the preaching of Buddhism. With the new gods we see the first appearance of definite and long-continued foreign influences. Civilization was transformed and took on new life." This impression can only have been increased by George Soulié de Morant's *A History of Chinese Art* (1931), which Arthur must have bought just after he arrived in Oxford, since the seal plate is there dated November 1935. The crossing of the ways is well illustrated by *A Year Book of Stanford Writing* (1935), for it includes an essay of Arthur's entitled "Carlyle and the Modern Temper,"[4] but in the biographical note at the back we read, "Arthur Wright, '35 is a member of the English Club. He has travelled widely in the Orient and is a student of Oriental religions. He plays golf. Next year he will enter University College, Oxford."

At Oxford he was initially lonely and distracted—as we may guess from dated inscriptions in various books, conveying such messages as "To Arthur Wright from his best friend . . ." or "To Arthur on his birthday," inscriptions that seem ordinary enough until we realize they are written in Arthur's own hand and that these gifts—of poetry or literature—were from himself to himself. But at the same time he began to deepen his knowledge of Chinese religion and history, working under the direction of E. R. Hughes. Hughes at this time must have been completing his study *Chinese Philosophy in Classical Times*, which was published in 1942. In a brief obituary of Hughes written in 1956, Arthur was to characterize him as "first and foremost a humanist, widely read in literature and philosophy, ever ready to explore new lines which promised to yield fresh insights or deeper understanding."[5] Despite the growing seriousness of his work in Chinese, Arthur continued to pursue the aesthetic tastes he had developed at Stanford. An Oxford friend from those days, Dr. Edward Lowbury, writes of first hearing Sibelius's Fifth Symphony in Arthur's rooms at University College, and of Arthur's analysis of the music as "a sound-painting of the dawn." Arthur became friends with Mr. and Mrs. F. V. Branford—they wrote both poetry and plays—and inscribed Branford's *The White Stallion* to Lowbury. He was also in one of the small undergraduate literary societies that were such a part of the Oxford and Cambridge of those days—this one, "The Martlets," restricted to twelve members (an elegant spoof, perhaps, of Cambridge's prestigious "Apostles," where many Bloomsbury group members had been enrolled). If the source of the club's name came from the well-known reference to "martlet" in Shakespeare's *Macbeth*, the quotation's context makes an elegant joke in the light of Arthur's developing scholarly preoccupations:

> This guest of summer,
> The temple-haunting martlet, does approve
> By his lov'd mansionry that the heaven's breath
> Smells wooingly here: no jutty, frieze,
> Buttress, nor coign of vantage, but this bird
> Hath made his pendent bed and procreant cradle:
> Where they most breed and haunt, I have observ'd
> The air is delicate. (*Macbeth,* act 1, scene 6)

Even in these Oxford days, Arthur's astonishing professionalism was evident: when it was his turn to address the Martlets, he not surprisingly chose the Japanese tea ceremony as his topic; more surprisingly, he had prepared for the occasion by writing to Fukukita Yasunosuke—whose book on the tea ceremony, *Cha-no-yu: Tea Cult of Japan* (1932), Arthur had read and enjoyed—requesting photographs of each phase of the ceremony. Fukukita obligingly sent a large batch of excellent plates, with lengthy explanations appended to each.

One may assert that it was this side of scholarship that Arthur always loved—the gregarious friendliness and cooperativeness of scholars sharing interests and willing to discuss and pool information. It was to keep such a dream alive that he devoted so much of his time, after he became an established scholar in the mid-1950s, to the holding and funding of conferences, in the most attractive places possible, with maximum time for conversation and relaxation and yet with the highest scholarly standards. (Perhaps such a dream can come true only when a field is still fairly small and some of those involved have private incomes, or regular access to institutional funds.)

With a block of scholarly work now completed, Arthur returned to the United States in 1937, this time to enter the Harvard Ph.D. program. Here he plunged into a full schedule of Chinese and Japanese language courses with Professors Serge Elisséef and James Ware and also took courses on aesthetics, on the sociology of religion (with Professor A. D. Nock), and on the religions of India. Despite his increasing skills in both the Chinese and the Japanese languages, he continued to immerse himself in the great tradition of European sinology, and he never lost the respect that he built up in these years for Chavannes, Pelliot, and Maspero, whose writings all his students were later called upon to study carefully. It was at Harvard, too, that he met Mary Clabaugh, who had recently graduated from Vassar and was working on modern Chinese history at Radcliffe with Professor John K. Fairbank. She and Arthur announced their engagement at the end of 1939. As Mary put it in a letter to her father, "Finances still indefinite, but where there's a will and all that tra la toodle do. Off to Widener." She noted with pride, in the same letter, "Fairbank thought my paper was excellent, a 'tremendous job,' 'an intellectual feat,' etc. My work absolutely first rate, on a level with that of the best men at Harvard."[6] Arthur and Mary were married in the National Cathedral, in Washington, on July 6, 1940, and sailed for Japan from Seattle in September of that year.

Despite all the uncertainties of the international situation, Kyoto life was clearly a marvel to both Arthur and Mary. The scholarly dialogue now came true in its ideal home—in the setting of a small house on Shiraumezushi Dori, off Kawara-machi, a downstairs room with sliding doors onto the garden, "four young oaks, four camellias, five bamboos, and azalea and cape jasmine, growing among three beautiful rocks."[7] They had just moved in, in October, when their families began urging them to come back to the United States, because of the danger of war. Both refused. By now they had seven tutors[8] between them, for instruction in Chinese and Japanese spoken languages and texts and in Buddhist history and the Lotus Sutra. They visited temples, walked[9] in the winter mountains, struggled with ration books and food shortages, resignedly accepted the government bans on dancing and alcohol, and searched everywhere for a stove. Arthur's final triumph is caught by Mary at the end of a letter to her father and sister: "Here comes Arthur, wet as a doodle, on his bike, with a big black stove tied to the rear. You should see it."[10]

By early 1941 their tutors numbered nine or more: Arthur had six, each of whom he saw for a two-hour session every week—a Buddhist historian (probably Tsukamoto Zenryū) for his thesis texts, a calligraphy teacher, a Sutra teacher in a nearby temple, a conversation teacher, and two teachers to help in reading current articles and books;[11] Mary had added a more advanced tutor in modern Chinese history to her roster, plus a student to help her read Japanese articles on China.[12]

It seemed an ideal setup, but the tensions within Japan grew, and in March, Arthur went to Peking to scout the possibilities of studying there—neither family was told, as both were quite alarmed enough already. Peking seemed less touched by the war than Kyoto, though it was now nearly four years since hostilities had moved into a harsher phase after the Marco Polo Bridge incident. In one of his few surviving letters from this period, Arthur summed up the trip:

My expedition to the continent was a complete success marred only by the absence of the Lady Mary. I went by train, via Korea and Manchukuo, and found that the number of frontiers to be crossed and officials not to be crossed was extremely burdensome. The country was still in the throes of winter and looked very bleak after the warm greenness of Japan. At Mukden there was a fresh fall of snow, and the train provided with heat but no ventilation was decidedly uncomfortable, especially as each seat was sold to at least three different people. However, we reached Peking on the evening of the third day, and I was met by my good friends with whom I stayed. They have an attractive apartment at the Peking Language School, and provided for me handsomely.

I met some of my old Harvard colleagues at a sumptuous feast, the night after my arrival. My host, who is the third generation of his family to live in Peking, ordered a dinner which lacked none of the sumptuousness of the days of the Empire, when the Empress dowager herself frequented the same restaurant. The menu, at least a yard long, ended with Peking duck and walnut soup. The meal was lubricated with a delicious Chinese wine, and toasts went round and round.

I soon embarked on a rather feverish schedule of book-dealers, silk dealers, and scholars. During my visit I read through the whole of my thesis work with a learned Chinese scholar with the curious name of Achilles Fang. He speaks impeccable English, teaches German and is translating Plutarch and some of the Latin poets into Chinese. Besides that he understands thoroughly the intricacies of his own language, and in many cases gave me invaluable suggestions. I bought mountains of books for Mary and for myself and some Chinese rugs (delayed wedding present). The latter are going to America with a friend later this month; the books we have at present filling our little house to overflow. While in Peking I met some of the famous old residents, among them Dr. John C. Ferguson, who was advisor to the Manchu dynasty and to most governments since. He is an enthusiastic scholar of Chinese things, and has a priceless collection of antiques, rare books, porcelins [sic], etc. His house is an old temple of several courtyards, with dozens of servants to look after it. He is a handsome, ruddy, white-moustached old gentleman with a rather heavy manner, but withal fatherly and very kind. His opinions on any subject are not to be trifled with, as I discovered after a few essays at argument. I had several noteworthy meals at his home, and also dined around with some of my old friends. All of them, save my host and hostess, live in parts of old temples, and the rooms are very spacious and attractive. A friend at the embassy whom I had not seen for seven years entertained beautifully in a magnificent apartment, also a temple. A combination of red damask from ceiling to floor and red leather furniture was a wonderful complement to the dark old beams and fine doorways.[13]

By June, Arthur and Mary were in Peking, with a language tutor three hours a day, and a wing of a Manchu palace as their home. Here their scholarship, for the last time, took place in the grand old manner, with separate studies, a huge, high-beamed living room, a separate bedroom, and a sewing room, all in a garden compound. Three servants attended them—two for heavy work and cleaning, one as the cook.[14] Mary estimated that the small wages they paid these three, and the three new tutors they had acquired, supported at the least another twenty people.[15]

As in Kyoto, the pressures and tensions began to absorb them, even as they added three more tutors for work on their dissertations. Mary wrote of the ethos that surrounded them, as she picked up evidence through observation and newspaper:

The stark brutality of life here, which so overwhelmed me at first, is gradually getting into proportion with other factors, although it is still terribly depressing. Horses fall dead as they are whipped to pull impossible loads. Mere children are pulling rickshas and everyone knows they will die from it in a few years. Children fall into the lakes and are drowned while no notice is taken. Then their mothers slit their own throats with a sickle in grief. A young policeman falls asleep at his post, wakes up, and hangs himself on the spot, knowing that his job is lost and that he will starve, whereupon his aged parents poison themselves with opium, as their support is lost. The struggle to survive is simply terrific, and life can obviously mean nothing. Yet while they hang on, they are cheerful, happy, and kind. I don't suppose we will ever understand it really.[16]

Both of them were under mounting family pressures to return to the United States, but in August they mailed their rationales for refusing—the cost, the damage to their careers, the need to hang in with other foreign students, and the fact that Peking was so delightful.[17] In October they were back in Peking after an autumn holiday on the beaches at Peitaiho, and in a lovely letter to her mother, Mary tried to summarize the feelings about the two cities that absorbed her:

> I wish I could keep on writing and write well, but you must come here in October yourselves. The nostalgic delicacy of Kyoto in the autumn is missing. There, there are soft hills everywhere, streams, waterfalls—here there is the open expanse of a much bluer sky, soaring golden roofs, proud massive walls, Kyoto brings the whole universe into an exquisite little garden which melts away into a hillside. It is on a comprehensible scale. Here the sky really is the limit. Expand as one may and must, one is still small in comparison. At first this vast weight is oppressive, as I think I wrote you when I first came. Then it becomes intoxicating—although it is a much bigger sphere, one tries to grasp it. Apparently the third stage, though we have not reached it, is admission of defeat of pretensions too grand, resignation, live and let live, and idle meditation on the folly of trying to understand. In Japan, around Kyoto and Nara, the buildings preserved are much older on the whole than what remains of Peking. Yet a 19th century Chinese palace or temple has a greater feeling of the passage of the centuries than a 9th century Japanese one. Japan always remained, for me at least, provincial, homey, familiar, reassuring. Peking *is* the capital of the "Middle Kingdom," the universal empire, all under heaven[;] it is superb, glamorous and slightly terrifying.[18]

This interest seems to have been confirmed—sealed, in a sense—by a visit to Ta-t'ung, in Shansi, later that month. Here Arthur had a chance to see both the famous grottoes of the Buddhas and the ancient, almost totally unchanged walled city, which made him realize how thoroughly Westernized Peking already was.[19]

Thus the war, when it came, marked a harsh break; but the break occurred after Arthur's crucial intellectual interests had been set and formed. After sending off the article on Japanese studies of Buddhism to the *Harvard Journal of Asiatic Studies,* Arthur continued to work on his thesis, which was finished in draft by late 1942. But life was grim enough, conducted now on a greatly reduced scale—all possessions and most books packed for shipment in case a chance of repatriation offered itself, friends leaving one by one, money running out, no more letters, the tutors departed,[20] with Arthur wearing the red armband of an enemy alien.[21]

The internment orders were confirmed on March 24, 1943, and Arthur and Mary moved to Wei-hsien camp, in Shantung, with several hundred other foreign prisoners. Arthur was initially made the camp butcher, and the blood and smells were bleak enough that hot summer; then he was made water pumper and handler for the kitchens, and had to pull a cart of heavy supplies—food, coal, and wood—around the camp.[22] He showed a splendid fix-it ability in the camp, building furniture and desks for their ten-by-twelve-foot home and setting up a kitchen stove with three neighboring couples. He arranged to have a copy of his thesis draft smuggled into camp so that he could work on it further, while Mary studied Manchu and Russian with camp residents.[23]

As Arthur had responded to the war's beginning by concentrating on Japanese Buddhism, so he responded to its close by attempting a review of the sinological works he had missed in the interim. This resulted in "Sinology in Peiping 1941–1945," a fifty-seven-page study which finally appeared in volume 9 (1945–47) of the *Harvard Journal of Asiatic Studies;* it is a thorough and still engrossing survey of the world of scholarship in wartime—dominated by German sinologists, who were able to continue their studies throughout the war, but also showing the tenacity of dozens of other scholars, Chinese and Western. By writing this review, Arthur assured himself that he had "caught up" after the wasted years of wartime. And in a long letter to Mary's mother that Christmas he tried to set out the motives that kept him on in Peking, instead of coming home to recover from the war years:

> We are so glad that at last mail is beginning to arrive. We had letters this morning, and no better Xmas present could we imagine. While we were at Weihsien we felt like war orphans when no mail came, and I still get boiling mad when I remember how that stupid American Colonel closed the use of the outgoing mail to us for 2 weeks at a stretch, with planes com-

ing in and out almost every day. Those conditions caused many people to make quite the wrong decisions as to where they would go from camp. We just couldn't bring ourselves to leave from there with our work at loose ends, our books and ·mss we knew not where, and our knowledge of the language inadequate and rusty from disuse. I wrote in the most gentle and measured terms to my family as soon as mail was permitted, late in August, but the letters just didn't reach them, and the heartbreak was all the worse. . . . I hope you don't think it was caddish of me to stay out here, and Mary and I nearly wept when you wrote of your deep disappointment. We just *must* attain that degree of knowledge which will satisfy our inmost selves, for without that our whole lives will be overshadowed by a sense of inadequacy. Things are so promising here. The return of the Chinese intellectuals, the mingling of peoples of all nationalities, races, and creeds all contribute to a vigorous and healthy intellectual climate which is the best antidote for our disused minds.[24]

He stayed on in China, with Mary, until the spring of 1947, and even then the decision to leave was difficult. But now, as he wrote to his father-in-law, Colonel Clabaugh, Arthur felt "that this country is going to hell in a large and precipitate manner, and among other things, antiforeignism is growing and will grow with the sense of utter frustration which is all-pervading."[25] This was as near to a political statement from his pen as I have seen; he had not particularly shared Mary's enormous enthusiasm for Yenan, which they visited together in October 1946, meeting Chu Te and Mao Tse-tung and exploring the jails, schools, and hospitals. One of Mary's letters home catches him at this time in a vignette:

As you can imagine, the university was one of the most interesting places to us. Caves. Poverty. Almost no books. But first rate teachers and plenty of enthusiasm have enabled them to do something. The president incidentally is a member of the Democratic League, not a Communist at all. He was shot, but not fatally, obviously, on the streets of Sian by the secret police and escaped to Yenan. He is a good scholar and he and Arthur got sidetracked into a discussion of ancient history. His ideas on the place and function of a university and academic freedom are the same as the traditional views of European and American universities. We questioned him pretty closely, and we know the Chinese university situation well enough to be fairly good judges of his answers.[26]

The next few years, after Arthur had settled at Stanford, saw the productive period in which he prepared a number of essays for publication. Here he was drawing on, and consolidating, work that he had begun over a decade before—indeed, he was so typed as a scholar of Buddhism that the offer that came to him from Yale University during this period was from the Department of Philosophy.[27] But his other broad areas of interest, also developed over the years as a Stanford student and in Kyoto, had begun to mature. We can trace the first printed expressions of these through book reviews and brief essays.

In 1949 he tackled F. S. C. Northrop's book *The Meeting of East and West: An Inquiry concerning World Understanding* (1946) and found it conspicuously lacking. The penultimate paragraph of this review, in which Arthur picked on a single word of Northrop's to drive home his own point, is an excellent example of his growing range and intellectual shrewdness:

> Professor Northrop says, ". . . Buddhism and Hinduism *occur* in India, Ceylon, the Malay Peninsula, and the Southwest Pacific Islands." The verb "occur" here reflects Professor Northrop's notion that the Far East is timeless. Buddhism was created, developed, and decayed in India through centuries of time; Buddhism replaced the native heritage of Ceylon and, in a relatively primitive form, still dominates that island, etc. etc. Each place, each time has had and will continue to have its particular kind of Buddhism or Hinduism conditioned by its particular history and circumstances. It is thus no more meaningful to say that Buddhism and Hinduism occur in certain areas than it is to say that Christianity and Mohammedanism occur in Europe and in the near and middle east.[28]

A subsequent review of volumes 7 to 10 of Arnold Toynbee's *A Study of History* shows that Arthur was in no way biased against generalization as such. Writing in 1955, Arthur notes,

> As one whose interest in Toynbee goes back more than two decades I have been moved to reflect on my own developing attitude towards his work, and I find that I was initially

attracted by the *system*, the sets of categories, the "laws" by which Toynbee orders the past experience of man. Now, with the passing of two crowded decades, I find that the system has lost much of its earlier appeal but that Toynbee the poet, the explorer, the speculative intellect is as compelling as ever.[29]

Later in the same review, Arthur develops his response to the artist in Toynbee, reminding us again of the Stanford and Oxford days:

> Reading Toynbee is an aesthetic pleasure. He has the poet's feeling for the sensuous and evocative quality of words. Phrases like "the nemesis of creativity," "the failure of mimesis," "the mirage of immortality" and paired terms like "withdrawal and return," "archaism and futurism," "Zealots and Herodians" are memorable. They evoke, with notable economy and effectiveness, the complex ideas they symbolize, and in this way they serve to knit the manifold of this vast work together. Metaphor and simile have a rich texture of cadence and symbolism. At their best they crystallize in imagery the play of forces, the drama of choice or the tragic inexorability of a causal nexus. . . . Toynbee's sense of the tragic drama of man's life is another source of aesthetic pleasure. He brings the great scenes and the great figures to life, while the Toynbeean "laws" preside, like the Greek Gods, over the inevitable denouements. Dramatic themes such as the consequences of hybris, *peripeteia* or the reversal of roles are sensitively perceived and brilliantly developed. Toynbee as literary artist gives pleasure and his work should be read for pleasure by those whose daily chore is to labor through the bald ungraceful prose of ill-constructed fact-laden monographs.[30]

This is the period when Arthur finished most of the Buddhist studies, brought out his own short but strikingly elegant book *Buddhism in Chinese History*,[31] and worked on studies of personality and stereotypes in premodern Chinese history.

I mentioned earlier Arthur's homage to French sinologists and cited his remarks concerning the danger of inadequate preparation. I would venture the suggestion that this homage and these self-doubts persisted throughout his life—and the two remarkable studies that he reviewed in 1957 reconfirmed them. The two were Etienne Balazs's *Etudes sur la société et l'économie de la Chine médiévale* (1953–54) and Jacques Gernet's *Les aspects économiques du Bouddhisme dans la société chinoise du Ve au Xe siècle*, (1956), and Arthur praised them more warmly than he praised any other books. Balazs's two-volume study, he felt, was "a monumental contribution," "a new bench mark" that contributed "interpretations of the highest importance for the understanding of Chinese civilization as a whole."[32] Gernet's work marked "one of those rare moments when a major new theme and an important period of Chinese history suddenly attain a new level of intelligibility. . . . This is the sort of volume of exploration and analysis which maps a whole field of inquiry." And echoing another side of his overall concern with the general level of Chinese studies, Arthur concluded, "I am certain that Professor Gernet's brilliant book has taken us a long way towards the time when it will be possible to write a history of China which meets the standards of modern Western scholarship."[33] One needs little imagination here to see Arthur looking over his shoulder at Guérard; yet at the same time it is important to note that in the body of both reviews, Arthur tackled with a new clarity a whole range of data and hypotheses concerning social and legal relationships, roles of the populace, coercion by the official elite, place of the money economy in the emergence of a new isolated class of farm workers, warfare, and racial tensions. In short, I would guess that we have here the key intellectual genesis, in Arthur's mind, of a synthesis that could link those early city experiences in Kyoto and Peking to the type of historical skills he had been developing—the results being visible in his subsequent essays on Chinese cities, the prototypes for a whole series of studies that Arthur was beginning to project at the time he died.

In his introduction to the collection of Balazs's essays, *Chinese Civilization and Bureaucracy,* Arthur noted the fact that Balazs had himself chosen the title for the book of essays that was fated to appear posthumously. By a poignant coincidence, Arthur's sudden death in the summer of 1976 occurred just as he also was beginning to think about publishing a collection of his own essays.[34] The fact that death came before he could do this points to a tragedy for our profession: had Arthur had fewer doubts about what he was doing, less interest in constantly fund-raising so as to develop his field—both internationally and at Yale— and spent less time on conferences and editing the works of others, then he would have had the chance to work out more of these ideas in more detail, and paint them on a vaster canvas. But then he would have been a different man, and few of us who knew and loved him would have wished for that.

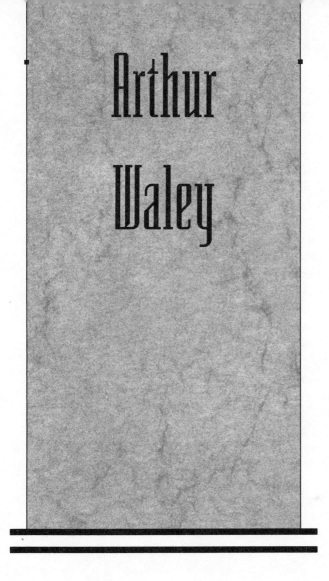

Arthur Waley

Arthur Waley selected the jewels of Chinese and Japanese literature and pinned them quietly to his chest. No one ever did anything like
it before, and no one will ever do so again.

There are now many Westerners whose knowledge of Chinese or Japanese is greater than his, and there are perhaps a few who can handle

This essay first appeared in 1970, in the *New York Times Book Review*.

both languages as well. But they are not poets, and those who are better poets than Waley do not know Chinese or Japanese. Also the shock will never be repeated, for most of the works that Waley chose to translate were largely unknown in the West, and their impact was thus all the more extraordinary.

Waley sat on a quiet edge of "Bloomsbury." Because he lived to a fine age—from 1889 to 1966—I have always associated him in some corner of my mind with E. M. Forster and Leonard Woolf, for they were all educated in the same special area of pre–World War I Cambridge, and all lived well into the 1960s, shrewd observers of a cataclysmically changing scene. All three were very talented, and none of them was gregarious. They might meet occasionally for tea at Lytton Strachey's house Ham Spray, or run into each other in Gordon Square, but they all defended their right to run their own lives. And all three, rather oddly one might have thought, had an interest in Asia. For Forster there was India; for Woolf, Ceylon; and for Waley, China and Japan. But though Forster worked in India and Woolf worked in Ceylon, Waley never even visited either of the two countries that gave him such extraordinary inspiration.

One can make all kinds of guesses concerning Waley's reasons for not going to Asia: that he didn't want to confuse the ideal with the real, or that he was interested in the ancient written languages and not the modern spoken ones, or that he simply could not afford the journey. Certainly we are safe in assuming that the trip would have been disconcerting, and it is worth reflecting on why this might have been so.

Waley was a classicist; and he was also in King's College at the time when Goldsworthy Lowes Dickinson—known as Goldie to generations of students—still presided over young minds, inculcating the virtues of an aesthetic humanism which are the heart of what people came to know as "Bloomsbury," virtues that were permanently captured in the essays and novels of E. M. Forster.

Dickinson was dejected by the ugliness and cruelty and insensitivity of the world that lurked just outside Cambridge; how could the Athenian ideals be preserved in such an appalling environment? Those men who valued decency, honesty, and compassion must state their values clearly lest the new Englishman—"Divorced from Nature but unreclaimed by Art; instructed, but not educated; assimilative, but incapable of thought"—inherit the earth.

This characterization of the Englishman was written by Dickinson in 1901, just after the Boxer Rising in China, and appeared in a little book of anonymous essays called *Letters from John Chinaman*, subsequently published in the United States as *Letters from a Chinese Official* (1903).

As Dickinson warmed to the theme, the inspirations came thicker, until his critique of his own society, his affection for his young friends, and shreds from the Chinese poets he had read in translation, all merged into a remarkable hymn to Chinese humanism, written in the first person by "John Chinaman" himself:

> In China . . . to feel, and in order to feel to express, or at least to understand the expression of all that is lovely in Nature, of all that is poignant and sensitive in man, is to us in itself a sufficient end. A rose in a moonlit garden, the shadow of trees on the turf, almond bloom, scent of pine, the wine cup and the guitar; these and the pathos of life and death, the long embrace, the hand stretched out in vain, the moment that glides for ever away, with its freight of music and light, into the shadow and hush of the haunted past, all that we have, all that eludes us, a bird on the wing, a perfume escaped on the gale— to all these things we are trained to respond, and the response is what we call literature. This we have; this you cannot give us; but this you may so easily take away.[1]

It is remarkable enough that William Jennings Bryan should have taken these letters literally, and written a stirring rebuttal (published in 1906), in which he defended labor-saving machinery, as well as the home and Christianity. What is perhaps even more remarkable is that Dickinson— the political scientist and expert in comparative governments—could visit Peking in 1913 and come away with his fantasy confirmed as reality! He wrote to E. M. Forster, "China! So gay, friendly, beautiful, sane, hellenic, choice, human. . . . Yes, China is much as I imagined it. I thought I was idealizing, but now I doubt it."

That China should be Hellenic comes hard on a modern graduate school product. But when Arthur Waley took his job in the Oriental Subdepartment of Prints and Drawings in the British Museum in 1913 such an aesthetic approach was very much in the air, and he breathed in a good deal of it. His first book, *A Hundred and Seventy Chinese Poems*, appeared in 1917, and in the introduction Waley wrote of the rationality and tolerance of the Chinese, of their powers of self-analysis, and of their friendship, in a way that could satisfy both Athens and Bloomsbury: "To the European poet the relation between man and woman is a thing of supreme importance and mystery. To the Chinese, it is something commonplace, obvious—a need of the body, not a satisfaction of the emotions. These he reserves entirely for friendship." And again, "For sympathy and intellectual companionship they looked only to their friends."

Furthermore, in the person of Po Chü-i, the great T'ang poet who lived from 772 to 846, Waley found someone who was immensely compatible, who spoke directly to the worries of Waley's time with a wise voice eleven hundred years old. It was a witty, warm, slightly melancholy voice, one that abhorred pretension, one that could both sympathize with the poor and excoriate the vulgar. On the death of his little daughter, Po Chü-i said, "At last, by thinking of the time before she was born, / By thought and reason I drove the pain away." When traveling through the dangerous Yangtze gorges, the poet wrote, "How can I believe that since the world began / In every shipwreck none have drowned but rogues?" And, with startling force:

> Sent as a present from Annam—
> A red cockatoo.
> Coloured like the peachtree blossom,
> Speaking with the speech of men.
> And they did to it what is always done
> To the learned and eloquent.
> They took a cage with stout bars
> And shut it up inside.

A second volume, *More Translations from the Chinese*, appeared in 1919. In a brief introduction, Waley noted that no reviewers had treated the first book of poems "as an experiment in English unrhymed verse, though this was the aspect of it which most interested the writer." I am not sure about that "most interested," but certainly Waley's touch was growing more sure, and he was writing his translations with total simplicity and total command of stress, as in these lines by Po Chü-i's contemporary Wang Chien:

> Poisonous mists rise from the damp sands,
> Strange fires gleam through the night-rain.
> And none passes but the lonely fisher of pearls
> Year by year on his way to the South Sea.

Astonishingly, in the same year of 1919, Waley had produced his first volume of translations from Japanese poetry, having taught himself that language as he had taught himself Chinese. Two years later he published *The No Plays of Japan*. This was an immense leap away from Po Chü-i, but here again Waley found a deeply personal echo. In No plays, he wrote in the introduction, "We get no possibility of crude realities; a vision of life indeed, but painted with the colours of memory, longing or regret."

In another passage of the same introduction, Waley shows his mastery of combining paraphrase, translation, and analysis, when he writes of the No dramatist Seami's usage of the Zen word *yugen:*

> It means "what lies beneath the surface": the subtle, as opposed to the obvious; the hint, as opposed to the statement. It is applied to the natural grace of a boy's movements, to the gentle restraint of a nobleman's speech and bearing. "When notes fall sweetly and flutter delicately to the ear," that is the yugen of music. The symbol of yugen is "a white bird with a flower in its beak." "To watch the sun sink behind a flower-clad hill, to wander on and on in a huge forest with no thought of return, to stand upon the shore and gaze after a boat that goes hid by far-off islands, to ponder on the journey of wild geese seen and lost among the clouds"—such are the gates to yugen.

Such a passage is art, as surely as the poetic translations themselves, or the originals from which the translations were taken. If one has a feeling that Waley found what he needed to find—a wryness, a delicacy, a languor, that seems to imbue Genji and Yüan Mei, Sei Shōnagon, and Monkey, even the imperial commissioner Lin Tse-hsü—one cannot cavil, and can immediately find other works that negate any simple generalization. He also translated the *Book of Songs* and Confucius' *Analects*, for example, and the Ainu poems.

The force of the impact that Waley had, over the fifty years of his creative life, upon a wide circle of artists, intellectuals, teachers, and students is now abundantly recorded in a risky but beautifully executed book that Ivan Morris has compiled: *Madly Singing in the Mountains: An Appreciation and Anthology of Arthur Waley.*[2] I say risky, because one may collect reminiscences, accolades, and passages of a person's works, without having any kind of a readable book. But this beautifully executed anthology is an exception.

Ivan Morris, himself an outstandingly good translator of Japanese literature, has somehow composed a book that is both intimate and distant, that manages to respect Waley's privacy and to be forthright. Much of the credit for the book's effect must go to the essay with which the book opens, "Intent of Courtesy," by Carmen Blacker, a wild, gentle, and beautiful example of the genus *Eulogy*, building up to a savagely romantic ending, that puts most other such pieces to shame.

As Carmen Blacker tells it, she came to Arthur Waley's house just after he had died, and was taken up to his old room by his widow, Alison Waley. Inside the door, Blacker stopped in surprise, for at first she imagined that the chair in which Waley used to sit had suddenly turned green:

> "I have changed nothing," she said. "But that chair by the window wasn't green, was it?" I asked. "Oh, that," she replied. "Yes, funny how the creeper has come in." I looked again. Through the window left open since he died the creeper had burst in like a lion. It had entirely covered the armchair with a thick coat of green leaves. It had flung tendrils across an entire wall. It had seized the long curtain and twined itself tightly round it in a spiral grip from floor to ceiling. It was as though the world of nature had flung itself into the room, and I thought of the swarms of bees which sometimes alight on the graves of saints or the birds which descend at the funerals of great men. That Arthur should have received this oblation seemed entirely fitting.[3]

As the book progresses, the range of Waley's talents becomes increasingly apparent. The more each modern specialist says how good Waley was in his particular field, the more one is conscious of Waley's independence; his remark that he "would rather be dead" than a professor at Cambridge dances in the air above those pages that sometimes grow a little solemn.

Waley's reputation grew steadily. In 1929 he was able to retire from the British Museum and devote himself full-time to writing—though how he could possibly have written more in the time past than he already had defies imagining. Fame brought its rewards, some conventional and some surprising. How very nice it must have been, when everybody who was anybody in England thought that Edith Sitwell was brilliant and rather dotty, to have Edith Sitwell think that you were the one who was brilliant and dotty. Having found a book written in some exotic language lying around her brother Sacheverell's library, she placed it next to Waley's bed (he was an overnight houseguest) in the hopes that he might prove unable to translate it. As she recorded the sequel:

> Next morning, Mr. Waley looked a little pale; his manner was languid, but as he placed the book on the breakfast table he announced in a faint voice: "Turkish. 18th century." The pages were few; and after an interval of respect we enquired: "What is it about?" Mr. Waley, with sudden animation; "The Cat and the Bat. The Cat sat on the Mat. The Cat ate the Rat." "Oh, it is a child's book." "One would imagine so. One would *hope* so!"[4]

It is an affectionate anecdote; all the Sitwells, indeed, seem to have been captivated by Arthur Waley. His ability to translate from the Chinese and Japanese languages so dazzled them that they spoke of all the works he translated as being his own work. Thus Edith Sitwell wrote in a letter about his translation of the fifteenth-century Chinese novel *Monkey*, "I don't really *know Monkey* yet, of course. But it has given me that sense of inevitability, of excitement with peace, that your work always does give me." "Your work"—whether it was Chinese poetry, *The Tale of Genji, The Nō Plays of Japan, An Introduction to Chinese Painting,* or *The Analects of Confucius.* There is a kind of negative side to this: if the work was Waley's, then no attempt had to be made to comprehend the cultures that gave him his raw material.

As Sir Osbert Sitwell (circa 1950) could write in a passage extolling Waley, "It is precisely in individuality that Western Europe has excelled. Not for us of the Occident the schools of poets and painters, almost indistinguishable one from another in style, and continuing for millenniums: our works of art are sharply differentiated and defined." Yet if Waley felt patronized he didn't show it. He dedicated his marvelous book on the eighteenth-century Chinese poet Yüan Mei to Sir Osbert.

The China and Japan that Waley gave to his readers were humane and balanced. From perusing their newspapers, Westerners knew from 1895 onward that China was a torn and wretched country, with its people in misery from famine and civil war, and that Japan was entering a strident and dangerous phase following its startlingly rapid and successful industrialization on the Western model. Later they could read of the 1911 revolution and the Manchurian crisis, of Tojo, Mao Tse-tung, and Hiroshima. But with Sei Shonagon and Po Chü-i they were back in a world where courtesy mattered and where good taste was not simply something connected with food.

Waley's translations enraptured readers—whether they were of the Sitwells' social class or of the comfortable upper middle—who felt that the forces of darkness and unreason were taking over. His oriental benedictions to a way of life so seriously threatened were in no way banal. They were, rather, the products of a prodigious energy and erudition, and of a belief that there are certain values that are not transitory, certain attitudes that can never be anachronistic, because they have always been (and always will be) true.

I find it very hard to take leave of Arthur Waley. This is, at least partly, because by reading *Madly Singing in the Mountains* I have learned that at the time I spent a long, happy afternoon with Waley when I was a graduate student just embarking on the study of Chinese history and literature, his lifetime companion, Beryl de Zoete, was dying painfully upstairs. It is clearly fitting that the last words should be his, not mine. So here are some lines from his translation of "The Bones of Chuang Tzu," by Chang Hêng.[5] This, he once told Carmen Blacker, was his favorite Chinese poem.

> Suddenly I looked and by the roadside
> I saw a man's bones lying in the squelchy earth,
> Black rime-frost over him; and I in sorrow spoke
> And asked him, saying, "Dead man, how was it?
> Fled you with your friend from famine and for the last grains
> Gambled and lost? Was this earth your tomb,
> Or did floods carry you from afar? Were you mighty, were you wise,
> Were you foolish and poor? A warrior, or a girl?"
> Then a wonder came; for out of the silence a voice—
> Thin echo only, in no substance was the Spirit seen—
> Mysteriously answered, saying "I was a man of Sung,
> Of the clan of Chuang; Chou was my name.
> Beyond the climes of common thought
> My reason soared, yet could I not save myself!
> For at the last, when the long charter of my years was told,
> I too, for all my magic, by Age was brought
> to the Black Hill of Death."

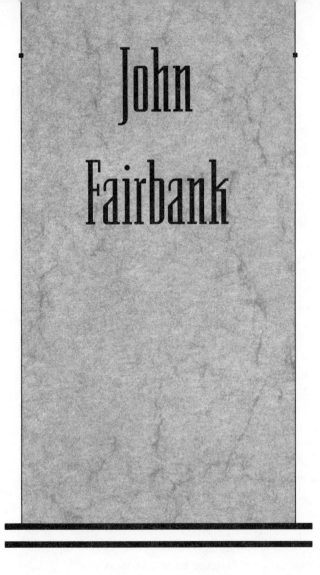

John Fairbank

For around thirty years, from the late 1940s to the late 1970s, John King Fairbank was the single most powerful force in the development of Chinese studies in the United States. Though he has now retired from his Harvard professorial chair, his influence is still formidable.*

The first part of this essay initially appeared in 1982, in the *Saturday Review;* the second part, in 1988, in the *New York Review of Books.*
*John Fairbank died on September 14, 1991.

One can confidently assert that the numerous books he edited, authored, or coauthored—they have ranged over the fields of Chinese diplomacy, institutional history, mission history, Communist organization, military history, and American foreign policy—will still be read and valued in the twenty-first century.

That could be enough achievement for most people, but Fairbank characteristically has chosen to subsume this record in the form of a personal memoir, *Chinabound*.[1] The memoir is a venerable genre with an honorable pedigree, but it has always been an ambiguous and hybrid form of writing. It potentially encompasses the triple zones of literature, history, and autobiography, yet lacks the true creative freedom of the first, the verifiable documentation of the second, or the intimate self-scrutiny of the third.

Fairbank, however, has the qualifications to succeed at the task: a voracious memory; a refusal to throw away any memo or letter; the good fortune to have survived into his seventies with his intelligence as acute as ever; a peripatetic career that extended from Huron, South Dakota, to Wisconsin, Harvard, Oxford, prewar Peking, and wartime Chungking; and a passionate and unshakable conviction that what he did was interesting and that we should all know about it. The result is an admirable example of the memoir genre—entertaining, discursive, detailed, and surprising.

Like many good books, Fairbank's is the account of a journey—a journey out into the world, a journey in which the wide-eyed and drivingly ambitious young man is transformed—by incredible tenacity, hard work, good fortune, and impeccably cultivated contacts—into a wide-eyed and drivingly ambitious middle-aged man. At seventy-four, Fairbank is content to have us believe that the ambition is satisfied. But he keeps the detached and eager expression of that young venturer still, while eschewing ideological commitment, supporting the forces of law over the forces of moralism, and claiming that "irrational faith appalls" him. "My acquired religion is Harvard," he writes, "and what it stands for in the secular world. That is, I put my faith in our ongoing institutions devoted to fostering the free working of the mind."

Fairbank's memoir is in seven parts: his childhood and education from 1907 to 1931; his studies in China from 1932 to 1935; his early teaching; China in World War II; developing Harvard's area studies and coping with McCarthyism; the Harvard East Asian Research Center years between 1953 and 1971 and the problems of the Vietnam War; later life reflections and his return visits to the People's Republic in the 1970s.

Perhaps because they deal with earlier eras—and so are both easier to digest and faded by the gentle air of time—I found the first four sections the strongest. They are consistently fascinating, even at times lyrical (not an attribute that Fairbank normally lays claim to). He is marvelous on his early Harvard mentors, on the exuberant chaos of his early years in China studies as a Rhodes scholar at Oxford, and on being the neophyte with his young bride, Wilma, in prewar Peking. Some of the vignettes here are lovely: the meetings with the great Hosea Ballou Morse, for example, or with Stanley Wright, Owen Lattimore, and Agnes Smedley. But the most powerful passages deal with Chinese friends—for it is a real article of Fairbank's self-perception that these friendships were among the most important aspects of his life and that the desire to help Chinese intellectuals in the desperate conditions of the 1930s and 1940s was one of the driving motives of his career. Here, among many splendid moments, I would single out his careful descriptions of Chiang Ting-fu (T. F. Tsiang), the haunting evocations of the married life of the scholarly and talented young couple Lin Hui-yin and Liang Ssu-ch'eng (Lin the former focus of the excitable poet Hsu Chih-mo's fancy, and Ssu-ch'eng, son of the great scholar-philosopher-reformer Liang Ch'i-ch'ao), and Fairbank's unforgettable evocation of his egregious wartime Mr. Fix-it, Ch'en Sung-chiao.

In fact, I think that the parts of this book that will have the most value for future historians of China will be the sections on Chungking, and even more the glimpses of the Chinese faculty exiled from their Peking universities, living in desperate poverty in Kunming as a deliberate result of the ruthless and shortsighted Kuomintang policy of Chiang Kai-shek.

Fairbank leads us clearly, and I believe honestly, through his wartime ideological peregrinations and on to his maturation as one of the slightly left of center liberals who grew to dislike the Kuomintang they knew and to reflect with increasing favor on the Communist party they only faintly understood. Wary of Stanley Hornbeck at the State Department—and suspicious of the aristocratic detachment of Hornbeck's deputy, Alger Hiss—Fairbank shows how he came to respect John Stuart Service and John Carter Vincent for their mixture of realism and compassion, and thus felt it all the more strongly when their careers were ruined by the attacks on their integrity made during the McCarthy period.

Yet his passages on the tormented years of the McCarthy period strike me as oddly flat—perhaps wounds are still too deep (and some disliked individuals too vigorously with us) to make total directness possible. But Fairbank does suggest that he did not always behave as he would have wished, and he is astute in showing how one of the most pernicious sides of McCarthyism was its unremitting pressure on liberals to apologize more than they had to, to express an ideological "purity" that was either an empty formula or hypocrisy, and thus to be forced full circle to adopt the protective devices of the very Communist intellectuals their democracy was trying to attack.

Fairbank also seems a little too hasty and unconcerned with the students' agony over the Vietnam War, the effect of their anguish on their thinking and their careers, and the nature of the rifts that developed between individuals in the East Asian Field. For many of this generation, the late 1960s were as bitter as the early 1950s had been to many of Fairbank's friends. "I replied, others joined in, and we had some lively exchanges," he writes of the battles within the pages of the *Bulletin of Concerned Asian Scholars.* There was a good deal more to it than that. And I find it very hard to accept that it was really a major factor in the war and its aftermath that no one had had the foresight to develop Vietnamese studies at Harvard. Fairbank apologizes too much here.

As I read steadily through this remarkable and absorbing memoir, a little echo hammered away somewhere at the back of my skull. It pounded more insistently whenever Fairbank gave a particularly amusing self-denigratory comment, sniped neatly at a target, avoided a direct confrontation with a charged emotional issue, spoke of long-term goals and the vagaries of human fate, and insisted on the importance of his efforts. It was almost on the last page that I recognized the voice of Sir Robert Hart—the inspector general of China's Maritime Customs from the 1860s to the 1900s, known to history as the "Great I.G."—who had been obsessed by such subtleties. "I hope this is something," Hart once write, "for otherwise I don't see much in return for all the work done and thought expended on it—except that the thought produced the work, and the work has succeeded as work!"[2] Hart had no need to worry about his work or his reputation, nor need John Fairbank worry about his own forty years' labor. It *was* worth it, and the achievement was lasting. In our own lifetimes there will not be another such I.G. of Chinese studies.

*   *   *

John King Fairbank's first book, *The United States and China,* was published in 1948. A careful blending of Chinese institutional history with diplomatic history, the book proved immediately popular among Americans seeking to place their present against the background of China's past. Over the next six years, as the Communists consolidated their hold over China and the Korean War effectively wrecked U.S.-China relations, Fairbank established his reputation as the leading expert on China in the United States, producing the astonishing number of five further books within that short period. One was a major bibliographical guide to recent Chinese historical writing; another, a meticulously translated and annotated collection of documents on the Chinese Communist party's rise to power. One, particularly useful for graduate students, was an analytical teaching manual on how to decipher and translate Chinese historical texts. Another was an important monograph published in two volumes, based on Fairbank's earlier Oxford Ph.D. dissertation, on the formation of the foreign powers' favored "treaty ports" on the Chinese coastline between 1842 and 1854.

This remarkable productiveness, made possible in part by Fairbank's unflagging energy and in part by his astute choice of unusually competent collaborators or coauthors, started a pattern of scholarly work that continued unbroken through the 1960s, 1970s, and 1980s as Fairbank edited, coauthored, or composed on his own a textbook on the Far East, volumes of essays on Chinese military history, Christian missionaries in China, the Chinese world order, Confucian belief and practice, and the workings of the traditional Ch'ing bureaucracy; along with several more annotated bibliographies, an enormous edition of Sir Robert Hart's letters, and five separate volumes of the *Cambridge History of China*. Asked to look at the works Fairbank has produced between 1983 and 1986 a reviewer may be bemused but hardly surprised to find that there seem to be at least six of them, and that doubtless there are several more he has failed to keep track of. At the age of eighty, Fairbank is as hard to keep up with as ever.

Fairbank continues, in his six most recent books, to command a wide range of scholarly subjects, just as he did at the beginning of his career. *Christianity in China*,[3] edited with Suzanne Barnett, consists largely of commentaries by modern scholars on the early writings of Protestant missionaries in China. Fairbank has always urged China scholars not to ignore the immense body of data on late traditional China that is preserved in missionary archives, and he has been indefatigable in gaining financial support for the preservation and examination of these documents. The essays collected in this volume prove his contention that missionary sources can help to illuminate Chinese society, especially the rather shadowy world where Chinese sectarian and secret-society practices edged away from conventional Confucian teachings and where the partially literate saw the chance for further education and to escape a self-perpetuating cycle of low status and hard work. Sometimes—as when

Liang Fa handed his Christian tracts over to the failed scholar Hong Xiuquan, who later emerged as the leader of the catastrophic Taiping Christian millenarian rebellion of the 1850s and 1860s—the results were awesomely dramatic. More often, however, the story is a quiet one, in which ideas are exchanged in a local setting and triumphs are small and deceptions petty. It may be, as Fairbank reflects in his introduction, that the missionary pioneers "had more intellectual impact on the West than they had religious impact on China."

Fairbank has kept up his interest in Western trade with China since his Oxford days. *America's China Trade in Historical Perspective*, which he edited with Ernest May, gives an excellent sampling of modern scholarship on such subjects as the tea trade, textiles, tobacco, and petroleum. In his introductory essay for this volume, Fairbank notes how little tangible economic profit either country drew from the relationship, and yet how charged emotionally the contacts often were. Paradoxically, he feels, it is only by seeing how little money was to be made in the trade that we can gauge the force of China "in the American imagination."[4]

In *Reading Documents* and *Entering China's Service*, Fairbank has continued to work, with skillful collaborators, in two other kinds of scholarship that he has always encouraged: the preparation of highly technical handbooks for teaching Chinese history and the transcription and analysis of relevant documents. But *Reading Documents*[5] shows how much the study of Chinese history has changed since Fairbank issued his first book of documents in 1952. Then he mainly concentrated on foreign policy, on the way that major officials in the Chinese and Manchu bureaucracy tried to comprehend, and to deal with, the baffling Western invaders, and the sea of problems that they brought with them. By 1986 the compilers' attention had swung to local Chinese history, to the study of rural hardship and land tax patterns, marriage and kinship, acts of protest against injustice, and patterns of small-scale and illegal military recruitment. The shift in U.S.-China relations, long a central component of Fairbank's work, is dramatized in this volume by the inclusion, for the first time, of photo-reprints of relevant documents from the vast holdings of the "Number One Ming-Qing Archive" in Beijing, as well as from the Palace Museum in Taipei.

Reading Documents is a technical work, and hardly the place to catch Fairbank's authentic voice. But one can surely detect it in *Entering China's Service*, the splendid edition of the early journals of the famous builder of the Imperial Maritime Customs in China, Robert (later Sir Robert) Hart, which Fairbank wrote jointly with Katherine Bruner and

Richard Smith.[6] It is a little more mischievous these days, a touch more sardonic. Fairbank enjoys wordplay and puns, is tolerant of human foibles—he presents us with a lighter-hearted version of the scholar whom we met in his autobiography, *Chinabound.* In two characteristic sentences, he sums up his relationship with the elderly last foreign inspector of the Chinese Maritime Customs, L. K. Little, then long retired and living in New Hampshire, concerning publication of Robert Hart's letters. As Fairbank puts it, "Mr. Little, being of cheerful and activist disposition, expected that it might be a year before they appeared in print. It took seven."

The transcription of Robert Hart's journals, which are now preserved in the library of Queen's University in Belfast, was itself something of a feat. Tapes were recorded directly from the manuscripts—often as gunfire and the other echoes of war rumbled in the background—and were then dispatched to Harvard for Fairbank and his collaborators to pore over. The journals edited by Fairbank cover the years between 1854 and 1863, the years Hart spent first as British consular official and then as customs inspector, before he became inspector general of the customs bureau organized by the Western nations to collect Chinese tariffs on Western imports. It was during these years that Hart gained the confidence of the Chinese; he was later to become a powerful force within the Ch'ing dynasty. Given the extraordinary difficulty of reading Hart's handwriting, and the problems of oral clarity in the less than ideal working conditions, a number of mistakes were made, but they were caught when the first typed transcript was flown back to Belfast and checked against the originals. With his lifelong interest in sources and their uses, such details always interest Fairbank.

The Hart journals also presented a different kind of historiographical problem, since the volumes from an important early phase of Hart's life in China were partially erased or entirely missing. Reflecting on this problem, the authors note that the vanished sections overlap with the period of Hart's long love affair with a young Chinese woman called Ayaou, which led to the birth of three children. In the mid-1860s Hart had these children separated from their mother and sent to England, so that there would be no danger of their existence being known to his new bride, Hester Jane Bredon, whom Hart married in 1866 in their native Belfast and brought back to China. The revealing journals were later cleansed of this sad story. The authors comment—and here one detects a truly Fairbankian cadence—that nowadays historians feel they have an obligation to examine and record such vanished moments of passion:

What the double standard of Victorian England would in Hart's day have called wild oats and swept under the rug, biographers of the late twentieth century are expected to scrutinize as meaningful experience. We can only regret that the moral standards and practical necessity of an earlier day deprived us of Hart's record of his coming of age as a resident of China during his service in the Canton consulate in early 1859 and his first years in the Customs from mid-1859 to mid-1863.[7]

What is "regretted" in this passage is not the fate of the children and the social climate that made it inevitable but the loss of a valuable source for nineteenth-century diplomatic history.

Another intriguing passage in the same volume concerns the slow unraveling of Hart's marriage to Hester, an unraveling that became apparent in the late 1870s. The authors build up the moment with a series of shrewd questions, and then pull the reader up sharply by challenging the validity of the questions themselves. It is, once again, a most Fairbankian technique:

Hart joined her and the children in Paris in the summer of 1878, and, after the exhibition, they went for a time to Bad Ischl in Austria and then to Baden-Baden. Hart was suffering from incapacitating headaches—a breakdown of sorts, never explained. Had he worked too hard, too uninterruptedly? Was there some unforeseen crisis in Chinese affairs which he found unnerving? Was the Chinese Customs Service, so rapidly expanding, becoming unmanageable for one man? Was it becoming clear that his marriage was never to be a close companionship—a development for which he could place blame nowhere except possibly on his own romantic naiveté at courtship and a simplistic acceptance of the marital state as consisting merely of its outward trappings? We cannot know; we cannot even know whether these are the right questions.[8]

Asking the right questions has been a central goal of Fairbank's long life as a professional historian, and one that he has struggled to express through a career of reviewing books that has been evidence of his industry as remarkable as that of his monographic labors. *China Watch* is a collection of twenty-six short essays, of which most were book reviews, many of them written for the *New York Review of Books*. But Fairbank has not simply put the reviews between hard covers. Instead, he has reedited, cut, rewritten, and reorganized the pieces, so that they are divided into separate major themes and can thus be seen as more that the sum of their parts. The five headings do indeed cover major aspects of China's recent history: the role of foreign imperialism, the harshness of China's revolutionary leaders toward their people, the "normalization" of relations with the United States after the twenty years of hostility, the Cultural Revolution, and the attempts by recent American visitors to decide what the Chinese experience is all about.[9]

Fairbank, of course, has his own, clear view of how the important questions should be put and where the answers should be sought: in history. He has spent much of his life arguing that China can be understood only through its past, and he is not about to give up his mission now. Those who receive his most telling gibes are those who do not understand the origins of the events they are allegedly analyzing. He does not believe that most of the recent work in the social sciences has been of much help in understanding China, and he is not especially sympathetic to the new practitioners of Chinese social history, even though his latest collaboration on the volume of *Reading Documents* might have alerted him to the richness of the sources now available to a new generation of scholars. "The records are too extensive for historians," Fairbank notes, "and too difficult for political scientists."

What then does Fairbank think are the great themes that historians should concentrate on as they conduct their inquiries? He is, for one, a firm believer in the relativity of current ideas on human rights as these are commonly voiced in the West. He believes the Chinese have a different approach to the relationship between the individual and the collective. In comparison with Americans, they tend to give different and higher values to ideas of harmony than to ideas of striving. They have a different perception of the role of both time and leadership in history. These differences, Fairbank has tried to show, spring from a host of past factors, among which are the patterns of China's agricultural work, the nature of the bureaucracy, the theories of rule and kingship, and the shaping of the historiographical record itself. Ignorance of these differences, and of their roots, I think Fairbank is saying, lies behind the various failures in the missionary, business, diplomatic, and military ventures that the United States has embarked on in China across the span of the last two hundred years. (Probably the best as well as the wittiest essays in this engaging collection are those on Douglas MacArthur and Joseph Stilwell, where Fairbank can contemplate at leisure the interplay of arrogance, incomprehension, and zeal in their experience in China.)

When trying to apply his views on the connections between past and present of some specific event, however, Fairbank often runs into trouble. To take one example, here is his analysis of the origins of the Great Leap Forward, which as we now know had a catastrophic effect on Chinese agriculture, industry, and public morale during 1958 and 1959:

> How could all this happen? Such harebrained romanticism would not mobilize American farmers in Fargo or Fresno or even Provo. The Great Leap was so bizarre a triumph of revolutionary fervor over common sense that one wishes the historical literature were adequate to connect it with its antecedents in Chinese history. Unfortunately the institutional history of China remains still underdeveloped. The great tradition of statecraft *(ching shih),* how the bureaucrats customarily organized and manipulated the populace, is neglected while researchers today swarm into social history as more suited to current concerns.
>
> Institutional and historical perspective on the Great Leap would no doubt begin with the parts of the written dynastic histories dealing with the economy. These detail how new regimes, upon reunifying China, commonly mobilized corvée labor for great public works (and often wore it out), how they assigned peasants, for example, "equal field" allotments of land, and organized them into responsibility groups for mutual surveillance. Dozens of ingenious devices, like "ever-normal granaries" in each locality or soldier-farmer encampments on the frontiers, stand in the record unstudied. The question of how these clever schemes of scholar-administrators actually worked out in practice remains largely unanswered. They represented the ruler's unquestioned prerogative to structure the life of the people by personal example, sumptuary regulations, moral exhortation, and condign punishments.[10]

All of this makes sense, of course, and much learning lies behind the words. But one can certainly argue that the very historians who are now doing that "swarming" into social history offer us the best chance we have ever had of making sense of the interconnections between past and present. They do so just because they are getting away from the Confucian-trained bureaucracy's own laundered record and are beginning really to discover what happened to patterns of landownership, to lineage organizations, to sojourners in China's cities, to women seeking a fair share of society's scarce benefits, and to a score of other local phenomena and values that might help us to see just why so many people were susceptible to this mode of manipulation.

"Sinology is of course the natural habitat of nitpickers," as Fairbank notes in one of the delightful lighthearted asides that ornament this book, and one picks up such issues as the one I have just raised only because Fairbank is challenging his readers to think about the larger historical factors and their implications. He challenges them even more directly in the opening lines of *The Great Chinese Revolution, 1800–1985*[11] which are surely designed to make most people interested in the field of modern Chinese history seethe with righteous indignation, for they blandly imply that only Fairbank is trying to link the People's Republic back to China's history. But he is a deft scholar, indeed, and at once observes that as "an ex-professor who is not up for tenure, and who doesn't care about reputation," he is going to assume the needed task of being "the doormat for the coming generation to step on." There are no notes to this "home brew," since Fairbank feels they would be "misleading, invidious, and inadequate." Nor is there any bibliography, since Fairbank has spent much of his life compiling such book lists and feels that "too much is quite enough." In addition, the romanizations follow his own personal inclination, since none of the extant systems is wholly satisfactory. In short, this is a high-spirited, informed, amusing, occasionally exasperating tour through China's revolutionary past. Fairbank clearly had great fun writing it, and it is fun to read.

Despite Fairbank's jocular rejection of scholarly trappings in *The Great Chinese Revolution,* the book is in fact very up-to-date, not least because he has been involved, either as editor or as coeditor, in all the recent volumes of the *Cambridge History of China* for the nineteenth and the twentieth centuries up to 1979. He has read the attempts to summarize this long span of complex history made by many of the best Chinese historians in the world. Fairbank acknowledges their help both by dedicating the book to all the contributors collectively and by providing the contents of the relevant volumes as an appendix to his own book. Thus we find discussed inside his broad chronological narrative such topics as indigenous Chinese commerce before the impact of the West, the nature of local uprisings against state power, the composition of the "Sino-liberal" elite, and the meaning of personal humiliation in the Cultural Revolution. Again and again, Fairbank vividly captures these experiences. Of the terrible humiliations of the Cultural Revolution, for instance, he writes,

> To Chinese, so sensitive to peer-group esteem, to be beaten and humiliated in public before a jeering crowd including colleagues and old friends was like having one's skin taken off.[12]

Such concision is powerful and effective. So, in its way, is the trick of describing a complicated social phenomenon in a couple of sentences and letting the reader slip from mood to mood. Thus

> eunuchs came mainly from North China and were manufactured by cutting off scrotum and penis, binding the wound with a plug in the urethra, and allowing no drinking water for three days. When the plug was removed, if urine gushed out, the eunuch was in business; if not, he would die fairly soon.[13]

The reader's attention is in fact often caught—does Fairbank fear that our minds are given to wandering?—by such racy asides, even when there is not very much evidence to support them. "Folklore," we are told, is the source for the charming details of how a concubine entered the royal bed. The size of a sexually notorious warlord's penis is presented, even though "this datum has never been verified." The thought of trying to verify this particular datum, of course, makes this both a nice joke and a parody of the scholar's normal disclaimers.

The Great Chinese Revolution is thus Fairbank's heady distillation of everything that struck him, amused him, irritated him, interested him, during a half century of incessant reading and thinking about China. He leaves us with the thought that the "revolution"—whether "great" or not—may itself be as much a dynastic cycle as a permanent change. The words "socialism" and "capitalism" are ours, not deeply China's, and we apply them at our peril. China has indeed been trying to "break the grip of history." But even a revolution may not be able to assure that. For as Fairbank suggested at the beginning of this same book, the rhythms and condensations at the heart of China's history, and their geographical concentration, confront us with a truly imaginative challenge if we are to gauge their weight correctly:

All the historic sites of four thousand years of Chinese history lie close together. For us it would be as though Moses had received the tablets on Mt. Washington, the Parthenon stood on Bunker Hill, Hannibal had crossed the Alleghenies, Caesar had conquered Ohio, Charlemagne's crowning in the year 800 was in Chicago, and the Vatican overlooked Central Park.[14]

No other scholar has produced so much of high quality on China during the last fifty years as Fairbank. It's good to know how much he can still enjoy his favorite subject.

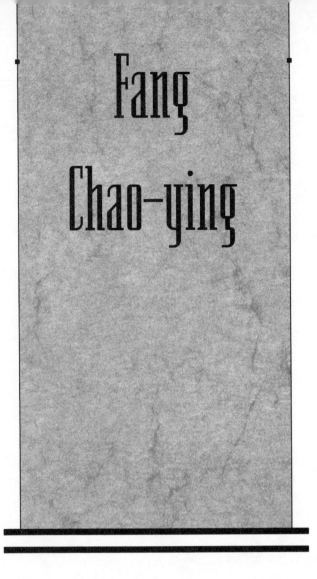

Fang Chao-ying

In February 1962, when I was a third-year student in the Yale Graduate School, completing basic Chinese-language work and wondering what to do next, Professor Mary Wright asked me if I was still determined to work on the early Ch'ing. I replied that I was, and she told me to consider with whom I should do some textual work, since she did not

This previously unpublished essay was delivered in 1985 at Mr. Fang's memorial service.

regard herself as fully qualified to teach all the documents of that era. Inspired by my readings in *Eminent Chinese of the Ch'ing Period,* I answered that there seemed to be only two great experts on the fields that interested me: one was Fang Chao-ying (1908–1985) and one was Tu Lien-che. Mary roared with laughter and said in that case I was in luck, since Tu Lien-che was in fact Mrs. Fang, and she knew them both. They were living in Australia, in Canberra, and I should write and ask if I could come to study with them. I did so, and Mr. Fang's answer was swift, courteous, and positive. In a wonderful way, in his opening paragraph, he managed to put me at ease by suggesting, of all unlikely things, that *I* could be of service to *him.*

> Your air letter of January 24 proposing to come to Canberra and work with me for a year on Ts'ao Yin was received two days ago. I must say I am flattered. As I have carried in my mind for several years a project of translations from the Chinese, Korean and Japanese sources on the Chinese society in the 17th century, our working together may be of benefit to both of us. Hence, my answer to your proposal is affirmative.[1]

He then continued by presenting a series of bibliographical questions and suggestions. In my reply of thanks, of which I have no copy, I must have made some comments about my geographical displacement as an intellectual, for Mr. Fang responded with this paragraph, tucked into an air letter brimming with more bibliographical advice:

> I like your remark about being too English to be American and too American to be English; if you substitute "Chinese" for English then that is exactly how I feel, not just concerning a fellowship but in many aspects of my life. I must say that I feel proud of being Chinese with an American outlook, and hope that I have selected in the way of life from both civilizations a little better than just an average.[2]

So I traveled to Australia, for the most memorable year of study and reflection in my life. Both Mr. and Mrs. Fang put their enormous learning at my disposal and treated me and my wife, Helen, with unfailing kindness. I remember vividly the meals *we* gave *them,* for *they* always brought most of the food. I remember the meals they treated *us* to, to which we were allowed to contribute nothing. I remember their merry, scampering dog, Ma-ma hu-hu, perfectly named;* and long drives through the lovely Australian countryside to Sydney or the beaches at Bateman's Bay.

And I will never forget the work that Mr. Fang expected me to do. I was introduced to a kind of scholarly standard the existence of which I had only guessed at—and, I hasten to add, which I was never even remotely able to approach. We worked through sections of the *Statutes* (the *Hui-tien shih-li*), the Chinese-language editions of the Manchu genealogies, and the analytical histories of the Eight Banners (the *Pa-ch'i t'ung-chih*). We read Ts'ao Yin's secret memorials, and Chou Ju-ch'ang's immense work on the eighteenth-century Chinese novel *Hung-lou meng* *(The Dream of the Red Chamber)*. Mr. Fang could be didactic or Socratic, depending on his mood or—perhaps—on what he thought I needed at the time. I remember his ending a spiraling series of my questions with the final, declarative statement "Because that's the way it is!" Once I came to him in great excitement with a section from the *Statutes* and said we must work on it, for I believed it solved all sorts of questions about the *pao-i* (the early Ch'ing bondservants). He looked the passage over, nodded, and told me to come back in two weeks with a careful translation. I worked and worked, with mounting dismay and frustration, for the two weeks, and kept our appointment in something of a state of rage. "I've done all that work" I said, "and it seems to have nothing to do with the kind of *pao-i* I'm interested in whatsoever." Mr. Fang beamed and said, "Excellent."

If there is to be a meaning in the term *lao hsien-sheng*, an essentially untranslatable Chinese term that means something between "revered teacher" and "honored friend," it is in the feeling I kept for Mr. Fang as I finished off the Ts'ao Yin thesis with his help and advice, and began my own teaching career and attempts to write further books on China. That feeling is a thorough mixture of awe, admiration, affection, and alarm—and he remains *Mr.* Fang to me, despite the friendship he developed with my mother, my sister, my wife, and even with my children, for after he settled in New York in the later 1960s he treated us all to wonderful meals at the Harbin Inn and elsewhere, and would always ask about them.

---

*The Chinese phrase can best be translated as "chaotic" or "uncontrollable."

I treasure many of his remarks, but perhaps none sums him up better than a small correction he made in a letter commenting on a piece of my research. "It shows much improvement," he typed. Then he must have reflected that that was going too far (I'm sure it was!), and he neatly inked out the word "much" and substituted "a good deal of."[3]

I treasure advice he offered me in the same letter about the problems of an audience for scholarly writing. It has not, to my knowledge, been said better by anyone.

> I have found that a researcher tends to write only for the initiated and experts (his own professors, etc.). It is perhaps a tedious job to include complete strangers in the audience but some consideration for general readers (including professors of other disciplines) seems necessary. . . . On the other hand if you are intending to write *only* for the experts, then it seems you have said too much.

One has to pry oneself away from a *lao hsien-sheng* eventually and follow one's own interests and judgment; otherwise the student has no room to grow and the *hsien-sheng* no room to breathe. But Mr. Fang will never cease to be a model to me of one kind of great preceptor, and I continued to treasure our occasional meetings and exchanges. I find in my file my annotations on a telephone conversation we had in 1976, when I had told him that I might go ahead and try and write on Matteo Ricci. My yellow-pad scrawl records, "Fang on Ricci: Scholarship without sincerity can be detected at once." In that case, I believe, Mr. Fang meant that the Ming Chinese had indeed admired Ricci because Ricci showed a sincere interest in their culture. If I could be equally sincere in my interests in Ricci, then I should go ahead.

But my most treasured of his letters, and the one in which he revealed a fresh dimension to me, was written by Mr. Fang on Christmas Eve in 1975, just after he had received a drawing of waving reeds in a snowy landscape which my wife sent him as a Christmas card. Let me take leave of him with these words, written in his always beautifully fluent and articulate English:[4]

> It reminds me of my childhood in Tang-ku, about ten miles from the mouth of Pei-ho [on the coast of north China]. My two brothers, nine and six years older than I, stayed most of the year at school in Peking, coming home only during sum-

mer and New Year's vacations. So most of the time I was alone with my parents who forbade me to play with other children. There weren't any anyway, for we were the only Chinese family in a large compound of office buildings. At the back of the house there were swamps and tidal ditches. One ditch ends in our backyard and filled up during high tide. I used to light a lamp to attract crabs at its bank. Further on I could see reeds and cattails stretching for miles. It was a lonely childhood, only at that time I had no idea what loneliness meant.

I had books for company. My father was busy during the day but sometimes he taught me to learn the characters with cards having illustrations at the back—very modern for those days. At six I could read Chinese translations of a world history (Myers *General History?*) and a world geography. Well, I could read to a certain extent. It was for fun and the illustrations, I suppose, but I still remember 留 尼 達 for Leonidas and the likeness of Napoleon. I also learned the English alphabets and spelling and the first dictionary I learned to use was the Pocket Dictionary by Chauncey Goodrich, Carrington's father. I looked up the form of a Chinese character through romanization when I first went to school to study the Analects.

Happy New Year!

Yours, Chao-ying

Notes

Introduction

1. C. R. Boxer, ed., *South China in the Sixteenth Century* (London, 1953), 145–46.
2. Ibid., 122 (with one tense change).
3. Ibid., 55.
4. Ibid., 56.
5. Knud Lundbaek, *T. S. Bayer (1694–1738): Pioneer Sinologist* (London and Malmö, 1986), 92.
6. Ibid., 152; the passage referred to by Bayer can be found in A. S. F. Gow, ed. and trans., *Theocritus*, vol. 1 (Cambridge, 1973), 113.
7. Lundbaek, *Bayer*, 43.
8. Ibid., 58–60.
9. Ibid., 60–68.
10. Ibid., 93; but see also his "boast" on p. 151, where he states that he hopes one day to be hailed as the "Father of Sinology."
11. Ibid., 208.

The Paris Years of Arcadio Huang

1. This essay is drawn mainly from manuscript materials in the Bibliothèque Nationale in Paris, especially MSS Fr. nouv. acq. 10-005, "Journal d'Arcade

Hoang, 1713–1714," in one volume; Arch. Ar. 69, "Papiers de Fourmont," "Memoire de ce que j'ay depencé pour le Sr. Arcade Oange, chinois . . . ," which has detailed inventories of Huang's personal effects; and MSS Orient. Ch. 9234, "Arcade Hoange, Dictionaire chinois-français." I am also especially indebted to the following works: André Masson, ed., *Montesquieu, oeuvres complètes,* vol. 2, *Geographica* (Paris, 1953), and accompanying commentary; Robert Shackleton, "Asia As Seen by the French Enlightenment," in Raghavan Iyer, ed., *The Glass Curtain between Asia and Europe* (New York, 1965), 175–87; Danielle Elisseeff, *Nicholas Fréret (1688–1749): Réflexions d'un humaniste du XVIIIᵉ siècle sur la Chine* (Paris, 1978), which contains lengthy transcripts of crucial material on Huang, and the same author's *Moi Arcade* (Paris, 1985); and Knud Lundbaek, *T. S. Bayer (1694–1738): Pioneer Sinologist* (London and Malmö, 1986). The essay printed here is the original version of one that appeared in a much truncated version in *Granta* (Spring 1990).

The Peregrinations of Mendes Pinto

1. Fernão Mendes Pinto, *The Travels of Mendes Pinto,* ed. and trans. Rebecca D. Catz (Chicago: University of Chicago Press, 1990).
2. Ibid., 1.
3. Ibid., 522–23.
4. See the splendid analysis and translation of several of these by Charles Boxer in his *South China in the Sixteenth Century* (London: Hakluyt Society, 1953).
5. Pinto, *Travels,* 501.
6. Ibid., 36–37.
7. Ibid., 54.
8. Ibid., 365.
9. Ibid., 287.
10. Ibid., 31.
11. Ibid., 32–33.
12. Ibid., 491.

Matteo Ricci and the Ascent to Peking

1. For the full background on Ricci's life and education and for the entire meticulously annotated text of Ricci's manuscript of the *Historia,* see Pasquale M. D'Elia, S.J., ed., *Fonti Ricciane: Documenti originali concernenti Matteo Ricci e la storia delle prime relazioni tra l'Europa e la Cina 1579–1615,* 3 vols. (Rome, 1942–49); Wolfgang Franke's fine essay in L. Carrington Goodrich and Chaoying Fang, eds., *Dictionary of Ming Biog-*

raphy, 1368–1644, 2 vols. (New York, 1976), 2:1137–44; and Jonathan D. Spence, *The Memory Palace of Matteo Ricci* (New York, 1984). Valignano is well analyzed in Josef Franz Schütte, S.J., *Valignano's Mission Principles for Japan*, vol. 1, *From His Appointment as Visitor until His Departure from Japan (1573–1582)*, pt. 1, *The Problem (1573–1580)*, trans. John J. Coyne, S.J. (St. Louis, 1980). The quotation from Ricci's letter to Fuligatti is in Pietro Tacchi Venturi, S.J., ed., *Opere storiche del P. Matteo Ricci, S.J.*, 2 vols. (Macerata, 1911–13), 2:214.

2. Schütte, *Valignano's Mission Principles*, vol. 1, pt. 1, pp. 30–35, and esp. 44 n. 106, 52 n. 122.

3. Ibid., 60, 67, 71.

4. Ibid., 76–68.

5. Ibid., 104–8.

6. Ibid., 131.

7. Tacchi Venturi, *Opere storiche*, 2:25.

8. Ibid., 26.

9. Ibid., 7–8, 10, 10 n. 2.

10. Schütte, *Valignano's Mission Principles*, vol. 1, pt. 1, pp. 269, 272–73, 279–80.

11. Ibid., 269–97, 308.

12. Ibid., 282.

13. Ibid., 286–287.

14. Ibid., 186.

15. Tacchi Venturi, *Opere storiche*, 2:27.

16. Ibid., 17.

17. Ibid., 27–28.

18. Ibid., 28.

19. Ibid., 29.

20. Ibid., 32–33.

21. See above, note 1.

22. Tacchi Venturi, *Opere storiche*, 2:49, 60, 65, 117, 122.

23. For bibliography, see Wolfgang Franke, *DMB*, 2:1144. See also John D. Young, *East-West Synthesis: Matteo Ricci and Confucianism* (Hong Kong, 1980).

24. Tacchi Venturi, *Opere storiche*, 2:67–70, 90, 234, 279.

25. Ibid., 75, 94, 106–7, 163. The identification of biblical quotations is from Tacchi Venturi.

26. Vergil, *Aeneid*, trans. William Francis Jackson Knight (New York, 1970), 151.

27. Tacchi Venturi, *Opere storiche*, 2:69, 117–18, 237.

28. Ibid., 45, 57.

29. Pasquale M. D'Elia, S.J., *"Il Trattato sull'Amicizia*. Primo Libro scritto

in Cinese da Matteo Ricci, S.J. (1595). Testo Cinese. Traduzione antica (Ricci) e moderna (D'Elia). Fonti, Introduzione e Note," *Studia Missionalia* 7 (1952): 425–515.

30. See Ricci's *Hsi-kuo chi-fa* (Western memory techniques) and Pliny's *Natural History*, 7.24.88–91. Ricci also drew his *Erh-shih-wu yen* (Twenty-five discourses) almost totally from Epictetus's *Encheiridion*, as has been graphically shown by Christopher Spalatin, S.J., "Matteo Ricci's Use of Epictetus' *Encheiridion*," *Gregorianum* 56, no. 3 (1975): 551–57. I am grateful to Father Spalatin for giving me a copy of this valuable essay at the Loyola University of Chicago conference in October 1982.

31. Pasquale M. D'Elia, S.J., "Musica e canti italiani a Pechino (marzo-aprile 1601)," *Rivista degli studi orientali* 30 (1955): 131–45. I am grateful to Thomas M. Greene for following up in correspondence the leads he first presented in his remarks on Petrarch in *The Light in Troy: Imitation and Discovery in Renaissance Poetry* (New Haven, 1982).

32. Ernest Cassirer, Paul Oskar Kristeller, and John Herman Randall, Jr., eds., *The Renaissance Philosophy of Man* (Chicago, 1948), 41–45.

33. Ibid., 43. Regarding St. Augustine, see his *Confessions*, translated with an introduction by R. S. Pine-Coffin (Baltimore, 1961), 216.

Gamble in China

1. Copies of Sidney Gamble's letters, his photographs, and sources on his life are held by the Sidney Gamble Foundation for Chinese Studies, in New York City. I am grateful to Gamble's daughter, Mrs. Catherine G. Curran, for making them available to me. A useful summary of material by Gamble is given in Nancy Jervis, ed., *China between Revolutions: Photographs by Sidney D. Gamble* (New York: China Institute in America, 1989). A helpful biographical essay is James Parry Eyster II, "A Princetonian in Asia: Sidney Gamble's Social Surveys in China, 1918–1934," *Princeton Alumni Weekly* (1986): 253–70.

Malraux's *Temptation*

1. André Malraux, *The Temptation of the West*, trans. Robert Hollander (Chicago: University of Chicago Press, 1992), 3.

2. Pierre Loti, *Les Derniers Jours de Pekin* (Paris: Calmann-Levy, 1914), 91–92 (author's translation).

3. Ibid., 406.

4. Paul Claudel, *Connaissance de l'est*, 4th ed. (Paris: Mercure de France, 1913), 28 (author's translation).

5. Paul Claudel, *The East I Know*, trans. Teresa Frances and William Benét (New Haven: Yale University Press, 1914), 45–46.

6. Victor Segalen, *Steles*, trans. Michael Taylor (Santa Monica: Lapis Press, 1987), no pagination.

7. Malraux, *The Temptation*, 13, 39, 65, 110.

8. Goldsworthy Lowes Dickinson, *Letters from a Chinese Official* (New York: McClure, Phillips, 1903), 15.

9. Ibid., 26.

10. Ibid., 57.

11. Ibid., 64.

12. Malraux, *The Temptation*, 101–5.

13. Ibid., 109–10.

14. Ibid., 118, 120.

15. Ibid., 120–22.

Looking East: The Long View

1. For these early works on China see Donald Lach, *Asia in the Making of Europe*, 5 vols. to date (Chicago: University of Chicago Press, 1965–); Pasquale d'Elia, ed., *Fonti Ricciane*, 3 vols. (Rome: Libreria dello Stato, 1942–49); and Jonathan D. Spence, *The Memory Place of Matteo Ricci* (New York: Viking, 1984). For Chinese criticisms of the Westerners see John D. Young, *Confucianism and Christianity: The First Encounter* (Hong Kong: Hong Kong University Press, 1983), and Jacques Gernet, *China and the Christian Impact: A Conflict of Cultures* (Cambridge: Cambridge University Press, 1985).

2. J. Bouvet, *Histoire de l'empereur de la Chine* (The Hague, 1699; reprint, Tientsin, 1940), 6–7 (my translation).

3. Margaret Hodgen, *Early Anthropology in the Sixteenth and Seventeenth Centuries* (Philadelphia: University of Pennsylvania Press, 1964), esp. 413–25; Basil Guy, *The French Image of China before and after Voltaire* (Geneva: Institut et Musée Voltaire, 1963); and David Mungello, *Leibniz and Confucianism: The Search for Accord* (Honolulu: University of Hawaii Press, 1977).

4. Voltaire, *Essai sur les moeurs et l'esprit des nations* (Paris, 1771), 1:13, 31, 33, 36 (my translation).

5. In addition to Guy, *French Image of China*, see J. H. Brumfitt, *Voltaire: Historian* (Oxford: Oxford University Press, 1958); Lord George Macartney's journal as edited by J. L. Cranmer-Byng, *An Embassy to China: Being the Journal Kept by Lord Macartney during his Embassy to the Emperor Ch'ien-lung, 1793–1794* (London: Longmans, 1962); and Jonathan Goldstein, *Philadelphia and the China Trade* (University Park: Pennsylvania State University Press, 1978), 35.

6. Daniel Defoe's critique appears in *The Further Adventures of Robinson Crusoe* (London: W. Taylor, 1719). The quotations are from Richard Walter

and Benjamin Robins, comps., *A Voyage around the World in the Years 1704–44 by George Anson* (Oxford: Oxford University Press, 1974), 351–52, 366, 368.

7. G. W. F. Hegel, *Lectures on the Philosophy of History*, trans. J. Sibree (New York: Dover, 1956), 120–21; Guy, *French Image of China*.

8. For background references see Stuart Creighton Miller, *The Unwelcome Immigrant: The American Image of China, 1785–1882* (Berkeley: University of California Press, 1969), and Mary G. Mason, *Western Concepts of China and the Chinese, 1840–1876* (New York: Seeman, 1939). For other specific examples see Charles Dickens, *The Pickwick Papers* (London: Chapman and Hall, 1837), 414; Johann Peter Eckermann, *Conversations of Goethe with Eckermann*, trans. John Oxenford (New York: Dutton, 1930), 164; F. I. Carpenter, ed., *Emerson and Asia* (Cambridge: Harvard University Press, 1930), 37, 239; and Dona Torr, ed., *Marx on China, 1853–1860* (London: Lawrence and Wishart, 1951).

9. For an introduction to the huge literature on this subject see Michael Hunt, *The Making of a Special Relationship: The United States and China to 1914* (New York: Columbia University Press, 1984).

10. See William F. Wu, *The Yellow Peril: Chinese Americans in American Fiction, 1850–1940* (Hamden, Conn.: Archon Books, 1982).

11. A good background to the growth of this sinological tradition is Arthur F. Wright's "The Study of Chinese Civilization," *Journal of the History of Ideas* 21 (1960). On Backhouse, see Hugh R. Trevor-Roper, *Hermit of Peking: The Hidden Life of Sir Edmund Backhouse* (New York: Knopf, 1977).

12. Harold Isaacs, *Scratches on Our Minds: Western Images of China and India* (New York: John Day, 1958), reprinted as *Images of Asia* (New York: Harper Torchbooks, 1972) and as *Scratches on Our Minds* (White Plains, N.Y.: Sharpe, 1980); the 1980 edition published by Isaacs contains a new preface. Isaac's periodization is outlined on p. 71 (same pagination in all editions).

13. Pearl Buck, *The Good Earth* (New York: John Day, 1931). An excellent evaluation of Pearl Buck is given by Michael Hunt, "Pearl Buck: Popular Expert on China," *Modern China* 3 (1977): 33–63.

14. See, for example, Ernest Bramah, *The Celestial Omnibus: Collected Tales of Kai Lung* (1940; reprint, Chester Spring, Pa.: Dufour, 1987), and *Kai Lung beneath the Mulberry Tree* (1940; reprint, Salem, N.H.: Ayer, 1978). See also van Gulik's Judge Dee stories, which are available in paperback editions by Scribner's, Dover, and the University of Chicago Press.

15. Hsia Chih-yen [pseud.], *The Coldest Winter of Peking: A Novel from Inside China*, trans. Liang-lao Dee (New York: Doubleday, 1978). See also *The Execution of Mayor Yin* (Bloomington: Indiana University Press, 1978).

16. Edgar Snow, *Red Star over China* (New York: Random House, 1938);

Graham Peck, *Two Kinds of Time* (Boston: Houghton Mifflin, 1950); Simon Leys, *Chinese Shadows* (New York: Viking, 1977); and Vera Schwarcz, *Long Road Home: A China Journal* (New Haven: Yale University Press, 1984).

17. John Hersey, *A Single Pebble* (New York: Knopf, 1956).

18. James Clavell, *Taipan* (New York: Delacorte, 1983), and Robert S. Elegant, *Dynasty* (New York: Fawcett, 1982).

19. Victor Segalen, *René Leys* (Paris: Gallimard, 1971).

20. John Hersey, *The Call* (New York: Knopf, 1985).

21. See Paul Scott, *The Chinese Love Pavilion* (London: Eyre and Spottiswood, 1960), reprinted in the United States as *The Love Pavilion* (New York: Carroll and Graf, 1985); James G. Farrell, *Singapore Grip* (New York: Carroll and Graf, 1986); and Han Suyin [pseud.], *A Many Splendoured Thing* (London: J. Cape, 1952).

22. Maxine Hong Kingston, *The Woman Warrior* (New York: Knopf, 1976).

23. See André Malraux, *Man's Fate*, trans. Haakon M. Chevalier (New York: Modern Library, 1965), and *The Conquerors*, trans. Stephen Becker (New York: Grove Press, 1977).

24. Bertolt Brecht, *Good Woman of Setzuan* (New York: Grove Press, 1966).

25. Franz Kafka, "The Great Wall of China," *Selected Short Stories of Franz Kafka*, trans. Willa and Edwin Muir (New York: Modern Library, 1952), 129–47.

26. J. G. Ballard, *Empire of the Sun* (New York: Simon & Schuster, 1984), 211, 228.

27. Canetti's novel, for which he later received the Nobel Prize in Literature, was first published in 1935 in German as *Die Blendung. Auto da fé* was the title he used in England, though an early U.S. edition was titled *Tower of Babel*. See *Auto-da-fé* (New York: Farrar, Straus & Giroux, 1984).

28. Edward W. Said, *Orientalism* (New York: Pantheon Books, 1978).

The Seven Ages of K'ang-hsi

1. *Journal of Asian Studies* 24 (1965): 229–43, citations from 229.

2. Act 2, scene 7, lines 139–66.

3. Much of the general outline below is taken from the biography of K'ang-hsi (Hsüan-yeh) by Fang Chao-ying in *Eminent Chinese of the Ch'ing Period*, ed. Arthur W. Hummel, 2 vols. (Washington, D.C., 1943–44), 1:327–31, and from related biographies in the same work.

4. *Ch'ing-shih lieh-chuan*, 80 *chüan* in 10 vols. (Taipei, 1962 reprint), 4:3b–4; *Ch'ing-shih*, 8 vols. (Taipei, 1961), 5:3494(2); *Eminent Chinese*, 2:796.

5. *Pa-ch'i Man-chou shih-tsu t'ung-p'u* (Genealogy of the Manchu clans in the eight banners), 80 *chüan* (1745), 74.8b for Ts'ao Hsi; Chou Ju-ch'ang, *Hung-lou meng hsin-cheng* (New studies on the *Dream of the Red Cham-*

ber) (Shanghai, 1953), 42, 205, 229, 319, on rewards to Sun; "Ch'ing K'ang-hsi chu-p'i yü-chih" (Vermilion endorsements of the K'ang-hsi emperor), in *Wen-hsien ts'ung-pien*, 2 vols. (Taipei, 1964 reprint), 1:290–302, for Ts'ao Yin as agent.

6. *Ta-Ch'ing Sheng-tsu Jen huang-it shih-lu* (Veritable records of the K'ang-hsi reign), 300 *chüan* in 6 vols. (Taipei, 1964 reprint), 43–44, 1572.

7. For printed examples of errors through dropped radicals or incorrect homophones, see "Su-chou chih-tsao Li Hsü tsou-che" (The palace memorials of the Soochow textile commissioner Li Hsü), in *Wen-hsien ts'ung-pien*, 2:855, 862.

8. *Ta-Ch'ing Shih-tsu Chang huang-ti shih-lu* (Veritable records of the Shun-chih reign), 144 *chüan* in 3 vols. (Taipei, 1964 reprint), 1695–97.

9. *Ch'ing-shih*, 5:3496(2).

10. Ibid., 3495(6). *Ta-Ch'ing Shih-tsung Hsien huang-ti shih-lu* (Veritable records of the Yung-cheng reign), 159 *chüan* in 3 vols. (Taipei, 1964 reprint), 1.

11. For an interesting and unstereotyped presentation of his prowess at archery, cf. *K'ang-hsi shih-lu*, 2587.

12. Short summaries of the tours are in *Ch'in-ting ta-Ch'ing hui-tien shih-li* (The collected statutes and precedents of the Ch'ing dynasty), 1220 *chüan*, 1899 (Taipei, 1963 reprint in 19 vols.), 9261, 9233–41. Fuller accounts are in the *K'ang-hsi shih-lu*.

13. Joseph Sebes, S.J., *The Jesuits and the Sino-Russian Treaty of Nerchinsk (1689)* (Rome, 1961). *Lettres édifiantes et curieuses, écrites des missions étrangères* (nouvelle édition, Paris, 1781), 17:306–10, on quinine. *Sheng-tsu wu-hsing Chiang-nan ch'üan-lu* (A complete record of the K'ang-hsi emperor's fifth southern tour), anon., printed in *Chen-ch'i t'ang ts'ung-shu*, 1st ser., corroborates Jesuit accounts, and gives invaluable extra detail on the 1705 tour to supplement the *K'ang-hsi shih-lu*.

14. As in the case of the exemplary scholar Chang Po-hsing, who was plucked from comparative obscurity by K'ang-hsi and became Kiangsu governor. In this post he was involved in a major scandal, and finally became deranged, recovering only when K'ang-hsi promoted him sideways to a literary position. I am now engaged in a detailed study of his career.

15. *Wen-hsien ts'ung-pien*, 1:294, interlinear endorsement to Ts'ao Yin's memorial dated K'ang-hsi 43 / 11 / 22.

16. As in the great examination-hall scandal of 1711–12. Cf. memorials by Ts'ao Yin and Li Hsü in *Wen-hsien ts'ung-pien*, 1:291–93, and 2:867–72; and *K'ang-hsi shih-lu*, 3306–58.

17. The development of K'ang-hsi's personal power through the use of bondservants in key positions is one theme in my book *Ts'ao Yin and the K'ang-hsi Emperor: Bondservant and Master* (New Haven, 1966).

18. Chang P'eng-ko's humiliation is described in *K'ang-hsi shih-lu*, 3051–57. For de Tournon, see Francis A. Rouleau, S.J., "Maillard de Tournon,

Papal Legate at the Court of Peking," *Archivum Historicum Societatis Iesu* 31 (1962): 264–323, esp. the appendix (312–21).

19. *K'ang-hsi shih-lu,* 3533; *Wen-hsien ts'ung-pien,* 2:896, 898–99; *Ch'ang-ku ts'ung-pien* (Taipei, 1964 reprint), 210.

20. *K'ang-hsi shih-lu,* 3969, 3977–78.

21. *Yang-chou shih-jih chi;* translations of this work are listed in *Eminent Chinese,* 652.

The Energies of Ming Life

1. Ray Huang, *1587, a Year of No Signficance: The Ming Dynasty in Decline* (New Haven: Yale University Press, 1981).

2. Ibid., 86.

3. Hok-lam Chan, *Li Chih, 1527–1602, in Contemporary Chinese Historiography: New Light on His Life and Works* (White Plains: M. E. Sharpe, 1980); Jean-François Billeter, *Li Zhi: Philosophe maudit (1527–1602)* (Geneva and Paris: Librarie Droz, 1979).

4. Billeter, *Li Zhi,* 243 (my translation).

5. Ibid., 260 (my translation).

6. The interconnections between the two men's backgrounds and writings are explored by Cheng Pei-kai in "Reality and Imagination: Li Chih and T'ang Hsien-tsu in Search of Authenticity" (Ph.D. thesis, Yale University, 1980).

7. Tang Xianzu, *The Peony Pavilion,* trans. Cyril Birch (Bloomington: Indiana University Press, 1980).

8. Patrick Hanan, *The Chinese Short Story: Studies in Dating, Authorship and Composition* (Cambridge: Harvard University Press, 1973); idem, *The Chinese Vernacular Story* (Cambridge: Harvard University Press, 1981).

9. For equivalent developments in the visual arts see the valuable essays on late Ming merchants' printing and collecting enterprises (including discussion of the *Fangshi mopu,* published in 1588) in *Shadows of Mt. Huang: Chinese Painting and Printing of the Anhui School,* ed. James Cahill (Berkeley, Calif.: University Art Museum, 1981).

10. Useful studies of such changes in plot and attitude during the Ming-Qing period can be found in the essays by Robert Hegel and Nathan Mao included in *Critical Essays on Chinese Fiction,* ed. Winston Yang and Curtis Adkins (Hong Kong: Chinese University Press, 1981). Though much of it is concerned with writing in the early Qing dynasty, Robert Hegel's admirable new study *The Novel in Seventeenth Century China* (New York: Columbia University Press, 1981) is also a valuable supplement to both Huang and Hanan. Particularly pertinent are Hegel's linking of new developments in the novel to the years following Emperor Wan-li's almost total withdrawal in 1589; his discussion of the literati audience for the novels and of rich merchants' reading habits; his study of the way imperial

prototypes were used to criticize Emperor Wan-Li; and his observations on the importance of the new genre of commentary on the novels.

Collapse of a Purist

1. This essay is based on material from the "Veritable Records" of the Ch'ing dynasty (the *Ta-Ch'ing Shih-lu*) for the K'ang-hsi reign, along with the collected memorials of Ts'ao Yin and Li Hsü. For full data on these and other relevant sources, see the bibliography in my *Ts'ao Yin and the K'ang-hsi Emperor: Bondservant and Master* (New Haven: Yale University Press, 1966 and 1988).

A Vibrant Doctrine

1. *Studies in Chinese Thought*, ed. Arthur F. Wright (Chicago: University of Chicago Press, 1953); *Confucianism in Action*, ed. Arthur F. Wright and David Nivison (Stanford: Stanford University Press, 1959); *The Confucian Persuasion*, ed. Arthur F. Wright (Stanford: Stanford University Press, 1960); *Confucian Personalities*, ed. Arthur F. Wright and Denis Twitchett (Stanford: Stanford University Press, 1962).
2. *Self and Society in Ming Thought* (New York: Columbia University Press, 1970) and *The Unfolding of Neo-Confucianism* (New York: Columbia University Press, 1975).
3. *The Limits of Change: Essays on Conservative Alternatives in Republican China*, ed. Charlotte Furth (Cambridge: Harvard University Press, 1976), 298–99.
4. Ibid., 250. In his own valuable recent book, *Neo-Confucian Thought in Action: Wang Yang-ming's Youth (1472–1509)* (Berkeley: University of California Press, 1976), Tu Wei-ming acknowledges his debt to T'ang Chun-i and writes of Wang Yang-ming in similar terms—as an "epoch-making" thinker, whose personal quest for sagehood involved that most fundamental of all struggles—the "struggle to be human" amid a "variety of depersonalizing forces."
5. Thomas A. Metzger, *Escape from Predicament: Neo-Confucianism and China's Evolving Political Culture* (New York: Columbia University Press, 1977).
6. Ibid., 134.
7. Ibid., 158.

The Dialogue of Chinese Science

1. Needham's collaborator Nathan Sivin seems to have been an important force in thinking aloud such problems: he broods about the inappropriateness of the word "biology," since the Chinese were not "asking the

same questions," warns about separating "advanced" and "retrograde" elements from the Chinese alchemical tradition so as to fit some convenient modern definition of "chemistry," and helpfully suggests that Chinese alchemy be seen as a "deductive proto-science" that should more usefully be compared to such other Chinese protosciences as medicine, acoustics, and magnetic geomancy (*SCC*, vol. 5, pt. 4, pp. xxxvi, 210, 298).

2. Compare Matteo Ricci, *Fonti Ricciane*, ed. Pasquale M. D'Elia, S.J., 3 vols. (Rome: Libreria della Stato, 1942–49), sect. 216, with *China in the Sixteenth Century: The Journals of Matthew Ricci*, trans. Louis J. Gallagher, S.J. (New York: Random House, 1953), 137. By 1664 the literatus and writer on science Fang I-chih was apparently taking for granted "watches only an inch across," made by a man and woman from the Sun family (*SCC*, vol. 4, pt. 2, p. 525).

3. See *Fonti Ricciane*, sects. 255, 259, 263.

4. Ibid., sects. 150–51; see *SCC*, vol. 4, pt. 1, p. 101, on glass, pt. 3, p. 26, on prisms.

5. Compare *Fonti Ricciane*, sect. 241, with *China in the Sixteenth Century*, 153. Cf. also, for example, the reports of the Florentine merchant Francesco Carletti in *My Voyage around the World*, trans. Herbert Weinstock (London: Methuen, 1964), 153.

6. Wang as trans. by Julia Ching, *To Acquire Wisdom* (New York: Columbia University Press, 1976), 246; Sung as trans. by Sun E-tu and Sun Shiou-chuan in *Chinese Technology in the Seventeeth Century* (University Park: Pennsylvania State University Press, 1966), 242. *Caveat lector*, however, since Sivin in *SCC*, vol. 5, pt. 4, p. 279, has found errors in another of their translations involving mercury and cinnabar matters. For information on many of the figures in this next section, see *Dictionary of Ming Biography, 1368–1644*, ed. L. Carrington Goodrich and Chaoying Fang, 2 vols. (New York: Columbia University Press, 1976), and *Eminent Chinese of the Ch'ing Period, 1644–1912*, ed. Arthur W. Hummel, 2 vols. (Washington, D.C.: Government Printing Office, 1943).

7. *Fonti Ricciane*, sect. 169.

8. *Ibid.*, sect. 364.

9. Sun and Sun, *Chinese Technology*, xii, xiv.

10. This bizarre "practice" was in fact an odd tribute to Chinese potency, since the eyes of barbarians were considered "useless" for those making this particular elixir; Chang Chen-t'ao as cited in Paul Cohen, *China and Christianity* (Cambridge: Harvard University Press, 1963), 31.

Being Chinese

1. Jerry Dennerline, *Qian Mu and the World of Seven Mansions* (New Haven: Yale University Press, 1988).

2. Jerry Dennerline, *The Chia-ting Loyalists: Confucian Leadership and*

Social Change in Seventeenth-Century China (New Haven: Yale University Press, 1981).

3. Dennerline, *Qian Mu,* 66.

4. Ibid., 149.

Food

My special thanks to Andrew Hsieh for much help with this essay.

1. Hsia Tsi-an, *The Gate of Darkness: Studies on the Leftist Literary Movement in China* (Seattle: University of Washington Press, 1968).

2. Peking United International Famine Relief Committee, *The North China Famine of 1920–21* (Peking, 1922).

3. The population figures for the *hsien* (county) show an increase of about 40 percent for the period between the printings of the two gazetteers. See *T'an-cheng hsien-chih* 1964, 5:19, working from *ting* equivalents.

4. Ho Ping-ti, *Studies on the Population of China, 1368–1953* (Cambridge: Harvard University Press, 1959).

5. His son later had these notes printed just as they had been written; they fill fifty-one printed pages. See Li Hua-nan, *Hsing-yüan lu,* in *Han-hai,* comp. Li T'iao-yuan (Taipei: I-wen, 1968), preface.

6. For the crops available in this area, see *Hsiu-shui hsien-chih* (1596).

7. George Macartney, *An Embassy to China, Being the Journal Kept by Lord Macartney during His Embassy to the Emperor Ch'ien-lung, 1793–94,* ed. J. L. Cranmer Byng (London: Longmans Green, 1962).

8. *Kuang-lu ssu tse-li* (Peking: Imperial Publications, 1839).

9. Robert Fortune, *A Resident among the Chinese: Inland, on the Coast, and at Sea* (London: John Murray, 1857).

10. J. MacGowan, *Sidelights on Chinese Life* (London: Kegan Paul, 1907).

11. Meng T'ien-p'ei and Sidney Gamble, *Prices, Wages and Standard of Living in Peking, 1900–24,* in *Chinese Social and Political Science Review,* special supplement (July 1926).

12. L. K. Tao, *Livelihood in Peking: An Analysis of the Budgets of Sixty Families* (Peking: Social Research Department, 1928).

13. Simon Yang and L. K. Tao, *A Study of the Standard of Living of the Working Families in Shanghai* (Peiping: Institute of Social Research, 1931).

14. Festival foods can be seen in any of the above gazetteers. See also Ku Lu, *Ch'ing Chia Lu,* Ch'ing tai pi chi ts'ung k'an ed. (Shanghai, n.d.).

15. S. Wells Williams, *The Middle Kingdom: A Survey of the Geography, Government, Literature, Social Life, Arts and History of the Chinese Empire and Its Inhabitants,* rev. ed., 2 vols. (New York: Scribner, 1893).

16. C. T. Wu, *The Scholars,* trans. Yang Hsien-yi and Gladys Yang (Peking: Foreign Language Press, 1957).

17. Yüan Mei, *Sui-yüan Shih-tan,* Hsiao-ts'ang shan-fang ed. (1824).

18. Arthur Waley, *Yuan Mei: Eighteenth Century Chinese Poet* (London: Allen and Unwin, 1956).

19. Li Yü felt that geese that had had their feet tenderized by being placed in hot oil while they were still alive should not be eaten—the practice was too cruel. See Li Yü, *Hsien-ch'ing ou-chi* (Shanghai: Chung kuo wen hsüeh chen pen ts'ung shu, 1936).

20. Lin Hsiang Ju and Lin Tsuifeng, *Chinese Gastronomy* (New York: Hastings House, 1957).

21. Shen Fu, *Chapters from a Floating Life: The Autobiography of a Chinese Artist*, trans. Shirley M. Black (London: Oxford University Press, 1960).

22. Ts'ao Hsüeh-ch'in, *The Story of the Stone*, vol. 1, *The Golden Days* (Harmondsworth, England: Penguin Books, 1973).

23. Nakagawa Shundai, *Shinzoku Kibun* (Tokyo: Tokyo Bunko, 1965).

24. One incident is translated in Waley, *Yuan Mei*, 197.

25. Liang Chang-chü, *Lang-chi hsü-t'an* (Taipei: Kuang wen shu chü, 1969).

26. Yü Huai, *A Feast of Mist and Flowers: The Gay Quarters of Nanking at the End of the Ming*, trans. Howard Levy (Yokohama, 1966, mimeographed).

27. P'u Sung-ling, *Contes extraordinaires du pavillon du loisir*, trans. Yves Hervouet et al. (Paris: Gallimard, 1969).

28. Kenneth Rexroth and Chung Ling, *The Orchid Boat: Women Poets of China* (New York: McGraw-Hill, 1972).

29. Hawkes makes this innuendo more direct in his translation.

30. Wang Yeh-chien, *Land Taxation in Imperial China, 1750–1911* (Cambridge: Harvard University Press, 1973).

31. Chang Te-ch'ang, "The Economic Role of the Imperial Household in the Ch'ing Dynasty," *Journal of Asian Studies* 31 (1972): 243–73.

32. Jonathan Spence, *Emperor of China: Self-Portrait of K'ang-hsi* (New York: Knopf, 1974).

33. Der Ling, *Son of Heaven* (New York: Appleton, 1933).

34. Su Chung [Lucille Davis], *Court Dishes of China: The Cuisine of the Ch'ing Dynasty* (Rutland and Tokyo, 1966).

35. Place settings for Mongol envoys in the Pao-ho tien can be seen in *Todo Meisho Zue*, 1:27.

36. John Bell, *A Journey from St. Petersburg to Pekin, 1719–1722*, ed. J. L. Stevenson (Edinburgh: Edinburgh University Press, 1965).

37. Shih Sheng-han, *Ch'i-min Yao-shu chin-shih* (Peking: Science Press, 1958).

38. Adrian Bennett, *John Fryer: The Introduction of Western Science and Technology into Nineteenth Century China* (Cambridge: Harvard University Press, 1967).

39. Teng Ssu-yü and John K. Fairbank, *China's Response to the West: A Documentary Survey, 1839–1923* (Cambridge: Harvard University Press, 1954).

40. William Ayers, *Chang Chih-tung and Educational Reform in China* (Cambridge: Harvard University Press, 1971).

41. See the passages on Western food in *Ch'ing-pai lei-ch'ao*, vol. 24, no. 56, pp. 49, 56; vol. 47, no. 92, pp. 2, 7, 8.

42. John K. Fairbank, *Trade and Diplomacy on the China Coast: The Opening of the Treaty Ports, 1842–54* (Stanford: Stanford University Press, 1969).

43. William C. Hunter, *Bits of Old China* (London: Kegan Paul, 1885).

44. Aisin-Gioro Pu Yi, *From Emperor to Citizen: the Autobiography of Aisin-Gioro Pu Yi*, trans. W. T. F. Jenner, vol. 1 (Peking: Foreign Languages Press, 1964).

45. G. E. Simon, "Note sur les petites sociétés d'argent en Chine," *Journal of the North China Branch of the Royal Asiatic Society*, n.s., 5 (1868): 1–23.

46. Hosea Ballou Morse, *The Gilds of China* (New York: Longmans, 1932), and Ho Ping-ti, *Chung-kuo hui-kuan shih lun* (Taipei: Hsüeh-sheng shu chü, 1966).

47. D. J. MacGowan, "Chinese Guilds or Chambers of Commerce and Trade Unions," *Journal of the North China Branch of the Royal Asiatic Society*, n.s., 21 (1886): 133–92.

48. Maurice Jametel, *La Chine inconnue* (Paris: J. Rouam, 1886).

49. Ku Lu, *Ch'ing Chia Lu*, Ch'ing tai pi chi ts'ung k'an ed. (Shanghai, n.d.).

50. Chiang-su po-wu-kuan, *Chiang-su sheng Ming-Ch'ing i-lai pei-k'o tzu-liao hsüan-chi* (Peking: Wen Wu Press, 1959).

51. Endymion Wilkinson, "Chinese Merchant Manuals and Route Books," *Ch'ing-shih wen t'i* 2, no. 9 (1973): 8–34.

52. China Imperial Maritime Customs, *Returns of Trade at the Treaty Ports for the Year 1884* (Shanghai, 1885).

53. Li Tou, *Yang-chou hua-fang lu*, 18 chüan (Tzu Jan An, 1795).

54. Maurice Jametel, *Pékin: Souvenirs de l'Empire du Milieu* (Paris: Plon, 1887).

55. Huang Liu-hung, *Fu-hui ch'üan-shu*, ed. Yamane Yukio (Tokyo, 1973).

56. Susan Naquin, "The Eight Trigram Rising of 1813" (Ph.D. diss., Yale University, 1974).

57. Fang Hao, "Ch'ien-lung shih-i nien chih shih-pa nien tsa-chang chi chia-chih-chang," *Shih-huo* 2, no. 1 (1972): 57–60.

58. Fang Hao, "Ch'ien-lung wu-shih-wu nien tzu Hsiu-ning chih Pei-ching lü-hsing yung-chang," *Shih-huo* 1, no. 1 (1971): 366–70.

59. Fang Hao, "Kuang-hsü yüan-nien tzu Hsiu-ch'eng chih Chin-ling hsiang-shih chang," *Shih-huo*, 2, no. 5 (1972): 288–90.

60. This brief section of the biography is not translated by Waley.

61. Yüan Mei, *Hsiao-ts'ang shan fang wen chi* (Shanghai: Chung Hua shu chü, 1933).

Medicine

I am indebted to Professor Nathan Sivin for his trenchant and helpful comments on the first draft of this paper.

The opening paragraph of the conference version of this essay ran as follows: "Since the broad theme of this conference is medicine and society in China, I will not narrow the topic unduly. Accordingly I will not deal with religious themes, but will treat "missionary" in the broad sense of one who is sent overseas to perform a stipulated service. Furthermore, I will at times be cavalier about whether I am discussing Americans or British, since it is the shared cultural and medical values that are of interest, rather than any specifically isolable traits."

1. Donald MacGillivray, *A Century of Protestant Missions in China, 1807–1907* (Shanghai: 1907).
2. *The China Mission Hand-book*, vol. 1 (Shanghai: American Presbyterian Mission Press, 1896).
3. Kenneth Scott Latourette, *A History of Christian Missions in China* (New York: MacMillan, 1929).
4. K. Chimin Wong and Wu Lien-teh, *History of Chinese Medicine: Being a Chronicle of Medical Happenings in China from Ancient Times to the Present Period* (Tientsin: Tientsin Press, 1922).
5. R. D. Rogers, "Progress Report, China Records Project" (July 24, 1972), and mimeographed catalog of general files, Day Missions Library, Yale Divinity School.
6. Ralph C. Croizier, *Traditional Medicine in Modern China* (Cambridge: Harvard University Press, 1968).
7. Joseph Levenson, *Confucian China and Its Modern Fate (1958–1965)* (London: Routledge and Kegan Paul, n.d.).
8. Paul Cohen, *China and Christianity* (Cambridge: Harvard University Press, 1963).
9. *Tien-shih-chai hua-pao* 3, no. 2 (n.d.): 71.
10. *The China Medical Missionary Journal* 7 (1893): 5; see also E. Gough, "Difficulties and Discouragements of Obstetric Work in China," ibid., 15 (1901): 249–54.
11. *Memorials of R. Harold A. Schofield* (London: Hodder and Staughton, 1898), 183.
12. Ibid., 219–26.
13. John G. Kerr, *The John G. Kerr Refuge for the Insane, Report for the Years 1907 and 1908* (Canton: n.p., 1909), 2.
14. Croizier, *Traditional Medicine*, 30.
15. Edgar Woods, "The Two Extremes," *China Medical Missionary Journal* 7 (1893): 11–13.
16. "Hospital Reports," *China Medical Missionary Journal* 7(1893): 43.

17. A. M. M., "Cases Illustrating What May Be Done for Chinese Patients in Their Own Homes," *China Medical Missionary Journal* 9 (1895): 62.
18. Editorial, "The Medical Missionary and the Anti-Foreign Riots in China," *China Medical Missionary Journal* 7 (1893): 110–16.
19. Frederick Porter Smith, *Contributions towards the Materia Medica and Natural History of China* (Shanghai and London: American Presbyterian Mission Press, 1871), 61.
20. Gough, "Difficulties and Discouragements."
21. V. P. Suvoong, "Observations on Opium," *China Medical Missionary Journal* 7 (1893): 172–79; for morphia "cures," see Hilary Beattie, "Protestant Missions and Opium in China," *Papers on China*, vol. 22A (1969): 104–33.
22. *Light-Giving School for Blind Girls and Boys, Canton, China: Report for 1906–1910* (n.p., n.d.).
23. Kerr, *Refuge for the Insane, 1907 and 1908*.
24. Ibid., 4; see also W. W. Cadbury and M. H. Jones, *At the Point of a Lancet: One Hundred Years of the Canton Hospital, 1835–1935* (Shanghai: Kelly and Walsh, 1935), 105–9.
25. See the thorough discussions of leprosy, mental deficiency, and mental disease in Herbert Day Lamson, *Social Pathology in China* (Shanghai: Shanghai Commercial Press, 1934).
26. John G. Kerr, *Refuge for the Insane: Report for 1909* (Canton: n.p., 1910).
27. John G. Kerr, *Refuge for the Insane: Report for 1916 and 1917* (Canton: n.p., 1918) 14.
28. Philip Cousland, "The Medical School," *China Medical Missionary Journal* 15 (1901): 199.
29. *Shen-pao (T'ung-chih*, 11th year), 2:780, 1339.
30. Ibid., 1103.
31. Ibid., 1002.
32. Ibid., 774.
33. Ibid., (*Kuang-hsü*, 9th year) 40:27,022–25.
34. Ibid., 27,106; 27,089; 2:685.
35. Ibid., 2:1354, 1485.
36. Beattie, "Protestant Missions"; Wong and Wu, *History of Chinese Medicine*.
37. *Shen-pao*, 2:654.
38. Ibid., 717.
39. Ibid., 766.
40. Ibid., 40:27,042.
41. Ibid., 27,033; 27,036; 27,028.
42. Ibid., 27,036.
43. Jonathan Spence, "Opium Smoking in Ch'ing China," in Frederic

Wakeman and Carolyn Grant, eds., *Conflict and Control in Late Imperial China* (Berkeley: University of California Press, 1975), 143–73.

44. Smith, *Contributions towards the Materia Medica,* vii.

45. H. W. Boone, "An Ambulance for Carrying Patients, Suited to the Conditions of Chinese Life," *China Medical Journal* 22 (1908): 167–68.

46. William Wilson, "The Use of Native Drugs," *China Medical Journal* 22 (1908): 300–310.

47. *Tien-shih-chai hua-pao,* no. 12, sec. 1, p. 26; see also John Fairbank, "A Chinese Look at Life in Shanghai of the 80's," *Harvard Bulletin* (April 1972): 44–49, which first introduced this source to me.

48. William Lockhart, *The Medical Missionary in China: A Narrative of Twenty Years' Experience* (London: Hurst and Blackett, 1861), p. 159.

49. *Tien-shih-chai hua-po* no. 2, sec. 1, p. 7.

50. Editorial Comment, "Drs. Ida Kahn and Mary Stone," *China Medical Missionary Journal* 10 (1896): 181–84; for other Chinese women, see Wong and Wu, *History of Chinese Medicine,* 363–64.

51. George C. Basil, "Dr. Strobel: The Successful Failure," in *Test Tubes and Dragon Scales* (Chicago, Philadelphia, and Toronto: John Winston, 1940), 205–20.

52. *China Medical Missionary Journal* 1 (1887): 29.

53. J. W. S. Johnsson, "L'Anatomie mandchoue et les figures de Th. Bartholin, étude d'iconographie comparée," *Kongelige Danske Videnskabernes Selskab* (Copenhagen), Biologiske Meddelelser, VII, 7 (1928, 3–42): 28.

54. John Dudgeon, "A Modern Chinese Anatomist," *China Medical Missionary Journal* 7 (1893): 245–56.

55. John G. Kerr, *A Guide to the City and Suburbs of Canton* (Hong Kong and Shanghai: Kelly and Walsh, 1904).

56. Ibid.

Taxes

1. Madeleine Zelin, *The Magistrate's Tael: Rationalizing Fiscal Reform in Eighteenth-Century Ch'ing China* (Berkeley: University of California Press, 1984); Philip C. C. Huang, *The Peasant Economy and Social Change in North China* (Stanford University Press, 1985); Benjamin A. Elman, *From Philosophy to Philology: Intellectual and Social Aspects of Change in Late Imperial China* (Cambridge: Harvard University Press, 1984).

2. Linda Grove and Christian Daniels, eds., *State and Society in China: Japanese Perspectives on Ming-Qing Social and Economic History* (Tokyo: University of Tokyo Press, 1984); Joshua Fogel, ed. and trans., *Recent Japanese Studies of Modern Chinese History* (Armonk, N.Y.: M. E. Sharpe, 1984).

3. Among the other recent studies that should be mentioned here are John B. Henderson, *The Development and Decline of Chinese Cosmology* (New York: Columbia University Press, 1984); Robert B. Marks, *Rural Revolution in South China: Peasants and the Making of History in Haifeng County, 1570–1930* (Madison: University of Wisconsin Press, 1984); Ng Chin-Keong, *Trade and Society: The Amoy Network on the China Coast, 1683–1735* (Singapore: Singapore University Press, 1983); Philip Chadwick Foster Smith, *The Empress of China* (Philadelphia: Philadelphia Maritime Museum, 1984); Peter Roebuck, ed., *Macartney of Lisanoure, 1737–1806: Essays in Biography* (Ulster: Ulster Historical Foundation, 1983); and Charles O. Hucker, *A Dictionary of Official Titles in Imperial China* (Stanford: Stanford University Press, 1985).

Opium

1. My special thanks to Andrew Hsieh, for much help with bibliography and translation; to Fu-mei Chen and Randle Edwards, for crucial legal references and for correcting several mistakes in the draft paper; to John Fairbank, for perceptive comments as discussant; and to Janis Cochran, for typing so often from my longhand without objections. Thanks also to many people who discussed this paper with me or supplied references: Leonard Adams, Charles Boxer, Edward Brecher, Rosser Brockman, Chang Te-ch'ang, Sherman Cochran, Herbert Kleber, Jao Tsung-i, Sue Naquin, Jonathan Ocko, Saeki Tomi, Jack Wills.

2. The most interesting studies include Hosea Ballou Morse, *The International Relations of the Chinese Empire*, 3 vols. (Shanghai and London, 1910–18); John King Fairbank, *Trade and Diplomacy on the China Coast: The Opening of the Treaty Ports, 1842–1854* (Cambridge: Harvard University Press, 1953); Chen Ching-jen, "Opium and Anglo-Chinese Relations," *Chinese Social and Political Science Review* 19:396–437; Yü En-te, *Chung-kuo chin-yen fa-ling pien-ch'ien shih* (A history of the prohibitions of opium in China) (Shanghai: Chung-hua shu-chü, 1934); Chang Hsin-pao, *Commissioner Lin and the Opium War* (Cambridge: Harvard University Press, 1964); Charles C. Stelle, "American Trade in Opium to China, prior to 1820," *Pacific Historical Review* 9 (1940): 425–45; idem, "American Trade in Opium to China, 1821–39," ibid., 10 (1941): 57–74; David Edward Owen, *British Opium Policy in China and India* (New Haven: Yale University Press, 1934); Michael Greenberg, *British Trade and the Opening of China, 1800–1842* (Cambridge: Cambridge University Press, 1951); and the documentary collection *Ya-p'ien chan-cheng*, 6 vols. (Shanghai, 1954), cited hereafter as *YPCC*.

3. Chang Lu, *Pen-ching feng-yuan* (Clear exposition of medical classics), in *Chang-shih i-shu* (The medical works of Chang Lu) (preface dated 1709),

3:11–12; Joseph Edkins, *Opium: Historical Note, or the Poppy in China*, Imperial Maritime Customs, China, vol. 2, special ser. no. 13 (Shanghai, 1898). As a febrifuge, especially for the poor in marshy areas or for boatmen, see *The Minutes of Evidence* and the *Final Report* of the British government's *Royal Commission on Opium* (London, 1894–95), cited hereafter as *RoyCom*, 1:112, no. 1637.

4. Most early-eighteenth-century sources mention its aphrodisiac quality. See Lan Ting-yuan, *Lu-chou ch'u-chi* (Collected works from Lu-chou) (1731 ed.); and Huang Shu-ching, *T'ai-hai shih ch'a lu* (Notes on a mission to Taiwan) (Taipei: T'ai-wan wen-hsien ts'ung-k'an, 1957). Liang Kung-ch'en cites a mid-Ch'ing prostitute for more graphic details. See Liang Kung-ch'en, *Pei-tung-yuan pi-lu* (Notes from the northeast garden), in *Pi-chi hsiao-shuo ta-kuan* (A broad view of random essays and fiction) (Taipei: Hsin-hsing shu-chü, 1962), 3rd ser., 2:21b. There are strong parallels with one element of heroin motivation here: both opium and heroin initially prolong male erection and postpone ejaculation, though in later stages of addiction, desire decreases markedly. See *RoyCom*, 1:167, for the interesting testimony furnished by the Sydney Police Department on Australian prostitutes consorting with Chinese addicts.

5. The epidemic is discussed in K. Chimin Wong and Wu Lien-teh, *History of Chinese Medicine* (Tientsin: Tientsin Press, 1932). For the extent of the epidemic, see *Ch'ing-shih* (Dynastic history of the Ch'ing), Kuo-fang yen-chiu-yuan ed. (Taipei, 1961), 1:671.

6. On opium smoking in circumstances of great prosperity, see the evidence for Szechwan collected by S. A. M. Adshead, "The Opium Trade in Szechwan, 1881–1911," *Journal of Southeast Asian History* 7, no. 2 (1966): 93–99.

7. The waning of eunuchs' power and their dissatisfaction is considered by Chang Te-ch'ang in "The Economic Role of the Imperial Household *(Nei-wu-fu)* in the Ch'ing Dynasty," *Journal of Asian Studies* 31 (1972): 243–73. Manchu nobles had little power after Yung-cheng's reign.

8. The interpretation that some soldiers became addicted so as to avoid dangerous combat assignments was suggested to me by Dr. Herbert Kleber.

9. A theme beautifully illustrated in Mao Tun, *Midnight* (Peking: Foreign Language Press, 1957). Charles de Constant guessed in the late eighteenth century that women smoked for similar reasons. See Louis Dermigny, *Les Memoires de Charles de Constant sur le commerce à la Chine* (Paris: Ecole Pratique des Hautes Etudes, 1964).

10. As mentioned by Benjamin I. Schwartz, *In Search of Wealth and Power* (Cambridge: Harvard University Press, 1964), 31.

11. *RoyCom*, 1:110, no. 1631, and 116, no. 1733.

12. *RoyCom*, 1:116, no. 1739, and 141, nos. 2026–32.

13. *RoyCom,* 1:30, no. 389.

14. *Hsia-men chih* (Gazetteer of Amoy) (1839), 15:17.

15. Jay Leyda, *Dianying, Electric Shadows: An Account of Films and the Film Audience in China* (Cambridge: MIT Press, 1972), 17–18.

16. Much data is in the collections by Wang Shih-han, comp., *Chin-ssu lu* (Notes on tobacco), in *Ts'ung-mu Wang-shih i-shu* (Collection of Mr. Wang's posthumous papers) (1886); Lu Yao, *Yen-p'u* (Notes on tobacco), *Chao-tai ts'ung-shu, ting-chi* (Chao-tai collection, 4th ser.) (1833), chüan 46; and Ts'ai Chia-wan, *Yen-p'u* (Notes on tobacco) in *Pai-mei shang-fang chi shang-shu* (Writings from the house on Pai-mei mountain) (1836). These discuss tobacco smoking as being good for health and relaxation and as an aid in forgetting sadness; all three presumably would have been emphasized by opium smokers had a *Ya-p'ien p'u* (Notes on opium) ever been written. The joys of opium in a Chinese literati setting of the 1930s are wonderfully caught in Emily Hahn's essay "The Big Smoke," *Times and Places* (New York: Crowell, 1970).

17. *RoyCom,* 1:48, no. 627 and *passim,* for Indian testimony.

18. Brief summary in *RoyCom,* 6:51. Again, there was much detailed study of the effects of opium on Indian laborers.

19. *RoyCom,* 1:47, no. 611.

20. *RoyCom,* 1:95, no. 1320.

21. Francis H. Nichols, *Through Hidden Shensi* (New York, 1902), chap. 5.

22. For examples, in order, see D. W. Y. Kwok, *Scientism in Chinese Thought, 1900–1950* (New Haven: Yale University Press, 1965), 50–60; David Roy, *Kuo Mo-jo, The Early Years* (Cambridge: Harvard University Press, 1971), 46 (Kuo's father also dealt in opium; ibid., 9); James Sheridan, *Chinese Warlord: The Career of Feng Yü-hsiang* (Stanford: Stanford University Press, 1970), 9; Chou Hsia-shou (Chou Tso-jen), *Lu Hsun ti ku-chia* (Lu Hsun's home) (Shanghai: Shang-hai ch'u-pan kung-she, 1953), sec. 26, p. 70; Donald Klein and Ann Clark, 'Ch'ü Ch'iu-pai," *Biographical Dictionary of Chinese Communism, 1921–1965* (Cambridge: Harvard University Press, 1971), 1:239.

23. Pa Chin, *The Family* (Peking: Foreign Languages Press, 1958), 91, 117–18.

24. *Fu-chou fu-chih* (Foochow prefectural gazetteer) (1754), 25:24; L. Carrington Goodrich, "Early Prohibitions of Tobacco in China and Manchuria," *Journal of the American Oriental Society* 58:638–57; Berthold Laufer, *Tobacco and Its Use in Asia,* Anthropology leaflet no. 18 (Chicago: Field Museum of Natural History, 1924).

25. "Wu-ch'an-chih" (Section on produce), 1:7b, in *Fu-chien t'ung-chih* (Fukien provincial gazetteer) (1870 ed.; reprint, Taipei), 632.

26. André Joao Antonil, *Cultura e opulencia do Brasil por suas drogas e*

minas, ed. and trans. Andrée Mansuy (Paris: Institut des Hautes Etudes de l'Amérique Latine, 1968), 333.

27. See the illustrations in *Wan-shou sheng-tien* (Compilation of K'ang-hsi's sixtieth birthday celebrations) (1717), showing the tobacco shops along Peking streets.

28. John Bell, *A Journey from St. Petersburg to Pekin, 1719–1722* (Edinburgh: Edinburgh University Press, 1965), 167.

29. Wang Shih-han, *Chin-ssu lu,* 2.

30. Arthur W. Hummel, ed., *Eminent Chinese of the Ch'ing Period* (Washington, D.C.: Government Printing Office, 1943–44), 1:53.

31. For 1617, see L. C. D. van Dijk, "Bijvoegsels tot de geschiedenis van het handle en het gebruik van opium in Nederlandsch Indië," in *Bijdragen tot de Taal-, land, en Volkenkunde van Nederlandsch Indië,* 211; for the resolution of 1671 to forbid further Chinese dealing, see Algemeen Rijksarchief, K.A. 586, fol. 256. Both of these references were supplied by Jack Wills.

32. Engelbert Kaempfer, *Amoenitatum Exoticarum politico-physico-medicarum* (Langoviae, 1712), cited in Edkins, *Opium,* 155.

33. Lan Ting-yuan, *Lu-chou ch'u-chi,* 2:16.

34. Huang Shu-ching, *T'ai-hai shih-ch'a lu,* 43.

35. Cited in Yü En-te, *Chung-kuo chin-yen fa-ling,* 16.

36. Dermigny, *Charles de Constant,* 207.

37. Clarke Abel, *Narrative of a Journey in the Interior of China* (London, 1818), 214–15.

38. Ch'en Ch'i-yuan, *Yung-hsien chai pi-chi* (Notes from the Yung-hsien study), in *Pi-chi hsiao-shuo ta-kuan* (A broad view of random essays and fiction) (Taipei: Kuang-wen shu-chü, 1960), 8:22.

39. *RoyCom,* vol. 6, pt. 1, p. 117.

40. Huang Shu-ching, *T'ai-hai shih-ch'a lu.*

41. *RoyCom,* vol. 7, pt. 2, appendix B, p. 33.

42. *RoyCom,* vol. 6, pt. 1, p. 117.

43. Chen Ching-jen, "Opium and Anglo-Chinese Relations," *Chinese Social and Political Science Review* 19:388.

44. Dermigny, *Charles de Constant,* 205, n. 1.

45. Morse, *International Relations,* 1:173–74.

46. Chang Hsin-pao, *Commissioner Lin,* 237, n. 6.

47. Chao Hsueh-min, *Pen-ts'ao kang-mu shih-i* (A continuation of the medical classic *Pen-ts'ao kang-mu*) (Hong Kong: Shang-wu yin-shu kuan, 1969), 34–35. Also, pp. 25–34 have a great deal of information on tobacco.

48. *Ta-Ch'ing hui-tien shih-li* (Collected statutes and precedents of the Ch'ing dynasty) (Taipei 1963 reprint, cited hereafter as *TCHT*), 15,442 (828:4b).

49. *YPCC,* 454–56; *CSL:*TK, 3562, 3579, 3587; *Hsing-an hui-lan* (Collection of Ch'ing penal cases) (Taipei 1968 reprint, cited hereafter as *HAHL*).

50. *YPCC*, 436. Chang Hsin-pao, *Commissioner Lin*, 34, shows that Pao Shih-chen had estimated 100,000 addicts spending about 10,000 taels a day in the Soochow of 1820.

51. *CSL:*TK; 3893, 3895, 3897, 3899; biography of Li Hung-pin in *Ch'ing-shih lieh-chuan* (Biographies of the Ch'ing dynasty) (Taipei: Chung-hua shu-chü, 1962), 36:46b; *HAHL*, 863.

52. Chang Hsin-pao, *Commissioner Lin*, 87–88; and *Chinese Repository*, 5:139–44.

53. *Chinese Repository*, 5:396.

54. Chang Hsin-pao, *Commissioner Lin*, 223, appendix B.

55. Morse, *International Relations*, 1:209–10.

56. Stanley F. Wright, *Hart and the Chinese Customs* (Belfast: Wm. Mullan, 1950), 544.

57. Morse, *International Relations*, 3:437.

58. Imperial Maritime Customs (cited hereafter as IMC), *Native Opium, 1887; with an Appendix: Native Opium, 1863*, vol. 2, special ser. no. 9 (Shanghai: Inspector General of Customs, 1888), 6, and app. on 1863; and IMC, *Opium: Crude and Prepared*, vol. 2, special ser. no. 10 (Shanghai: Inspector General of Customs, 1888), 38.

59. *Ku-chin t'u-shu chi-ch'eng* (Historical encyclopedia of the Ch'ing) (Shanghai: Chung-hua shu-chü, 1934), as cited in Edkins, *Opium*.

60. *Fu-chou fu-chih: Kuei-chou t'ung-chih* (Kweichow provincial gazetteer), 1741 ed.

61. *YPCC*, 474; for Kwangtung, *YPCC*, 440; for Chekiang, *YPCC*, 465.

62. Chang Lu, *Pen-ching feng-yuan*, 3:11.

63. *RoyCom*, vol. 1, app. 6, pp. 168–69.

64. Ibid., 169.

65. *YPCC*, 471. For the much higher earlier prices, compare Chang Hsin-pao, *Commissioner Lin*, 21–22. In 1821 Bengal had been over $2,000.00, and in 1817 Patna had been $1,300.00.

66. Fairbank, *Trade and Diplomacy*, 242.

67. IMC, *Native Opium*, app. on 1863.

68. *RoyCom*, 1:39, no. 503; 47, no. 611; 112, no. 1637. Also IMC, *Native Opium*, 40.

69. *RoyCom*, 1:44, nos. 553–54.

70. IMC, *Opium: Crude and Prepared*, 5.

71. Ibid., 16.

72. IMC, *Native Opium*, 8.

73. Ibid., 6.

74. John Lossing Buck, *Land Utilization in China* (Shanghai: Commercial Press, 1937), 234.

75. IMC, *Native Opium*, 41; *RoyCom*, 2:384.

76. *RoyCom*, 2:383. A photograph of opium and tobacco growing in alternate rows is in Buck, *Land Utilization*, facing p. 206.

77. W. D. Spence, acting consul at I-chang, claims to have investigated tenancy relations in 1882; see *RoyCom*, 2:383–84. His report is fascinating, but it is by no means clear how thoroughly his investigation was conducted.

78. *RoyCom*, 2:384.

79. *RoyCom*, 1:17, no. 212; 2:386.

80. *Peking Gazette, Translations* (cited hereafter as *PGT*), published by the *North China Herald* (Shanghai), (1892), 125.

81. *PGT* (1878), 45.

82. *RoyCom*, 1:44–45, nos. 559–60, and 129, nos. 1977–79.

83. *RoyCom*, 1:15–17, nos. 193 and 212.

84. *RoyCom*, 1:113, no. 1643.

85. *RoyCom*, 1:18, nos. 221–22. Estimates of annual consumption vary widely; one observer in 1865 thought two pounds per year a better guess for medium smokers, with four pounds for heavy smokers. See "Opium-Raucher and Esser in China und Japan," *Wiener Medizinische Wochenschrift* 15:1568–69.

86. *RoyCom*, 2:387. Alexander Hosie, *On the Trail of the Opium Poppy* (London, 1914), 265, estimated that 200,000 piculs were produced in Szechwan in 1904, of which 180,000 piculs were smoked locally.

87. *Agrarian China, Selected Source Materials from Chinese Authors* (Chicago: University of Chicago Press, 1938), 118. "Catties" in this source appears to be a misprint for ounces.

88. *Agrarian China*, 124.

89. Hosie, *On the Trail*, 237.

90. Ibid., 242–43.

91. S. A. M. Adshead, *The Modernization of the Chinese Salt Administration, 1900–1920* (Cambridge: Harvard University Press, 1970), 13.

92. Walter Fuchs, "Koreanische Quellen zur Frühgeschichte des Tabaks in der Mandjurei zwischen 1630 and 1640," *Monumenta Serica*, 5:89.

93. Fuchs, "Frühgeschichte," 96, and edict of 1639 in Goodrich, "Early Prohibitions," 652.

94. Fuchs, "Frühgeschichte," 99.

95. Ibid., 93.

96. Chang Chieh-pin, *Ching-yueh ch'üan-shu* (Complete medical works) (n.d., 17th-century ed.), 48–25.

97. Goodrich, "Early Prohibitions," 650–51.

98. Ibid., 651.

99. *T'ing-hsun ko-yen* (K'ang-hsi's conversations), translated in Goodrich, "Early Prohibitions," 654.

100. Yü Min-chung, *Kuo-ch'ao kung-shih* (History of the Ch'ing palace) (Taipei: Hsueh-sheng shu-chü, 1965), 26.

101. Yü En-te, *Chung-kuo chin-yen fa-ling*, p. 16; *TCHT*, 828:1.

102. Ibid.

103. *Tu-li ts'un-i* (annotated edition of the Ch'ing legal code), ed. Hsueh Yun-sheng (Peking, 1905), cited hereafter as *TLTI*, 22:63b–64; Fang Pao, *Fang Wang-chi hsien-sheng ch'üan-chi* (Fang Pao's collected works), 1746 ed. (Shanghai, 1935), 457.

104. Yü En-te, *Chung-kuo chin-yen fa-ling*, 15; F. Hirth, "The Hoppo Book of 1753," *Journal of the North China Branch of the Royal Asiatic Society*, new ser., 17:221–35.

105. The case is in *Yung-cheng chu-p'i yü-chih* (Vermilion endorsements of the Yung-cheng emperor) (Shanghai, 1887), 14:22b, and has been translated by Fu Lo-shu, *A Documentary Chronicle of Sino-Western Relations, 1644–1820*, A.A.S. Monographs and Papers no. 22 (Tucson: University of Arizona Press, 1966), 1:162–64. I am grateful to Professor Saeki Tomi for using his index of the *chu-p'i yü-chih* to check that there were no other Yung-cheng references to opium cases.

106. H. B. Morse, *The Chronicles of the East India Company Trading to China, 1635–1834* (Oxford: Oxford University Press, 1926), 1:215.

107. Yü En-te, *Chung-kuo chin-yen fa-ling*, 22. Fu Lo-shu, *Documentary Chronicle*, 1:381–83, has a translation of the 1811 prohibition edict and the Liang-kuang governor-general's reply.

108. *TCHT*, 15,442 (828:4b).

109. Chang Hsin-pao, *Commissioner Lin*, 20.

110. *TCHT*, 15,443 (828:5).

111. *YPCC*, 439, interlinear endorsement.

112. *TCHT*, 15,443 (828:6); *HAHL*, 905–6.

113. *TCHT*, 15,443 (828:6b); *HAHL*, 904, 906–8.

114. *HAHL*, 482–83.

115. *HAHL*, 484.

116. *HAHL*, 906.

117. *TCHT*, 15,443 (828:6b); *TLTI*, 22:60b–61b; Morse, *International Relations*, 1:548.

118. *TLTI*, 4:42b.

119. *TLTI*, 22:62b–63.

120. *TPCC*, 458.

121. *Chinese Repository*, 5:396.

122. See the survey for the 1840s in Fairbank, *Trade and Diplomacy*, 240–41.

123. *PGT* (1874), 141.

124. *PGT* (1882), 132.

125. *PGT* (Sept. 12, 1878).

126. Continuation of the *Hsing-an hui-lan* (cited hereafter as *HAHLF*), 4971.
127. *PGT* (1881), 32.
128. *PGT* (1872), 115.
129. *HAHLF*, 4971.
130. *PGT* (1879), 98.
131. *PGT* (1872), 130.
132. *PGT* (1877), 175.
133. *PGT* (1881), 135.
134. Algemeen Rijksarchief, K.A. 589, fol. 55, council resolution of May 8, 1674. This reference is also courtesy of Jack Wills.
135. *RoyCom*, vol. 7, app. B, p. 35; memorandum by F. C. Danvers on the Dutch trade in opium during the seventeenth century.
136. Fu Lo-shu, *Documentary Chronicle*, 1:163.
137. Chang Hsin-pao, *Commissioner Lin*, 32.
138. Ibid., 33, and map on 25.
139. Fang Chao-ying and Tu Lien-che, eds., *Tseng-chiao Ch'ing-ch'ao chin-shih t'i-ming pei-lu* (Index to the Ch'ing dynasty *chin-shih* holders), Harvard-Yenching Institute Sinological Index Series, Supplement no. 19, reprint (Taipei: Ch'eng-wen, 1966), p. 151, 2d rank, 76th name in class of 1820.
140. *YPCC*, 433–34.
141. *YPCC*, 444.
142. *YPCC*, 447.
143. *YPCC*, 449.
144. *YPCC*, 451–52.
145. *YPCC*, 453.
146. *YPCC*, 455.
147. *PGT* (1872), 79 and 89.
148. *PGT* (1874), 141.
149. *PGT* (1875), 49.
150. *PGT* (1890), 189.
151. *PGT* (1882), 46. In this instance wine was the smuggled article.
152. *PGT* (1887), 12.
153. IMC, *Opium: Crude and Prepared*, 18. For Swatow men, see also Edward Le Fevour, *Western Enterprise in Late Ch'ing China: A Selective Survey of Jardine, Matheson and Company's Operations, 1842–1895* (Cambridge: Harvard East Asian Research Center, 1968), 23–24.
154. Li Hung-chang, *Li Wen-chung kung ch'üan-chi* (The complete works of Li Hung-chang) (Shanghai, 1905), 41:32. For Samuel's role in the deal, see Morse, *International Relations*, 2:385.
155. Robert Hart, "Letters to James Duncan Campbell" (MSS at Harvard University), 413 and 697.
156. Hart, "Letters," 701 and 706.
157. *RoyCom*, 2:384.

158. *PGT* (1887), 182–83.

159. Yen-p'ing Hao, *The Comprador in Nineteenth-Century China* (Cambridge: Harvard University Press, 1970), 103.

160. IMC, *Opium: Crude and Prepared,* 18.

161. Ibid., 7.

162. *YPCC,* 467.

163. IMC, *Native Opium,* 6.

164. *RoyCom,* 1:47, no. 618.

165. *RoyCom,* 1:45, no. 562.

166. *RoyCom,* 2:386.

167. Emile Bard, *Chinese Life in Town and Country,* adapted by H. Twitchell from the French (New York, 1907), 159–60. It is possible that these divans catered to peasants visiting town in connecting with their periodical marketing journeys; if so, this would be another item to add to the analysis of market structures made by G. William Skinner, "Marketing and Social Structure in Rural China," in 3 pts., *Journal of Asian Studies* 24 (1964): 3–43, 195–228, 363–99.

168. *Chiao-hui hsin-pao* (Mission news) 2:65 (Dec. 11, 1869); Kuo Sung-t'ao, *Yang-chih shu-wu wen-chi* (Collected prose works of Kuo Sung-t'ao) (Taipei: Wen-hai ch'u-pan she, 1964), 12:21b.

169. Fairbank, *Trade and Diplomacy,* 297.

170. *RoyCom,* 1:47, no. 611.

171. *RoyCom,* 1:45, no. 567.

172. *RoyCom,* 1:114, no. 1670; 115, no. 1693.

173. *RoyCom,* 1:59, no. 836.

174. Hilary Beattie, "Protestant Missions and Opium in China," *Harvard University Papers on China,* vol. 22A (1969): 104–13.

175. *PGT* (1888), 88.

176. Yen-p'ing Hao, *The Comprador,* 77, 79, 82.

177. Ibid., 81.

178. Fairbank, *Trade and Diplomacy,* 405–6.

179. A graphic case is in *PGT* (1888), 160; another in Fairbank, *Trade and Diplomacy,* 405–6.

180. Fairbank, *Trade and Diplomacy,* 238.

181. IMC, *Native Opium,* 16.

182. *RoyCom,* 2:385.

183. *PGT* (1881), 52.

184. *PGT* (1874), 46.

185. *PGT* (1874), 87.

186. *PGT* (1875), 36.

187. *PGT* (1875), 147.

188. *PGT* (1878), 225.

189. *PGT* (1876), 105.

190. Kuo Sung-t'ao, *Yang-chih shu-wu wen-chi.* 12:18b.

191. *PGT* (1877), 184–86.
192. *PGT* (1878), 13.
193. *PGT* (1878), 176.
194. Morse, *International Relations*, 1:549.
195. Ibid., 551–55.
196. Ibid., 2:375.
197. Ibid., 2:379.
198. Ibid., 2:376.
199. Chang Chung-li and Stanley Spector, eds., *Guide to the Memorials of Seven Leading Officials of Nineteenth-Century China* (Seattle: University of Washington Press, 1955), 364, 379, 391, 396.
200. Ibid., 173–74.
201. Ibid., 231.
202. Ibid., 245, 277, 311, 328, 329, 335.
203. *PGT* (1874), 87.
204. *PGT* (1877), 116–17.
205. *PGT* (1880), 58.
206. *PGT* (1887), 197.
207. *PGT* (1887), 142.
208. *PGT* (1879), 200–201.
209. *PGT* (1881), 52–53.
210. *PGT* (1888), 88.
211. *PGT* (1889), 117, and (1890), 232.
212. *PGT* (1877), 88.
213. Beattie, "Protestant Missions," 121.
214. Hart, "Letters,' 1957–58.
215. Ibid., 1830.
216. Ibid., 1968.
217. Ibid., 1971.
218. Ibid., 2089.
219. An excellent account of his suppression campaign in Yunnan is in Roger V. Des Forges, "Hsi-liang, A Portrait of a Late Ch'ing Patriot" (Ph.D. thesis, Yale University, 1971), 252–81.
220. With some reservations, as noted in Mary C. Wright, ed., *China in Revolution: The First Phase, 1900–1913* (New Haven: Yale University Press, 1968), 14–15.
221. There are intriguing data in Edward Friedman, "Revolution or Just Another Bloody Cycle? Swatow and the 1911 Revolution," *Journal of Asian Studies* 29 (1970): 289–307, esp. 301–2.
222. These are among the themes in a recently registered Yale Ph.D. thesis by Leonard P. Adams III, "The Tarnished Crusade: Opium Suppression in China, 1880–1930."
223. The Communists had also learned a great deal about local option and minority group sentiments, as can be seen from their February 1950 anti-

opium provisions: *Chung-yang jen-min cheng-fu fa-ling hui-pien* (Collection of laws and decrees of the People's Republic of China) (Peking: Fa-lü ch'u-pan she, 1952), 1:173–74.

Cock's Blood and Browning Pistols

1. Charles W. Hayford, *To the People: James Yen and Village China* (New York: Columbia University Press, 1990).
2. David Strand, *Rickshaw Beijing: City People and Politics in the 1920s* (Berkeley: University of California Press, 1989).
3. Marie-Claire Bergère, *The Golden Age of the Chinese Bourgeoisie, 1919–1937*, trans. Janet Lloyd (New York: Cambridge University Press, 1989).
4. Wen-hsin Yeh, *The Alienated Academy: Culture and Politics in Republican China, 1919–1937* (Cambridge: Council on East Asian Studies, Harvard University Press, 1990).
5. Phil Billingsley, *Bandits in Republican China* (Stanford: Stanford University Press, 1988).

Film and Politics: Bai Hua's *Bitter Love*

This essay is a slightly emended version of a lecture given to the British Association for Chinese Studies at the School of Oriental and African Studies in the University of London on March 11, 1982.
1. A full translation of *Chaguan* is in *Chinese Literature*, no. 12 (1979): 16–96.
2. The script of *Ku Lian* first appeared in the Beijing literary magazine *Shiyue*, Oct. 1979, 140–71 and 248, attributed to the joint authorship of Bai Hua and the film director Peng Ning, with illustrations by Lin Yong. The date and place of composition were given as "April 1979 Guangzhou and May 1979 Beijing." I follow the text of *Ku Lian* as translated in *China Report* (Political, Sociological and Military Affairs, no. 248), JPRS 79676, Dec. 6, 1981, which was in fact taken from the Chinese version that appeared in the Hong Kong journal Cheng-ming, June 1, 1981, 82–98. For help in tracking Bai Hua materials, I would especially like to thank Mark Sidel and other members of the Yale-China Association discussion group, Mr. and Mrs. Basil Clarke, and analysts at the Far Eastern section of the BBC.
3. See the speech by Bai Hua, *People's Daily*, Nov. 13, 1979, from the BBC's *Summary of World Broadcasts* (cited hereafter as *SWB*) (F3/6282/B11), Nov. 27, 1979, 1–7, which includes some biographical details; Wolfgang Bartke, *Who's Who in the People's Republic of China* (Brighton: Harvester Press, 1981), s.v. "Bai Hua"; and *Qishi niandai* (The seventies), June 1981, 38–41, and Oct. 1981, 93–94.
4. Bai Hua's speech (see note 3 above), 1.
5. Ibid.

6. Ibid., 2–7.

7. *Ku Lian* translation in *China Report*, JPRS (see note 2 above), 8. Various commentators (for example, Xiao Jin in *Qishi niandai*, Oct. 1981, 93) have pointed out that the model for Ling Chenguang seems to be the painter Huang Yongyun, who returned from Hong Kong to Beijing in 1951 and was later persecuted. The inside cover of the issue of *Shiyue* that carried Bai Hua's script has a reproduction of Huang Yongyun's famous owl painting, which gazes at the viewer with one eye open and one closed.

8. *Ku Lian* translation, 13.

9. Ibid., 19.

10. Ibid., 20.

11. Ibid., 25–26.

12. Ibid., 30.

13. Ibid., 33.

14. On its first appearance see Isabel Hilton, "A Hundred Flowers or Poisonous Weeds," *Index on Censorship*, no. 4 (1981): 19.

15. Bartke, *Who's Who in the People's Republic of China*, s.v. "Bai Hua."

16. For the Wuhan connection see *SWB* monitoring report (FE/6718/i), May 8, 1981.

17. *SWB* (FE/6729/B11), May 21, 1981, 1–6.

18. Ibid., 1.

19. In order, ibid., 1, 3, 4, 5.

20. Ibid., 6.

21. *SWB* monitoring report (FE/6718), May 8, 1981.

22. *SWB* (FE/6734/B11), May 28, 1981, 12.

23. Reuters, June 8, 1981, Beijing. *People's Daily* stated that they wanted "a free debate without intimidation" and "critics have the right to criticize, while those being criticized have the right to state their own opinions."

24. *China Quarterly* 87 (1981): 554.

25. Interview summarized in *SWB* (FE/6776/B11), July 16, 1981, 9–10, from *Ta Kung Pao* of July 10, 1981.

26. *SWB* (FE/6817/B11), Sept. 2, 1981, 1–2.

27. *Beijing Review*, Sept. 21, 1981, 3; and Oct. 19, 1981, 28.

28. *SWB* (FE/6916/B11), Dec. 31, 1981, 5–8.

29. *New China News Agency*, English ed. (122925/1311), Dec. 29, 1981, 40–41.

30. The full poem is in *Chang'an*, no. 1 (1981): 7–9. One could include in this group Ye Wenfu, whose "General" poems were criticized in Dec. 1981. See Foreign Broadcast Information Service (FBIS), *Daily Report—China*, Jan. 27, 1982, K13–K17.

31. *SWB* (Fe/6898/B11), Dec. 5, 1981, 1–5.

32. *Daily Report—China*, FBIS, Jan. 26, 1982, K9–K14, quoted passage on K11.

33. Ibid., K10 and K13.

34. Ibid., K10.
35. Sketches of all these figures are presented in my book *The Gate of Heavenly Peace: The Chinese and Their Revolution, 1895–1980* (New York: Viking, 1980).
36. *Ku Lian* translation, 34–35.

Tiananmen

1. For help with locating historical materials, illustrations, and maps of Tiananmen, I am grateful to Joan Judge, Ellen Johnston Laing, Peter Wang, Andrea Worden, and the staff at Asia Watch.

Poetry and Physics: The Spirits of Opposition

1. Bei Dao, *Waves*, edited by Bonnie S. McDougall and translated by Bonnie S. McDougall and Susette Ternent Cooke (New York: New Directions, 1990). Also Bei Dao, *The August Sleepwalker*, translated by Bonnie S. McDougall (New York: New Directions, 1990).
2. Fang Lizhi, *Bringing Down the Great Wall: Writings on Science, Culture, and Democracy in China*, edited by James H. Williams and translated by James H. Williams and others; introduction by Orville Schell (New York: Alfred A. Knopf, 1991).

Arthur Wright

For use of all manuscript letters cited, I am profoundly grateful to Colonel Sam Clabaugh and Mrs. Henry Hiles. For access to Arthur Wright's personal book collection, photograph collection, and student essays, I am similarly grateful to Mrs. Arthur F. Wright.
1. *Harvard Journal of Asiatic Studies* 7 (1943): 261–66, dated Peking, March 18, 1942; quotations at 263 and 266.
2. AFW MSS, "Balzac and the Historical Spirit," bibliography, 2.
3. Essay dated autumn 1934 and enclosure "Revision for Possible Publication." Guérard's two-page comment is also in the essay.
4. AFW, "Carlyle and the Modern Temper," *A Year Book of Stanford Writing* 6 (1935): 11–13.
5. *Journal of Asian Studies* 2 (1957): 333.
6. MCW to Sam Clabaugh, Cambridge, Mass., Jan. 18, 1940.
7. MCW to Family, Tokyo [*sic?*], Oct. 5, 1940.
8. MCW to Family, Kyoto, Oct. 12, 1940.
9. MCW to Family, Kyoto, Jan. 16, 1941, 3.
10. MCW to Daddy and Betty, Kyoto, Nov. 13, 1940.
11. MCW to Family, Kyoto, Feb. 4, 1941.

12. MCW to Family, Kyoto March 1, 1941.
13. AFW to Col. Sam Clabaugh, Kyoto, April 5, 1941.
14. MCW to Mother, [Peking], June 15, [1941].
15. MCW to Mother and Daddy, Peking, Aug. 5. 1941.
16. MCW, Peking letter no. 5, Aug. 2, 1941.
17. MCW to Sammy and Family, Peking, Aug. 12. 1941; AFW to Mr. Clabaugh, Peking, Aug. 15, 1941.
18. MCW to Mother and Family, Peking, Oct. 7, 1941. Even here, Mary could not cease to scrutinize herself. The next sentence of the letter reads, "All this drivel of course is certainly not a careful estimate of the two countries."
19. MCW to Family, [Peking], Oct. 23, 1941.
20. See especially MCW to Family, Peking, June 4, 1942.
21. These and other camp details are in MCW to Family, Wei-hsien Camp, Aug. 31, 1943.
22. Ibid., 9. See also one very brief letter, AFW to Mother and Dad, [Wei-hsien Camp], Sept. 10, 1943.
23. Ruth Kunkel to Mr. and Mrs. Wright, Motorship *Gripsholm*, Nov. 9, 1943, and Betty to Family, Albany, N.Y., Jan. 4, 1944, relaying William Christian's comments.
24. AFW, Letter 22 to Mary Bacon, Peking, Dec. 25, 1945.
25. AFW to Sam, Peking, Feb. 14, 1947.
26. MCW to Family, Yenan, Oct. 31, 1946.
27. MCW to Daddy, Portland, April 22, [1947], and Blanshard communication.
28. *Journal of the History of Ideas* 10 (1949): 148–49.
29. *Far Eastern Quarterly* 11 (1955): 105.
30. Ibid., 106–7.
31. AFW, *Buddhism in Chinese History* (Stanford: Stanford University Press, 1959).
32. *Far Eastern Quarterly* 11 (1955): 295, 298.
33. AFW, "The Economic Role of Buddhism in China," *Journal of Asian Studies* 16 (1957): 408, 414.
34. One volume of these essays was eventually published, under the title *Studies in Chinese Buddhism*, ed. Robert M. Somers (New Haven: Yale University Press, 1990).

Arthur Waley

1. Goldsworthy Lowes Dickinson, *Letters from a Chinese Official* (New York: McClure, Phillips, 1903), 38.
2. Ivan Morris, comp., *Madly Singing in the Mountains: An Appreciation and Anthology of Arthur Waley* (New York: Walker, 1970).

3. Ibid., 28.
4. Ibid., 96.
5. Ibid., 176.

John Fairbank

1. *Chinabound: A Fifty-Year Memoir* (New York: Harper and Row, 1982).
2. Stanley F. Wright, *Hart and the Chinese Customs* (Belfast: William Mullan, 1950), 864.
3. Suzanne W. Barnett and John K. Fairbank, eds., *Christianity in China: Early Protestant Missionary Writings* (Cambridge: Council on East Asian Studies, Harvard University Press, 1985).
4. Ernest R. May and John K. Fairbank, *America's China Trade in Historical Perspective: The Chinese and American Performance* (Cambridge: Council on East Asian Studies, Harvard University Press, 1986).
5. Philip A. Kuhn and John K. Fairbank, with the assistance of Beatrice S. Bartlett and Chiang Yung-chen, *Reading Documents: The Rebellion of Chung Jen-chieh*, 2 vols. (Cambridge: Council on East Asian Studies, Harvard University Press, 1986).
6. Katherine F. Bruner, John K. Fairbank, and Richard J. Smith, eds., *Entering China's Service: Robert Hart's Journals, 1854–1863* (Cambridge: Council on East Asian Studies, Harvard University Press, 1986).
7. Ibid., 231.
8. Ibid., 322.
9. John K. Fairbank, *China Watch* (Cambridge: Harvard University Press, 1987).
10. Ibid., 147.
11. John K. Fairbank, *The Great Chinese Revolution, 1800–1985* (New York: Harper and Row, 1986).
12. Ibid., 336.
13. Ibid., 26.
14. Ibid., 2.

Fang Chao-ying

1. Fang Chao-ying, letter to J. Spence, the Library, the Australian National University, Feb. 2, 1962.
2. Fang Chao-ying, letter to J. Spence, the Library, the Australian National University, Feb. 21, 1962.
3. Fang to Spence, Columbia University, March 4, 1965.
4. Fang to Spence, n.p., Dec. 24, 1975.

Acknowledgments

Grateful acknowledgment is made to the following for permission to reprint previously published material:

"The Paris Years of Arcadio Huang," *Granta* 32 (Spring 1990): 125–132, reprinted by permission.

"Matteo Ricci and the Ascent to Peking," in *East Meets West: The Jesuits in China, 1582–1773*, ed. Charles Ronan and Bonnie Oh (Chicago: Loyola University Press, 1988), 1–18. Reprinted by permission of Loyola University Press. Copyright © 1988.

"A Picaresque Hero: The Travels of Mendes Pinto," *New York Review of Books*, April 12, 1990, 38–40. Reprinted by permission of the *New York Review of Books*. Copyright © 1990 by Nyrev, Inc.

"China between Revolutions," in *Sidney D. Gamble's China, 1917–1932: Photographs of the Land and Its People*. Reprinted by permission of the Sidney D. Gamble Foundation for China Studies. Copyright © 1989.

Preface to *The Temptation of the West*, by André Malraux. (Chicago: University of Chicago Press, 1991). Reprinted by permission of the University of Chicago Press, copyright © 1991. All rights reserved.

"Western Perceptions of China, from the Late Sixteenth Century to the Present," in *Heritage of China: Contemporary Perspectives on Chinese Civilization*, ed. Paul Ropp (Berkeley: University of California Press, 1990), 1–14. Copyright © 1990 by the Regents of the University of California.

"The Seven Ages of K'ang-hsi (1654–1722)," *Journal of Asian Studies* 26 (February 1967):205–12. Reprinted by permission of the Association for Asian Studies, Inc.

"Take Back Your Ming," *New York Review of Books*, April 30, 1981, 53–55.

Index